DESERT WARRIOR

Two weeks before the start of the Gulf War, King Fahd inspected a
parade of troops from 24 nations.

DESERT WARRIOR

A Personal View of the Gulf War by
the Joint Forces Commander

HRH GENERAL
KHALED BIN SULTAN

Written with Patrick Seale

HarperCollins*Publishers*

HarperCollins*Publishers*
77–85 Fulham Palace Road
Hammersmith, London W6 8JB

Published by HarperCollins*Publishers* 1995
1 3 5 7 9 8 6 4 2

A catalogue record for this book is
available from the British Library

ISBN 0 00 255612 X

Set in Linotron Meridien by
Rowland Phototypesetting Ltd,
Bury St Edmunds, Suffolk

Printed in Great Britain by
HarperCollinsManufacturing Glasgow

TO MY FATHER

CONTENTS

LIST OF ILLUSTRATIONS

(Photographs are from the author's KSA Library, unless otherwise stated.)

Frontispiece: With King Fahd

LIST OF MAPS AND CHARTS

LIST OF ABBREVIATIONS

ACC	Arab Cooperation Council
ADC	Aide de Camp
ANGLICO	Air Naval Gunfire Liaison Company
APC	Armored Personnel Carrier
ARAMCO	Arabian-American Oil Company
ASOC	Air Support Operations Center
ATO	Air Tasking Order
AWACS	Airborne Warning and Control System
C3	Command, Control and Communications
C3IC	Coalition Coordination Communications and Integration Cell
CAS	Close Air Support
CENTCOM	Central Command
CEP	Circular Error Probable
CIA	Central Intelligence Agency
CINC	Commander-in-Chief
CMTS	Central Maintenance and Technical Support
CNN	Cable News Network
CRC	Combat Reporting Center
CSS	Combat Service Support
FAR	Force d'action rapide, France
FMS	Foreign Military Sales
GCC	Gulf Cooperation Council
GPS	Global Positioning System
HARM	High-Speed Antiradiation Missile
HET	Heavy Equipment Transporter
HUMINT	Human Intelligence
ICRC	International Committee of the Red Cross
JFACC	Joint Force Air Component Commander
JFC	Joint Forces Command

KKMC	King Khaled Military City
KTO	Kuwait Theater of Operations
MBE	Member of the British Empire
MLRS	Multiple Launch Rocket System
MODA	Ministry of Defense and Aviation
MRE	Meals Ready to Eat
NATO	North Atlantic Treaty Organization
NBC	Nuclear, Biological and Chemical
NCO	Noncommissioned Officer
PGM	Precision Guided Munitions
PLO	Palestine Liberation Organization
POW	Prisoner of War
PSO	Program Supply Office
PSYOPS	Psychological Operations
R&D	Research and Development
RCC	Revolutionary Command Council
RSAF	Royal Saudi Air Force
RSLF	Royal Saudi Land Forces
SAM	Surface-to-Air Missile
SANG	Saudi Arabian National Guard
SAS	Special Air Service, UK
SOP	Standard Operating Procedure
TACP	Tactical Air Control Party
UAV	Unmanned Aerial Vehicle
USAF	United States Air Force

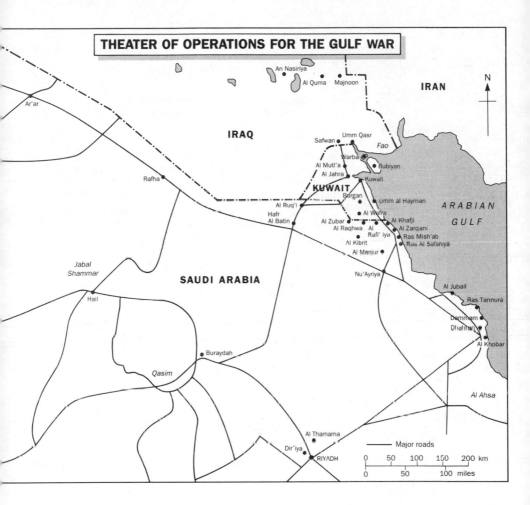

THEATER OF OPERATIONS FOR THE GULF WAR

An Nasiriya
Al Quma
Majnoon

IRAN

Ar'ar

IRAQ

Safwan
Umm Qasr
Fao

Warba

Al Mutl'a
Bubiyan

Al Jahra
Kuwait

Rafha

KUWAIT

Burgan

Umm al Hayman

Al Ruq'i

Hafr
Al Batin

Al Wefra

*ARABIAN
GULF*

Al Zubar
Al Khafji

Al Raqhwa
Al
Al Zarqani

Rafi' iya
Ras Mish'ab

Al Kibrit
Ras Al Safaniya

Al Manjur

Jabal
Shammar

Nu'Ayriya

SAUDI ARABIA

Al Jubail

Hail
Ras Tannura

Dammam
Dhahran

Al Khobar

Buraydah

Qasim

Al Ahsa

Al Thamama

Dir'iya

RIYADH

Major roads

0   50   100   150   200 km

0   50   100 miles

N

FOREWORD

THE GULF CRISIS OF 1990–91 was the greatest threat in my life-
time to the independence of our region and to the free flow of
oil to the world. No fewer than 37 nations joined in a Coalition
to reverse Saddam Hussein's aggression against Kuwait, under-
lining the worldwide importance of the Gulf and the need for
an international effort to protect it.

The war demonstrated the absolute centrality of the Kingdom
of Saudi Arabia in the defense of this region. It is no exaggeration
to say that without our military infrastructure and strategic
depth, which allowed friendly forces to mass and deploy in preparation for Operation Desert Storm, and without our financial
and material contribution, the war to free Kuwait could not
have been waged, or could only have been waged with the
greatest difficulty. We were the linchpin of the Coalition, its
essential cement.

Saudi Arabia is also the living heart of the Muslim world and,
by virtue of its geopolitical position, plays a key role in the
stability of the Middle East.

I have written this book because, although there have been
many published accounts of the Gulf War, none in my view
does justice to Saudi Arabia's massive contribution to victory.
There is an untold story which I feel it is my duty to tell. Unless
I do so, I do not think others will. I owe it to my country, to
our allies, and to our brave and loyal soldiers, to set the record
straight.

I hasten to add that this is not an official account of the war
or of my country. I am not speaking for the government of Saudi
Arabia or for the Royal Family. It is a personal view of what I
witnessed and what I and my colleagues achieved.

I have included some chapters about my family background
and early career to help the reader understand where I come

from and what preparation I received for the task King Fahd entrusted to me. Hence this is in part a war book, and in part the story of my life. However, it is neither a complete military history of the war, nor is it a full-scale autobiography (which might be considered premature in a man of 45).

There are many lessons to be learned from the Gulf War and I trust I have absorbed some of them. I hope that relating my own experiences will be of some use to others. With an eye to the future, I have also put forward some ideas about Gulf security.

The world's dependence on Gulf oil will last for at least another generation. To protect our region and its resources, we need to build real military power of our own, as well as an effective system of alliances, both regional and international. I am confident that we will rise to the challenge if we take careful note of what the crisis has taught us.

It remains for me to express my warm thanks to all those who have helped me research and write this book. The names of some of them appear in the text, but I am also deeply grateful to many others, for the most part close and valued colleagues in my military career, whom I have not mentioned.

Finally, I would like to acknowledge a debt of gratitude to Brigadier General Farouk Abd al-Karim, whom I first met when we both attended the U.S. Army Command and General Staff College at Fort Leavenworth, Kansas, and who has been my loyal adviser and tireless aide over the past dozen years.

KHALED BIN SULTAN
Riyadh, February 1995

DESERT WARRIOR

CHAPTER I

In the Eye of the Storm

A SANDSTORM WAS BLOWING. An invisible hand was scooping hot orange dust from the desert floor and throwing it in our faces. It stung like a whip. Great ugly swirls of sand climbed high into the sky, then fell back as the wind changed, lashing the windshield of the scout car and settling in heavy drifts across the road. The noisy turmoil of the elements seemed to match the turmoil in my mind.

We were heading up Saudi Arabia's north–south coastal highway towards Kuwait. To our right, marshy salt flats, glistening and treacherous, merged into the waters of the Gulf. We had just driven through the small town of al-Khafji and just ahead of us, some eight miles up the road, was a Saudi border post. This desert border post, the main gateway from the Kingdom to Kuwait on the coastal road, is usually a pretty busy place. But that day, to my amazement, a vast crowd of people, wailing and gesticulating, huddled around the customs house looking for a bit of shade and for protection from the dust – and from Saddam Hussein.

The road beyond the post was jammed with cars, parked five or more abreast, stretching back towards Kuwait as far as the eye could see. I thought one would have to go up in a helicopter to get the whole picture. And what a picture of chaos it was! For, as we came closer, we could see that the entire landscape of dune and marsh was dotted with abandoned cars, most of them embedded up to their axles in the soft, slippery ground. Unable to move on the road, the drivers had taken to the desert, racing for a gap in the berms which marked the frontier – and had run out of fuel or had sunk into the marshland. Taking what they could carry, they had struggled on foot towards the border, dragging women and children behind them, until exhaustion had forced them to abandon bulging suitcases, mattresses, cardboard boxes, cassette players, plastic carrier bags and a host of other possessions, so that the whole area looked like a squalid and disorderly picnic interrupted by rain.

Border guards were collecting the stragglers and evacuating them to the road leading into the Kingdom. They had erected a number of large tents where food and cold water were being handed out to wild-eyed and hungry families, while a rough attempt was made to record the names of the flood of visitors.

This was August 1990, two weeks after Saddam's invasion of Kuwait. On August 10, King Fahd had appointed me Joint Forces Commander with wide responsibilities for the defense of the Kingdom. This was my first visit to the field to assess the deadly threat we faced.

How many Iraqi infiltrators, I wondered, were hidden in this unorganized desperate mass of Kuwaitis, fleeing their own country by the tens of thousands? It was an intelligence nightmare. Clearly we would have to improve the filtering and screening process.

For reasons I could not fathom, Saddam had not closed the frontier and people were still swarming across it. Was it his deliberate policy to empty Kuwait of its inhabitants? It was not long before we had to find homes for 360,000 Kuwaitis. Saddam let out anyone who wanted to go, generals and senior government servants among them. It surprised me that he allowed the most important people to leave. The Iraqis even failed to secure Kuwait's two air bases in the first 24 hours, and planes were still taking off long after the capital had fallen. It remains a puzzle to this day. About 40 Kuwaiti aircraft, some coastal vessels and the best part of an army brigade reached Saudi Arabia safely.

At that border post north of al-Khafji, I had a glimpse of the great civilian influx. As I looked on helplessly at the distraught crowd milling around the customs post, the thought crossed my mind that I was witnessing a tragic sight all too characteristic of the world we lived in. These were ordinary people driven from their homes by fear, trying to save themselves and their children from the indiscriminate savagery of war. The once confident –

perhaps overconfident – Kuwaitis, proud of their well-ordered state, boasting one of the highest per capita incomes in the world, were now reduced to being exiles. Were we, in Saudi Arabia, to be the next victims?

I presumed that when Saddam attacked Kuwait he intended to kill or capture the Al Sabah ruling family. As any one of his advisers would have told him: "You want to take Kuwait? Get rid of the ruling family. The place will be yours. You can then pull out or stay as you please." Without the Al Sabah, there would be no focus for loyalty, no symbol of state legitimacy. When the army seized power in Iraq in 1958, one of its first moves was to kill the young King Faisal and members of his family, much as Lenin's Bolsheviks slaughtered Czar Nicholas II and other members of the Romanov family in the civil war which followed the Russian Revolution of 1917.

But, if Saddam's intention was to destroy the Al Sabah, he did not go about it the right way. Why did he attack Kuwait frontally? Why did he not go around the back and block the escape routes? That was the first question in my mind. I reckoned he could have done the job with two divisions only – one against Kuwait itself, the other to cut the al-Khafji and al-Ruq'i roads, the two exits which lead out of the city and south into Saudi Arabia, and secure the airport and the two air bases. Had Kuwait been cut off and the frontier sealed, he would have held the ruling family in the palm of his hand. Perhaps he expected more resistance. Perhaps he thought the Kuwait government would not leave but would stand and fight. Instead, the Amir, the Crown Prince and other members of the ruling family withdrew to Saudi Arabia on the day of the invasion, with an hour or two to spare before the Iraqis arrived in Kuwait City – a wise decision which was to prove of great benefit to their country as they were able to set up a government-in-exile and lend encouragement to the underground resistance movement in occupied Kuwait.

On the fateful day of the invasion, my cousin and close friend Prince Muhammad bin Fahd, Governor of Saudi Arabia's

Eastern Province, was directly involved in rescuing the Amir of Kuwait: in fact, as he later recounted to me, he went to fetch him at al-Khafji on instructions from King Fahd, and personally drove him by car into the Kingdom. As the story is little known, it is worth relating in somewhat greater detail.

Prince Muhammad had learned of the Iraqi invasion in the early hours of August 2. At 6:30 that morning, he received a call from a lieutenant at the Saudi border post north of al-Khafji who, to his astonishment, informed him that the Amir of Kuwait was there and wished to speak to him. It turned out that the Amir wished to speak to the King but did not have his number at Jeddah! Muhammad gave it to him and the Amir was soon in direct communication with the King.

King Fahd then rang Muhammad with instructions to urge the Amir to come to Dammam, a city to the south where his security could be guaranteed. It was dangerous for him to stay at the border post which might, at any moment, be overrun by the Iraqis. Over the next two hours, Muhammad called the Amir repeatedly, but the latter was reluctant to leave. He had sent couriers into Kuwait City to find out what was happening and was awaiting their return. The Crown Prince of Kuwait, Shaikh Saad, was still in the city. Muhammad urged the Amir at least to move to the governor's palace at al-Khafji where he would be safer and where he could more conveniently make his phone calls. But the Amir still hesitated to leave the border post.

At 11 a.m. King Fahd instructed Muhammad to go personally to al-Khafji and escort the Amir farther into the Kingdom. By the time he arrived after a two-and-a-half-hour drive, the Crown Prince, several other members of the Al Sabah family and most of the government ministers had joined the Amir. "For the sake of Kuwait and for the sake of your people," Prince Muhammad told the Amir, "you should come with me." He had not been there long when he received another call from King Fahd inquiring why he was still there! But the Amir was waiting for the couriers he had sent into Kuwait.

At last, at 4 p.m., the Amir was persuaded to leave. They set off for Dammam, with Muhammad at the wheel and the Amir seated beside him. It was an extremely hot August day.

Muhammad had not slept for 24 hours. The Amir held himself well but, perhaps overcome by the momentous events of the day, he said very little. It was no time for small talk. Fighting off sleep – in fact very nearly dozing off half a dozen times – Muhammad finally brought the Amir to safety at the royal guest palace at Dammam, where he tightened security and doubled the guard. He stayed with him a couple of hours before driving home to snatch some sleep. But he had not been in bed an hour when he received a call from the government representative at Hafr al-Batin with news that other members of the Al Sabah had managed to escape through al-Ruq'i, the second crossing point into the Kingdom.

The Amir and his entourage stayed two weeks at Dammam. On the first day, the Kuwaiti's party numbered about 150 persons from the ruling family, to be joined over the next couple of weeks by some ten to twenty people a day, several of them in a state of shock. Some had escaped with nothing but the clothes they had on. Concerned to see to the comfort of his guests, King Fahd gave instructions that they should be provided with whatever they needed in the way of household goods, personal effects, clothes and the like. A nearby building was turned into a small hospital for their exclusive use.

As with the Amir and his party, the task of looking after the vast numbers of Kuwaiti refugees fell most heavily on the Governor of the Eastern Province. Accommodation, beds and bedding, air conditioning, food, medical services and much else had to be provided. Fortunately it was summer when schools and university campuses were empty. These, together with sports stadiums and empty apartments, were used to provide temporary housing for the refugees. Committees of volunteers sprung up all over the province to help the Kuwaitis. Some Saudis took Kuwaitis into their own homes and went themselves to stay with relatives. Many of the refugees eventually moved on to Riyadh, Jeddah, Abha and elsewhere in the Arab world, but about 110,000 stayed on in the Eastern Province for the duration of the crisis.

After a day in the Eastern Province, being briefed at the operations center of the King Fahd Military City by the Eastern Area commander, Major General Salih al-Muhaya, and his staff, I flew up the Gulf coast to Ras Mish'ab, a small naval station and airstrip some 30 miles from the Kuwait border. And from there I proceeded by scout car to see for myself what was happening on the border and to inspect my troops.

My troops? A terrible shock awaited me. The northern border of the Kingdom was very lightly defended. When, before the crisis, we had evaluated the potential threats to our Eastern Province, we had discounted the early possibility of being exposed to a land threat from our northern Arab neighbors. We had, of course, considered the real possibility of air, naval, missile and terrorist threats from across the Gulf and we were well prepared to face these dangers – but not a land threat, not tanks and troops pouring across our borders in a land war. For this reason, we maintained only small land forces in northeastern Arabia. However, to allow for rapid reinforcement in an emergency, we had taken the precaution of building a strong military infrastructure in the form of "military cities" at strategic locations around the Kingdom, of which the King Khaled Military City (KKMC) at Hafr al-Batin was one of the largest. Situated at the "hinge" of the frontiers of Saudi Arabia, Iraq and Kuwait, KKMC lay astride the Wadi al-Batin, a wide, dry stream bed which was the natural invasion route into the Kingdom from the north. It is said that, during the Ice Age, the Wadi al-Batin was one of the largest rivers in Asia. But, unfortunately for us, it dried up about 10,000 years ago with the ending of the heavy rains.

Small infantry, armored and air force units were routinely stationed at KKMC, but the modern, well-equipped base was large enough to house tens of thousands of troops if the need arose. Other such military cities included King Faisal Military City at Khamis Mushait in the south and King Abd al-Aziz Military City at Tabuk in the northwest. These elaborate complexes of barracks, offices, supply depots, maintenance areas, warehouses, hospitals and schools were real towns. Our military cities were, in fact, the modern equivalent of the desert forts with which rulers of ancient Arabia defended their frontiers.

Before the crisis over Kuwait, our intelligence and our general staff had paid little attention to Iraq because, in the politics of the 1970s and 1980s, no one had anticipated that a threat to the Kingdom might come from that direction. No one had imagined that Iraq, a brotherly Arab country which Saudi Arabia had helped enormously in its long war with Iran, could suddenly turn into an enemy. When people criticize Saudi Arabia for having been taken by surprise, they fail to realize that no one had seriously thought it possible that Iraq might invade Saudi Arabia, and no one in their wildest nightmares had conceived that Kuwait, our small friendly neighbor and fellow member of the Gulf Cooperation Council, could under Iraqi occupation become a potential jumping-off point for an aggression against us. Is France's frontier with Belgium defended?

In the east, close to the border, the only unit we had immediately available was the 2nd Mechanized Brigade of the Saudi Arabian National Guard, which found itself well within range of Iraq's artillery. Further west, at KKMC, was a small GCC force, known as "Peninsula Shield," itself of limited military capability. Made up of a Saudi brigade group and a few disparate companies and battalions from other GCC members, it hurried to take up defensive positions.

Also at KKMC was a newly arrived contingent of Moroccan desert rangers – 962 men in all – who, together with a regiment of Egyptian Special Forces, had been the first friendly Arab forces to fly to our aid within days of Iraq's invasion. When I visited the Moroccans, I could see at once that they were a fine body of men, battle-hardened by their country's long struggle with the Polisario Front for control of the Western Sahara, but they were still in camp and their support units had not yet arrived.

To reinforce this thin line, Saudi troops were being rushed up from all over the place. The 8th Brigade of the Royal Saudi Land Forces was racing across country from Tabuk, in northwestern Arabia, via al-Qasim, a journey of over 700 miles, while the 10th Brigade was rushing up from Khamis Mushait in the south, an almost equally long journey. It would take a military man to appreciate the tremendous effort demanded of these troops to travel such vast distances across country in the heat of August. Priority had rightly been given to moving combat units first, leaving the support units to follow, but this meant that the advance columns faced some interruption in supplies and a shortage of maintenance and workshop personnel.

When I went to inspect these brigades, some of their units had already reached the front and were taking up defensive positions, but other units were still on their way, strung out for miles along the roads. In the long journey to the front, vehicles had to be refueled, some had broken down and needed repair, while the men themselves, tired from hours of traveling, needed rest, fresh water and hot meals. The top-speed deployment to face the Iraqi threat from the wholly unexpected direction of Kuwait meant that our troops, racing up from Tabuk and Khamis Mushait, had to make do without water points or fuel dumps, without warehouses along their route to hold supplies or workshops to repair vehicles. As I reported to my father, Prince Sultan, second deputy Prime Minister* and Minister of Defense and Aviation, we had to make defensive plans and combat preparations virtually from scratch in facing what was a totally new situation.

I visited all three brigades – the National Guard brigade and the two Land Forces brigades – and listened to a briefing by the brigade commanders. I wanted to know how many troops had already arrived and how many were still to come, what difficulties they faced, and, above all, what was their state of readiness. The National Guard units faced fewer problems, because they were already in the Eastern Province and did not have so far to travel. But, as they were light brigades and their firepower was not considerable, I could not conceive of using them in checking an Iraqi armored thrust. Each of our two Land Forces brigades had an armored battalion, but even these were merely a handful of tanks with which to confront Saddam's heavy divisions. To my alarm, some of our tanks had already been positioned along the frontier berms where they seemed to me like sitting ducks, providing live targets for Iraqi gunners.

The Iraqis were just across the frontier in overwhelming strength. They had massed about 200,000 men and 2,000 tanks in Kuwait and, according to our intelligence, were resupplying

* Under our system, the King is the Prime Minister; Crown Prince Abdallah is the deputy PM; and Prince Sultan, the third most important man in the Kingdom, is the second deputy PM.

their attack formations as if preparing to advance against us. Meanwhile, the first American soldiers were only just beginning to arrive: they were still at Jubail, some 160 miles to the rear and they were certainly not ready for battle at this stage. Alone in the front line were the Saudis and a few hundred GCC troops.

That trip to the field made me recognize the magnitude of the challenge we faced. It was a matter of life and death. I tried to put a brave face on it but, once I was alone back in my quarters in the port of Ras Mish'ab, I stamped about my room, raging with frustration and pondering what to do. I needed to put on a show of force. I needed to show that the Saudi army was in the field confronting the aggressor, and that a commander was there taking charge.

But I knew well enough that if Saddam moved – and if he were prepared to take heavy losses from air strikes – he could within days reach Jubail and the eastern oil fields. I reasoned gloomily that if he meant to hold Kuwait, he could not stay cooped up in that small theater and expose himself to a counter-attack. He would soon need to move down the coast and disperse his forces. No military strategist would expect him to stop at the Saudi border.

In those early anxious days and weeks, we sent agents into Kuwait and Iraq to bring back what information they could glean about Saddam's intentions. Showing great initiative, a brave two-star general, the third most senior man in our General Intelligence Directorate, ventured himself into occupied Kuwait. Disguised as a Bedouin, he spent three days on his mission, traveling right up to Safwan under the noses of the Iraqis. It was a risky and not wholly wise adventure, as his capture would have caused us much embarrassment. But he brought back the most precise information about the deployments of Iraqi units.

Saddam already had far more troops than he needed in Kuwait, but all the reports we received indicated that he was steadily reinforcing his vast army there. Why was he building up his strength? Inevitably, it suggested he had some further objective.

In the meantime, we seemed to be witnessing an operational pause, which was not unexpected – a pause in which Saddam could secure his first-stage objective, resupply his forces, move in combat support elements such as artillery and missile launchers, give his field commanders a chance to complete their operational plans and then assign them combat missions for the next stage. Politically, he may have paused to gauge the reactions of the Arab and Islamic world and of the international community, as well as to make the necessary local administrative arrangements to control the captured territory. He may also have wanted to reassure us that seizure of *our* territory was not part of his plan.

But could we believe him? Was he aiming for our oil fields in the Eastern Province and the important Dhahran air base, or, still more ambitiously, did he plan to topple all six GCC states? Did Saddam mean to redraw the whole map of Arabia? These somber questions buzzed around in my head.

Studying my charts and trying to put myself in his shoes, I thought he would make a frontal attack on our oil fields and our ports, and perhaps use special forces in our rear. We could throw our air force at him and we would no doubt have to sacrifice it in doing so. We could also expect some immediate help from the U.S. Air Force, seeing that some American wings had already arrived and two U.S. carrier battle groups had deployed to the region. But once Saddam seized control of more than 40 percent of world oil reserves, the West might think twice before challenging him. It might have to deal with him – and that could have been his ultimate intention. This I found extremely worrying.

August was the best time for him to attack before our friends had time to rally to our help but, on the ground, I knew that I had little with which to stop him. I tried to keep smiling, but the situation seemed highly dangerous. Compared to the enormous force Saddam had assembled, we seemed very weak in numbers and equipment. It was the worst moment of my life.

Back in Riyadh a few days later, Lieutenant General John Yeosock, the Central Command's army commander, who was in the Kingdom to prepare for the arrival of U.S. forces, asked me anxiously what I had seen at the front.

"It's as if we already fought the war – and lost!" I exclaimed.

It was my way of saying that much remained to be done to safeguard our independence.

❖

On August 20, two days after my return to Riyadh after my first field trip, I went back up to the front to have another look and see what immediate measures could be taken. On this occasion, I accompanied Crown Prince Abdallah, deputy Prime Minister and head of the Saudi National Guard, who wished to see for himself the situation on the ground.

Crown Prince Abdallah was the first senior member of the Royal Family to visit the troops in the field. He came from August 20 to 22. It was the first time that his National Guard and the Royal Saudi Land Forces were together under one command, and the first time that I, as the newly appointed Joint Forces Commander, accompanied him on a tour of inspection.

As I mentioned, the situation in the Northern Area Command was better than in the Eastern Area. The troops up north, having only traveled some thirty miles from King Khaled Military City, were in good shape, with access to fuel and ammunition, to supply depots and repair workshops. The main problem lay in the east. My first priority was to boost the morale of the brigades which had crossed the peninsula at great speed and were now living rough in the desert, facing sandstorms, extremes of heat and shortages of supplies. I was struck by the universal demand for ice. I contacted the chief government representative at al-Khafji and asked him to rush me several truckfuls.

I badly needed finance. I called Prince Sultan and begged him to send me some emergency funds. I explained that I did not want to have to go through military channels. There was no time for that. He was a great help. I was able to give each brigade commander the equivalent of $20,000 in petty cash to top up the rations of his men and buy ice on a daily basis, and $2 million to each of the two area commanders in emergency aid. The Eastern Area Commander in particular had to cope with the swelling army of Kuwaiti refugees: Arab hospitality – and political necessity – demanded that they be cared for. Among the troops, small comforts resulted in an immediate change of mood. I shared a meal with one of the units under a canvas awning slung between two vehicles to create a patch of shade. Wind howled between the trucks, raising swirls of sand, but failed to dampen spirits.

But these were mere stop-gap measures. Clearly, forward supply bases would have to be established, one in the east and another in the north – and if possible they had to be below ground out of harm's way. I got people to start digging. In the east, north of the village of al-Nu'ayriya, was a promising range of hills, some 45 miles back from the frontier. Caves could be dug in the flanks of this high ground to store fuel, ammunition of all calibers, and other supplies. The flow up there soon got underway. But, at the start, everything was under canvas – food, water, fuel, ammunition. Sorting that out kept me busy in those first few days.

In the desert, transporting water for large numbers of men was a problem, which made me think that if it was difficult for me, I was going to make sure it would be doubly difficult for Saddam. I gave orders to identify every waterhole in the desert, and called up experts from the Ministry of Agriculture to help. I wanted to make sure that, if Saddam attacked and we were forced to withdraw, these water points would be damaged. If that was the price for stopping Saddam, it was worth paying. At al-Khafji itself, some 15,000 inhabitants were heavily dependent on a desalination plant. Should it too be destroyed, I wondered, if the Iraqis invaded? It was a difficult decision, but I felt it had to be done.

What if the Iraqis used gas, as they had against Iran and against their own people? I worried about the supply of protective clothing and masks for our troops. Some of the units in the Northern Area had been issued with masks, but others farther back had not. On examining the masks in our stores, we discovered that some of the filters were out of date, and would have to be replaced. Rarely in wartime do things go according to plan.

At this stage, I had fewer than 8,000 men in a state of combat readiness to defend the long northern frontier. I deployed the two ready battalions I had as a screening force, while we hurried to prepare heavier units farther back.

My staff urged me to lay minefields to check any Iraqi

advance, and presented me with maps of where the minefields should be. The Americans, too, were in favor. But, in what turned out to be one of my best decisions, I refused. I did not want inhabitants of this region to be plagued with unexploded mines, as in the Western Desert after World War Two, or even the Falklands. I argued to myself that if the political contacts then underway with Iraq persuaded Saddam to withdraw, clearing the minefields would pose a threat to my troops, with a potential loss of life. In the event, when diplomacy failed to dislodge Saddam and the Coalition had to attack, our own minefields might again have been a great nuisance and might even have hindered our advance.

The only exception I later allowed was in the Egyptian sector. The Egyptian commander begged me to permit him to lay a minefield of several hundred yards on the al-Ruq'i approach road to check any Iraqi advance into the Kingdom. I agreed on condition that every mine would eventually be lifted before Egyptian troops left the location and that, when the time came, they would themselves advance through that sector on their way to liberate Kuwait.

Perhaps the most important point I grasped from my first trip to the front was the sheer folly of trying to defend the frontier itself. It would be to condemn to death the troops manning it.

The defensive plans drawn up by the Land Forces Command had to be amended. My brigades were tactical forces not border guards. I felt there was no need to disperse them along the border. On the contrary, it was imperative to pull them back, out of range of Saddam's artillery, so as to create some space for our air force to intervene against any enemy advance. (Yet I was worried about the coordination between my forces and the Ministry of Interior border guards who man posts every fifteen miles around our land frontiers. They needed to remain on the border to assert our sovereignty. But I wanted to be sure that, if we had to withdraw, they would pull out with us.)

I established a defense line at Ras Mish'ab. North of that and up to the border would be a 30-mile "killing zone." The desert was our greatest asset. It gave us depth. If the Iraqis came in, their supply lines would be stretched and we could cut them up. I took my decision regarding these deployments on August 18, and two days later it was implemented.

The town of al-Khafji, only eight miles from the border, was wholly indefensible if the Iraqis attacked in strength. Even if they did not, they could destroy the city with artillery fire from their side of the border if they chose to. I knew that, if I positioned any military forces in the city, the Iraqis might use that as a pretext to shell it. So I declared al-Khafji a "dead city." We did not want to cause panic by moving civilians out there and then, but we needed to have ready a contingency plan to evacuate the population the moment Saddam made a move. The evacuation plan, by road and sea, was drawn up by the civil defense authorities with help from the Governor of the Eastern Province and the Eastern Area Commander. Gradually, without our making a formal announcement, most of the town's inhabitants reached their own conclusion that it would be safer to move out.

With all this on my mind, I regrouped my forces after appraising the situation with the Northern Area commander, Major General Abd al-Rahman al-Alkami, and the Eastern Area commander, Major General Salih al-Muhaya. I was extremely happy to find these two fine officers in my theater of operations.

I returned to Riyadh with the grim overall picture clearer in my mind. The country was in grave physical danger, something I could not possibly have imagined before the crisis erupted just three weeks earlier. As I reviewed the problems to be faced and the tasks to be done, I was acutely aware of the huge burden of responsibility I had assumed. As I reported to Prince Sultan, I had urgently to improve the combat readiness of our troops in their new positions. I had to train them, supply them and devise an effective defense plan. I had to set up an effective headquarters and deal with the friendly forces then beginning to flow into the Kingdom.

For a moment I was seized with the idea that I was sitting in a darkened theater, waiting for the curtain to go up on an unfolding drama, full of blood and violence and uncertainty. No one could tell who would survive it or what the final act would bring.

CHAPTER II

The Historic Decision

WHEN KING FAHD WAS FIRST TOLD of the Iraqi invasion of Kuwait – just before 2 a.m. on Thursday, August 2 – he refused to believe it. An hour later reports came in to confirm that heliborne Iraqi commandos had seized key government buildings in Kuwait City. It eventually became clear that they were the spearhead of an invasion force of three Iraqi Republican Guard divisions: one armored and one mechanized infantry division mounted the main attack on Kuwait, while a second armored division provided support farther west.

Still in a state of disbelief, King Fahd put through a call to Saddam Hussein in Baghdad on one of his ten or fifteen private numbers, but was told that the Iraqi president could not be reached. It was not until 10 a.m. that day that the King managed to talk to Saddam and found him in a jovial mood, seemingly on top of the world. I understand the conversation went something like this:

"What is this I hear?" the King asked him.

"Don't worry about it!" Saddam replied. "I am sending Izzat Ibrahim* to explain it all to you."

That same morning, King Fahd also tried to reach King Hussein of Jordan by telephone but was told the King was asleep. It is more likely that Hussein did not wish to take the call.

Izzat Ibrahim, the Iraqi envoy, was received by King Fahd at 3 p.m. on Friday, August 3, and, to the King's surprise and irritation, insisted on relaying Saddam Hussein's assurance that the Kingdom was safe and had nothing to fear from Iraq.

---

* Vice President of Iraq's Revolutionary Command Council.

17

"I am discussing Kuwait, not the security of Saudi Arabia," King Fahd said.

To which Izzat Ibrahim replied, "I am not here to discuss Kuwait. The status of Kuwait has now been rectified. The clock cannot be turned back. I merely want to reassure you about the safety of Saudi Arabia."

These early exchanges, which I believe are substantially accurate, shaped the King's perception of the crisis. He was extremely angry and upset at Iraq's occupation of Kuwait. It had shattered the status quo in Arabia, which he had striven to preserve throughout his reign, and broken all the rules of Arab politics. The King had a special feeling of consideration for Kuwait: his father – my grandfather – Abd al-Aziz, known as "Ibn Saud," had found refuge there in his youth from his adversaries, the Al Rashid, rulers of Hail and northern Arabia, and had in January 1902 set off from Kuwait on his momentous raid to recapture Riyadh for the Al Saud.

But there was also something very personal about the King's distress. He had felt genuine friendship for Saddam and had helped him greatly over the years – for instance, during Iraq's war against Iran, Saudi Arabia had given Saddam loans of $16 billion and further large sums in outright grants. Now this false friend had stabbed him in the back! The King's acute feeling of hurt can be clearly sensed in the many speeches he made at later stages of the crisis, in which he recounted time and again how Saddam had let him down.

As always with disputes between Arab states, the King's first instinct was to try to solve the Iraqi–Kuwaiti quarrel by mediation. But by Friday evening, after two days of telephoning and consultations with Arab and foreign leaders, he saw no use in pursuing the matter any further.

He realized on that Friday that Saddam Hussein meant to stay in Kuwait and that no Arab force could expel him. All talk of an "Arab solution" was, therefore, illusory. It was whistling in the wind. The traditional instruments of Arab diplomacy – the brotherly chats, the choice of a go-between to reconcile the warring parties, the mutual concessions, the agreement to kiss-and-make-up – were this time inappropriate. The crisis was just too big.

On moral and humanitarian grounds, the King was outraged at the aggression against Kuwait, our neighbor, close friend and fellow member of the six-nation Gulf Cooperation Council.* But he was also quick to grasp its geopolitical implications. If Saddam were allowed to get away with the seizure of Kuwait, the independence of Saudi Arabia, and indeed of the whole Arab Gulf, would be threatened. The combination of Iraq and Kuwait together would be so powerful as to dominate the Gulf and indeed the whole Middle East system. Once he had digested Kuwait, Saddam would become the undisputed master of the area – and Saudi Arabia would face pressure to bend to his will.

From this perspective, whether or not Saddam attacked the Kingdom was in a sense irrelevant. On all important matters – particularly oil policy and foreign affairs – he would be in a position to dictate terms.

The King's somber conclusion was that the occupation of Kuwait was little different from the occupation of Riyadh itself, and the disappearance of Kuwait would, sooner or later, pose a great threat to the security and identity of Saudi Arabia.

It was this lucid grasp of the impact of Saddam's move on the regional balance of power that made King Fahd impatient with King Hussein and PLO chairman Yasser Arafat, who later maintained that Saddam had no intention of attacking the Kingdom. "Why are you so nervous?" they said. "Saddam has told us himself he has no hostile intentions towards you . . ." The King also dismissed those innocent souls who argued that Saddam would have pulled out of Kuwait had his action not been immediately condemned by the Arab League Council, meeting in emergency session in Cairo.

From the King's point of view, those who thought in this way were blind to the consequences of what Saddam had already done. By invading Kuwait he had threatened the Kingdom's survival as an independent nation! I do not think anyone in the Kingdom could have doubted that, once Kuwait had gone, Saudi Arabia would have come under unbearable pressure from Saddam Hussein, whether he chose to leave it alone for a while or attack it straight away.

* A regional grouping, formed in 1981, of Saudi Arabia, Kuwait, Bahrain, Qatar, the United Arab Emirates and Oman.

Iraqi Forces compared to those of the GCC, Egypt and Syria

WEAPONS		IRAQ	BAHRAIN	OMAN	QATAR	SAUDI ARABIA Armed Forces	SAUDI ARABIA National Guard	UAE	EGYPT	SYRIA
Total Armed Forces	ACTIVE	1,000,000	6,000	29,500	7,500	67,500	55,000	44,000	450,000	404,000
	RESERVE	850,000							623,000	
Main Battle Tanks (MBT)		5,500	54	39	24	550		131	3,190	4,000
Light Tanks		100			36			76		
Infantry Fighting Vehicles (AFV)		1,500		2	30	>500		30	470	2,250
Armored Personnel Carriers (APC)		6,000	103	6	160	1,100	1,100	510	2,745	1,500
Self-Propelled Artillery (SP)		500		12	6	275		20	>140	186
Towed Artillery		3,000	14	63	>8	200	68	77	1,120	2,000
Multiple Rocket Launchers (MRL)		200				>14		58	300	250
Combat Aircraft (CBT AC)		689	24	57	18	189		91	475	558
Attack Helicopter (AH)		159	12	20				19	74	100

Source: The Military Balance 1990–1991, IISS

Once the war was over, Saddam was quoted several times as saying, "We made a vast mistake in not proceeding forthwith to invade Saudi Arabia" – which at the very least suggests that, at the back of his mind, he may have envisaged an attack on the Kingdom at a later stage. We cannot know his intentions for certain, but – from our vantage point at the time – what he had done was threatening enough.

With the Kingdom in jeopardy, it was therefore more or less inevitable that the King should turn for help to the United States, the one power strong enough to evict Saddam from Kuwait and restore the status quo ante. "The Kuwaitis delayed asking for help, and they are now our guests," the King remarked at the time. "We do not want to make the same mistake and become someone else's guests!" We had learned that, a day or two before the invasion, the Kuwaitis had received an American warning of Iraqi troop movements, but had delayed calling for help until it was too late.

In the hectic hours and days after the Iraqi invasion, the sobering conclusion reached after an appraisal of the political and military situation was that the ratio of Saudi land forces to Iraqi land forces was one to fifteen; while the ratio of all GCC land forces to Iraqi land forces was one to seven. If the whole Egyptian army could have come to the aid of the GCC, the ratio would still have been one to two. If we had been able to bring in both the Egyptian and the Syrian armies, the ratio would have been about one to one. But, of course, it was wholly unrealistic to imagine that either Egypt or Syria, or indeed our GCC partners, could have lent us all their land forces. The Syrians, in particular, were tied down on the Israeli front and in Lebanon, and had themselves to keep troops facing Iraq. Moreover, these difficulties apart, we and our Arab friends lacked large-scale means of strategic transportation, as well as an integrated defense policy.

Could we have hoped for help from the rest of the Islamic world? An Islamic state like Pakistan was deeply preoccupied by its confrontation with India, while Bangladesh and Malaysia were not very strong and, in any event, a long way away. Ours was a hostile environment. In the east, Iran would no doubt welcome any aggression against the Kingdom; Yemen in the south and Jordan in the northwest were sympathetic to Iraq and were linked to it in the recently formed Arab Cooperation Council, which seemed to us at the time like a riposte to our own Gulf Cooperation Council; in the northwest, too, was Israel, with its long history of hostility to the Arabs. And on our northern borders, Iraq was massing troops, with their numbers increasing by the hour. Moreover, Iraq was led by a man who had shown that he had no respect for his word. His deputy, Izzat Ibrahim, had refused even to discuss the invasion of Kuwait, where Iraqi troops were already committing ugly crimes.

In their analysis of this situation, our leaders determined that the friendly forces we invited to come to our aid would have to meet a number of conditions which could be summarized as follows:

1. They would have to be capable of high mobility and a speedy response.
2. They would need to have a deterrent capability, even before reaching the Kingdom.
3. They would need to be able to protect supply lines to the Kingdom, especially maritime routes.
4. They would have to be strong enough to defend the Kingdom and confront any possible Iraqi attack.
5. They would have to be able to contemplate launching an offensive operation to free Kuwait in the not too distant future.

The inescapable conclusion was that only the forces of the United States could meet these conditions.

King Fahd's decision to invite in American and other friendly troops – a decision which has rightly been termed "historic" – will no doubt be seen as one of the crowning achievements of his reign. It was also a decision dictated by logic. At a moment of peril, he was brave enough to put national survival first, thereby challenging the taboos and popular slogans that sometimes pass for Arab nationalism. He was not impressed by the argument that calling on the West for help could set the region on fire. Did Arab nationalism demand that Saudi Arabia bow to the will of an aggressor?

The King considered that some Muslims would no doubt

object to our seeking assistance from foreign troops, especially as this would be the first time that non-Muslim forces entered our territory. Unlike other parts of the Arab world, we had never been colonized by a Western power. He was aware that some Muslims might fear that foreign troops would stay on in Saudi Arabia after fulfilling their mission. There was also concern that some Saudi citizens, and some citizens from other Arab and Muslim countries, might react negatively. But the King judged that, in the threatening circumstances created by Saddam's invasion of Kuwait, such risks had to be taken. In everything he did, the King was acutely sensitive to Muslim opinion, not just in the Kingdom but around the world. His Islamic credentials were globally recognized. It needs to be recalled that he had carried out the greatest expansion in history of the holy shrines at Makkah and Madina. And it was at Madina on October 27, 1986 (or 24 Safar 1407 A H in our Islamic calendar), that he had expressed the wish, in an official letter to Crown Prince Abdallah, that henceforth he be addressed only as "Custodian of the Two Holy Mosques," and no longer as "Your Majesty" or any other secular title.

There has been much speculation about how and when the King made up his mind to invite the Americans in. Some writers have claimed that his decision was taken on August 6 when Dick Cheney, the American Secretary of Defense, arrived in Jeddah at the head of a large delegation, which included General H. Norman Schwarzkopf, Commander in Chief, U.S. Central Command; Robert Gates, later CIA Director; Paul Wolfowitz, Under-Secretary for International Affairs at the Defense Department; Lieutenant Generals Charles Horner and John Yeosock from the U.S. Central Command; and a small army of senior aides and staff members. They were received at the royal palace by the King, by Crown Prince Abdallah, by Prince Abd al-Rahman bin Abd al-Aziz, the deputy Minister of Defense, by the Foreign Minister Prince Saud al-Faisal, by Othman al-Humayd, assistant Minister of Defense, and by the Chief of Staff, General Muhammad al-Hammad, while my brother, Prince Bandar, our ambassador in Washington, translated for the King. Prince Sultan, the Defense Minister, who had been recovering in Morocco from knee surgery and was consulted by telephone at

every stage and on every aspect of the crisis, flew to Jeddah
on the evening of the 6th, and met with Cheney the next day.

According to some accounts, the determining factor in the
King's decision is said to have been satellite pictures produced
by Cheney purporting to show Iraqi forces massing on the Kingdom's borders. In other accounts, the ball started to roll some
days earlier on the other side of the Atlantic when Margaret
Thatcher, Britain's "Iron Lady," met George Bush at Aspen,
Colorado, on the very day of Saddam's invasion, and stiffened
the American President's resolve to intervene.

These fanciful accounts omit some essential background.

The King's decision to invite in the Americans was not taken
on the spur of the moment, nor was it the subject of dissent
within the family, nor indeed did any one person, other than
the King himself, and certainly no foreigner, play a determining
role. Decisions vital to the national interest are not taken on the
basis of a casual remark here or there. The survival of our
country did not depend on Mrs. Thatcher happening to be in
Aspen nor on the fact that the King was shown a few pictures.

The decision was the result of a consensus among leading
members of the royal family, arrived at and reinforced over the
years, that if our security and the integrity of our territory were
threatened, and if our own forces were in danger of being overwhelmed, then we would not hesitate to request assistance from
any friendly nation with which we had common interests —
including the United States.

Under Prince Sultan's direction, Saudi Arabia's defensive
capability has improved vastly over the past decade — especially
the air force and the air defense forces, as well as military infrastructure generally, including the building of "military cities" at
strategic sites around the country. But, in spite of these dramatic
advances, the continued vulnerability of our large and thinly
populated country and its rich oil reserves is a fact of life that
cannot be disguised or ignored. As a result, the widely shared
assumption among Saudi decision-makers was that we would
have to depend on our friends, and on those with whom we
have common interests, specifically on the United States, if we
faced a massive aggression from, say, the ex-Soviet Union, which
would be beyond our capability to handle on our own. We

calculated that, in such circumstances, it would be in the West's own interest to help us. Friendship is to be found between individuals, but between nations interests prevail.

It is no secret that the Americans tried hard over the years to persuade us to formalize this security relationship and allow them to pre-position war materiel in the Kingdom. President Carter, shocked by the fall of the Shah of Iran in early 1979 and fearful that this would trigger general instability in the region, wanted us to sign a defense treaty. President Reagan even went so far as to offer us a deal identical to the "strategic alliance" he concluded with Israel. "Everything I am offering Israel, you can have," he told us.

But King Fahd, even when he was still Crown Prince, saw no need to formalize the relationship with the United States. His often expressed view was that, if ever we faced a problem that constituted a threat to both ourselves and the Americans, we would not need a formal alliance. We would fight together. But if their interests were not endangered, no formal alliance would compel them to help us.

His reading from the beginning was that the Kingdom faced two sorts of potential threat: one which endangered American interests, in which case they would come, and one which did not, in which case they might be reluctant to come. So it was pointless, in his view, to tie ourselves to an alliance which was likely to arouse the hostility of the Arab and Muslim world. I do not think any leading member of the family disagreed with this analysis – even though journalists and other outsiders are always looking for points of dissension.

Although the King refused American requests for a formal alliance, we were nevertheless kept fully informed of American defensive preparations in the region. We took note of the new resolve under President Carter – known as the Carter Doctrine – to project force into the region if American interests were threatened. We watched the birth of the U.S. Rapid Deployment Force and its evolution in 1983 into the U.S. Central Command (CENTCOM) which, for the first time, made an American commitment to defend the Gulf look credible. At the same time, U.S. arms sales to the Kingdom gathered pace. But, rather than sign a defense treaty with Washington, the King together with our neighbors in the Gulf continued to prefer an "over the horizon" American defense umbrella, to be opened only in the event of a real threat.

This, then, was the background to the King's decision: Saddam posed a grave threat to our security, to the stability of the region, and to the international economy of which our oil-producing Eastern Province was a vital nerve center. As only the Americans could stop him and reverse his aggression, they were welcome to come. It was acknowledged that calling in the Americans would be a great risk, but this would be reduced by the King's determination to keep control. For example, a condition for accepting U.S. help was a signed commitment that U.S. forces would withdraw at the King's request.

The real question, therefore, with which the King and his advisers had to wrestle was not whether or not to call in the Americans. Rather it was: could the Americans be relied upon? Would they come in sufficient numbers and with sufficient determination to finish the job? This was the question which occupied the first four or five days after the invasion and which was debated back and forth across the Atlantic.

To gain time for the answer to be clarified, the King continued the process of consultations with Arab and non-Arab leaders. Before taking the momentous step of issuing an invitation, he had to be sure he could truly count on the United States, and then on Britain. In those early days, I understand he spent several hours talking on the telephone to President Bush and Mrs. Thatcher. I do not know whether the liberation of Kuwait was mentioned in so many words, but we must assume that, had the King not received firm assurances from American and British leaders that they would fight, he would have clung publicly to the hope that the Arabs could work something out among themselves. He believed that this time an "Arab solution" could not be counted on, but he could not afford to risk losing both the Arabs and the West.

In a sense, therefore, the Cheney mission to Riyadh of August 6 merely put an official, public seal on something which had already been decided. The King had already made up his mind. President Bush's order to two carrier battle groups to deploy to the region was issued before August 6 and the 82nd Airborne

Division was already preparing to move when the American delegation was received by the King.

As I have suggested, I do not think there was the slightest disagreement among the Kingdom's three key policymakers – the King, Crown Prince Abdallah and Prince Sultan – that this was the right course to follow.

Some commentators have portrayed the Gulf War as a Western imperialist war, waged in defense of Western economic interests. Other commentators, several Arabs among them, have portrayed the war as a cynical American–Israeli conspiracy to destroy the one Arab country able to challenge Israel's military power.

What these writers overlook is that Saddam Hussein did not threaten only Western and Israeli interests. Had he done so, the Coalition against him would have been very different. He threatened the vital interests of every major player in the region – Arab states like Saudi Arabia, Syria, and Egypt, but also non-Arab powers like Turkey and Iran. None could tolerate his bid for regional hegemony, because that is what his aggression amounted to.

It was because so many countries – not all by any means on good terms with one another – saw his move as a deadly threat to themselves that George Bush was able to put the Coalition together and inflict on Iraq the punishment that he subsequently did. To see the war only in terms of Western interest in the defense of oil or the protection of Israel obscures the true nature of the crisis by overlooking the impact of Saddam's move on regional politics and on the interests of regional players.

Saddam's folly was to threaten the interests of all the neighboring states, as well as of several further afield. In defense of their own vital interests, a number of Arab states, in alliance with foreign friends, were forced to make war on him – although they were aware that this would no doubt be to the advantage of adversaries such as Israel. It was a dilemma from which Saddam's aggression allowed them no escape.

CHAPTER III

✦

The Battle for Authority

WHILE THE KING, the Crown Prince and Prince Sultan dealt with high policy at this supreme moment of national peril, the Kingdom's military commanders struggled to find the right response to the war raging close to our borders.

I recall that I first heard the news that Iraqi troops had crossed the Kuwaiti border when I was at my farm, an hour by road from Riyadh, and I raced to my office at the Air Defense Command placing on full alert our nationwide air defense network. It was 4 a.m. on August 2.

Shortly afterwards, I made my way to the office of the Chief of Staff, General Muhammad al-Hammad, where I was soon joined by the other members of the Higher Officers' Committee – the commanders of the land forces, the air force and the navy, respectively Lieutenant Generals Yusuf Abd al-Rahman al-Rashid, Ahmad al-Buhairi and Talal al-Mufadhi.

As military commanders, we were faced with the immediate problem of making practical arrangements to receive, and provide logistical support for the troops which friendly governments were proposing to send us. The Egyptians, the Moroccans and the Syrians had indicated their willingness to send troops. But as yet no preparations had been made to receive them. We needed to reply to inquiries from friends who were eager to assist us. Clearly, a major reorganization of our land and air bases, and indeed of our whole support structure, was required. From a military point of view, that first week was very trying. Saddam's objectives were unclear and the response of the international community was uncertain.

My wife and family had gone abroad on holiday at the end of July and I was due to join them on August 4. Of course, I could no longer do so. But I persuaded them to stay away for a while, not because I wanted them out of danger, but because I needed to be free to devote my whole attention to the crisis.

When I saw the difficulties we were facing in putting our peacetime military establishment on a war footing, it became clear to me that we had to think innovatively. I believed that we needed to create a separate command, alongside our existing military structure, and assign to it the officers and men required for the mission at hand. The concept I had in mind was that of a task force, set up to deal with a particular problem: this was the procedure followed by other armies and even by businesses when faced with an unexpected emergency. I envisaged that, to do the job, such a command would need to be given full authority.

After a more or less sleepless night pondering these questions, I put my proposals in writing to the Chief of Staff, and appealed to him to consider them. My starting point was that our existing command structure was having difficulty coping with the crisis. I urged the Chief of Staff to set up a Joint Forces Command, separate from the existing military hierarchy, to take the situation in hand and deal with the Americans and other friendly forces.

To assist the Chief of Staff in that first week of the crisis, I also asked my staff to prepare flow charts to determine the number, size and type of units we might require from friendly countries, the preparations we would have to make before their arrival, and the procedures to be followed until the stage of their combat readiness in the field. I submitted these charts to the Chief of Staff.

On August 5, I telephoned Prince Sultan in Morocco to seek his advice. As the architect of our armed forces, and as Defense Minister for more than three decades, he knew the worth of every commander and the exact extent of our capabilities. He was the only man who could solve the problems we were facing. Although a civilian, Prince Sultan has had more military experience than any general in our armed services.

But, as ill luck would have it, following his knee operation

Prince Sultan could move only with the greatest pain and difficulty, so much so that the King, out of compassion, had advised
him to remain where he was until he made a full recovery.
But there was no way Prince Sultan could stay away from the
Kingdom at such a desperate moment, and to my relief I learned
that he had already made preparations to fly back immediately.

At any moment, American troops were expected to start
arriving in the Kingdom in massive numbers. To prepare the
way for them, U.S. Defense Secretary Dick Cheney and General
Schwarzkopf had left behind Lieutenant General Charles
Horner, the Air Force Commander of Central Command, and
Lieutenant General John Yeosock, the Army Commander. As
the senior American officer present, Chuck Horner was appointed acting CENTCOM Forward Commander. Like myself,
he was very conscious of the fact that between Riyadh and the
massed Iraqi divisions on the border there was nothing except a
thin Saudi screening force. Horner's air force deputy was already
busy deploying U.S. air wings which would have to go into
action, side-by-side with our own air force, if the Iraqis crossed
our frontier. Yet, in those early days, it had not even been
decided where U.S. headquarters were to be located. John Yeosock's main task was to deal with various Saudi government
agencies in preparing for the reception of U.S. ground troops at
our ports and airports and then see to their onward movement
to the field. In those dangerous and turbulent days of early
August, the Americans needed decisions about where to put
their people and how to support them. They had to get their men
to where they would be most useful should the Iraqis attack. The
incoming transport planes could not hang about in the air.

Friendly forces coming to our aid needed to work with a Saudi
team – and with a Saudi commander who had sufficient authority to make things happen. Clearly, there was a vacuum to be
filled. I proposed that the new Joint Forces Command fill this
vacuum.

Even before such arrangements could be made, I had already
intervened in a number of small ways. I had secured Prince
Sultan's agreement that the American headquarters should be
located in the new command center in the basement of our
Ministry of Defense where they could interface with our own

people. My staff also gave Lieutenant General Horner what help they could. It is amusing to remember that, in those early days, he was driving about in a rental car without a telephone: we provided him with a car, and a car phone so that we could keep in close touch with him.

I was anxious, however, for the Chief of Staff and the other force commanders to understand that I was not seeking to promote myself. I did not want the job of heading the proposed new command, I told them, but they must put someone capable in charge and we would all support him. Within a day or two, with the need to accommodate the incoming Americans becoming ever more urgent, the Chief of Staff was won around to my ideas. He sent a letter to Prince Sultan endorsing the idea of a Joint Forces Command and recommending me as the officer best suited to head it. Prince Sultan promptly returned the letter with the advice that they look for someone else! Perhaps he did not want to appear to be favoring his son. He suggested another commander. To which the Chief of Staff replied that, in his opinion, none of the other commanders could do the job. Considering the upset I was proposing in his military hierarchy, it took a great man to say so.

The matter was put before the King and, on August 9, he approved my appointment as Joint Forces Commander to take effect 12 noon on Friday, August 10. No royal decree was issued or official announcement made. The King's decision was conveyed in a letter to Prince Sultan – a discreet way of doing things which was just as well, considering the opposition the idea of a Joint Forces Command soon aroused among senior officers, several of them more senior than myself. I would have liked my appointment to have been made by royal decree to underline the importance of the responsibilities the King was giving me. In retrospect, however, I see that this was perhaps unrealistic.

I must in passing correct Norman Schwarzkopf's version of these events in his book *It Doesn't Take a Hero* where he writes that my appointment "was Horner's and Yeosock's first victory." He claims that, needing to deal with a Saudi general who had the authority to spend money, they "appealed in frustration" to Prince Sultan who, after conferring with the King, put me in charge. "Simply put," Schwarzkopf concludes, "Khaled had the authority to write checks." This is an inaccurate outsider's view of the reasons for my appointment as Joint Forces Commander, and the steps which led to it. As Lieutenant Generals Horner and Yeosock would confirm, they did not meet Prince Sultan or discuss my appointment with him, or indeed have anything to do with it.

I immediately set about structuring my organization and putting my team together. From the very start, I saw that my task would involve three quite different aspects which will be further explained in this and subsequent chapters: the first was practical, smoothing the way, in every sense of the word, for the vast inflow of foreign forces to the Kingdom; the second, symbolic but nonetheless crucial, was making sure our all-powerful American allies did not swallow us up; the third was to get my fellow force commanders to agree that I needed overall operational authority if I was to have the flexibility necessary to fulfill my mission.

I can perhaps best explain the tension which surfaced between me and other force commanders at this time if I say that our differences revolved around the different levels of operational and tactical command. I believed the job of Joint Forces Commander required operational command of all our land forces in the Theater of Operations, as well as of the air force and the navy – that is to say, I wanted to be free to assign missions to any of our forces and insist on their execution. In contrast, the other force commanders saw the new Joint Forces Command as a mere tactical headquarters, to which liaison officers from the air force and navy would be assigned. These liaison officers would pass on my requests to the force commanders – which they would then comply with or veto as they saw fit, leaving them in effect in ultimate command of their respective services.

Prince Abdallah, the Crown Prince, was to give me some very welcome encouragement in my battle for authority. As I have mentioned, I accompanied him on a visit to the troops in the field on August 20.

Protocol demanded that I fly ahead to Hafr al-Batin to receive him there. Accordingly, I arranged to leave an hour before he did. But when my plane was about to take off, a messenger came hurrying out onto the runway. The Crown Prince wanted to speak to me urgently. I thought it must be something serious, and ran from the plane to the nearest phone in the terminal building. One of his senior advisers, Prince Turki bin Abdallah, was on the line. He explained that the Crown Prince wanted to propose a change in the hour at which we were to take lunch with the troops at Hafr al-Batin. He wanted to give himself more time to visit the units, but he did not want to change the program without first consulting me.

What a boost to my morale! That gentle word of courtesy was balm after the problems I was facing. The Crown Prince was confirming my new authority in the nicest possible way, while others were seeking to question it. I felt I had been awarded a medal.

❖⊰×⊱❖

Lieutenant General John Yeosock, the CENTCOM Army Commander, was a good soldier with a gruff, straightforward manner who had some knowledge of our country, which is no doubt why he was chosen for the job. I grew to like him. A decade earlier, he had spent two years in the Kingdom advising the Saudi Arabian National Guard on its modernization. He had some familiarity with our government bureaucracy which, like bureaucracies everywhere, was not built to cut corners or deliver swift decisions. But now that we faced an emergency, I had to get the Saudi government machine to speed up its way of doing business. As there was no existing codification governing U.S. –Saudi relations, we had to make things up as we went along.

In the first few days of the crisis, the two countries had simply agreed that the U.S. would deploy troops and that the Saudis would facilitate the operation. But how was this to be done? No formal instruments were exchanged at Secretary Cheney's meeting with the King, no detailed guidelines were laid down. We had to work it all out. U.S. forces had been used to operating in a NATO environment where every move made – down to loading a train or crossing a border – is governed by regulations built up over 45 years. Between the various members of NATO there are treaties, memoranda of understanding, bilateral and multilateral arrangements, status of forces agreements. But Saudi Arabia and the United States had entered into an alliance for a combined operation in the Gulf with absolutely none of that. I soon discovered this was actually an advantage because it allowed us to invent the ground rules as we needed them.

I came to the job with certain advantages. I felt I had enough insight into the cultural differences between Westerners and Saudis to be able to bridge the gap and make the actions we had to take palatable to both sides. I knew what compromises were possible, and when it was necessary to draw the line.

Yeosock put together a staff drawn from the U.S. army, navy, air force and marine corps. As his deputy, he called in Major General Paul Schwartz, who knew the Kingdom well as he had also spent some years with the National Guard. A man of great tact and charm, he had a gift for human relations. I, in turn, picked bright men from across the Saudi armed services to staff my Joint Forces Command. The main focus of my attention in those first few days was to build an organization on a par with the American command, and able to plan, manage and execute missions jointly with it.

As my deputy, I appointed Major General Abd al-Aziz al-Shaikh, the Deputy Commander of Land Forces, a good field officer with whom I had occasionally clashed over the years but whom I admired for his honesty, toughness, sense of initiative and fearlessness in speaking his mind. I wanted someone brave enough to give me frank advice.

Yeosock and I needed a point of fusion between our two organizations – a place to which problems could be sent to be resolved – so we invented a body known as the C3IC, an acronym which stood for the Coalition Coordination Communications and Integration Cell. In charge of it on a 24-hour-a-day basis, we put Major General Schwartz and Major General Salih al-Garza'i, a fine front-line officer. After a short while, however, I gave Major General Garza'i command of the 8th Brigade, and replaced him in the C3IC with Brigadier General Abd al-Rahman al-Marshad, a capable, self-confident officer. Between them, Major General Schwartz and Brigadier General Marshad did a superb job. This was where the capability for combined Saudi–U.S. operations was first generated. The C3I cell became a war-winning organization, for it was here that all the many problems between CENTCOM and the Joint Forces Command were resolved – problems such as logistics, intelligence sharing, training, the allocation of firing ranges, and so on. Eventually, as our coordination expanded, it was decided for greater efficiency to split the cell into ground, air, naval, logistics, special operations and intelligence sections.

As I have said, in those early weeks I had the title of Joint Forces Commander but still not complete authority. The Chief of Staff and the forces commanders did not yet recognize my responsibilities. While fighting for my authority, I was at the same time Yeosock's counterpart as Land Forces Commander. In other words, I was wearing two hats: first as Joint Forces Commander, and second as Commander of Land Forces in the Theater of Operations.

In those anxious August weeks when it looked as if Saddam might attack, General Schwarzkopf had not yet arrived. While CENTCOM headquarters was still at its base at Tampa, Florida, Lieutenant General Yeosock and I hammered out the basic relationship between our forces on the ground. I was determined that the Saudis should remain in front of the Americans, and that if the Iraqis attacked, the Saudis would be the first to shed blood. So we worked out where the U.S. troops would be deployed behind the Saudi units and where the boundaries between them would lie. I knew Yeosock needed time to deploy his forces. I therefore never suggested that U.S. troops should go forward to act as a tripwire.

At all-night working sessions, Yeosock and I tackled a thousand problems (keeping ourselves awake with cups of extra-strong cappuccino). The U.S. needed large-scale debarkation facilities at our airports and seaports and it needed them at once. One night Yeosock told me he needed 30 clear berths at Dammam, as well as access to nearby warehouses. Respecting his professionalism, I knew that I did not have to query his requirements. But it meant moving people and ships out of Dammam in a hurry, with the risk that civilian trade and traffic would be disrupted. To go through bureaucratic channels would have taken weeks. I was able to resolve the matter in a few hours.

In Dammam, the Americans could not cope with a situation

in which one man was in charge of warehousing, another of pier space, and a third of the handling equipment. To get things to happen, I felt I needed one man at the port with total authority over every function there. I was able to find such a man in Major Ali Al-Shu'aybi.

According to Saudi regulations, everything the Americans brought into the Kingdom had to be checked through customs. But this would have created a monstrous bottleneck: Yeosock was ordering supplies from the States and Germany in astronomical quantities, 3,000 of this and 5,000 of the other. To check the containers through our customs in the normal way would have meant mobilizing the whole nation as customs officials! Fortunately, I was able to find my way around what might have been a serious problem.

One night at eleven o'clock Yeosock called me to say that his logistics commander in Dhahran was in a state of high frustration. Costs of local contracts – whether for food, water, trucks or what have you – were spiraling out of control. "If I offer $200 a day for a truck," he complained, "the next day it's $400." This was something we had to stomp on at once – especially as Saudi Arabia was paying the bills! The following morning, price controls were in effect.

Yeosock and I recognized that the U.S. and Saudi Arabia had vital, if different, contributions to make to the Coalition. No one could match the advanced weapons, the technology or the capability of the U.S. armed forces, but similarly, few countries had our vast resources. We each had to give of our best but, as the host country, we had to lay down the rules.

At one of our late-night cappuccino sessions, Yeosock asked me how I conceived our relationship.

"All you need are terms of reference," I replied.

"You make the terms," he said with a laugh, "and everyone else has to refer to them!"

He was right. As the hosts, the Saudis had to lay down the terms of reference, and the other members of the Coalition had to refer to them. If they did not like the terms, they could negotiate and try to change them. But, at the end of the day, that is how it was.

From the very start, the King, Crown Prince Abdallah and

Prince Sultan were agreed that Saudi forces were not to serve under any command but their own. They could not serve under American command: the need to protect the sovereignty of the Kingdom was paramount. It was in this spirit that, in the first few days of August, the King had asked the Americans for a legally binding, written undertaking that they would leave the Kingdom, no questions asked, whenever he wanted them to.

I feared that, whatever promises the Kingdom secured from Washington, once the war started the Americans would be in the driver's seat. We needed to establish from the start how military orders would be given.

My worry – even before I was appointed Joint Forces Commander – was that Saudi Arabia would not long retain its unique identity if it were seen to be passively under the U.S. umbrella. That is why, in dealing with Horner and Yeosock, and later with Norman Schwarzkopf, I strove to put together a credible, effective and professional staff which could work with the U.S. command, yet hold its own. I needed to defend the good name of the Kingdom. I was not playing a game of tennis in which I could afford to let the other man win. It was a matter of life and death.

It was essential that my staff grasp the seriousness of this point. When I first assembled them, I asked them one question. "Who was the military commander in Vietnam?" "Westmoreland," they answered. "And who was the commander in Korea?" "MacArthur," they replied. "But were not Vietnamese and Korean commanders also involved on the allied side?" I inquired. No one knew their names! I told them I did not want a repeat in Saudi Arabia of what had happened in Vietnam and Korea, where an American was the all-powerful supreme commander who could do what he liked.

I believed my King and my country would not forgive me if history were to record that we had been commanded or controlled by a foreigner on our own soil. My main concern, therefore, was to make sure that, in this conflict, there would be no supreme commander.

It was with this in mind that, after long discussions, I proposed that my title should be "Commander of Joint Forces and Theater of Operations." From a military point of view the title was eccentric, even wrong. I should have been called one thing or the other, but not both.

Why then was the "and" put in?

The first intention was to preempt any attempt to name General Schwarzkopf as Supreme Commander or even Joint Forces Commander. He was then the Commander in Chief of Central Command – known in U.S. military jargon as CINC-CENTCOM – and was due to arrive in the Kingdom in late August. The second objective was to prevent him calling himself Theater of Operations Commander, which he might have done seeing that he had troops not only in Saudi Arabia but also in Bahrain and elsewhere in the region. It was, in fact, a double blocking operation! For the sake of the country's dignity and independence, as well as for sound operational reasons, it was necessary to ensure that my command was strictly on the same level as that of the American commander – in other words a parallel command. It was not to be 49 percent, not 49.5 percent, but 50–50.

Moreover, in my letter of assignment from Prince Sultan a phrase was inserted in brackets. It read that "Theater of Operations" meant not just our Eastern and Northern provinces facing Kuwait and Iraq, but any area of the Kingdom to which combat operations might extend. Wherever a threat materialized on the territory of Saudi Arabia – from Yemen, say, or from Jordan, or from Israel in the northwest – I would be in charge. By rank, I was not the senior officer in the Saudi armed forces, but I wanted to be given overall authority.

The Americans were unhappy with my title. Clearly, there was some resistance in a part of the American bureaucracy to the notion of a parallel command. They preferred to call me the Commander of Arab and Islamic Forces. Failing that, they pressed for my title to be "Joint Forces Commander in the Theater of Operations" – "in" rather than "and" – which would have substantially limited my authority. In the end, although the American press was slow to catch on, the American authorities accepted the title I wanted – as indeed did President Bush himself in his generous letter of citation to me on the award of the Legion of Merit at the end of the campaign.

However, while noting that I had united the forces of 14 Arab and Islamic countries into a single army, even he failed to mention, probably unintentionally, the many non-Islamic troops under my command.

❖

In those early months I had to fight a stiff battle with my colleagues on the Higher Officers' Committee to convince them of my ideas. I wanted overall operational control while they wished to limit me to a tactical command.

In coopting officers to my staff, I looked for men who could plan and act, whereas they wanted to assign mere liaison officers to my command. They wanted me to have the title of Joint Forces Commander while themselves retaining direct control over their own forces. At first, they tried to limit my powers to the land forces in the Eastern and Northern Area Commands – and even there I was supposed to bow to the authority of the Land Forces Commander. If I wished to assign missions to the air force or the navy, I would have to negotiate with their respective commanders.

I argued that it was not a matter of taking the credit, but of doing the job. On one occasion, after a particularly heated argument, I went home in a fury. But I soon had second thoughts. "By God," I said to myself, "I can't give up now. If we don't talk again, what will happen to this country?" So I went back and, inch by inch, week by week, fought for the powers I needed. Eventually my colleagues agreed that I should handle the Americans. But what of the Egyptians, the Syrians, the Moroccans who had already arrived, and the long list of others who were expected? Who was to be responsible for them?

I sent a letter to Prince Sultan who, although still suffering from a painful knee, was firmly back in charge of the Ministry of Defense. In my letter I explained the nature of my disagreement with the Higher Officers' Committee. "Let the Chief of Staff take command," I wrote. "I will serve as his adjutant or as his junior in any capacity. But let us get on with the work." I pointed out that, among other difficulties, our disputes were creating problems for the Americans: for example, a man like

Lieutenant General Horner, the acting CENTCOM Commander, did not know with whom to deal.

Our disagreement placed Prince Sultan in an awkward position. Although I was his son, he did not wish the other commanders to think that he favored me for that reason. He asked the Assistant Minister of Defense, Shaikh Othman al-Humayd, a highly respected soldier and former Chief of Staff, to mediate, but it was to no avail. I wanted operational command of all our forces, but they were reluctant to let me have it. Relations became somewhat tense. In the early days of the crisis, I had been in the habit of lunching almost every day with the other force commanders in the Chief of Staff's office. But I grew so distant from them that I stopped going.

Finally, on November 5, I sent a top-secret letter to Prince Sultan, a strong five-page letter. I poured into it all my fears and complaints. The country was in danger. I had been coping as best I could, but it could not go on. Problems were mounting up. Hundreds of thousands of men were on their way. Our responsibilities were becoming greater. He had to decide whether I was to have an operational or a tactical command. Three weeks later, on November 27, he broke the deadlock by summoning us to a meeting at the Air Force Operations Center. It was his habit to visit the headquarters of every force on a rotating basis to see what was going on. He used to listen to briefings by the commanders, review the operational plans, and examine the combat readiness of the troops. He would also send inspection teams to carry out spot checks of individual units. This time he may have chosen Air Force Headquarters because the air force was where the main opposition to granting me operational control was to be found, based on long-held fears of a land forces commander being placed over the air commanders, rather than being coequal with them. I knew, however, that no war had ever been fought with an air force commander in overall control. Be that as it may, the Air Force Headquarters was where the main struggle for authority was being fought. The Air Force Commander, Lieutenant General Ahmad al-Buhairi, was a friend, but we had on this issue a professional disagreement.

About two dozen generals were present – the Chief of Staff,

the force commanders, the base commanders from various parts of the Kingdom, and other senior commanders. It was late morning and the lights in the large room were dimmed.

The meeting opened with an air force briefing for the Prince, followed by interventions by other generals. Usually Prince Sultan has a smile on his face but, as he explained to us the unprecedented dangers facing the Kingdom, his face darkened. I had rarely seen him so somber. Then, looking from one general to the other, he burst out angrily: "You are quarreling among yourselves while the safety of the country is in the balance. It is intolerable."

"I want the navy, the air force, the land forces, everybody, under a single command," he declared. "If you don't think Khaled can do the job, get him out! I don't care whether he is my son or not. You are all my sons. I will not take sides in your disputes. You must solve this matter now!

"I want you all to know that I will not endanger the country because of your differences. Is anyone here capable of assuming command? If he is, then let him speak up and I will support him to the end and give him full operational authority. But if no one is ready, then let Khaled have the powers he needs!"

Prince Sultan spoke in this vein for half an hour. I had never seen him in such commanding form. He was the general of the generals. Firm and yet unbiased by family feeling, his words created a profound impression. Not one of the generals presented himself as a commander. Everyone realized that a turning point in the crisis had been reached.

That speech was the key to my success. It was the first time I had felt in complete charge. From that moment on I was fully supported. I was given the authority I needed to prepare for war. On November 30, Prince Sultan officially delegated wide powers to me.

I knew then that I could head a command of which the country would be proud.

CHAPTER IV

Grandson of Ibn Saud

FROM MY BOYHOOD, I have wanted to be a soldier. Even as a young teenager, I realized I did not want to live a civilian life, but longed for a tougher and more exciting existence in which I dreamed of winning fame and performing great feats of arms.

This must have had something to do with my personality which was — and I fear still is — stubborn and combative. As a child, I always wanted to get my own way and was ready to fight for it. I used to pride myself on never crying, even if I fell down and hurt myself. When I was eleven or twelve, I was thrown from my horse and broke a leg, but my brother Fahd, who was riding with me at the time, will testify that he never saw a tear in my eye. I must have been a tough kid, and not very easy for others to get on with. I have always preferred to be a leader than a follower.

Almost certainly, the main factor which shaped me as I was growing up was the fact that I was the eldest son of Prince Sultan. As Minister of Defense — a post he has held without interruption for more than thirty years — my father was very busy with his government responsibilities. My memory of him as a child was that he was always working at his papers or talking on the telephone. This meant that, in a way, I had to undertake some family duties, which contributed to the sense of responsibility my father implanted in me when I was very young. In our large family, with brothers and sisters bound together by bonds of affection and real warmth, there were always domestic problems to attend to, the need for someone to give advice, to talk things out, or simply to be there. From a very early age I was aware that, as the eldest son of a very important man, I had to play this role.

Although I was still a boy in the early 1960s, I think I was also greatly influenced by the leadership and intimidating personality of King Faisal who came to the throne in 1964 at a critical time for the Kingdom. He greatly enhanced the strength of the family, as well as Saudi Arabia's reputation in the world, but he was a ruler who was more respected than loved. A stern man, he set high standards for himself and expected a lot from others. There is no doubt that his example marked many of the younger members of the family, myself among them.

But perhaps still more formative in my make-up was the fact that I was the grandson of King Abd al-Aziz, known as Ibn Saud, our great forebear who, with faith, gun, sword and skillful diplomacy, united this huge country – over which he ruled for half a century and to which he gave the name of Saudi Arabia. King Abd al-Aziz died in 1953 when I was only four so, although I have heard a great deal about him from my father and my uncles, my personal recollection of him is vague. I can just sense his towering presence. He was a very large man with very big hands and a tender smile.

When I was fifteen I wrote an essay, which was published in our school magazine, about his daring recapture of Riyadh in 1902, when he was only 24 years old. Surging out of the deep desert to achieve surprise in what we would today call a commando raid, Abd al-Aziz and his men scaled the walls of the city with palm trunks and overwhelmed the garrison. In this feat of arms, his main associates were four members of a branch of the House of Saud known as Al Jiluwi. Three were sons of Prince Jiluwi – Abdallah, Abd al-Aziz and Fahd – and the fourth was a grandson, Abd al-Aziz bin Musa'id, then a youth in his teens, who was to be my own mother's father. The Al Jiluwi were renowned for their fighting prowess. Indeed, in the recapture of Riyadh, it was Abdallah bin Jiluwi who chased Ajlan, the ruler of the city, across the courtyard of his fortress and felled him with his sword, thus deciding the battle in favor of the Al Saud. On that same morning, Abd al-Aziz was proclaimed ruler.

Over the following several decades, the Al Jiluwi earned a further reputation as dedicated servants of the Saudi state,

My Family Tree

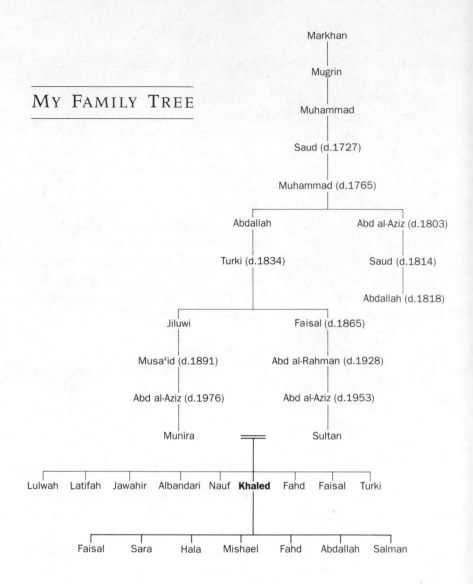

Markhan

Mugrin

Muhammad

Saud (d.1727)

Muhammad (d.1765)

Abdallah — Abd al-Aziz (d.1803)

Turki (d.1834) — Saud (d.1814)

Abdallah (d.1818)

Jiluwi — Faisal (d.1865)

Musa'id (d.1891) — Abd al-Rahman (d.1928)

Abd al-Aziz (d.1976) — Abd al-Aziz (d.1953)

Munira === Sultan

Lulwah Latifah Jawahir Albandari Nauf **Khaled** Fahd Faisal Turki

Faisal Sara Hala Mishael Fahd Abdallah Salman

Markhan and Mugrin are my distant seventeenth-century ancestors. Saud (d. 1727) is the ancestor who gave the name to the family. Muhammad bin Saud (d.1765) contracted the key alliance with Shaikh Muhammad bin Abd al-Wahab, founder of the religious reform movement.

Turki (d. 1834) liberated Najd from the Turks and moved the capital of the Al Saud to Riyadh after the old capital of Dir'iya was sacked by the forces of Muhammad Ali, ruler of Egypt.

Abd al-Aziz (d. 1953), founder of the modern kingdom of Saudi Arabia, had many children. For the sake of brevity, the chart shows only one of his sons, my father Prince Sultan.

King Abd al-Aziz, founder of the modern Kingdom of Saudi Arabia, photographed in the 1930s with some of his sons. My father, Prince Sultan, is on the far left of the picture. As a very young man he was already serving as Governor of Riyadh.

The launch of the long-standing Saudi–American relationship may be dated back to the five-hour meeting between King Abd al-Aziz and President Franklin D. Roosevelt on board the USS *Quincy* in Egypt's Great Bitter Lake on February 14, 1945. The interpreter was Colonel William A. Eddy, Minister at the American Legation in Jeddah. Born in Sidon, Lebanon, he spoke fluent Arabic.

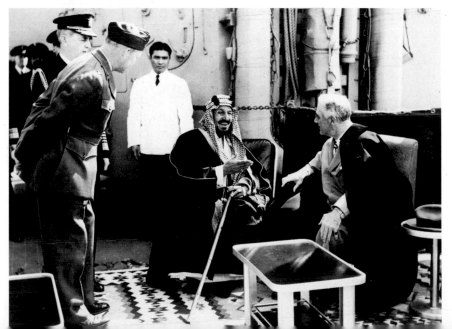

ABOVE LEFT: This rare early photograph of my great-grandfather, Imam Abd al-Rahman bin Faisal al-Saud, was probably taken at the turn of the century. In 1891, following a clash with his adversaries, the Al Rashid, he was forced to flee from the Saudi capital Riyadh and take refuge in Kuwait. In 1902, Riyadh was recaptured by his 24-year-old son, Abd al-Aziz. Imam Abd al-Rahman died in 1928.

ABOVE RIGHT: My mother's father, Prince Abd al-Aziz bin Musa'id al-Jiluwi, was the Governor of Hail in northern Nejd for half a century, from 1922 until his retirement in the 1970s when he was well over 90. As a young man in 1902, he took part in the fight to recapture Riyadh.

RIGHT: Myself, age three, outside my father's old house, al-Aziziyya, in Riyadh.

RIGHT: I am standing in the middle of the front row next to my younger brother Fahd, my closest childhood companion. Another playmate, Nader, son of my nanny Bushra, is crouching on the right of the picture.

BELOW LEFT: My brother Fahd and myself (age about eight) with retainers.

BELOW RIGHT: Fahd and myself (age about ten) in the garden of al-Aziziyya, our old house in Riyadh. I am carrying my baby brother Faisal.

King Saud *(in dark glasses)* and my father, Prince Sultan, on a visit to the young King Hussein of Jordan in Amman shortly after the latter's accession to the throne in 1953.

King Faisal *(seen in profile on the left of the picture, and below)* consolidated the Kingdom's finances and its international reputation during his rule from 1964 to 1975. Seated one chair away from him is Prince Turki bin Abd al-Aziz, then the deputy Defense Minister. I am leaning on the back of the empty chair between them (and earned a reprimand from my father at that time for sitting so casually).

ABOVE: In 1990, King Fahd took the courageous decision to ask for Western help in repelling Saddam Hussein's aggression against Kuwait which threatened the independence of Saudi Arabia and its Gulf neighbors.

RIGHT: King Khaled, who ruled from 1975 to 1982, presided over a period of prosperity and ambitious development planning.

Army Form B.2606.
(REVISED)

MILITARY
IDENTITY CARD No.   C   079838

Surname   HRH PRINCE KHALED .

Christian Names (and rank or
designation at time of issue)

Sex   MALE

Personal No.

Height   6'

Colour of Eyes   BROWN

Colour of Hair   BLACK.

THE ROYAL MI~~

Other Distinguishing Marks (if any)

Date of Birth   1948.

Signature of Issuing Officer   *R.L.Rule*

Signature of Bearer

Date   28/2/67

ABOVE: From my early teens I dreamed of going to
Sandhurst. Although I was born in September 1949, I
gave my date of birth as 1948 to gain admittance early.
I was 17½ when this military identity card was issued.

RIGHT: At Sandhurst, in the year I graduated.
I am a proud corporal in the Cadet Government of
Gaza Company.

BELOW: The old building and parade ground at
Sandhurst with, in the foreground, the Adjutant on
his traditional gray horse.

RIGHT: My father Prince Sultan and Egypt's leader Gamal Abd al-Nasser are seen clasping hands amicably. Their friendship was interrupted during the Yemen civil war of the 1960s when they found themselves on opposite sides.

BELOW: My first field command in 1970. Commanding a Hawk battery at Tabuk in northwestern Saudi Arabia at the age of 21.

On a visit to the United States in 1973 to negotiate the purchase of Raytheon's Improved Hawk missile, I met Elliot Richardson, President Nixon's Secretary of Defense. The visit marked a watershed in my career.

RIGHT: In June 1988, as Commander of Saudi Arabia's Air Defense Forces, I paid an official visit to the Lexington, Massachusetts headquarters of the Raytheon Company, manufacturers of the Hawk and Patriot missiles. *From left to right:* Dennis J. Picard, then Senior Vice President and General Manager, Raytheon Missile Systems Division; Thomas L. Phillips, then Chairman and CEO, Raytheon Company; myself; James J. Lewis, the Senior Vice President and Program Manager, Raytheon Middle East Systems Company.

The multibillion-dollar contract for a command, control and communications system which I negotiated with "Tex" Thornton, Chairman of Litton Industries – seen here at his California ranch – was to prove one of the biggest headaches of my military career.

fighting in numerous wars against the Turks and local adversaries and being rewarded for their valor by their appointment as provincial governors once Saudi rule had prevailed in different parts of Arabia. Thus, King Abd al-Aziz made the Al Jiluwi governors of the Eastern Province, a post members of their family held until fairly recently. The Al Jiluwi were strong people, and a firm hand was required at al-Hasa to maintain law and order in the years when the oil industry was being established.

In 1922, my maternal grandfather, Abd al-Aziz bin Musa'id al-Jiluwi, after a glorious career as a military commander, was named governor of Hail, the principal center of northwestern Arabia which, a year earlier, had been captured by King Abd al-Aziz from the Al Rashid, traditional adversaries of the Al Saud. Abd al-Aziz bin Musa'id was to rule in Hail for the next half century, until his retirement in the early 1970s, when he was well over ninety. It was there, in the Jabal Shammar region of northern Najd, that my mother grew up. Abd al-Aziz bin Musa'id had two sons, Abdallah and Jiluwi, and seven daughters. Of these daughters, one was to marry King Fahd – and give birth to my milk brothers Faisal, Muhammad, Saud, Sultan and Khaled; another, Princess Munira, was to marry my father, Prince Sultan, and give birth to me and my brothers Fahd, Faisal and Turki, and to my sisters Nauf, Albandari, Jawahir, Latifah and Lulwah, for all of whom I have the greatest affection. We grew up as a happy and united family and remain very close. But, of course, I have other brothers and sisters, born to my father's other wives, to whom I am tied by strong bonds and for whom I also have the greatest affection. A third Jiluwi sister was to marry my uncle, Prince Naif, and give birth to my cousins Saud and Muhammad bin Naif, who were also my milk brothers. So our network of family relationships is very tight.

It was King Abd al-Aziz himself who named me Khaled. I was born in Makkah on September 24, 1949. In our tradition, the naming of a child usually takes place seven days after birth. But in my case, the seventh day coincided with what we call *yawm al-waqfa*, that is the solemn day during the annual *hajj* when the massed ranks of pilgrims stand before God on Mount Arafat, just outside Makkah. Being a profoundly religious man, the king postponed my naming until the eighth day after my birth. To be the grandson of this exceptional man, to be linked to him by direct descent, is to have something very deep and solid in one's background. To me it is a source of immense pride.

The Al Saud family is in many ways a remarkable family, and I am not saying this because I am a member of it. It is not like other royal houses, either in this area or in other parts of the world. Its origins, its history for hundreds of years, are rooted in the heart of Arabia, this extraordinary desert land of clans and tribes, which has bred warriors and poets and in which God revealed the Arabic Quran to his Prophet Muhammad.

In Arabia, the Al Saud are closely linked to other great families from whom they do not differ much by blood or background. Indeed, some of these families have a history at least as long as ours. But what brought our family to the fore in the last two hundred and fifty years was a compact between two outstanding men. In 1744, my ancestor, Muhammad bin Saud, forged an alliance with Shaikh Muhammad bin Abd al-Wahab, a religious reformer whose declared mission in life was to rescue Islam from the widespread corruption of the age.

Arabia, the birthplace of Islam, was at that time experiencing some slackening of religious practice. In the then prevailing anarchy, with the country aflame with tribal and regional conflict, Islamic learning and religious teaching were being neglected.

This was the situation that Shaikh Muhammad bin Abd al-Wahab vowed to correct. However, to spread his reformist message, the Shaikh needed the backing of a strong man, able to raise armies and control the tribes. He found him in my ancestor, Muhammad bin Saud, then the ruler of Dir'iya, our ancient capital (the ruins of which are to be found today on the outskirts of Riyadh). Together, armed with sword and Glorious Quran, they brought the people of central Arabia back to the true path.

In the second half of the eighteenth century, one of my ancestor's sons married the daughter of Muhammad bin Abd al-Wahab, thus sealing an alliance between the families of Al Saud and Al Shaikh which, with further intermarriage and close association over the years, continues unbroken to this day. An example in my own life is my very close friendship with Abd al-Muhsin bin Abd al-Malik al-Shaikh, who has demonstrated his affection and loyalty to me over the years.

The defense of Islam, in its pure and uncorrupted form, which was initiated in the eighteenth century is thus an important source of our family's legitimacy.

Another major family asset is that the Al Saud are also the recognized champions of Arab virtues which for countless generations, before and after the coming of Islam, have provided the ethical code of the desert. By Arab virtues, I mean generosity, nobility, courage, the unquestioned defense of one's own people, and also, I would add, a determination to protect one's honor and one's interests. Adherence to this code of behavior allowed people to stay alive in the harsh desert environment: departure from it meant death. Today, the desert has been tamed by modern communications and other amenities, but I believe our family's record in preserving the essence of the old virtues has contributed to the support we now enjoy.

Ours is a family of some five thousand members – male and female, princes and princesses, stemming from different branches – all gathered around the sons and grandsons of King Abd al-Aziz and their descendants who alone are in line for the throne. If I had to name a single principle which unites this large family it is respect: essentially, respect for members older than oneself, even by a few weeks or months. In practice, this means that if a difference of opinion arises between you and another member of your family – whether it be your father, your uncle, your brother, your cousin, or some other relative – there is always a line you cannot cross, a line imposed by deference. Some people object to this deeply ingrained tradition. They say you should act and speak your mind without hindrance or restriction. But when you stop to think, it makes a lot of sense to have a line drawn in the sand where you have to stop.

I am not saying that all is harmony in our family and that there are never any quarrels. Nor am I claiming that we have not made some bad mistakes. There are some black sheep in any family who are a disgrace to all. You find them in families of four or five members, let alone of five thousand. That is human nature. But the good things we have done as a family can, in my view, serve to mitigate some of the mistakes. And

our respect for one another prevents disputes within the family
from getting out of hand.

At moments of crisis we stick together, which is one of the
reasons the family has remained strong. If we are to face problems in the future, it will be as a result of differences within the
family. We must, therefore, bring up our children to believe
in the overriding importance of family unity, and in the
notion that achievement will be rewarded, however young
or old a person may be, so as to avoid disruptive jealousies
and hatreds.

If I had to sum up, therefore, the characteristics which have
contributed to the strength of the House of Saud, I would list
the following:

- First and foremost, strict adherence to and defense of
  Islam, as a faith and a legal system.
- Respect and appreciation for the King, the head of the
  family, who is considered the father of every single
  member of the family.
- Dedication to public service and to raising high the
  name of the Kingdom in the world.
- Concern to husband the Kingdom's wealth, to spread
  its benefits widely among the citizens, and put it to the
  best possible use in the internal development of the
  country, which has resulted in the great leap forward of
  recent years.
- Respect by younger members of the family for their
  seniors, however small the age gap between them
  may be.
- A determination to solve disputes within the framework
  of the family, and the nurturing of bonds between family
  members on the understanding that the interest of the
  family is greater than that of any individual member.
- The application of the Shari'a to members of the family
  on the same basis as it is applied to the Saudi
  population as a whole.
- The allocation of some top government jobs to the most
  qualified members of the family, on the understanding
  that those with and those without jobs are entitled to
  equal respect.

To infringe any one of these principles would, in my personal view, endanger the family, jeopardize our ruling system and fragment the nation.

I am confident that the Saudi people are aware that, without our family's commitment to public service and its pool of talent, without the cement of the Al Saud, our country could once again be divided as it was before King Abd al-Aziz united it.

I have always been inspired by the fact that my grandfather, King Abd al-Aziz, was brought up as a warrior, skilled in horsemanship, in hunting, in the use of dagger, sword and rifle, and in the art of surviving in the desert. Long before modern practitioners of guerrilla warfare – such as David Stirling, a British pioneer in such warfare, whose Long Range Desert Group raided behind German lines in the Western Desert during World War Two and was the inspiration for Britain's elite Special Forces, the SAS – Abd al-Aziz had perfected night raids like the one which secured Riyadh, and which he was to repeat with success against the Turks and local adversaries in subsequent decades. Perhaps my own admiration for Special Forces springs from this heritage.

Always ready to absorb new military technology, King Abd al-Aziz was acutely aware of the value of the weapons he captured from the Turks. He knew that ammunition was a key to success and, as I was intrigued to learn, he would himself count out the rounds of ammunition he distributed to his marksmen. Anxious to improve the military skills and equipment of his men, he sent his son, Faisal – who as a boy of seventeen in the 1920s had already covered himself in glory fighting in Yemen – to buy arms from Poland and the Soviet Union in 1930–31. He brought in instructors to train his men, like the Nigerian Tariq al-Afriqi, who was in effect our first Chief of Staff, as well as experienced soldiers from Syria. Later, in the 1940s and 50s, when money was more plentiful, training was continued by British and American military missions. In 1942, King Abd al-Aziz sent his son Mansur, Saudi Arabia's first Defense Minister, to visit Indian troops serving in the British 8th Army in North Africa. As a ruler, he was always open to advice and eager for information, relying on the talents and experience of a wide circle of trusted men drawn from many parts of the Arab world and farther afield.

As a boy I used to thrill to hear stories of Abd al-Aziz, of his
brothers Muhammad and Abdallah, and of his fighting sons, my
uncles Turki, Saud, Faisal and Muhammad, who fought bravely
in tribal wars in the first decades of this century. Unfortunately,
I was never to know Turki as he died in the great flu epidemic
of 1919 which ravaged Arabia thirty years before I was born.
These were all military men, bred in a military tradition. In 1922,
Abd al-Aziz described to the Lebanese-American writer, Amin
Rihani, the regime he imposed on his sons:

> We have to be always ready and fit. I train my own children
> to walk barefoot, to rise two hours before dawn, to eat but
> little, to ride horses bareback – sometimes we have not a
> moment to saddle a horse, leap to his back and go.*

Living in a world full of perils, where courage, military skills
and military technology are still all-important, I draw strength
from the legacy of such a grandfather.

⟡

I spent my entire school career at a school for the education of
young princes founded in the early 1950s by King Saud and
housed, in its early years, in al-Nasiriya, his palace in Riyadh.
It was called Ma'had al-Anjal, the "Institute for (Royal) Sons."

When we were young, in the days before asphalt roads, the
journey from our house to the King's palace would take about
three quarters of an hour, which meant a long journey home
for lunch and then back to school for the afternoon classes. But
King Saud was an exceptionally kind and generous man. When
he noticed that we were under a bit of a strain, he decreed that
my brother Fahd and I were to eat lunch in the palace itself
with his own son, Prince Mansur – and that is what we happily
did thereafter, resulting in our long friendship and mutual
respect. In 1964, when King Faisal came to the throne, the
school was moved out of the palace and its funding transferred
to the Ministry of Education.

* Amin Rihani, *Ibn Saud*, London 1928, quoted in Leslie McLaughlin, *Ibn Saud:
Founder of a Kingdom*, London, 1993, p. 33.

When it first opened, the school had a single class of some 25 pupils, but by the 1990s it had grown to a large institution of over 1,200 pupils in classes ranging all the way from kindergarten to secondary school. By this time commoners far outnumbered princes, and a separate girls' wing had been established in a separate building, although as teenagers we were never able to discover its exact location.

The name of the school has now been changed to the Capital Institute and, with the founding of other private schools, it has lost its monopoly of young princes.

From its foundation and for its first 31 years, the school was run – ruled would be a better word – by a man of unassuming appearance but iron will, Mr. Othman al-Salih. He had been chosen as headmaster by King Saud but, once in office, he would tolerate no interference in the running of his establishment, not even from the King himself. If anyone, and I mean anyone, tried to tell him what to do, he would threaten to resign immediately. It was only later in life that I appreciated what a great man he was. After his retirement, I tried to pay him regular visits in gratitude for what he had done for me, and indeed for a whole generation of young Saudis.

He was, I suppose, what one would call a headmaster of the old school – strict discipline, no food or sweets permitted on the premises, a deferential demeanor to teachers at all times, and no politics allowed in the classroom. The pupils were known simply by their names with no princely titles.

When I was fourteen I staged a minor rebellion against this iron regime. "Don't be so strict!" I once exclaimed. "We are only boys, not puppets to be drilled. Let us live like boys!" Instead of reaching for his cane, Othman al-Salih actually smiled. He was apparently so impressed by my outburst that he decided not to punish me.

My brother Fahd, eleven months my junior, is the closest person to me in my life, closer than a twin. As children we quarreled and competed, but our friendship was cemented as we approached manhood. We spent our whole school career together, always, as we moved up, side by side in the same classroom. Fahd and I were not top of the class, but we were above average. One summer, Othman al-Salih gave us some extra coaching which allowed us to jump a year. He felt we were clever enough to do so. My father once asked Othman which of his sons was better at his studies. Othman replied that Fahd was slightly ahead. But, after the examinations, my father checked our marks and, to my great satisfaction, discovered that I led by a short head. The truth is that Fahd was always in front – except in the last two years of high school when, with luck turning in my favor and a bit of hard work, I was able to edge ahead of him. In recent years, I have not seen my brother Fahd as much as I would like. When I was in the armed services, he was working at the Ministry of Social Welfare, rising to become Deputy Minister. He was then appointed Governor of Tabuk, far away in northwest Arabia, where over the past eight years he has established what is said to be a model administration.

Another very close childhood friend was Prince Muhammad bin Fahd, Governor of the Eastern Province, a key post he has occupied with distinction for several years. As I have mentioned, Muhammad and I were milk brothers, having shared a wet nurse. We were playmates and companions from kindergarten onwards. As his father King Fahd – then not yet Crown Prince – was married to my aunt, my mother's sister, we literally lived and played together most of the time, day and night. At school, I was not very keen on sports, but it was Muhammad who persuaded me to play handball, and I became quite good at defense, at blocking attackers. On one occasion, both Muhammad and I put our names forward as candidates for class leader. Then, another cousin, Prince Sultan bin Muhammad (now a highly successful businessman for whom I have great affection and respect) put his name forward as well. It was obvious that the vote would be split and Sultan would get in. So I withdrew my name and forced my supporters to cast their votes for Muhammad, who was duly elected.

We were sometimes unruly students. Once, when we were teasing our teacher, the headmaster suddenly walked into the classroom.

"Are you satisfied with the boys' behavior?" the headmaster asked sternly.

"Except for those two!" the teacher replied, pointing at Muhammad and me.

Othman al-Salih called us to his study. Unwisely, I tried to argue and defend our behavior, while Muhammad remained silent. Othman dismissed Muhammad but gave me a good beating. It was an early lesson not to be argumentative, a lesson I have still not fully absorbed.

During the Gulf War, my close friendship with Muhammad proved of great value to me. As we knew each other's minds, we were able to solve problems easily as they arose. This was a source of comfort to both of us. I knew I could always count on his help. He was invaluable whenever I needed to bypass bureaucratic procedures and get something done in a hurry.

Prince Muhammad is six months older than me, which according to our tradition means that he takes precedence and that I have to defer. I was therefore very touched by one of his gestures during the war which he may not even remember. As a civilian provincial governor, his chain of command goes up to Prince Naif, the Minister of Interior. Yet one day, needing to go to Jeddah for some reason during the crisis, he telephoned to ask whether I would mind his being absent from his post for a day or two. He had absolutely no need to ask me, but it was a nice gesture of recognition of my command.

❖

Although the memory of my grandfather was very important, my immediate role model as I grew up was my father, Prince Sultan. He has been an inspiration to me throughout my life. During the Gulf crisis, when I was in the very exposed job of Joint Forces Commander, he was my shield and my protector. He protected me from the left and from the right. If we were playing American football and I was running with the ball, he would be the man ahead of me, knocking down anyone trying to stop me. I had a secure telephone line to him and talked to him more than once every day. His directives were my daily guidelines. In the accounts of the Gulf War I have read, I was sorry to note that he has not been given the credit he deserves for a role as important as that of Defense Secretary Cheney in the United States.

When I was a boy, I sometimes used to feel that my father

did not love me as much as my brothers, that he gave them greater favors. But as I came to manhood I realized that he loved me dearly, and that what I had taken for harshness was only an attempt to shape my character which he knew to be strong and willful. I, in turn, have the greatest love and respect for him and, to this day, cannot confront him strongly on anything, but have to defer.

When I was nine or ten years old, my father took me falconing in the desert, a week-long hunting trip. He also put me in the charge of one of his friends and followers, an important tribal figure by the name of Shaikh Muhammad bin Khalid al-Hithlain, a man of my father's generation, even slightly older. Shaikh Muhammad liked to hunt and accompanied me and my brothers Fahd and Bandar, teaching us the rules of the desert.

In those days, before the surge in oil wealth, a mango was a real luxury and the only sweets we knew were tins of condensed milk which you could puncture with a hunting knife and then suck. We did not have much air conditioning, and so in the hot season we used to drive out to the desert late at night and sleep there until awakened by the sun. Later on, as an adult, I used to go hunting in the deep desert for a month or six weeks nearly every year. You drive out in caravans, establish your camp and then go out looking for game from sunrise to sunset. I enjoyed it very much but stopped falcon hunting altogether in the late 1970s. On my last trip, in the winter of 1976–77, I went north through our border town of Ar'ar and spent a month hunting in the Iraqi desert. I know the terrain there rather well, knowledge which I was able to put to some use during the Gulf War.

My father is a very organized person, with a career in public life which stretches back to his youth when King Abd al-Aziz made him governor of Riyadh. He is very punctual, a trait he is thought to have picked up from King Faisal, whose right-hand man he was for many years. King Faisal was a man of such strict habits that it is said people used to set their clocks by his movements. So, from my father, and indirectly from King Faisal, I inherited punctuality, a sense of organization and a dedication to public service, in my case in the armed services for a quarter of a century.

But what I remember most from my childhood is that my

father always set time aside to see us, however busy he might be. Lunch was a very important occasion. It was served every day at the house of my grandmother, Hussa bint Ahmad al-Sudairi, widow of King Abd al-Aziz, a remarkable old lady universally known as Umm Fahd, "Mother of Fahd," after her eldest son, King Fahd. All of us would go there to eat – the King, my father, my other uncles and aunts, and all their sons and daughters, invariably a very large gathering. Of all my uncles, I am perhaps closest to Prince Salman, the Governor of Riyadh, a friend and wise counselor who has helped me with many problems, including personal ones. More than any other single person, he has been responsible for the remarkable development of our capital city.

Umm Fahd was a strong and highly respected figure, but her strength was always tempered with kindness. My only regret is that I did not listen to her more closely as a child, to learn about her past. The West is wrong in believing that women do not enjoy respect in our society, for it is the very opposite of the truth. In the home, their influence is enormous. When Umm Fahd died in 1970, my father continued the tradition of lunching every day with his family at my mother's house, in either Riyadh or Jeddah. All his sons and daughters attend as a matter of course, if they happen to be there, accompanied by their own wives and children.

My father thus manages to bring us all together, encouraging us to talk, to discuss anything we like, to express our opinions but always with a lot of respect. It is a wonderful institution, wonderful to behold and to be part of. It means that every day, unless I have an inescapable engagement, I see my mother, kiss her hand, sit beside her, and chat happily with her and my brothers and sisters.

My mother, Princess Munira, has played a great role in my life. As I have said, she is the eldest daughter of Abd al-Aziz bin Musa'id al-Jiluwi, a cousin and companion of King Abd al-Aziz, who fought side by side with him, and lived to the grand age of over ninety. I am proud that I have a double dose of noble blood in my veins, through my two grandfathers, King Abd al-Aziz and Abd al-Aziz bin Musa'id al-Jiluwi, both outstanding military commanders. Together they played the major roles in capturing Riyadh and afterwards in unifying the Kingdom.

My mother is an extremely kind and tender woman, incapable of bearing a grudge against anyone. God has not put anything but goodness in her heart. But she is also extremely frank, giving voice to everything she feels, an important feature of her character which keeps everyone around her up to the mark. I never leave the country without first bidding her goodbye, and on my return I always call her first, even before my own wife and children. It is her pride and mine that, rather than being called Princess Munira, she prefers to be known simply as Umm Khaled. People in Saudi Arabia have come to know that if they want something from me, and fear that I might refuse them, they go to see my mother because they know that, if my mother were to ask me a favor, there is no way I could refuse her.

During the Gulf War, after every attack on Riyadh by Saddam's Scuds, my mother would call for her car and ask to be driven around the Defense Ministry where I was working just to assure herself that the building – and her son – were still there!

Apart from my mother, the important woman in my life as I grew up was my nanny, Bushra. She was short, plain, black and very tough. She was so strong that even my mother tried to avoid clashing with her. She had been a slave with my mother's family in Hail (long before, that is, the formal abolition of slavery in the Kingdom in 1962) and, when my mother married Prince Sultan, came with her to Riyadh. She herself had been married for a year or two, but her husband had died in an accident several years earlier, and she had then devoted herself to our family. She could neither read nor write, but she was a nanny in a thousand, with a gift for bringing up children which I was fortunate to enjoy. She looked after me and my sister al-Bandari, and then my younger brother Turki until he was ten years old.

Bushra, and her son Nader, were very much part of our family, and I would say that, as much as anyone else, she was one of the determining influences in my life. She cared for me throughout my youth and taught me to be a man. She had a mind of her own and was extremely stubborn – not just stubborn, mulelike. When I was five or six years old, I was given a gun by Abdallah bin Mas'ud who had been assigned by my father to look after me. Bushra gave him some of her own money to buy ammunition and urged him to teach me how to use the gun. When the recoil knocked me over, she got Abdallah to pick me up and make me fire again. She used to urge her son to be my sparring partner: "Hit him! Come on! Toughen up!" Whenever she saw me slouching, she would explode: "Stand up straight, or I'll break your neck!" If I strolled into my father's sitting room, and did not behave as she thought proper, she would leap on me like a tigress and slap my face. "Don't ever look down when you talk to people," she would scream. "Look them in the eye!"

Of course she had less to do with me when I finished high school, but we remained very attached to each other. By the time I went to the Royal Military Academy at Sandhurst, she was suffering from cancer and had been brought to London for treatment. I used to escape from Sandhurst at eleven o'clock at night, drive up to London to stay with her all night in the hospital, and then drive back before dawn. They told me, and I think it is true, that when she died a little while later in Saudi Arabia, she had my picture with her. I was really like a son to her.

❖≫≪❖

One way and another, events in Yemen, our southern neighbor, have had a considerable impact on my life. It so happened that I grew to manhood in the 1960s at the time of the seven-year Yemen civil war, which undermined Saudi security, deeply preoccupied my father, brought King Faisal to the throne and determined my own choice of a career.

I was only thirteen when the Imam Badr, ruler of Yemen, was deposed by a military coup in Sanaa on September 26, 1962, but I well remember the shock waves it caused in the Kingdom and inside our royal family. As it was the first overthrow of a monarch in the Arabian peninsula, it was a precedent we did not relish. The new republican regime called for Egyptian help and Gamal Abd al-Nasser, then the idol of radical Arab nationalism, immediately sent his army to defend it. A country which had been our friendly neighbor for thirty years suddenly became a deadly threat – a situation not unlike that which developed when Saddam Hussein invaded Kuwait. I am not, of course, saying that Saddam Hussein is another Nasser who, for all his faults, was a genuine hero of Arab nationalism in the eyes of his supporters.

The danger to us was physical, humiliating and immediate. By sending an army to Yemen, Egypt was positioning itself to give direct help to the various opposition groups who were already beginning to spread mayhem throughout the Arabian peninsula. It was not long before Egyptian aircraft were attacking our villages in the border areas of Jizan and Najran, which we could do nothing to defend. We simply did not have an army, or an air force or an air defense system able to take on the Egyptians. I vividly remember my father's deep anxiety at our weakness and vulnerability. I was very young, but I too felt a sense of hurt, of wounded pride.

Nasser also posed a disturbing ideological challenge. He had been our hero. All the young princes loved him. We used to fight over who loved him most. We were all Nasserites, in fact all the Arabs were. I could see it in my own family. My uncles, my father, all admired him and were intrigued by his speeches and his new ideas. His picture was everywhere and everyone praised him. By nature, we in Saudi Arabia love Egyptians. We have always had an affinity with them, and many Egyptians have come to live in the Kingdom, especially in the Hijaz. Egypt was the place for Saudis to go on vacation and, as a result, numerous marriages with Egyptian women were contracted.

But, by sending his army to Yemen to threaten us, by vowing to overthrow our family, Nasser forced us to oppose him, and this was painful. We had to learn the hard way that Nasser's Arab nationalism was little more than a cloak for his political ambitions. It dawned on us that he did not want only Yemen: he wanted to be the undisputed master of the Arab world. Our opinion of him underwent a radical change, in fact a complete 180° turnabout. In the 1950s he had been a hero, but by the early 1960s he had become a threat — at least to us. We were only children at the time, but we could tell what our parents were thinking. To preserve our independence, we had to resist the Egyptians in Yemen by all the means in our power, just as a generation later, and for much the same reason, we had to resist Saddam's hegemony. In fact some people would say that the proxy war we fought in Yemen against Nasser's regime in the 1960s was a first test of our national will, while a second test of will was the Gulf War we fought against Iraq. In both cases an Arab ruler threatened to put intolerable pressure on our decision-makers, and therefore had to be resisted. In both cases, the King of Saudi Arabia – King Faisal then and King Fahd this time – had the necessary strategic vision to confront the danger before it reached our heartlands.

During the first test of will, King Saud had to hand over control of affairs to Crown Prince Faisal in October 1962 – the first step in the process which led Faisal to ascend the throne two years later. Faisal promptly named Prince Fahd Minister of Interior, Prince Abdallah head of the National Guard, and Prince Sultan Minister of Defense. My father thus became the senior member of the family most intimately involved in the struggle to expel the Egyptian army from Yemen.

Yemeni tribal leaders were always quarreling, but Prince Sultan was a maestro at bringing them together. Imposing figures in turbans, with curved daggers in their waistbands, they used to come up to Jeddah and Riyadh to see him. Of course, I could not hear the actual negotiations, but watching my father's skill and patience from afar, I learned a great deal. It helped me when I came to deal with the widely different members of the Gulf War coalition.

I believe the experience in Yemen was formative for my father and my uncles. It was, of course, King Faisal who carried the heaviest political and diplomatic burden in the trial of strength with Nasser. The Kingdom then stood alone in the face of a heavy Nasserite wave. And it held out until the Arab defeat in the 1967 war showed that Nasser, for all his hypnotic charisma, was himself vulnerable. Faisal's great advantage was that, unlike Nasser, he understood the strategic fundamentals of Yemen – its powerful tribes, its formidable mountains, its tormented history – because he had personally learned about them in the military campaigns he conducted there on behalf of his father, Ibn Saud, in 1926 and in 1932.

But in the 1960s, Prince Fahd, Prince Abdallah and Prince Sultan also gained experience of war – experience of what today

would be called "crisis management." They learned that when
the chips are down you have to fight, that the defense of the
country and the family is not something which can be delegated
to others. I believe that underpinning our successful efforts to
build a coalition during the Gulf crisis – not only with the U.S.,
Britain and France, but also with Egypt, Syria, our GCC partners,
Morocco, Niger, Senegal, Czechoslovakia, Poland, the Philip-
pines and the others – was the clear evidence of our readiness
to fight in our own defense, to give our blood. The issue of
confronting Saddam could not be dodged, however tempting
some might have found it, and this was a lesson I think we
learned in Yemen nearly thirty years earlier.

Under the psychological impact of the Yemen war, several
young royal princes joined the armed services in the 1960s. No
doubt I was inclined in that direction by seeing my father always
surrounded by military officers. I too wanted a military career.
So, from the age of fourteen or fifteen, I started begging my
father to send me to Britain's Royal Military Academy at Sandhurst, a tough and celebrated school which I had heard about
and which a dozen or so Saudis had already attended.

But, on reflection, I think it was our inability to defend our
country which really drove me into the army.

CHAPTER V

―――――❦❦❦―――――

A Taste of British Discipline

ET IN 900 ACRES of green Surrey parkland, Britain's Royal
Military Academy at Sandhurst, some 30 miles from
London, is one of the best – and the toughest – officer
training schools in the world. It is equal to Saint Cyr in France
or West Point in the United States, two other military institutions
famous for turning raw youths into leaders. At first sight, the
noble façade of Sandhurst's Old Building, the landscaped gar-
dens and ornamental lakes, suggest that this is the gracious
home of an English duke. But, as I was soon to discover, behind
the elegant exterior, the Academy has some of the features of
a prison for young offenders.

The Sandhurst method can be summed up simply: first they
break you, mentally and physically, reducing you by harsh treatment to a quivering jelly. Then they build you up again, teach
you discipline and good manners, restore your confidence,
inflate your self-esteem, and hopefully turn you, in the classic
English phrase, into "an officer and a gentleman."

I spent two years at Sandhurst in the late 1960s, between the
ages of seventeen and nineteen and, although I would be lying
if I said the experience was entirely pleasant, I found it one of
the most valuable of my life.

Not everyone, by any means, makes the grade. Some drop
out, others are weeded out. Simply to finish the course is an
achievement. When I started at Sandhurst, I was one of half a
dozen cadets from the Arab world, but at the end only two of
us remained, myself and Shaikh Khalifa bin Ahmad al-Khalifa,
now Bahrain's Defense Minister, and a dear friend ever since.
We were the only survivors. We kept talking to each other
throughout the course to give each other courage.

For most cadets, the fear of failure, the dreaded humiliation of returning home without an officer's commission, is what enables them to endure the hardships of the training.

The story is told – and I believe it is a true story – that one of my Saudi predecessors at Sandhurst, one of the first six Saudis to be admitted to the Academy in 1948, was sent home after a few months because he did not like sports. Before leaving, he had to appear in front of the commanding officer, General Sir Hugh Stockwell (who was later to achieve fame, or perhaps I should say infamy, by commanding British troops in the tripartite aggression on Egypt in 1956).

"What can I do for you, my boy, before you go?" the general growled.

"Just one thing, sir."

"Well, what is it?"

"Shoot me!"

As I have related, long before finishing high school I started to press my father to send me to Sandhurst. Not knowing the rules, I wanted to go straightaway. Four of my cousins had gone to British training establishments before finishing high school. Why was I being held back?

But Prince Sultan was strict. "Forget about the others," he told me. "Finish your high school first. If you really want to go to Sandhurst, I want you to do it the right way, just like an English boy. You must get the same qualifications as the British cadets. The military will not accept anything less than the twelfth grade . . ."

Two years later when I had graduated from high school, my father said to me, "Now is the moment of choice. You can give up the idea of Sandhurst if you like, and go to a university. No one is forcing you. It is something you have chosen to do yourself. But if you do go to Sandhurst, make sure you stay to the end. If you quit, I never want to see your face again!

"I want you to think of Sandhurst as a horse with a mind of its own. If it runs away from you, run after it. Whatever the difficulties, chase after it!"

Many times in my first weeks at Sandhurst I wanted to give up the chase, but my father's words kept me going.

I was what was termed an "overseas cadet," that is to say a non-British cadet who had been offered a place because the British government was on friendly terms with my government. There were a number of such overseas cadets in each platoon. Apart from myself and Shaikh Khalifa from Bahrain, there were others, including a cadet from Thailand, one from India and another from Pakistan, one from Ceylon, one from Zambia and one from Iraq. For some of us foreigners, the English language was a considerable barrier. As a teenager, I had spent three brief summers studying English at a school in London, and then two happy months in two successive years with an English family, Colonel and Mrs. Dent and their two children at Stockbridge, Hampshire, in the south of England. That was the extent of my exposure to English.

Therefore, before starting at Sandhurst on January 3, 1967, I and some other cadets with poor English were sent in September 1966 to a British army educational establishment at Beaconsfield for a three-month language course. Called the "Sandhurst wing," it prepared overseas cadets for Sandhurst by giving them four or five hours a day of language teaching and a good deal of army drill in the rest of the time. What made the experience challenging was that we were billeted, twelve to a hut, with the Gurkhas, tough soldiers from the mountains of Nepal who had a 200-year-old tradition of serving the British Empire. Like the Yemenis, also a mountain people, the Gurkhas wear a curved dagger – known as a *kukri* – in their belts, and we were cautioned that if a Gurkha draws his *kukri* in anger he will not put it away again until blood flows. Living with these men was my first training in toughness.

At Beaconsfield, I was accompanied by my nanny's son, Nader, who had been sent along by my parents, because he was as keen as I to attend. But Nader was thin, small and frail. As ill luck would have it, rain coming through the roof of our leaky, icy, pre-World War Two hut, fell on his bed. I did not mind the damp, so I swapped beds with him, but he fell ill, developed TB and had to go home. But not before he had done me a service.

Prince Sultan had given instructions that no one, not even my mother, was to send me money. The small allowance I received from the Saudi military attaché in London, Major General Mashhur al-Harithi, was supposed to be enough. (Major General Harithi and his wife were extremely kind to me in those years and their son, Na'il, himself a Sandhurst graduate from the intake before mine, has remained a lifelong friend.) One day two letters arrived from my mother, one addressed to Nader, the other to me. In her letter to me, my mother wrote how much she missed me and how earnestly she prayed that I was well. To Nader, she wrote a short note – and enclosed a draft for £100. I caught a glimpse of it as he opened his envelope.

"Look here," I said to him. "Nader, you are like my brother. There is no difference between us. Why don't we pool our funds and spend them together?"

Nader thought for a moment. If Umm Khaled had sent him £100, she must have sent me £1,000. He readily agreed to my proposal. I pocketed his money, gave him a fiver and, I must confess, spent the balance on myself. I am glad to say that I more than made it up to him thereafter.

In later life I did not forget the Gurkhas whose fearlessness, discipline and smiling faces had impressed me greatly. When I heard that, because of financial cuts and a dwindling empire, the British were beginning to phase them out, I recruited a score of them to serve as security guards at my farm outside Riyadh. And every time I pass through the main gate, it always gives me a thrill to receive the salute of a well turned-out soldier with the *kukri* emblem on his cap.

The two-year course at Sandhurst is divided into six terms, each of 14 weeks. The "breaking" process I have mentioned, which is widely acknowledged to be a foretaste of hell, occurs in the first term, and is accomplished in two ways. First, in the sacred cause of "fitness," the cadet is subjected to unremitting physical hardship in the form of a daily three-mile run in full battle order, with rifle, webbing and helmet; hour upon hour of drill as the platoons are marched or doubled back and forth across the square; assault courses in which one has to climb 12-foot walls, ford rivers, swing on ropes and scramble in nets; and night exercises in which, frozen to the marrow and numb with pain, lying face down in the mud of a trench, one longs for an end to the misery. Then, on returning to barracks, weak from exhaustion, one has to spend hour upon hour polishing boots, cleaning equipment, whitening belts and slings, "blanco-ing" gaiters and green webbing, shining brass fittings, and generally preparing oneself and one's kit for inspection – which is, more often than not, followed by still more punishment in the form of pushups and extra drill, in highly polished full guard order, up and down the square. There was then, and no doubt still is, something called a "Sandhurst shave." They used to come with a card and rub it up your face to see if you had shaved both ways. But that is nothing compared to the mental and physical roughing up you can expect if you are captured on a survival course. Although you know you are not really going to be tortured, it is unnerving nonetheless. When I was there, punishment of captives could be severe. There was the threat of being tied up and dragged on the ground behind a vehicle. Fortunately, "POWs" were given the opportunity to escape and attempt to survive in open country. On one such exercise, I managed to escape my captors and, after stumbling about in the dark, found a small hut in a field and bedded down in the warm hay. When dawn broke I discovered I was sharing my bed with a pig.

What makes the trials at Sandhurst almost unbearable is not just the physical strain but the humiliation which accompanies it, which is the necessary second ingredient in the breaking process. The cadets are treated like dirt. They are screamed at, bullied, insulted, punished by fierce sergeant instructors from the Brigade of Guards and by their willing accomplices – that is to say, sadistic senior cadets who, having suffered themselves a year earlier, are anxious to inflict equal suffering on their juniors. Square bashing, weapons training, shooting, map reading, radio instruction, first aid – these are the basic skills which the cadet must acquire as his body and his mind fight to survive the rigors of those first 14 weeks.

I was not used to being told what to do every moment of the day, to be shouted at on and off the parade ground, to be called names and insulted. Being stubborn by nature, I found it difficult to take and I often longed to shout back – which would have quickly brought my Sandhurst career to a premature end.

In my time, one cadet who faced dismissal because he could not meet the standard expected of him, killed himself by firing a blank round into his mouth. But other cadets were an example to us. One such was Officer Cadet Shami from Pakistan, who studied hard and was totally devoted to serving his country. He was rewarded by being made an Under Officer. His father had been killed in the Indo–Pakistan war of 1965 and he himself lost a leg in the 1971 Indo–Pakistan war – but he is still serving. He was the first foreigner I invited to Saudi Arabia to perform the pilgrimage.

At Sandhurst, I had a particular and very painful problem: I had developed a fistula in my rectum which required surgery. In London, I went to see Dr. Norman Tanner, one of the foremost abdominal surgeons of the day, who had successfully operated on members of the Saudi royal family. He diagnosed an abscess, but it turned out to be an infection of the passage between the skin and the inside of the rectum. He cleared out what he thought was the abscess but not the inside of the whole track. Later I had to have repeated operations, about six in all. Finally, Dr. John Ind, a gifted physician, recommended that I consult another specialist, a Dr. John Griffiths. The problem was soon cleared up, never to recur. But, in the meantime, it was a nightmare. I had to pad up the wound with bandages and tissues to make sure that discharge did not trickle down. I feared that if my problem were discovered I would be expelled from Sandhurst on grounds of ill health. I had to conceal it completely.

One day we were taking part in an assault course in full combat gear. It involved, as I have explained, running for two or three miles while negotiating various obstacles. I was staggering along, exhausted, when another cadet came up from behind and pushed me. "Lay off!" I said. But then he pushed me again: "Come on, you stupid Arab!" Had he been my senior, I might have taken it, but he was in my own platoon. It was unbearable. I saw red. I hit him hard with the butt of my rifle and really hurt him. When I was asked why I had hit him, I said he had insulted my race. I was punished, of course – confined to barracks for three weeks and given extra drills – but it was better than being kicked out.

As it happened, my mother was then being treated in London for a severe attack of asthma. But I could not go up to see her as I was confined to barracks. To my great surprise and joy, she drove down to see me, accompanied by one of my sisters. My mother did not realize that I was being punished and therefore could not spend more than ten minutes with her. As she was extremely sick and could not walk, we just sat in her car while I tucked into a small Saudi dish of meat and rice, known as *kabsa*, she had brought me. Like most mothers, she was worried that I was not getting enough to eat.

After the incident on the assault course, I decided to fight back. One of the overseas cadets, who came from an Asian country, was one of the nicest men you could hope to meet. But because he was weak and polite, members of the platoon used him like a slave. Not having had the experience of an English boarding school or encountered the prefect system before, I did not know that this was standard behavior between older and younger boys. But I realized that one had to fight for one's rights or go under.

When I first went to Sandhurst and joined Intake 42, I was an innocent. If another cadet asked me for a cigarette or a six-pence to make a phone call, I would hand it over. If he offered to return it, I would of course refuse. But I realized after a while that the cadets thought me an easy touch. They were laughing at me. Trying very hard to remember to whom I had given money or cigarettes, I went to each in turn and said, "Pay up! I want it back *now!*" The cadets soon started treating me differently.

I must confess, however, that I came to Sandhurst overweight, unfit and somewhat spoiled. As a young prince in Saudi Arabia, I had not had to do a great deal for myself. Although my nanny Bushra had given me a hard time, I was not used to cleaning out lavatories nor to being abused as a "bloody idle sod, sir." Our platoon was often addressed by a certain Sergeant Major Ray: "I call you, sir, and you call me, sir," he would bawl. "The only difference is that you mean it, while I don't!"

The story goes that when King Hussein of Jordan was at Sand-hurst, some twenty years before me, he had faced much the same treatment. "What an idle little king we are today, sir!" the company sergeant major is said to have screamed at him when carrying out an inspection. "Idle," I learned, is a word much used in British army training to mean any activity short of the maximum that muscle and sinew can achieve. My brothers and cousins were at various universities, living in luxury and enjoying themselves. I was nursing my blistered feet and crawling on my knees with boot polish and cleaning mop. Had I made the wrong choice?

I had not been at Sandhurst very long when I was picked on by a junior cadet sergeant blessed with the name of Barney Rolfe Smith, a member of the so-called "cadet government." He clearly did not like the look of me.

"Report to me for a physical fitness test tomorrow at 6 a.m.," he commanded.

I knew the test involved a cross-country run which I was bound to fail. I was not built for speed. The wound in my rectum was giving me great pain. In my imagination, failure meant possible dismissal from Sandhurst. My father would kick me out of the family, or so I feared.

So that night, sitting with my friend Shaikh Khalifa, I anxiously pondered what to do. I had to do something. I needed a breathing space. On impulse, I pulled off my boot and sock and, taking a razor blade, hammered it into my big toe with the heel of my boot. Soon my whole foot was covered in blood. Shaikh Khalifa was outraged. He turned pale with shock. "You're mad!" he cried. I left the wound undressed and, the next morning, hopped to the hospital, my toes swollen and still bloody. I said I had been walking barefoot and had had an accident. Funnily enough, instead of putting a dressing on the injured big toe, they put the bandage on the toe next to it! At any rate I could not possibly run that morning. Smith must have known that I had hurt myself deliberately but he could not prove it. "Who would do a crazy thing like that?" I asked him brazenly. I had beaten the system.

When confronted by a no-win situation such as that first term at Sandhurst, I learned to survive. I learned to be crafty. I might be boiling inside with rage and injured pride, but from the outside I managed to look as if I were in no trouble at all. In other words, I learned how to smile in adversity — an extremely valuable lesson which I have needed to remember at various times of my life.

Somewhere at home in Riyadh I have two photographs, both taken at the same spot in Barcelona (where on two occasions I accompanied one of my younger sisters who needed to consult an eye specialist). One picture, taken just before I went to Sandhurst, shows a plump, carefree youth, no doubt idly looking forward to his next ice cream. The other, taken only six months later, shows a striking difference: I am standing very straight, the surplus pounds have melted away, my smile is confident but my eyes are narrowed as if anticipating danger . . .

My brother Fahd came to visit me at Sandhurst at the end of my first term. As I marched up to the main gate, I found him waiting for me outside. But I was so skinny and undernourished that the sight of me brought tears to his eyes. He thought I must be ill. "Let us go quickly and have a proper meal," he cried as I climbed into his car.

Things improve vastly at Sandhurst after the punishing first term of basic training. By this time the cadets are treated like human beings rather than animals. The next four terms, more leisurely and more civilized, are principally devoted to the academic study of war, strategy, military history, and international affairs. The cadet is regarded more like a university student, and recovers something of his self-respect. Once the day's lectures are over, as well as the couple of hours of compulsory sports, he is allowed to go out, wearing civilian clothes of a gentlemanly cut and a hat. The object of the outing is usually fish and chips or chicken and chips in Camberley. But if he has the time, the means and the inclination, evening spins up to London are not uncommon at weekends.

I had a red Chevrolet Corvette in those days and took full advantage of it. I used to roar up to London and, on occasion, sit in the lobby of the Royal Garden Hotel, which had only just opened, to give the impression to my cousins and friends that I had money and was staying there. I was young but I was nevertheless keen to keep up appearances. In fact, there were occasions when I was living in my car: when I was tired, I would drive somewhere quiet and sleep. I would sometimes frequent small hotels behind Madame Tussaud's where in those days you could get a bed for one pound a night – without bath, of course. Emerging one morning from one of these establishments I found that my car had been splashed all over in psychedelic paint. I had it resprayed in white. This was the 1960s, the era of Flower Power, love, long hair and antimilitarism. That was what was going on in English society at the time. As I discovered from my English friends, being an officer cadet with short hair and a black-and-white Sandhurst view of things was not all that fashionable.

And back at the Academy, I was still finding English a problem. I could talk fluently enough, but I could not always follow the lectures. Battles the British army had fought and which we had to study – such as Waterloo or the Somme – were very familiar to the English cadets but totally alien to me. This was another country's history, not my own.

My company commander, Major D. B. Carnie, MBE – a man whose kindness I will never forget – noticed that, although I was trying hard, I was falling behind. All the odds were against me: my lack of fitness, my painful and embarrassing illness, my lack of preparation at school for the rigors of Sandhurst, the cold and alien environment, my poor English. But fearing dismissal, I was determined to succeed, if only because my father's words were still ringing in my ears – and Major Carnie spotted my determination.

He came to the rescue. After consulting the Saudi military attaché in London, he arranged for me to go to Eastbourne on the south coast of England for an intensive six-week language course. It helped a great deal. On my return, I was able to follow the lectures and, although I never shone academically, I made good progress. Major Carnie was keen on swimming and water polo. Anxious to impress him and earn a good report, I attempted both sports, but with only indifferent results. A decade and more later, when I was studying at the U.S. Army Command and General Staff College at Fort Leavenworth, Kansas City, Kansas, Major Carnie, then a British military attaché in the United States, paid me a visit. We had a good laugh over old times.

The great strength of Sandhurst is that it is thoroughly impartial in the way it treats its cadets, whether English boys or foreigners, kings or commoners, the sons of generals or the sons of the working class. All are treated fairly and no favors are given. Every man knows where he stands. All are taught to conform to a code of behavior, a set of standards, an ethos which cannot be compromised and which is greater than the individual, summed up in the Academy's motto, "Serve to lead." Thus, it is hoped, are young men inculcated with the great military virtues of courage, discipline, self-control, and integrity – "integrity" is a key word at Sandhurst – as well as the ability to think and act quickly under pressure. Because, in that country house setting of fine vistas and immaculate lawns, we were not allowed to forget that we were there to learn how to lead men in battle, in other words how to kill – but always, within the formal, depersonalized context of the rules of war.

But this did not come all at once. Carefree boyish exuberance was not easily quelled. On one occasion, as a proof of resourcefulness, three cadets and I volunteered to go hitchhiking to Morocco. It was the spring of 1967. We had enough money to buy camels which we were planning to ride to the Algerian desert and back again. We got to Rabat, bought four camels at a market outside the town, and set out on our journey. But things soon started to go wrong. One camel died. Our money drained away. We were forced to return to the city, and set up camp in a garden – not too far from the Rabat Hilton! My companions left for home. Reluctant to follow them, I telephoned the Saudi ambassador who was good enough to inform King Hassan's brother, Prince Abdallah, of my presence. The Prince invited me to call on him and, for the next ten days, the harsh rigors of Sandhurst were forgotten. I remember conveying my respects to the Moroccan monarch himself while he was playing golf. It was the first time I had met King Hassan whom I consider one of the most astute, and certainly the best educated, ruler in the Arab world.

I had barely got back to England when the June War of 1967 broke out in the Middle East. For an Arab, it was a terrible time to be at Sandhurst. Israel's victory over the Arabs – achieved by an early air strike which destroyed Egypt's air force on the ground – carried it to a peak of pride and conceit and plunged the Arabs into the very depths of despair. The struggle for independence which the Arabs had waged since World War Two was seen to be hollow. Having achieved total air supremacy, Israel proceeded to overrun vast tracts of Arab territory, including Egypt's Sinai Peninsula, Syria's Golan Heights, and the Palestinian territories of the West Bank, Gaza and East Jerusalem. More than a quarter of a century later – and largely as a result of the Gulf War – I am happy to see that the peace process is at last making real progress.

In a military academy like Sandhurst, there was tremendous applause for Israel's exploit at trouncing its Arab neighbors within a week. The cadets and indeed their instructors knew little or nothing of the politics of the region. They viewed the war solely from a military point of view. Few, if any, understood that this was only one round in a long struggle. Although the long-drawn-out conflict in Vietnam was raging at the time, the Middle East war was more dramatic, and was much discussed at Sandhurst. It captured everyone's attention. Perhaps because the memory of their empire was then still fresh, the British had little respect for Arabs. And, as an Arab at Sandhurst, I was not spared. I was mocked and taunted. I was the target of the most vicious jokes. I did not know where to hide. Among officers – officers from opposing armies – a certain code of behavior applies, in defeat as in victory. But cadets know no such code. It was probably the most embarrassing and humiliating moment of my life. What made matters worse was that Shaikh Khalifa and I – he shared my torments – had at the start believed Egyptian communiqués. We had thought that the war was going our way. We had listened to the "Voice of the Arabs" from Cairo and believed we were winning. Then disaster struck. Had bad news come at the beginning, it might have been easier to accept.

At any rate, the psychological impact on us was profound. It was a bitter blow to begin our military careers with a catastrophic defeat for Arab arms.

In 1967, and again a year later, the annual Sandhurst exercise, usually involving about half the Academy, or some 600 cadets, was held in Cyprus where Britain, in agreement with the Cyprus government, maintains a number of sovereign base areas. We were divided into opposing teams and, having been issued with blank ammunition, spent strenuous hours practicing tactics and fighting each other among the rocks and thickets of this Mediterranean island.

Then, to our immense surprise, Turkey threatened to invade the island, apparently to protect the Turkish minority in the northern part of the island from the Greek majority. As Turkish warships massed offshore and Turkish jets strafed Greek Cypriot military targets, Greece and Turkey were brought to the brink of war. Nicosia, the island's capital, was divided into Greek and Turkish sectors. There was consternation in the British camp. No one knew if the Turks planned to land and advance on the base areas, which were manned by only a small garrison. In the absence of regular British troops, the Sandhurst cadets were thrown into the breach. Blank ammunition was withdrawn and replaced with live rounds. Our instructors became serving officers commanding real troops. What had been an exercise looked like becoming a real confrontation between Britain and Turkey.

Refugees poured in from the threatened invasion zone and we were detailed to look after them. We established a camp for displaced families where we served as cooks, mess servants and nursemaids. I remember peeling a lot of onions and potatoes.

When the troubles broke out, I heard that the Saudi military attaché in Beirut, then Major-General Ali al-Sha'ir, wanted to send a plane to evacuate me. But I refused to go. It was not in the Sandhurst tradition – or indeed in the Arab and Islamic tradition – to turn one's back on danger, and I would have suffered a terrible loss of face had I run away.

But we were soon back in England and immersed in our studies once again. The essence of the Sandhurst teaching method is to reduce every military activity to a set of rules – to Standing Operating Procedures (or SOPs), as they are called. Whether it is marching, or shooting, or stripping down a weapon, or issuing orders, or radio signaling, or reading a map, or writing a military "appreciation," or fighting, or taking pris-oners – there is always a right way and a wrong way of going about it. Every move is documented meticulously. And, what-ever the subject, everything is taught in the same way. First you are given a theoretical explanation, then a practical demonstration, then you are asked to do it yourself, then your performance is reviewed and criticized – and then you do it all over again, and again, and again, until you get it right. And at every stage, the cadet's skills are monitored to see whether he is reaching the required standard. If he is not, he is either put back a term or two, or thrown out.

The ultimate aim of all these rules is to help an officer control himself, and control his men, in the stress and panic of battle. As John Keegan, a former Sandhurst instructor and military commentator, put it in his excellent book, *The Face of Battle* (London, 1976), the aim "is to reduce the conduct of war to a set of rules and a system of procedures – and thereby to make orderly and rational what is essentially chaotic and instinctive."

To surmount the natural fear of death, to keep cool under fire, to make quick decisions, all these demand mental and physical robustness. But this is not a quality most people are born with. It has to be acquired and developed. Looking back on what I learned at Sandhurst, I would say the most valuable lesson was not just how to behave as an officer, but how to behave generally. I learned to take things seriously and to discipline myself – self-discipline of the mind, of the body, but also of the emotions, which is perhaps the most difficult of all.

On Sundays, there were a few spare hours to fill and, not wanting to waste time, Shaikh Khalifa and I decided to learn to fly. We spent several Sundays flying Cherokees at a nearby flying school at Blackbush airport. On other weekends, we simply drove up to London to enjoy some good food, see friends, and catch up on lost sleep. In spite of the pressure of work, there were festivities and days of leisure to enjoy. I wanted to attend the June ball at Sandhurst – a lavish and colorful affair – but one needed a dinner jacket and I did not have one. Muhammad Asem, an Egyptian friend who worked behind the reception desk at the Royal Garden Hotel, wore a version of a dinner jacket when on duty. I borrowed it for the ball.

In those days, Sandhurst was composed of three colleges – Old College, New College and Victory College – each college made up of four companies. I started life in New College in a company commanded by Major Carnie and named after the World War One battle of the Somme. But, just before my last term, the Academy was reorganized and the companies in each college were reduced from four to three. My Somme company was scrapped and its cadets dispersed among New College's other three companies. I was moved to Gaza company, named after a battle fought by the British against the Turks in World War One, under a Major Henry Trigear. Before I left Somme, Major Carnie summoned me: "You are unlucky," he said. "If the Somme company had lived on, you would have become a junior Under Officer. I wanted to promote you because, although everything was against you, you tried hard and made the grade." I much appreciated his words of commendation. In each company only four cadets are promoted to the exalted rank of junior Under Officer, and only one to senior Under Officer.

I still have a letter Major Carnie wrote about me to Prince Sultan on July 30, 1968:

> . . . He has tried hard and shown a very keen interest and ability in all he has been taught.
>
> It is unfortunate that Somme Company is being disbanded as I had intended that he would be an Under Officer in his final term. However, he will be a Corporal in his new Company and I know that he will do the job with enthusiasm and skill.
>
> I am convinced that his time in England has been very well spent. He has matured considerably and I know that he will make an excellent young officer when he is commissioned. The most important thing is his ability as a leader. He has all the confidence, diplomacy and intelligence to be a great asset to Saudi Arabia in the future when he has gained more knowledge and experience.

The last, sixth, term at Sandhurst is once again entirely military and extremely arduous. The work done in the first term is revisited, but the difference is that, this time round, one is no longer a junior but a senior. That is to say, one is a member of the cadet government which runs the life of the first-year intake with a rod of iron – as our own life was once run. It is now one's turn to treat juniors like dirt and to inflict punishments.

The essential aim of the last term is to bring cadets up to speed before they are commissioned, to develop their robustness of mind under pressure. This is done by putting them through numerous exercises and simulated battles, forcing them to make plans and appraisals, and above all to take military decisions against the clock.

The triumphant climax of the two-year Sandhurst course is an elaborate passing-out parade. At one of the passing-out parades during my time at Sandhurst, Viscount Montgomery of Alamein came to inspect the cadets. Although he had retired from the army ten years earlier, he was still a trim, alert figure of immense authority. As chance would have it, he stopped in front of me and uttered a word of commendation. After the parade was over, I was rewarded with 24 hours' leave, a standard reward if a cadet attracts favorable attention from an inspecting officer.

On these passing-out parades, the immaculately turned out cadets show off their drill on the square, wheeling and turning about in review order, before marching proudly up the broad steps of the Grand Entrance and into the Old Building. Behind them up the steps rides the adjutant on his gray horse.

It was a moment I had worked for very hard. I celebrated the proud acquisition of the pip on my shoulder with a party for thirty of my fellow second lieutenants at the Royal Garden Hotel.

In my "End of Course Report," Colonel A. W. Mathew, commanding New College wrote:

> He is a proud man, fully aware of his heritage . . . He is a
> leader of great charm, and is well able to take control and
> be decisive when the need arises. He remains cheerful, and
> an example to others, under the worst conditions. He has
> enjoyed Sandhurst, and I believe he will be a good officer.

Sandhurst, I am told, is no longer what it was. The two-year course has been drastically cut, the juniors are no longer humiliated, the dreaded cadet government is no more, training and discipline are now entirely in the hands of Guards officers and NCOs. But, from what I saw of British officers during the Gulf War, the essential virtues of Sandhurst evidently continue to flourish.

CHAPTER VI

To Fly Like a Hawk

I HAD JUST GONE TO SANDHURST, aged seventeen, when I heard that the Hawk had, in my absence, arrived in the Kingdom. I did not know what the Hawk was. It was a wholly new weapon. I had never heard of air defense. But I remember the stir it caused: the Hawk was going to defend our air space, it was going to make us strong and lift us into the world of modern technology. Everyone in the armed services was talking about it. Saudi Arabia had entered the missile age and, although I did not realize it at the time, the pattern of my own future career was being established.

As already related, the arrival of the Egyptian army on our doorstep in Yemen in late 1962 caused a great shock. It forced us, perhaps for the first time, to think hard about how to defend our vast country against outside aggression. Until then, security had been essentially an internal matter – preventing disputes between tribes from getting out of hand, striking a balance between the interests of different provinces. Apart from Yemen, on which we kept a wary eye because of an ongoing border dispute, the possibility of aggression from outside did not enter seriously into our calculations, no doubt because we imagined that the size of our country, its waterless deserts and the seas on our eastern and western borders were barriers and buffers enough against any would-be enemies. In the field of Arab politics, we were cautious players, always relying on a regional balance of power to prevent any one Arab country from becoming overambitious. But our gaze was on the affairs of the Arabian peninsula rather than on the world outside. Before the oil-price explosion of the 1970s, our financial resources were scant, our manpower was unskilled, our society was still traditional, and we had barely begun the process of modernization which, in the past two decades, has put us ahead of most of our neighbors.

In terms of military force in the early 1960s, we had a few aging tanks, about the same number of aircraft, and a few thousand troops. We had some antiaircraft guns in our artillery corps – 20mm, 40mm, 90mm and 120mm – guns which are today museum pieces, and which were then scarcely better than that. Air defense as such was nonexistent. When the Egyptian air force bombed our frontier towns of Najran and Jizan, as well as the airport at Khamis Mushait and a hospital at Abha, we could do nothing about it. We were in no shape to contemplate fighting even a small-to-medium-sized force such as Egypt had in Yemen.

Such was the unpromising situation when Crown Prince Faisal appointed my father, Prince Sultan, Defense Minister in November 1962. His immediate task was to confront the threat from Nasser in Yemen.

According to a family story, Prince Sultan assured the Crown Prince that he would go at once to the operations room at the ministry, summon the general staff and review the Kingdom's defense plans. Prince Faisal smiled, but did not comment. So Prince Sultan went to the office and asked to be directed to the operations room. "What operations room?" his puzzled staff inquired. He called for the general staff. "What general staff?" He asked to see the plans. "What plans?" He ordered the air force to engage the Egyptians, but none of the planes could fly. He went back to see Prince Faisal.

"There's nothing there," he said, "no maps, no plans, no tanks, no officers, nothing at all . . ."

"That's why I've given you the job," the Crown Prince replied. "You can start working on it now."

The British, who were then still holding their colony at Aden and its tribal hinterland, were as worried as we were by Nasser's eruption into Arabian politics. Accordingly, in 1963, Britain agreed to send us a dozen combat aircraft – Hunters and Lightnings – as well as a battery of Thunderbird surface-to-air missiles, which we positioned at Khamis Mushait, then a small air base in our southwestern province of Asir, just north of Yemen. The

Thunderbird was an old-fashioned, World War Two weapon –
its crew had to pull the missile into position with ropes – and
it would have done little to deter the Egyptians. But its purchase
marked the beginning of Saudi air defense.

The unopposed freedom of the skies enjoyed by the Egyptian
air force must have made a profound impression on Prince
Sultan because, from then on, he gave high priority to
expanding our air force and improving our air defenses. It was
evident that any aggressor, wishing to leapfrog our natural barriers of the Gulf and the Red Sea, or cross our vast deserts north
and south of Riyadh, would have to come by air. The essential
threat to the Kingdom was an air threat, not a land threat such
as we would face some twenty years later with Iraq's invasion
of Kuwait. This became, as I understand it, the underlying
assumption of our defense policy.

It was given concrete expression in 1966 when, with the Egyptians still in Yemen, Prince Sultan contracted to buy a more
substantial air defense package which included over 50 British
combat aircraft and twelve American Hawk surface-to-air
batteries, together with associated radar and communications
networks. As I have mentioned, it was the arrival of the first
Hawk battery in 1966, and its siting at Jizan, which caused great
excitement, echoes of which reached me at Sandhurst.

The Americans started by saying that the new weapon – a
surface-to-air guided missile system designed to provide air
defense coverage against low-to-medium-altitude air attack –
was too sophisticated for the Saudis, and in truth no Saudis were
technically ready to handle it. Young candidates had to be sent
to Jeddah for a nine-month English language course, followed
by a three-month course in electronics before they could be
posted to the air defense sites. In the meantime, the sites were
manned by American engineers. In view of this situation, which
was not altogether flattering for the Kingdom, Prince Sultan
instructed the Chief of Staff to choose the best officers we had
to train on the new weapon. The Hawk program was to get the
cream of the crop.

On being commissioned, officers in our army are usually
allowed a choice of three branches of the military. In fact, a few
months before my graduation, the Saudi military attaché had

sent me a form in which I had to name my three preferred choices. I put down Special Forces first (and still have moments of regret that that was not to be my career), followed by armor and artillery. But when I graduated from Sandhurst in 1968 and returned to Saudi Arabia, I was not given a choice. I found myself posted to air defense as a platoon commander. They were still looking for English-speaking officers for the Hawk, and being a Sandhurst graduate I seemed to fit the bill.

I enrolled at once for a basic electronics course at the air-defense school in Jeddah, but to my distress the school commandant did not seem overjoyed to see me. He gave me no courses to follow, no duties to perform. When I reported to him for instructions, which I did almost daily, he would tell me to go away and relax, which he no doubt thought a more suitable occupation for a prince. After the high professional standards and demanding work schedule at Sandhurst, returning to a more relaxed pace proved something of an anticlimax. Looking for something to do, I moved across to the air defense language school as assistant to the director, but not finding this task up to my expectations either, I passed a test to go on a course to the United States. I soon found myself at the U.S. air defense school at Fort Bliss, Texas, located near the Mexican border at the town of El Paso. Nearby were the White Sands missile testing range and the McGregor range.

This, my first visit to the United States, took place early in 1969. I was still a very young man of 20, a British-trained, newly commissioned lieutenant, keen to master the American way of doing things, but also keen to have a good time. I worked hard and played hard. It was at El Paso that I first made the acquaintance of another young Saudi officer, Salih al-Muhaya, now the Land Forces Commander. Over the next 18 months I completed three courses, all to do with missiles and air defense – an electronic warfare course, a Hawk officers' course, and a trouble-shooting Hawk maintenance course. As part of a U.S. team, I also did practical, on-the-job training at the McGregor range.

All this stood me in good stead, because on my return to the Kingdom in 1970, I was given a job as an air defense inspector, one of a team of six whose task it was to visit and assess the operational readiness of the Hawk batteries which by then had been deployed at key sites around the Kingdom, among them Riyadh, Dhahran, Jeddah, Taif, Khamis Mushait and Tabuk. The inspection team had originally consisted of three American experts and three Saudi sergeants. I replaced one of the Americans, the first Saudi to do so. The job involved almost constant movement from one site to another. It was the first time I had traveled extensively in my own country and I got to know every corner of it.

Some months later, in late 1970, our team went to inspect a Hawk battery at Tabuk, which in those days was a small and primitive garrison town up in the northwestern corner of the Arabian peninsula, not far from Jordan's port of Aqaba and Israel's adjoining port of Eilat. Tabuk was then little more than a dot on a map, a mere desert staging post for pilgrims coming south to Makkah by the overland route from Syria and Jordan. But, because of its location close to Israel, it was a strongpoint of obvious strategic importance.

We found the Hawk battery out in the desert, its crew and support units in a wretched state. After a careful evaluation, I pronounced the battery "nonoperational" and, in a severe report, the team recommended the removal of the battery commander. As the Hawk was still a high-priority weapon, this negative assessment — the first one our inspection team had issued — went straight up to the top. A directive came down from the Defense Ministry to the effect that whoever had written the report should take over command of the battery. It was me. Prince Sultan tried to give me the impression that he only learned of my appointment when I went to bid him goodbye!

So began one of the happiest and most fulfilling periods of my life. I was 21 and it was my first field command. I was in charge of about 180 men, four officers and six launchers, each equipped with three missiles. I began by doing away with all the existing procedures and put my men, who were sloppy, bored and undisciplined, through a Sandhurst-type course: plenty of physical exercise, plenty of drill, plenty of inspections. Within a very few days, everyone knew who was in charge.

I discovered that my unit was ravaged by drugs which were being smuggled into Tabuk through the Gulf of Aqaba, about 70 miles away, and which in turn bred all sorts of other crimes.

I went after the dealers, and with help from the local police, caught and jailed three of them. I then went after the men, punishing offenders severely, but also handsomely rewarding good performance and good behavior. "Rewards and punishments" became my watchword which I have regularly applied, with I think good results, in various commands and at different stages of my life. I got to know the men individually. I thought up three sorts of punishment of different degrees of severity: one was confinement in a cell above ground, another in a hole below ground and a third in a pit near the sewage pit. The stench was so terrible that no one put there could stand it for more than six hours without fainting. I was as rough and tough as a one-man Sandhurst cadet government. I became known as the man who restored order.

Within a very few weeks, as pride and self-confidence were restored, the change in the fitness, bearing and appearance of the men was remarkable. Within seven months, this "non-operational" battery had come second in the nationwide annual firing competition. In spite of the total lack of amenities at Tabuk, our unit gradually acquired a reputation for excellence and, on one of his tours of inspection, Prince Sultan came to see us and was suitably impressed. I think he was proud of me.

It was at Tabuk that I realized I was able to exercise leadership and that I first took my military career seriously. In a small command like mine, it was possible to see at once the results of one's work. In a brigade, it might take months to see any real change, but in a battery, you can see the difference in a matter of days. Those 20 months in harsh conditions at Tabuk turned me into a professional soldier. It could so easily have been otherwise. My uncle was King. My father was Minister of Defense. I guess I could have got any plush job I wanted in Riyadh or downtown Jeddah. But I preferred to be out there in the desert with my troops. I wanted to prove I could do it. The real turning point in my military career was not Sandhurst, nor was it commanding Saudi air defense forces, nor being named Joint Forces Commander. It was commanding an air defense battery at Tabuk.

Aged twenty, when I was still part of the air defense inspection team, I had married my first cousin, Lulwa, a charming girl of seventeen. She was the daughter of my uncle, King Fahd (or Prince Fahd, as he then was).

Within a year of our marriage, my wife gave birth to a daughter, whom we called Reem. Mother and daughter were staying at my father's house in Taif where I would call in to see them for a few days at a time between my tours of inspection. On one such visit, when the child was about four months old, I got up in the middle of the night, woke my wife, and told her that I felt a strong urge to take Reem to Riyadh the next day to show her to my father and mother who had not seen her since her birth. As my wife was unable to make the journey, I was accompanied by the child's nanny. We flew to Riyadh and called on my parents. My father said, "This child is like an angel. She has the most beautiful face and skin. I am afraid for her. May God preserve her!" Reem and the nanny then returned to Taif by air, while I followed by road, as I had something to do on the way. I stayed overnight on the journey, but on arriving home found that the child had caught a cold. She died the next day. Something like a premonition had made me take her to Riyadh, to the people I loved most in the world, my father and mother.

I was a young man and she was my first child. Her death was a great sadness. It was the most painful wound I had suffered.

Trying to keep my composure, I buried her. I did not want to show any weakness. But an incident happened which depressed me further. Before the child was even buried, a man called at the house. He sent word that he needed to see me urgently. I came down from my room where I had been trying to hold back my tears.

"I want to ask you a favor," he said. "I know you have just bought your daughter a car. I would like to ask for it first, before anyone else does. Can I have it?"

It was true that I had bought a car to allow Reem's nanny to take her out, and it was also not uncommon for perfect strangers to ask one for presents. But in the tragic circumstances of the child's death, my visitor's words provoked in me a surge of anger. I thought I would tear him limb from limb. I do not know how I controlled my feelings. "You had better go at once," I said, and left the room. I am glad to say I have forgotten his name and what he looks like.

My brother Fahd and some friends came that night from Riyadh to console us, and the next day I went to Makkah to perform the *Umra*, or smaller pilgrimage. I felt I needed it. I then went on to Jeddah and back to work.

Later my wife and I had two more children of whom I am very proud. Our son Faisal was born in 1973 and our daughter Sara in 1976. But in 1978 my wife and I decided to part. Our children have my enduring affection. Their mother remains my cousin, of course, almost my sister. We are all very much part of the same family. When she needs something, I am always there to help, but our lives have taken a different course.

In 1971, when I was still commanding my battery at Tabuk, I received a telephone call from Prince Turki bin Abd al-Aziz, then the Deputy Defense Minister, who enjoyed great respect and affection in the armed forces. He ordered me to come to Riyadh straight away to help negotiate a contract with Northrop, the U.S. aircraft manufacturer, for the supply of pilotless aircraft, known as drones, used in air defense target practice. Two developments had led to that phone call. First, King Faisal had issued a directive that there should be no further subcontracting of main weapons systems, but that the Kingdom itself should deal direct with each manufacturer. Previously, we tended to have one main, all-embracing contract with a company, such as Raytheon, the makers of the Hawk, and Raytheon would in turn subcontract with other companies for the many items – from air defense sites, to catering, to housing, to air targets – which were necessary for the full deployment of the weapon. But under King Faisal's new directive, for reasons of economy and efficiency, the Kingdom was itself to perform this function, shopping for the additional items it needed. The proposed deal with Northrop for drones was a case in point.

The second reason I was summoned to Riyadh was that I was the only person in the Kingdom who had had some direct experience of drones, having encountered them in on-the-job training at the McGregor range in Texas. As an assistant inspector with the American army, I had spent three months in that featureless desert, watching from the control tower as U.S. batteries, which had come up from bases in Miami where they had been confronting Cuba, fired their missiles at air targets.

Wanting to stay at Tabuk, I begged Prince Turki to release me from the new assignment, but he insisted. So I went to Riyadh, formed a negotiating team of two officers and a finance man, sat down with Northrop's people in the Defense Ministry, and within eight months we had a deal which Prince Turki was able to approve. To everyone's satisfaction, I managed to bring the prices down. It was a small contract, but for me – and for my future career – it was very important. I had learned to negotiate.

The pattern in those days was for the Saudis to appoint a project officer for each defense contract. Each weapons system had its own project officer, whose task it was to liaise with the foreign supplier, monitor the implementation of the contract, accept the equipment, and even oversee the training of our own troops in the new weapon. Being a project officer for a major weapons system was therefore a position of considerable power and responsibility. For example, my cousin Prince Abd al-Rahman al-Faisal, who preceded me by half a dozen years at Sandhurst (where he had captained the fencing team) had specialized in armor and had become the project officer for the AMX-30 light tanks we had bought from France.

It was therefore with great satisfaction and excitement that, following my successful negotiation with Northrop, I learned in 1972 that I was to be appointed project officer, not just for the Northrop drone but for the Raytheon Hawk as well.

My Tabuk days were over: the young field officer had now to learn office management. At a very young age, I was being entrusted with handling our relations with Raytheon, the major American company which had initiated us into the missile age and on which we were dependent for the defense of our air space. In everything but name, Raytheon was running the show. Someone had to bring control into Saudi hands. My ambition was fired.

Officers in our armed services often inscribe a message to themselves on the back of the nameplate on their desk. It is usually an inspirational saying of one sort or another. Some inscribe a verse from the Quran, others a proverb. I chose a line from a famous Arabic poem: "He who dares not climb mountains will spend his life in the pits." I kept that line on my nameplate from my first appointment in Riyadh until my retirement from the armed services of the Kingdom. It was the only thing I took with me when the Joint Forces Command was dissolved after the Gulf War.

CHAPTER VII

Taming the Company

W HEN I WAS NAMED project officer for the Hawk in 1972, I found that Raytheon, the manufacturer of the Hawk, was like ARAMCO (the Arabian–American Oil Company*) – in other words, it was a power not to be challenged.

Just as ARAMCO ran our oil industry, so Raytheon ran our air defense. One provided revenue, the other protection. These two important American companies controlled vital sectors of the Kingdom. Vast powerhouses of wealth and expertise, closely associated with the U.S. government, they were directed by powerful boards back in the United States. In Saudi Arabia, few people were prepared to talk tough with them.

Raytheon had come to Saudi Arabia in 1966 with the purpose of introducing the Hawk missile to the Kingdom. It had not been subject to Saudi control for the simple reason that no Saudi understood how this high-technology weapon worked. Raytheon supplied the missiles, the spare parts and the maintenance. Their engineers manned the air defense sites and the central maintenance point. They supplied the training instructors. They managed the contract, with little if any oversight by us. In other words, we were totally dependent on Raytheon engineers, Raytheon instructors, Raytheon managers, Raytheon technicians of all sorts. At Jeddah, where the company had established its headquarters, its staff lived in a Raytheon compound of over a hundred villas built on a

---

* In the 1970s, ARAMCO was gradually taken over by the Saudi government until it became a 100 percent Saudi company.

promontory off the coast, known as the Peninsula, and to which no Saudi had access without permission from Raytheon's general manager, Mr. Glen Grubbs, a robust, no-nonsense American. Also on the Peninsula was our Air Defense School, known to local taxi drivers as the Raytheon school and a small hospital, known as the Raytheon hospital.

The chain of command was also very much in their favor. Mr. Grubbs, the representative of such a key company, had direct access to Prince Sultan and, even on occasion, to the King himself. But, if a senior Saudi officer – such as the commander of the Air Defense School – wished to meet Raytheon's General Manager, he had to come down to the company offices and ask for an interview.

This was not a situation to the liking of King Faisal, austere and ardent nationalist that he was, or indeed of Prince Sultan. Accordingly, the directive I was given was to curb the powers of the company and put some order into the relationship – no easy task for a young captain in his early twenties, but one which I tackled with gusto and a good deal of innocence.

I realized, of course, that I had a great deal to learn before I could impose myself on the company, nor could I afford to clash with an outfit so vital to our national security. But, nevertheless, at an early meeting with Glen Grubbs, I managed to start out on the right footing.

"I have been asked to handle our relations with you," I began. "If you have a problem you wish to discuss with the Saudi government, please come to me. If I cannot solve it for you, I will send it up to the air defense commander, and if he cannot handle it, it will then go higher still. But I plan to take over the relationship. One of us has to be in charge." I then added, for good measure: "From now on, we will not meet in your office. If you need to see me, we will meet in my office."

This last remark was particularly daring because I did not have an office at that time. I was working out of a briefcase. If I needed an office for a meeting, I would move into the first available one I could find.

I will not claim that from that moment on I was in charge. Old habits die hard. Not unnaturally, Raytheon resisted being pushed around by a young princeling, and it took four or five years of hard maneuvering – two steps forward and one step back – before I achieved real control. But it was a start.

Two things helped me a great deal, the first being that Glen Grubbs was quick to sense that change had to come. Instead of fighting to preserve Raytheon's dominance, he gradually persuaded the company to adapt to the new circumstances and become the partner, indeed eventually the junior partner, of the Saudi government. The second factor was that, in forging this new policy, he won the support of Tom Phillips, then president of Raytheon.

Saudi Arabia had signed for the Hawk in 1966 under a five-year contract worth, I believe, $112 million – a considerable sum in those days but not an enormous amount in view of Raytheon's overall activities. Yet Tom Phillips had the vision to see that it was only the first of many contracts in what was to be a great marriage between his company and the Kingdom.

Glen Grubbs – with whom I was to work closely for the next twenty years and more – later related to me that when that first contract was put before him, Tom Phillips said, "Let me tell you, gentlemen. With the exception of the U.S. Army, Saudi Arabia will be the finest customer we will ever have. That's my feeling, and I expect you to treat the Saudis accordingly." And, in the following years, whenever Grubbs went back to the United States, he would be summoned in front of the Chairman of the Board, who would ask him, "Are we doing a proper job for those people?"

The answer was that Raytheon did do a proper job. They made a great deal of money in Saudi Arabia, especially in the early years, but they also gave us a great deal – not just in equipment, but, what was more important, in terms of training and technology transfer. In the end, they helped us create an ultramodern, highly sophisticated, nationwide air defense network, the like of which any country could be proud, and, what is more, one which we could operate ourselves. But that was a decade or two down the road.

For the record, the architects of the new relationship – Phil Phallon, Raytheon's senior negotiator, and Glen Grubbs, their general manager in the Kingdom – deserve a good deal of credit. But I must also pay tribute to Jim Lewis, a giant of a man and a remarkable troubleshooter, who started out as Grubbs's assistant in the early 1970s which was when I first met him. He then went off to the Shah's Iran, to head Raytheon's operations there, before returning to the Kingdom in 1977 as chief Raytheon representative, a post he held with distinction until his retirement at the end of 1993.

Unlike the representatives of many other companies working in the Kingdom, it was refreshing that Raytheon representatives were empowered to make decisions on the spot, even when they involved tens of millions of dollars, without always having to refer back to their superiors in the United States. One of the keys to Raytheon's success with us was that they appointed managers with real clout, who could make independent judgments and carry them out.

❦

My work as a project officer was interrupted by the October War of 1973 when, in a dramatic bid to recover some of the territory lost in 1967 and bring Israel to the negotiating table, Egypt and Syria launched simultaneous attacks across the Suez Canal and on the Golan Heights. Their initial success was great and Israel fell back reeling. But having crossed the Canal and stormed Israel's Bar Lev line – a great feat in itself – the Egyptian army chose not to advance on the Sinai passes. (I was among those observers who thought this was an operational pause before a further advance.) As a result, Israel was able to throw all its weight against the Syrian front, driving Syrian forces off the Golan plateau and advancing on Damascus. Too late, Egyptian armored units then ventured out from their defensive positions east of the Canal but, having dealt with the Syrians, the Israelis were ready for them. To their immense advantage, the Israelis had by this time been urgently and heavily reinforced by the United States, with tanks, guns and other equipment flown straight to the battlefield by means of an air bridge from American bases in Germany and as far afield as Kelly Air Force Base, Texas. If the Soviets had attacked then, the U.S. would have been at a serious disadvantage.

President Anwar al-Sadat's offensive into the wastes of Sinai was dictated by political not military considerations. His top commanders were to a man against committing Egypt's reserves to the battle, leaving the west bank of the Canal vulnerable. It also meant attacking uphill. Major General Saad Ma'mun, the Second Army Commander, first threatened to rebel against Sadat's orders then, when he saw that the President insisted on his plan of action to relieve the pressure on Syria, he had a heart attack. Having made the mistake of committing its front-line reserves to the battle, Egypt was caught off balance. The sad sequel is known to everyone.

The initial Arab victory ended in stalemate. Unlike 1967, Arab armies fought bravely in 1973 and proved that they had mastered most of the arts of modern warfare. But the final outcome was not what the Arabs had hoped for.

The Saudi authorities were anxious to send a brigade up from Tabuk to stiffen Syrian resistance at Sa'sa, a point on the road to Damascus where the Israeli thrust had been held, and Major General Muhammad Badira, one of the finest officers in our army where tactics were concerned, was chosen to command it. The brigade was equipped with TOW antitank missiles mounted on jeeps, a new weapon at the time and an effective one. With five other officers, I was sent to Tabuk to organize the air defense battalion which was organic to the brigade. I was hoping to go to Sa'sa with a Hawk battery, but Major General Badira decided instead to take 40mm Bofors antiaircraft guns. As I had not been trained to use the guns, I would not have been of much use. In any event, the brigade's preparations were prolonged and, by the time it was on the road, the war was more or less over. It arrived in Syria after the cease-fire and did not see any action. But it stayed for nearly two years, helping the Syrians defend their front.

From Tabuk, we followed news of the war with intense interest. Having been conned in 1967 by overoptimistic reports, this time we were highly skeptical of Egyptian and Syrian claims. But what particularly impressed me, when I was later able to study the war in detail, was Egypt's effective use of short-range surface-to-air missiles – mobile SAM-6s and shoulder-carried SAM-7s – as well as antiaircraft guns such as the radar-guided, four-barreled, 23mm Shelka, which during the Canal crossing played havoc with the much vaunted Israeli air force. Instead of pitting plane against plane, Egypt, with these new weapons, had turned it into a contest of missile against plane, which was apparently the result of a decision, taken in 1966, to detach air defense from the artillery and make it, on the Soviet model, into a separate force, supported by its own early-warning network. Egypt's use of the portable antitank missile, the Malotka, also turned the ground battle into a contest of missile against tank.

I became absorbed, almost obsessed, by the potential of missiles. I felt that to defend our vast air space we needed air defense more than we needed planes. In any event, I was convinced that the United States, anxious to reassure Israel, would put a ceiling on our acquisition of combat aircraft, and would make sure that the British and the French did so too. None of the Western powers would allow Saudi Arabia to develop a really powerful air force. But they were not likely to put the same restrictions on air defense weapons. If there was a magic number for the planes we could buy, there was no such magic number for air defense batteries. That was, therefore, the way we should go. It seemed to me an irrefutable argument. So was planted in my mind the germ of an idea which, as will be seen, was to occupy me for several years.

As is well known in the arms business, nothing becomes obsolete more quickly than an expensive weapons system – and nowhere is this more true than in the realm of air defense. Missile manufacturers are engaged in a ceaseless struggle with manufacturers of combat aircraft to see who can outsmart the other. No sooner is a missile developed that can bring down an aircraft at a range, say, of 30 or 40 miles than countermeasures are devised to neutralize it. By 1973, the basic Hawk we had bought in 1966 was beginning to look old-fashioned. To keep in the game, we had to think seriously about buying the Improved Hawk, which could do a lot of things the basic Hawk could not do. As project officer for the Hawk, it was my responsibility to keep abreast of these developments and to prepare for the inevitable negotiation with Raytheon once we decided to upgrade our systems.

To get the negotiation started, it was mutually agreed with the company that Saudi officers should go on a working visit to the United States to meet Raytheon representatives, learn more about the Hawk system, view the improved equipment and visit the plants where it was being made. It was decided that I should lead the small Saudi team. The trip took place just after the 1973 war and lasted two and a half months. It was one of my most important journeys.

From the start, we were given red-carpet treatment. We were met by the Chairman of Raytheon, Mr. Adams, grandson or perhaps great-grandson of John Quincy Adams, sixth President of the United States. We were received with suitable ceremony at company headquarters at Lexington, near Boston. We visited the missile systems division at Andover nearby, before going on to Huntsville to view the software and maintenance facilities for the Improved Hawk. We traveled to test sites in Alabama and to El Paso, where I was able to revisit old haunts, including the range where I had first seen the basic Hawk in action. I was accompanied by Captain Salih al-Hajjaj, then the U.S.-based Saudi liaison officer with Raytheon (who has since retired as a brigadier general and who remains a good friend), and by Captain Muhammad al-Kayyal, an air defense officer who was to be one of my closest associates in my military career. Kayyal spoke good English. He had spent some years at school in England and had been to Sandhurst a couple of years before me. As a first lieutenant, he had then commanded the so-called English department of the air defense school where enlisted men were taught the language before moving to the Hawk, and it was there that I had got to know him in 1969. We became friends.

There was no money in the country at that time and our pay was very low. I remember that we wanted to buy a tape recorder, but could not afford it. Kayyal's grandmother had tucked away some money to pay for her shroud. She gave it to us, and we bought the tape recorder. Years later, when she developed cancer, I was able to repay the debt by sending her to the United States for an operation. At the time of writing, she is over 100 years old and still in good health.

On that visit to the U.S. in 1973, Kayyal and I, two young officers still in our early twenties, with no experience of meeting important foreign personages, were wheeled in to see numerous generals, managing directors and high government officials, such as Joseph Sisco, the Assistant Secretary for Near Eastern affairs at the State Department. But the climax of the trip was a call which Mr. Adams, the Raytheon Chairman, who had considerable pull in Washington, arranged for me to make on Elliot Richardson, President Nixon's Secretary of Defense.

For me at the time, it seemed the biggest thing that could happen to anyone. As a youth barely out of short pants, I was to meet a Secretary of Defense, not just of any country but of the mighty United States of America, within the context of the negotiation of an important contract which was going to change the face of Saudi air defense and enhance our military preparedness.

Curiously, when I was ushered in to Elliot Richardson's office, Mr. Adams, who had anticipated coming in as well, was asked to wait in an anteroom. I could see that he was displeased: there was fire in his eye. He was a friend of Elliot Richardson and I suspect he later gave him hell. Apart from his eminence as head of a great American company, he was highly respected in the Kingdom because of a courteous gesture to King Faisal in 1966. Accompanied by Prince Sultan, the King had visited New York in June of that year but the Mayor, no doubt anxious to please his Jewish electors, had refused to host a dinner for him. Stepping into the breach, Mr. Adams had gathered top business leaders from around the country and given the King the best and biggest dinner reception ever given to a visiting head of state in New York City. It had cemented their relations. With me, in turn, he was politeness itself: he was kind enough to wait for me while I saw Elliot Richardson, and we left the Pentagon together.

But there was an embarrassing aspect to the visit: I had no authority to make such high-level contacts. In fact, I had no permission to meet anyone in the U.S. government at all. During King Faisal's reign, no one was allowed to meet a top foreign official without his knowing about it. Moreover, it is worth recalling that ours was the first Saudi military delegation to visit the United States after the imposition of the oil embargo by King Faisal during the October War, and we expected some hostility from the public. This demanded extra-special discretion on my part.

I called my father to ask for guidance. It was purely a courtesy visit, I told him, which I had to make as it had already been arranged. "Go ahead," he said, "but make sure you don't commit yourself to anything. And no press!"

To my apprehension, Elliot Richardson had a long list of questions for me. A tall, lean, bespectacled man with the sharp intelligent look of a New York lawyer, he seemed to be putting me through some sort of a test. I noticed he seemed very curious about Saudi Arabia and about King Faisal, in particular, whose independent policy, oil embargo, and support for Egypt and Syria during the war had given Americans a jolt.

Several of Richardson's aides were taking notes of my replies. I glanced at Kayyal who, not to be outdone, took a pad out of his briefcase and started taking notes as well. That briefcase! It was stuffed full of confidential documents to do with our negotiations for the Improved Hawk. I had entrusted it to Kayyal, jokingly adding that if he lost it, he would be court-martialed. Kayyal took my remark literally, and the heavy case never left his side. He took it everywhere – and ended up bent double with a back problem.

Then, Richardson threw a sensitive political question at me. He wanted to know my views about Israel and the Palestinians.

"The views of His Majesty King Faisal are well known to you," I replied. "I am not here to comment on them. In any event," I added, "I am only a captain, and captains are not allowed to talk politics!" This cut him short. It also protected me from any rebuke from the King who would certainly have heard about it had I spoken out of turn.

That visit to the United States marked a watershed in my life. It fueled my ambitions by introducing me to a different league of player and by giving me an insight into what top Americans were thinking. I was eager to make my way up in my job, and I sensed that the contract which had been entrusted to me would be a great boost to my career.

The negotiations with Raytheon over the next three or four months were difficult and complicated. They were punctuated by rows. But we ended up as friends and the contract for the Improved Hawk was signed in Riyadh by Prince Sultan on April 8, 1974. But to get to this point, I had to master a great deal of technical detail – to do with the Hawk system itself and its cost, but also to do with the legal side of the contract, with its numerous clauses and side letters. It took a lot of study, a lot of reading at night, to be able to amend the terms and conditions of just one of the paragraphs. Whereas the company could call on scores of experts, I was virtually on my own. I needed to get advice.

For advanced know-how on the Hawk, I began by hiring four former U.S. government officials – a warrant officer called Mr. Bourn (who later worked for Raytheon in Saudi Arabia) and three civilians. I was happy to note that they gave me honest advice and did not side with Raytheon.

In addition to Kayyal, I was able at that time to recruit another valued associate, Captain Abdallah Justaniyah, who had spent two and a half years in Boston, from 1968 to 1970, as our first air defense liaison officer with Raytheon, during which time he had graduated as an engineer and acquired a knowledge of electronics. Being technically competent, he was assigned on his return to Central Maintenance and Technical Support in Jeddah, as acting commander. It was then that I met him. In addition to being project officer for the Hawk, I was also working as range commander, arranging for batteries from around the country to practice firing their missiles. It was Justaniyah's responsibility to make sure that the various systems at the Jeddah range were working and that spare parts were available if the units needed them. Inevitably, we saw a good deal of each other whenever I came to Jeddah in the early 1970s, and I came to appreciate his expertise.

He was, therefore, an obvious choice when I came to form a technical committee to advise me on the negotiations for the Improved Hawk. But, to get a thorough grasp of every aspect of the contract, I did not need only technicians. I needed to consult people who understood contracts, people with wide experience of business, finance and international affairs. To help me, Prince Sultan brought in two men from the Ordnance Corps who were university graduates – Colonel Nasser al-'Arfaj, later to be awarded a Ph.D., and his colleague Colonel Ali Khalifa – as well as Colonel Ahmad al-Malik, who had a Ph.D. in finance. (All three have since become generals.) Prince Sultan then added three distinguished civilians – Dr. Ghazi al-Gosaibi, later Saudi

Minister of Industry and, at the time of writing, ambassador to
Britain; Dr. Muhammad al-Milhem, later a government minister
without portfolio; and Dr. Muhammad Omar al-Madani of the
Foreign Ministry (who was to serve on my staff during the Gulf
War) whose expertise in international law was valuable to the
committee. I sometimes used to keep these gentlemen up until
two o'clock in the morning going over our requirements and
preparing our position. This then was the powerful team with
which I confronted the Raytheon negotiators.

In conducting the negotiation, I learned some basic tricks, one
of which being that first impressions are all important: that is
when your strength or weakness is determined. It is vital to
impress the team opposite and seize the initiative. The men
across the table have to be made to understand that you are
someone of stature and that you have a lot behind you. And it
helps, I believe, if you do things in style. At any rate, that is
how I like to do things. On one occasion in early 1974, during a
hiccup in the negotiations, I had to fly to the U.S. to see the
head of Raytheon. Having got as far as New York, I decided to
charter a plane for the onward flight to Boston. I knew I would
be met by the Chairman and wanted to make an impression.
But we did not have much money. One of my friends got up
early and worked the phone for an hour or so with the charter
companies to get us the best deal. He managed to save $1,000.

But penny-pinching was not my style.

"How many crew are there on board?" I asked him as we
approached our destination.

"Just the Captain, the First Officer and the Steward," he
replied.

"Give the Captain and the other two a handsome tip!"

My largesse made nonsense of my friend's hard bargaining
with the charter companies that morning. But we arrived in
style and were given a royal sendoff by the crew, just as we
were being greeted by the top-level Raytheon delegation.

With hindsight, it was not so much the advanced weaponry
we bought from Raytheon which, in the long run, proved important – although it cost us a tidy $264 million. Rather, it was
the extra concessions I was able to wrest from the company
with the contract. For example, in those days the air defense

compound in Jeddah was occupied by Raytheon employees and their families. Saudi officers lived outside and came to work on the base. This I believed was the wrong way around: I could not tolerate a situation in which a Saudi colonel lived in two rented rooms in town while a Raytheon employee lived in the luxury of the compound. Our own people should live on the base together with Raytheon employees. I refused to initial the contract until the company agreed to surrender forty of its villas, of which it had about one hundred, to Saudi officers. Although several of my colleagues at the Ministry of Defense urged me not to make a fuss over what they thought was a secondary matter, to my mind it was a nonnegotiable item. I dug in my heels. It was a hard tussle, but Raytheon agreed in the end. And with the next contract I took more villas. Today, the compound is entirely Saudi, and there are some 800 to 900 houses in it.

Another clause I wrote into the contract, on the suggestion of a member of the committee – and I believe it constituted a landmark – stipulated that any shipment air-freighted to the Kingdom in connection with the contract would have to be carried by our national airline, Saudia – then Saudi Arabian Airlines. I insisted that if our airline could not do the job itself, then it should make the necessary arrangements with another carrier. I went running to the airline to get its backing, and its managers were very appreciative. Raytheon fought this hard, but agreed to it in the end. About two years later, the clause became the subject of a royal decree and it now figures in all the Kingdom's contracts.

The multimillion dollar deal with Raytheon for the Improved Hawk was my first big project. It opened doors for me in defense ministries and defense industries overseas. It taught me to think big and to manage large budgets. Above all, it laid the foundations from which Saudi air defense was to grow.

There was in those days a small Projects Office at the Air Defense Command to which the various project officers reported – myself included. But my handling of the Improved Hawk contract, which was generally considered successful, gave me a certain standing. It enabled me to persuade the Air Defense Commander, then Colonel Muhammad al-Hammad (the present Chief of Staff), to allow me to take over as director of the

Projects Office. I proposed renaming it the Air Defense Projects and Planning Office, expanding its functions – and using it as my base. The main lesson I had learned from the Raytheon deal was that in a high-technology force like ours, heavily dependent on foreign manufacturers and foreign instructors, contracts were the crucial instrument of control. Through the contracts one could control the companies and then the system as a whole. This was a scheme I had nursed and matured at late-night sessions with several of my colleagues over many months. We used to borrow Glen Grubbs's meeting room and, sitting down together after working hours, strive to clarify our plans and goals.

Accordingly, in June 1974, the new office was set up in Jeddah, within easy reach of Raytheon, and I, newly promoted to major, was named its head with Kayyal as my assistant. I pressed Glen Grubbs to relinquish a room for us in one of the company villas and established my office there. Eventually a second office was acquired to which Kayyal moved, and a translator and a typist were hired.

For the Projects and Planning Office to be effective and to exercise some control over the company, Kayyal and I had to become efficient ourselves. It took a lot of work. The company employed large staffs, so keeping up with it was not easy.

Quite soon I realized that, to exercise real authority, our main office had to be at the Air Defense Command in Riyadh close to the Defense Ministry rather than at Jeddah close to the company. I therefore needed to expand my staff, and looked around for suitable recruits among air defense officers. I had my eye on Abdallah Justaniyah, the technically competent CMTS Commander who had been helpful to me during the Improved Hawk negotiations. I remember calling in at the Air Defense School one day for a chat with Colonel Hussein Saber, the Commandant, a quiet man of far-sighted intelligence and fine administrative abilities. Justaniyah and some of our colleagues were there with us in the small meeting room.

"I'm looking for an officer to serve in my new Projects and Planning Office," I told Colonel Saber. In those days, I always carried around in my pocket a small notebook in which I wrote down the names of officers in air defense I had met in the course of my work. As I put the question to Colonel Saber, I opened the notebook, leaned across towards him, and pointed to a certain name. "What do you think of this man?" I asked. "You couldn't make a better choice," Colonel Saber replied.

The Colonel and the others then left the room to go about their duties, leaving me alone with Justaniyah. I took off the jacket of my uniform, hung it on the back of a chair, rolled up my sleeves, and said to him, "Let's talk about serious matters." I outlined the functions of the new Office and then told him I had chosen the man I wanted to join me in Riyadh.

"Good luck to you!" he said.

"It's you!" I said. "You're the man. I want you to join us, and I want your answer within three days."

I could see that Justaniyah was not entirely happy. His family and friends were in Jeddah. It was where he had grown up. A posting to Riyadh, in the heart of the country away from the sea, would seem to him like a hardship post.

"What answer do you expect from me?" he asked with a wry smile.

"I want you to say yes."

"Well then, I won't need three days."

So we moved to Riyadh and started organizing our new department. There was just myself, Justaniyah and a civilian employee by the name of Muhammad Aita, who is still in the Projects Office. Kayyal was assigned to run our branch office in Jeddah.

Not everyone in air defense appreciated the powers our office was acquiring. When we first moved to Riyadh, my own office was the size of a broom cupboard, about two yards long and one and a half wide. Next door was a somewhat larger meeting room. My first request to Justaniyah was that he convert the meeting room into my office. At the same time, he established himself in a small storage room next door. I wanted everyone to be aware that the air defense command now had a Projects and Planning Office. Tactfully, we then set about expanding by evicting people from neighboring offices, either by gentle persuasion or by finding them alternative accommodation.

When the basic Hawk contract was awarded to Raytheon back in 1966, the company was also given a contract to maintain all the Kingdom's air defense facilities. Some years later, however, this maintenance contract was taken away from Raytheon and awarded to Dallah, then a newly formed Saudi company owned and managed by Mr. Salih Kamil. This followed the general directive by King Faisal which I have mentioned that, in the case of major projects, the Kingdom should deal with each company direct, rather than allowing foreign companies to subcontract. In addition, he ruled that preference should be given to Saudi companies if they were capable of doing the job. Accordingly, maintenance of the Kingdom's air defense facilities was put out to tender – and Dallah, having submitted the lowest bid, was awarded the contract. Raytheon's maintenance contract had been worth over $30 million: Dallah's bid was a little over $5 million. Moreover, whereas Raytheon's expenditure had been more or less uncontrolled, Dallah's was subject to strict supervision. Perhaps because of this lack of flexibility, Dallah's first year in the job was not successful and some people started to say that Raytheon should be brought back. In due course I managed to convince the government to give Dallah a fairer deal – greater flexibility and a better contract, although one still worth less than half that of Raytheon's. Thus was launched a career which was to make Salih Kamil one of the biggest contractors in the Kingdom, if not in the Arab world. Dallah's first customer was air defense, a fact which, to my satisfaction, Mr. Kamil is always ready to admit.

So when the Projects and Planning Office was set up, we found we had two companies to deal with – Raytheon and Dallah. But we were soon busy day and night, racing back and forth between Riyadh and Jeddah. The very creation of the new Office started to attract offers from a great variety of firms. I was invited by potential suppliers to visit their plants and headquarters in different parts of the world.

Gradually our goals became more precise and more ambitious. We wanted to assume responsibility for building up the air defense forces; proposing new systems for purchase; selecting and surveying new air defense sites; building the facilities; installing the equipment. We wanted to put Saudis in the right places, and make sure that know-how was transferred to them, so that they could eventually take over maintenance of the equipment and teaching at the Air Defense School. We wanted to become the sole channel of communications, the principal point of contact, between the company and the Kingdom. If Raytheon wanted anything from the Saudis it had to come through us and, conversely, any Saudi wanting something from Raytheon had to come through us. This was the chain of command I insisted on, which was no more than normal practice in most countries.

Another instrument of control was the Program Supply Office (PSO) created as part of the Projects and Planning Office. The job of the PSO was to receive all the equipment and materials from the companies against acceptance certificates; store everything; and then issue the stuff to the units and air defense groups around the country. Deliveries were thus centralized, allowing for greater accountability and control.

With these developments, I was slowly able to turn things around in our relations with Raytheon. It was now a matter of course that company representatives would come to us rather than our going to them. "I am the customer and their job is to serve us," I used to tell my colleagues. "They are giving us a service and we are paying them well for it. We are not asking for loans or favors. This is our country and they should come to us." Raytheon was not overpleased at having to deal with someone like me. But I was not competing in a beauty contest. I did not particularly care if I was liked. I wanted Raytheon to respect us and, in the end, that is what I got. Many people urged me to be more cautious and diplomatic and I did try to soften the impact of what I was doing by going about it gradually. As I have said, I could not afford to mount a direct challenge. It had to be done little by little.

My approach was to gain knowledge, to understand the business thoroughly, before seeking to impose leadership. My view was that the company was there to provide us not so much with hardware as with knowledge. We had to gain as much of that knowledge as we could, but without compromising our air defense capability which was still in its infancy. In the 1970s, we ourselves were in the first stages of growth and technological development. Whatever pride demanded, there was no point in trying to run before we could walk.

About a year after the Projects and Planning Office was set up, the time came to negotiate an even bigger contract with Raytheon, the so-called Triad contract worth a little over $1 billion. As its name suggests, the Triad added a third fire unit to each Hawk battery, allowing for a wider spread or a different configuration. My aim throughout was to seek more and more modern weaponry, greater and greater sophistication, and at the same time provide for a tremendous amount of training to ensure that our people could use these weapons and become autonomous and self-sufficient.

I will not weary the reader with the technical details. Suffice it to say that negotiations for the Triad started in late 1974 and, after a year and a half of hard work, the contract was signed in early 1976. By this time, the Ministry of Defense had established a foreign contracts department staffed with legal and other experts to formulate terms and conditions of defense contracts so as to safeguard the Kingdom's interests.

I put a great deal of time and effort into this contract. As my colleague Abdallah Justaniyah will remember, we would sometimes start a work session in the meeting room at 10 a.m. to go over our requirements and not leave the office until 10 p.m. Someone would go out and order sandwiches.

When I set up the Projects and Planning Office, Glen Grubbs was still the Raytheon chief representative in Saudi Arabia, and we worked closely and amicably together. I remember that on one occasion I asked him to continue fulfilling a contract for six months without the Saudi government yet signing it – and Raytheon agreed, just trusting my word. But, with the large and complicated Triad contract, Saudi Arabia had become Raytheon's biggest foreign customer. Accordingly, Glen Grubbs was promoted and recalled to Andover to run a newly established Saudi program office, in effect to become the manager at Raytheon of all the Saudi projects.

In the meantime, however, and overshadowing the Triad negotiations, was the undeniable fact that the Improved Hawk program had run into trouble. To put it in layman's terms, Raytheon engineers were having trouble converting the equipment from a basic Hawk configuration to an Improved Hawk configuration, which involved tearing the system down and putting new electronic guts into it. To my growing alarm, I found that the conversion from basic Hawk to Improved Hawk was falling behind schedule, and that while it was in progress we had virtually lost our regional air defense capability. One system had been taken out and the new system was not in place. Raytheon urgently needed a high-level troubleshooter in Saudi Arabia to sort things out if disaster were to be avoided.

Jim Lewis – a man I had come to admire – was then in Tehran, running Raytheon's Iranian program. On my prompting, Phil Phallon, a senior Raytheon executive, called him from the States and asked him if he would like to transfer to Saudi Arabia and take the problem in hand. He jumped at it, and within days he had arrived as operations manager. This was in August 1977.

On arrival, Jim Lewis stopped everything and started to put together a new schedule of work with a whole new manufacturing and engineering team he brought out from the States. To my growing impatience, he spent weeks preparing the new schedule. He came to me with a schedule, but I really did not like it. I said it had to be done quicker.

"Look, Prince Khaled," he said. "I am not going to give you a schedule which I won't be able to keep."

Finally, he came to my Projects Office with a schedule which he had already signed and dated.

"Can't you do better than this?" I asked.

"No, I can't!"

"You have to. You have got to get the equipment out to the sites."

"I'm not going to tell you something I can't do," he protested. "I know what can be done. I have the people here. We know what material we need. I can't do any better."

"You really mean that?" I pressed him.

"I mean it from my heart. I can't do better."

I took out my pen and signed the schedule. It was a year and a half of work, but in the end he beat it by six weeks. The conversion to the Improved Hawk was successfully accomplished, at considerable cost to Raytheon. By the time the Shah was overthrown in 1979, and the Gulf region was plunged into apprehension and turmoil, our systems were fully operational. And when the Iraq–Iran war broke out the following year, our troops and our equipment were ready if we needed them. All the effort and urgency and training we had put into the programs over the years were now justified.

Jim Lewis, a great expatriate, won my trust. Together we negotiated contract after contract and solved problem after problem. Inevitably we had rows over costs – there were times when he felt we owed them money and times when I felt he owed us services. But there was no difficulty which he and I did not enjoy solving together.

By the mid-1970s, the government was putting all the air defense contracts through my Projects and Planning Office. I was managing all the air defense projects – all the way from guns to catering. I had to choose officers to assist me and train them in negotiation and in other arts. Thousands of young men were being put through our Air Defense School. In 1976, I was able to arrange for Abdallah Justaniyah to go to Arizona to get his master's degree and then his Ph.D. in industrial technology management – planning, technology transfer, that sort of thing – skills which our air defense needed. He was away for six years and was replaced by Lieutenant Colonel Ahmad Lafi, an able air defense officer who had attended an Improved Hawk course in the United States in 1975.

Above all, Saudi Arabia's relationship with Raytheon – which had so far been the backbone of my career – turned out to be a considerable success. I believe it was to the benefit of both parties that I had made Raytheon understand that it was not dealing with a banana republic, but with a new Saudi Arabia, a very different place from what it had been at the start of the relationship in the 1960s. Now it was a rapidly modernizing country, stuffed with Ph.D.s, with computers, with good records, with powerful negotiators, with a highly professional, well-organized Ministry of Defense where Prince Sultan had established proper systems of control. In other words we were now a self-respecting country well able to monitor the performance of the company which, more than any other over the years, had helped us build and equip our air defense forces.

CHAPTER VIII

Command, Control and Communications

O N MARCH 25, 1975, the day King Faisal died, I had been out at the range, some 50 miles from Jeddah, attending a practice firing of the Hawk. On hearing the news, I went immediately to the airport and flew to Riyadh. It was only on the plane that I learned that the King had not died of natural causes but had been killed – and, to my horror, shot by my cousin, Prince Faisal bin Musa'id, whom I remembered from school as a quiet and polite boy. How could he have done such a terrible thing?

Rumors of all sorts flew about. Some people, recalling that he had been a student in Beirut and then at the University of Colorado, went so far as to say that he had been brainwashed and programed by the CIA to kill the King because powerful men in the United States detested King Faisal's nationalist policies in support of Egypt and Syria during the October War, and of the Palestinians under Israeli occupation, and were outraged by the oil embargo he imposed on the West. But I could not believe such a conspiracy theory. It seemed more likely that the young assassin, who had forced his way into the King's office when the Kuwaiti Minister of Oil was being presented at court, was motivated by revenge. His brother, Khaled, had died some years earlier in a shootout with the police. Khaled had been a religious fanatic. He and a group of fellow zealots had attacked the Riyadh television transmitter, which they considered an infringement of God's Law. They had then barricaded themselves in a house and opened fire on police who came to arrest them. As the police had orders not to return the fire, the shot which killed Khaled may well have been fired by one of his own group. In any event, Faisal bin Musa'id was later tried and executed for the premeditated murder of the King.

As may easily be imagined, King Faisal's death at the hands of a member of the royal family was an unmitigated catastrophe which plunged the whole family into deep shock. I remember it vividly and with a sense of humiliation because when he was buried 24 hours later, in the presence of numerous heads of state, Anwar al-Sadat among them, I was overcome with grief and had to be reprimanded by my father who told me to take hold of myself. To many of us younger princes at that time, King Faisal had been a revered figure of immense authority, the unquestioned leader who had restored international respect for the family and the nation. His loss was very deeply felt.

A man to whom we owed a great debt at that critical time was my uncle Prince Muhammad. As the eldest surviving son of Ibn Saud, he could have claimed the throne for himself had he wished to do so. But Prince Muhammad was a man without pretension. He had no ambition to be a ruler and shunned the responsibility of kingship. So he voluntarily renounced the throne in favor of his younger brother, Prince Khaled and, by so doing, established the important precedent that the choice of king need not necessarily go to the oldest candidate, but rather to the most capable.

As our tradition demands, the family met within an hour or two of King Faisal's death to swear loyalty to King Khaled, who in turn had to pledge to uphold the teachings of the Glorious Quran and follow the path of the Prophet Muhammad and his companions. I was standing in a great line waiting to pronounce the oath and witnessed what happened. Prince Muhammad stepped forward, grabbed hold of the first man in the line and said, "I want you also to pledge your loyalty to Prince Fahd, the Crown Prince!"

Prince Fahd was then the second Deputy Prime Minister and was, in any event, likely to become Crown Prince, but in the emotional circumstances following the death of King Faisal he preferred to delay his formal appointment. He protested that this was not the time for it. But Prince Muhammad insisted. "Yes," he said, "this is the time!" In naming Prince Fahd Crown

Prince, Prince Muhammad passed over three other brothers, Prince Nasir, Prince Sa'd and Prince Musa'id, all three older than Prince Fahd but younger than King Khaled. As the oldest of them all, Prince Muhammad was able to impose his view of the succession, thereby preempting any possible future disagreement and establishing yet another precedent. By announcing it in the way he did, he made it official and from that moment *mubaya'a*, the pledge of loyalty, was made to both King Khaled and Crown Prince Fahd together. In my view, the action Prince Muhammad took at that time to ensure a smooth transfer of power was of the greatest value and deserves to be recognized.

The 1970s were a decade of great excitement in Saudi Arabia, but also of grave anxiety. Excitement because the oil price explosions of 1973 and 1979 made us very rich. Within living memory – indeed in the 1950s when I was growing up – we had been poor: suddenly we could afford just about everything the world could offer. Our dreams of becoming a developed country could now be realized. In a very short time, we acquired modern roads and modern phones; airports in every corner of our continent-sized country; the latest planes and the fastest cars; world-class hospitals, hotels and universities; elegant public buildings designed by the world's best architects; industrial plants of all sorts around our new state-of-the-art ports of Jubail on the Gulf and Yanbu on the Red Sea, and many other improvements and facilities. Our standard of living which had been austere in the 1940s, modest in the 1950s, and comfortable in the 1960s, now became opulent and luxurious.

We also felt compelled to spend a great deal more on defense because these dramatic changes, which touched every aspect of our lives, took place against a background of considerable uncertainty and insecurity. At home, as I have mentioned, King Faisal's death suddenly robbed us of a strong leader on whom we had relied totally, while in the region, Egypt's drift towards a separate peace with Israel set Arab against Arab and created an atmosphere of tension. Few people in the region at that time appreciated what President Sadat had done but when, 15 years later, the peace process began to move forward again, his vision was proved to have been correct. More than a decade before Sadat's move, President Habib Bourguiba of Tunisia had, in the mid-1960s, called for a peaceful settlement with Israel, urging the Arabs to take what was on offer and then, in due course, ask for more as the Zionists had done before them. But his plea fell on deaf ears, and the bitter Arab–Israeli confrontation, punctuated by full-scale wars, continued remorselessly.

By the late 1970s, tension in the region was greatly heightened by the coming to power in Israel of Menachem Begin's right-wing Likud bloc, aggressive, hard-line champions of a "Greater Israel." We could not be indifferent to the threat of war on our northwestern approaches. Then two years later, in 1979, the overthrow of the Shah and the emergence of the Islamic Republic of Iran were other grave shocks which brought turmoil to the Gulf itself and compounded our fears for the security of the Kingdom. I should stress that we had no fear of Iran as an Islamic country; rather we were concerned by Iran's radical political views and its attempt to export its revolution.

As a military man I took no part in politics. But, as I rose in the Air Defense Command, with widening responsibilities for the procurement of new weapons, I was increasingly preoccupied by the ever-lengthening list of key cities, plants and facilities which had to be defended against potential air attack. Hostile aircraft could enter our airspace at any moment.

The central problem with which I wrestled was how to build a complete air defense system in the total area of the Kingdom. The job never seemed to finish. New units were constantly required because there were always new areas to defend. It was a question of establishing priorities, but the priorities themselves kept changing. Potential targets in Saudi Arabia included the capital and other major cities, the oil installations, the refineries, the desalination plants, the headquarters of the armed services, the air bases, the ports, the new industries on the east and west coasts . . . I had to pick the assets and then determine which of them were the most vulnerable. The job was one of planning, of coordination, of the management of resources, and above all of training – of different types of training. As we were desperately short of highly trained personnel, I considered training to be all-important, more so even than the expensive equipment we were buying, and this meant a steady expansion of the Air Defense School which Raytheon had built in Jeddah in 1962, and the sending for training abroad of hundreds of young men: our air defense troops, our technicians, our operators, our managers, our engineers, our researchers. There was no end to it. And, as we were all too aware, electronic warfare was changing by the day, as anyone can see for himself in the field of consumer electronics.

Being a vast country, Saudi Arabia needed a variety of overlapping air defense systems – long range, medium range, short range, local defense. But air defense is never foolproof: there are never enough systems to provide 100 percent security. Drug smugglers flying small aircraft still manage to cross the Mexican–U.S. border undetected, and not so many years ago a young German flew a small plane to the heart of Moscow and landed in Red Square, making a monkey of Soviet air defenses and forcing the resignation of the commander.

Before I came on the scene, we had antiaircraft guns like the manually operated Spanish 40mm Bofors guns, one of the first artillery systems we acquired in air defense, and still working. To these we later added excellent, state-of-the-art artillery, the low-altitude Oerlikon 35mm antiaircraft guns, under a contract originally negotiated by Salih al-Muhaya, but which I took over and renegotiated in a bid to standardize all our air defense contracts. A shell fired from a gun is faster than a missile but it does not have the same range. Whereas the maximum range of some guns is about seven miles, a missile can be effective at five times that distance. But, if the enemy has crossed your border and is already overflying your vital assets, guns have their uses. If he has jammed your missile systems by electronic warfare – as Iraq's missiles were crippled in the Gulf War – guns can sometimes save your neck. To fire a gun you do not always use radar, you use your eyes, as the Iraqis demonstrated when their guns, some of them sited on top of tall buildings, brought down several Coalition planes. In fact most Coalition aircraft losses were to guns.

In the 1970s we moved, as I have related, from the basic Hawk – a medium-range weapon – to the Improved Hawk and then, in the 1980s, as we needed still more Hawk systems because there were more to defend, to the six Triad batteries, each with three fire units, making a total of 18 fire units. And as we deployed these batteries, so they required constant, annual service practice and training. I insisted that the batteries come in from the sites and fire at the range; I was the first to institute night firing of missiles on the move, thus enhancing competition between the units to improve standards.

Weapons to be purchased were always tested in August, at the height of summer, to make sure that they would work in our desert heat. And with every new project, I instituted a six-month review covering every aspect – construction, technical operability, finance, training. These reviews, held alternately in the Kingdom and at the suppliers, were useful for resolving some 90 percent of the problems we encountered. It was the occasion for top people – on our side and on the company side – to resolve problems of delays, spare parts and training.

The painful transition from the basic Hawk to the Improved Hawk taught me that some programs could take years to implement. As head of the Projects and Planning Office, I chose the programs and worked hard to convince the various committees, the technical advisers and the higher echelons of the armed services to approve my plans. I wanted to create an effective air defense network and integrate it with the systems of the air force. It was a goal to which I gave my total commitment over many years.

Before entering a negotiation with a foreign supplier, I would make studies, seek the best possible advice, analyze. I did my best to select good people, to put the right man in the job. I wanted the best officers in air defense, chosen solely on the basis of merit and experience. I know that I was a very demanding boss, a hard taskmaster, and this meant setting an example myself. There were always boxes of paper to work on at home. I developed a back problem, and spent months working standing up. But I noticed that some of the people who worked most closely with me also seemed to be afflicted with certain types of illness. Abdallah Justaniyah, for instance, developed a perforated ulcer on one occasion and had to go to the hospital in Jeddah. Another close colleague, Colonel Muhammad al-Grafy, who was to be my right-hand man in my negotiations with the French, suffered a heart attack. Such was the pressure of work.

Ours is a vast country, virtually a continent, of over 850,000 square miles – an enormous rectangle about 1,000 miles long and 800 miles wide. Because of our limited manpower, a land-based defense of this huge area made little sense. But there were limitations, too, on the size of our air force. However skillful our pilots – and some were very skilled indeed – I suspected that there would always be a ceiling, imposed by the United States and by Israel's American friends, on the number of combat aircraft we would be allowed to acquire. Our offensive capability would always be circumscribed. In other words, we could not realistically hope to match the air power of our neighbors. As I mentioned in Chapter Seven, I had been deeply impressed by Egypt's use of mobile SAMs against Israel's air force during the crossing of the Suez Canal in 1973, and the way this seemed to change the rules of the battlefield. I concluded that salvation lay in a powerful air defense force which, if strategically deployed, fully integrated and equipped with its own early-warning system, could provide a fair measure of defense.

By 1974, I began to argue that our air defense forces, which were then still part of the land forces, should be constituted as a separate "Fourth Force" – separate, that is, from our land, air and naval forces – and should be given high priority. But I ran into a good deal of opposition. I should mention that the debate about the ultimate command and control of air defense forces is one which has engaged armed services in different parts of the world.

To summarize the issue in broad terms, one might say that there are two main schools of thought. In the West, the predominant view is that, as the interception of hostile aircraft is essentially an air force mission, air defense forces should be under the operational control of the air force. The rival view, developed by the ex-Soviet Union, is that the use of assets and facilities such as early-warning stations, ground radars, and short-range interceptors are all properly part of the mission of air defense forces and should therefore be controlled by a separate air defense headquarters rather than by the air force, still less by land forces. The choice between these two schools largely depends on the resources available, such as the number of warplanes, and on the traditions of the respective forces. Influenced by Russian military thinking, Egypt had opted for the "Eastern" or Soviet school of thought. As I had myself been impressed by Egypt's missile air defenses in 1973, I argued in favor of detaching our air defense forces from the land forces and setting them up as a separate force.

My critics maintained that a force which then consisted of a mere 200 officers and less than 2,000 men could not credibly constitute a separate force. However, the expansion of our air defense assets robbed this argument of some weight. Utterly convinced of the soundness of my views, I continued to agitate for a "Fourth Force," raising the matter at meetings whenever I could. I must have been a great trial to my colleagues.

By 1976, however, I realized I was getting nowhere. Far from promoting my cause, I was mobilizing opinion against it. I changed my tactics. Instead of a frontal attack I decided on an indirect approach. I went about pursuing my goal in gradual stages. Step by step, with the approval of the military high command, I distanced air defense from the land forces, taking over whatever authority and budgetary control I could, in the belief that a point of no return would eventually be reached.

But I soon realized that, for air defense to be credible as a separate force, it had to be internally integrated. Above all, it needed communications between its diverse parts. So far, program by program, I had put together a considerable armory of air defense weapons, and deployed them in a number of air defense groups around the country and at critical sites in such vital areas as our Eastern Province. But the weapons systems could not communicate with each other, nor could the commander in Riyadh get a complete air picture of the country at any one time. What was evidently required was a C3 system – nationwide Command, Control and Communications – linking early-warning radars and the various guns and missiles in our armory to a central control facility.

I convinced the authorities to allow me to start negotiations in 1976 with Litton Industries, a major American corporation, for the construction of such a C3 system. Signed on April 8, 1979, after more than two years of hard work, the contract was worth over $1.6 billion. Vast and technically complex, the project was due to be completed and operational by February 7, 1985 – that is, in 70 months or two months less than six years. On the day the contract was signed, I was jubilant at my achievement. But I would have been less satisfied had I known that it was to take over 14 years to implement, becoming in the process one of the biggest headaches of my military career.

⇜⇝

I negotiated the broad outline of the contract with Litton's Chairman, a remarkable man named Charles Bates Thornton who hailed from Texas and was universally known as "Tex" Thornton. Already fairly advanced in years when I met him, he had had a distinguished career in the American air force during World War Two, and then at the Ford Motor Company, before becoming, as I understand it, the moving genius behind the creation of Litton Industries, a $5-billion-dollar corporation. He was a brilliant manager with a remarkable grasp of figures and, had he lived, I am sure we would have had no problems with Litton. But "Tex" Thornton died of cancer shortly after the contract was signed and was replaced as Chairman by Fred O'Green, a warm, earthy farm boy from Iowa with whom I also got on famously – at the start at least.

I feel compelled to give some account, however brief and schematic, of our dealings with Litton if only because they overshadowed my last years at air defense before the Gulf crisis and indirectly affected our attitude towards foreign defense contractors in general.

For nontechnical readers, I should explain in simple terms what Litton's C3 system promised to do. It was designed to tie all the air defense elements around the Kingdom to a central control facility. Essentially it was a nationwide communications network, connected both to long-range radars able to provide an air picture of the Kingdom, and to missile minders, known as TSQ73s, which had the ability to analyze the air picture, identify an incoming threat and automatically instruct the best positioned weapon to intercept it. In other words, by means of its electronic, fully automated technology, the system could detect targets in real time, track them, and then order the firing batteries to engage. The communications network – known in engineering jargon as a tropo-scatter system – was centered on Riyadh but extended all over the Kingdom, from Tabuk in the northwest, to the southern border with Yemen, to Dhahran in the east and Jeddah in the west. The system as a whole was intended to give the Air Defense Commander an overview of his entire air space and control of all his weapons systems.

The lawyers and technical committees negotiated the nuts and bolts of the contract, but I was the prime mover in determining the content of the program and assumed responsibility for it: under my direction, a committee of senior air defense officers drawn from all departments identified our communications requirements, decided the number of TSQ73s we wanted, and outlined the training schedule our people would need.

Quite apart from the complex electronics, the system required a great deal of construction – to house the missile minders, the radars and the communications, all within reasonable distance of the Hawk batteries and other weapons. I had originally hoped that local contractors could do the building work but, because of the sophisticated technical aspects of the project, local firms could not handle it, and the construction was eventually subcontracted by Litton to the Frankfurt firm of Philip Holzman, which was to delay the program by some eighteen months.

It was indeed soon evident that the original 70-month contract schedule was too optimistic, and was not likely to be met. For one thing, Litton had run into technical difficulties with the long-range radars on the east and west coasts, apparently due to the very humid air, the huge temperature differences and other peculiar meteorological conditions. The engineers puzzled over what they called "anomalous propagation" which meant that you might turn on a radar set on the shore of the Arabian peninsula and see all the way across to India. The resulting radar picture was cluttered and very difficult to interpret. This happened in both Dhahran and Jeddah and required major modifications to the radar system. Eventually radars were installed to cover the Kingdom, with repeater sites to link up the radars to the big screen in the operations room at headquarters in Riyadh.

A second serious problem was that Litton failed to order

adequate supplies of spare parts. In my view this was to be a major cause of the delays. At one point there was close to a $100 million shortfall of parts, a situation which took years to put right: and the shortage became acute just when the radar problems became apparent at Dhahran and when the rest of the equipment started to arrive for installation in the buildings constructed by Holzman.

I appreciated that Litton faced nagging technical problems, but I was growing increasingly concerned about its overall performance. This inevitably impaired my once cordial and trusting relations with Fred O'Green. After a wearisome series of meetings and an increasingly frosty exchange of letters, schedules were made and remade and amendments negotiated to the original contract. Later, I made the strong suggestion that Litton's chief representative in Saudi Arabia, Robert Seitz, be withdrawn. He had in fact lost my confidence. Seitz was replaced by Glen Grubbs, a good manager with a sound grasp of technical matters who had by this time left Raytheon to become an executive vice president, and then a consultant, with Whitaker, a company that used to manage hospitals in the Kingdom.

But I would not wish to leave the reader with the impression that Litton could do nothing right. The crown jewel of the company's efforts was an extensive training course in California taken by hundreds of young Saudis. In general it was a very successful project. To protect my cadets from the temptations of Los Angeles, Litton bought a small motel to house them a good long way out of the city. Inevitably, there were one or two regrettable escapades by the teenage students. On one occasion, two of them ran away to Mexico and had to be brought back under duress. But quite apart from the training in command and control systems which Litton organized, the equipment the company was supplying was on the whole very good indeed, and Holzman's buildings which housed it were excellent.

However, the management problem was aggravated with the arrival on the scene of Dr. Orion Hoch, a cold, strong-minded man of German extraction with a doctorate in physics, who took over as Chairman in 1987 following Fred O'Green's retirement. I remember he came to see me in Birmingham, Alabama, where

I had gone to accompany my father who was having an operation.

"Prince Khaled," Dr. Hoch said, "I want to turn a new page. Let us put our problems behind us." I was delighted. We had a good discussion and I said I would help Litton in every way I could. However, the problems would not go away. I noticed in particular that Dr. Hoch's apparent stragegy to resolve the problems was to maintain tight control of the program from the United States by himself and his staff. But a program of Litton's size could not easily be managed from 10,000 miles away.

When the equipment was in place, Litton offered us the whole system for acceptance. But there was no way I and my colleagues in the Air Defense Command could possibly accept the package before a complete systems integration test had proved that it was 100 percent operational. Experience had taught me that only an extensive, in-depth test of the entire system would reveal the true condition of what we had bought.

After a good deal of argument, a further amendment to the contract was signed in August 1988 which extended the completion date to January 31, 1989, and provided for Litton to perform a Kingdom-wide "System Integration Acceptance Test." We brought in outside consultants to oversee the test, notably Brigadier General Joseph Fimiani, U.S. Army retired, a former Director of Air Defense at the Pentagon. (He was also known in some circles as the "godfather" of the Patriot as he had been program manager of the Patriot in its earliest days when it was called the SAM-D.)

The test required, as I had anticipated, a very considerable effort by the company and also by our Air Defense Command. Representatives of both sides were present at all the sites. We engaged the Royal Saudi Air Force to fly fake raids, and planned raids, and surprise raids against the system to see if it worked. There was a lot at stake.

The scoring procedure for the test was complex, but by December 1988 the test was completed. Litton thought it had passed. We agreed that the hardware had performed better than anticipated, but we and our consultants detected a number of operational discrepancies, largely to do with the driving software package. I very much wanted the system to work: we needed it for our defense in a highly unstable region. I also wanted my original decision to buy the C3 system to be vindicated. But I took the view that having waited so long for the system to work, we could afford to wait a little longer. I could not afford to give my acceptance to anything less than a system in perfect working order. I decided that until each one of the discrepancies had been rectified, we would not consider the contract completed.

Dr. Hoch was not pleased, to say the least, and it took several more months of sometimes acrimonious negotiation for the company to agree to complete the contract to our satisfaction. Glen Grubbs, the new Litton representative in the Kingdom, proceeded to compile a volume of every missing part and every discrepancy. But the situation was not fully rectified until Litton, in 1991, appointed Alton J. Brann, a dynamic young man in his mid-forties, as its President and Chief Operating Officer. But by this time the Gulf crisis had intervened and I had assumed my duties as Joint Forces Commander. Command of the Air Defense Forces passed to my deputy, Major General Majid al-Otaibi.

However, to complete the story, it must be said that Al Brann was like a breath of fresh air. He immediately set about changing the company's philosophy. He evaluated the program and concluded that Litton must assume responsibility for completing it at its own expense. Today, at the time of writing, the whole system is 100 percent operational.

I have been accused of picking on Litton, but I think I was well justified in demanding that Saudi Arabia get reasonable performance for the very large sums we had paid out. And, having spent years to arrive at a balanced relationship with Raytheon, I was not going to allow Litton, or any other company, to push us around. We were a sovereign state and could not be browbeaten by a corporation, however influential it might be and however much we needed its products.

But we, too, must take our share of blame. Very probably we gave Litton too much freedom. It is not a mistake we are likely to make again. After the difficulties with Litton we have been a good deal more careful in our negotiations with foreign companies. For our own protection, we have put into our contracts a great many terms and conditions. But it is, after all, by ironing out problems that one ends up with a deal that everyone recognizes as sound and fair.

I learned many things and broadened my experience immeasurably as a result of the Litton program. I hope that Litton also learned a few things about Saudi Arabia.

CHAPTER IX

Creating a Fourth Force

A S MY WORK GREW MORE DIFFICULT, and as the systems we were buying became more sophisticated, I was forced to recognize that I too needed some upgrading. In my first decade after leaving Sandhurst, I had had a good deal of what might be termed on-the-job training: as a battery commander at Tabuk, as project officer for the Hawk, but especially as Director of the Air Defense Projects and Planning Office which I had created. Negotiating and managing multimillion-dollar contracts had in itself been a great education. But, by the late 1970s, I sensed that I needed some more theoretical military training. In air defense, one tends to spend one's time looking up at the sky, to the neglect of the tactics of other players on the potential battlefield, notably land and naval forces. I wanted to widen my horizons.

As a young lieutenant colonel, still a shade under thirty, I set my heart on attending the U.S. Army Command and General Staff College at Fort Leavenworth, Kansas, and was delighted when the relevant authorities in both Saudi Arabia and the U.S. agreed. I enrolled for the one-year course, starting on August 1, 1978, and running through June 1979.

But feeling a little underprepared for it, I decided to pay a brief visit to Egypt in the early summer of 1978 to bring myself up to speed. Egypt was, and remains, the best place in the Arab world for strategic thinking and for books in Arabic on military subjects. I spent some fruitful days browsing in bookshops in Cairo and catching up on some reading (and enjoying some stirring games of backgammon in the evenings with my Egyptian friends).

In 1978, relations between Egypt and the rest of the Arab world were strained because of President Sadat's controversial visit to Israel the previous November but, in spite of the ups and downs of Saudi–Egyptian relations, I personally have always been a great believer in close ties with Egypt. I consider that country – with its wealth of manpower, skilled technicians, and well-established military traditions – to be our natural ally in the region. A few years earlier, in January 1974, fired by my study of the October War, I conceived the ambition to visit the Bar Lev line, Israel's once formidable defense line along the Suez Canal. I am not alone in considering Egypt's storming of the Bar Lev line in 1973 one of the peaks of Arab military endeavor in our time. So I went to Egypt to learn more about it.

During that visit, at 8 o'clock one morning in Cairo, our defense liaison officer arranged for me to pay a courtesy call on Egypt's Air Force Commander with whom I spent an agreeable half hour. His name was Major General Husni Mubarak (later Vice President and then President of Egypt since October 1981, following President Anwar al-Sadat's assassination). Later that day, a high-ranking Egyptian officer, Major General Ahmad Badawi, commander of the Third Army, kindly accompanied me on a visit to what was left of Israel's fortifications on the Suez Canal, and briefed me on the meticulous preparations and immense effort which resulted in the successful crossing of the Canal. I reached the conclusion that there was no such thing as an impregnable defense line. Any fortification, however formidable, could be stormed and breached, given the will and the right approach. Afterwards, I lunched with Egyptian troops. It was my first encounter with Egypt's armed forces. Regrettably, my escort Major General Badawi, who was to become Egypt's Defense Minister in May 1980, died in a helicopter crash in March 1981.

To gain an insight into the armed services of another country – to understand the values, procedures and arcane language of its soldiers – there is probably no better way than to attend one of its military schools. Just as Sandhurst initiated me into the special ethos of the British army, so Fort Leavenworth taught me a great deal about the U.S. armed services. I had of course met a good many U.S. officers in the course of my career and

had even briefly been a member of a U.S. team during my early
training on the Hawk at the U.S. Army Air Defense School at
Fort Bliss, Texas, but I had never before been so deeply immersed
in an American military environment.

In the course I attended there were some 900 American
officers, aged between thirty and forty-five, of the rank of major
and above, and all potential high-flyers. There were also 96
officers from allied or friendly countries, including about 20
Arabs from places as diverse as Sudan, Lebanon, Jordan, Kuwait,
the United Arab Emirates, Egypt, Morocco, Tunisia and, in my
case, Saudi Arabia. I think I was one of the youngest, and by
no means the best qualified. Most of the non-American officers
at Fort Leavenworth had already attended a staff college in their
own countries. Some had even been instructors but had chosen
to become students again. I had done no preparatory work at
all. Apart from my brief visit to Egypt, I had come straight from
my project office in Riyadh. I realized at once that I would have
to work very hard to make the grade. I knew I could not hope
to be first, but I did not want to be last either.

One of the reasons I found Fort Leavenworth difficult was
because, in addition to my studies, I had unfinished business
with Litton to attend to. What with meetings, telephone calls
and paperwork, it took a couple of hours each day. The technical committees in Riyadh had finished their work, but some
of the terms and conditions remained to be settled, as well
as some important financial details. As I had ultimate responsibility for the contract, I had to provide the liaison between
the experts on the one hand and Prince Sultan on the other.
King Khaled, attended by Prince Sultan, was then receiving
medical treatment at Cleveland, Ohio. On Saturdays, I used
to fly there for the day to brief them on progress. Eventually
they went home and, as I have already related, the agreement with Litton was signed a few months later, in the spring
of 1979.

The course, for which I was awarded a master's degree in
military science, rounded me out as a soldier, opening my mind
to tactics and strategy, to problems of management – which took
up some 25 percent of our time – to the political background
of military decisions and to the overwhelming importance of

studying history if the present is to make any sense. It also taught me a great deal about how the U.S. military see the world. Inevitably, the threat posed by the Soviet Union, then still the main adversary, was very much the focus of our attention. As far as we were concerned, the Cold War was still raging.

One way and another, it was a tough year, but one which I found extremely worthwhile. I made many friends and, by my bearing and seriousness, attempted to project a good image of the Arabs which, I must confess, was something of an uphill task. If my spell as a field officer at Tabuk was one of the determining experiences of my life, my year's hard work at Fort Leavenworth was certainly another.

One of the course programs, called "Know Your World," required each of the foreign officers to make a presentation about his country. When my turn came, I managed with the help of good visual aids to attract a large audience, many people driving in from Kansas City itself. I suspect that, for some at least, part of the attraction was not so much to learn about Saudi Arabia than the chance to see a live prince in action! The lecture was such a success that I was asked to repeat it in a larger auditorium.

A day before the repeat performance, Major General Arter, the commandant, summoned me to his office and with a solemn face told me that he had received a report that I might be the target of an attack during my lecture. He gave no clue as to the source of this intelligence or who the enemy might be. However, he told me he had arranged for Secret Service protection in the shape of two agents who, from behind a curtain, would keep the audience under observation as I spoke. He instructed me not to sit by myself before or after the presentation and to keep moving during it so as not to present a stationary target!

For the first time in my life I felt really important.

However, these were not ideal conditions in which to address a public audience, and I tried to keep as calm as possible. The lecture passed without incident, although under the stress of the occasion I forgot my instructions to keep moving and stood still when I was not meant to.

At Fort Leavenworth there was a church and a synagogue, but no mosque – in other words no special place of worship for the Muslims, of which there were thirty or forty, if the families of the officers were included. I raised the matter with the commandant of the college. I said I was prepared to organize it, even to build a mosque on the base at my expense. Freedom of worship was enshrined in the American Constitution, so there could be no possible objection. He promised to seek higher authority but, shortly before I completed the course, he acknowledged that he had failed to secure it. He suggested assigning a prayer room for our use inside the college, but we dispersed before we were actually able to pray together as a group. I have not given up hope that one day the authorities at Fort Leavenworth will invite me to build a mosque there!

Fort Leavenworth aroused my taste for study. I knew that if I returned to the project office in Riyadh I would soon be sucked in again and would not be able to emerge for several years. So, on a brief visit to the Kingdom during the summer holidays, I called on the Chief of Staff and requested him to allow me to attend the Air War College at Maxwell AFB, Alabama. I knew that if I were to advance in air defense, I needed to learn more about the tactical and strategic problems of other services, and especially of the air force. Luckily for me, I was one of only two officers that year in Saudi air defense to have attained the required educational level. Both our applications to Maxwell were approved. It was as if God were guiding my career to prepare me for what was to come.

The course at Maxwell lasted ten months and focused on global strategic issues as well as on problems of management and economics which, as it turned out, was what I most needed during the Gulf crisis. War games loomed large in our curriculum, clarifying for me some of the difficulties of reconciling air force missions with those of surface-to-air missile forces on the ground. Had I had some inkling of the challenge to come, I would have worked still harder and not have dozed off during some of the lectures.

In my first week there, I learned that some officers in my course were also preparing to follow a parallel course for a master's degree in political science which Auburn University at Montgomery provided in the evenings in an annex of the Air War College. I considered doing the same. My instructor warned me that "even American officers" found it difficult to do both courses at once, but that was a challenge I could not resist. On the contrary, it fired my determination to enroll. At least, I thought I would give it a try for two or three weeks, but would give it up if my military studies suffered. I took a small exam in American Government and was not encouraged by my score – a dismal C minus, awarded to me by Dr. Anne Permaloff, a demanding woman professor. I was not used to writing, as at air defense I had got used to dictating letters, reports and memoranda. By coincidence I made the acquaintance of a retired college professor who had been a colonel in military intelligence and I hired him to give me extra coaching. But despite his help, I came very close to giving up.

It was then that I got a call from a friend in Saudi Arabia.

"I hear you've enrolled for a master's!" he cried.

That was it. There was no going back. I was not a good student, but I had to see it through. If I dropped out now, everyone would know about it.

I spent the best part of a year at Maxwell – at the Air War College during the day and at night in the Auburn University annex – and I can say without exaggeration that it was the only year of my student life when I worked a steady fifteen to seventeen hours a day. I was rewarded with both degrees. I was designated a "distinguished graduate" of the 1980 class at the War College, an honor reserved for the top 24 percent of the class, and received the degree of Master of Political Science from Auburn.

Then, such is the excitement of acquiring knowledge, I could not resist the chance to go on to California in the fall of 1980 for a three-month course in international defense management at the Naval Postgraduate School at Monterey. This dealt with the choice of defense priorities, with the allocation of scarce resources, with the need to draw up a balance sheet of resources and needs, with military budgeting – all of which concepts and disciplines I was to find extremely useful. Yet, at all these courses, I found I learned as much from my fellow officers as from the instructors. Each officer had a special area of expertise which he would be encouraged to outline at seminars, and I too gave a number of lectures on Middle East security questions.

Throughout my two and a half years of study in the United
States, 1978 to 1981, I kept in the closest touch with my comrades in Saudi air defense, telephoning them several times a
week for news. To take over my job as Director of the Projects
and Planning Office in my absence, I had chosen Colonel Salih
al-Hajjaj, a man of strong personality and managerial gifts. Each
vacation I went back to see for myself what progress was being
achieved on the ground. By January 1982, I was back at my desk
in Riyadh to monitor the uneven course of the Litton contract, to
fill gaps which had opened up in our air defenses, and to take
up once more the battle for the "Fourth Force" on which I had
set my heart.

＊≫≪＊

The Raytheon Hawk (whether basic, or Improved, or in its Triad
configuration) had for many years absorbed my attention as an
air defense officer. We first acquired it, as I explained, in the
1960s during the Yemen civil war. As a medium-range missile,
with a reach of some thirty miles, it helped defend our border
cities.

Another war twenty years later – the Iraq–Iran war of the
1980s – spurred us into taking another step forward in air
defense. With the danger that fighting might spread to our Eastern Province, we decided we needed short-range weapons. So
we acquired U.S.-built Stingers, a very short-range weapon –
effective to almost three miles – which had proved itself against
Soviet forces in Afghanistan. It is a "fire-and-forget" weapon
operated by a two-man crew. One carries the weapon and fires
it, the other maintains contact with the operations center to
identify targets and distinguish friend from foe.

But, in addition to the Stinger, we had already in the mid-
1970s decided that we needed a light, mobile, short-range, low-
altitude weapon to support our mechanized units. Our choice
fell on the French-built Crotale. In the total scheme of surface-
to-air missiles, the medium-range Hawk, and the long-range
Patriot which we were to acquire during the Gulf crisis, are more
important weapons. By the time you get to use a Stinger or a
Crotale, you are in trouble, because the enemy is already deep

in your territory. But, once the Iraq–Iran war broke out, we were glad of the Crotale to help defend our oil installations and other vital facilities from any overspill from the conflict then raging at the head of the Gulf.

Built by Thomson CSF, with a range of three or four miles, the Crotale can be mounted on the chassis of a wheeled vehicle or on a tracked chassis for greater cross-country mobility. It can also be airlifted into position by C130 or C5 carriers. At our request, the French government had first installed some Crotale fire units in the Eastern Province as an emergency measure. The engineers were French but the crews were Saudi. Impressed by the performance and the all-weather capability of this weapon, the Saudi high command decided that we should have our own Crotale program and I was deputized to do the deal.

I traveled to Paris to meet Alain Gomez, Thomson's very able Chief Executive. I was to get to know him well. A graduate of France's prestigious Ecole Nationale d'Administration and a personal friend of President François Mitterrand, Gomez was that rare species, a socialist entrepreneur. When Thomson CSF, a leading French defense manufacturer, was nationalized, France's socialist government appointed Gomez as its head. I found him a tough but charming negotiator, as indeed were the French as a whole. Once a deal had been struck, they honored their obligations to the letter.

To help me in these negotiations, I chose Major Muhammad al-Grafy of the armored corps, a man of great ability who spoke French and had experience in dealing with the French since he had been involved with the AMX light tanks we had purchased from France a decade earlier. I had him transferred to air defense and assigned him to the Crotale project which he soon mastered, becoming my right-hand man.

It was not an easy negotiation. For one thing, the Americans and the British did not want us to buy French. Instead they tried to persuade us to buy their own short-range weapons. But the American missile, the Chaparral, designed to counter high-speed, low-altitude threats, was being phased out while the British Rapier was no real match for the Crotale. We noticed that, in the Falklands War of 1982, the British themselves used the Crotale rather than the Rapier, which was not a very good advertisement for their own weapon. The Americans went right up to Prince Sultan to try to undercut me, but the truth was that the Crotale was the best short-range weapon available and I wanted it.

I like all-embracing, self-sufficient contracts which have everything in them – equipment, plentiful supplies of spare parts, training, technology transfer, the lot. They take longer to negotiate but, in the end, are less wasteful of time, effort and finance. It took years to get the French, who had their own way of doing things, to agree to sign a standardized contract of which most of the terms and conditions were drawn from our contracts with Raytheon. It was much the same problem I had faced with Oerlikon, the Swiss gun manufacturer, when I renegotiated and rewrote their contract on standard terms, making it easier to manage and supervise.

Eventually, and after a lot of hard work, the deal with Thomson was done, and in due course, the Crotale 2000, the first-generation weapon with which we began, was replaced by the more powerful Crotale 4000, with a short range of six to eight miles, and the numbers were increased.

Throughout these protracted negotiations, I did my utmost to retain the initiative. As I have explained, I believe it is important in a negotiation to do things in style. I did not wish our negotiating team to be overwhelmed by the French. On my visits to Paris, I appreciated being received at a high level. And although our contract was with the French government, I was always able to have direct dealings with the French companies concerned and, as the customer, impose my views.

Then I was asked to head a committee to negotiate a $4 billion contract with the French – the biggest arms deal the French had ever done – for more advanced air defense weapons. Some years earlier, Saudi Arabia had agreed to participate in the development of the Shahine, an improvement on the Crotale. The Shahine is a self-propelled missile system mounted on an AMX 30 armored vehicle, powered by a special turbine engine. Whereas the Crotale has four missiles to each launcher, the Shahine has six, with a range of nine miles. The Shahine scored over its competitors by being an all-weather weapon equipped with night vision, making it a 24-hour efficient system. The French performed well, our relations with them were excellent and the weapons they delivered were first-rate.

In all these contracts, my main target was not just to buy advanced weapons. It was to improve the caliber and qualifications of my officers. Early in 1984, when the negotiations for the supply of an improved Shahine version, known as Shahine 2, had been successfully completed, I declared that I would refuse to recommend the agreement to Prince Sultan unless the French agreed to provide thirty places a year for Saudi cadets at the military academy of Saint Cyr. Such a request was unheard of. Friendly countries had, at most, been allotted one or two places. Special permission had to be sought from the President himself. Finally, in 1984, the French agreed to take 106 Saudi cadets over a five-year period; and in 1988 they agreed to take a further 100 cadets. There was some overlap between these two programs, but they averaged out at between 20 and 25 cadets a year. Over 100 young Saudis have already graduated from Saint Cyr, and they proved their worth as instructors at our Air Defense Institute, as officers commanding Shahine and Crotale fire units, and also as liaison officers with the French contingent during the Gulf War. I predict that one of these French-trained officers will in due course rise to command our air defense forces.

At Saint Cyr, I did not want my people to be fobbed off with a simplified course for "overseas cadets": I wanted them to receive equal treatment with the French. But this meant they had to be ready. It was agreed that they would spend three preparatory years in France, studying French language in the first year and higher mathematics in the next two, before embarking, on a par with their French contemporaries, on the two-year course at Saint Cyr. In selecting candidates for the course, we chose men who had completed high school with grades of 80 percent and above. They then appeared before a selection board, were made to take a written test and pass a medical examination. Those that survived this weeding-out process were then interviewed individually by me, before undergoing a really tough basic training course at the Air Defense Forces Institute. As well as mathematics, map reading, intelligence, small-arms firing and military training generally, the accent there was on physical fitness, cross-country running, swimming and so forth: we reckoned that nothing at Saint Cyr would be physically more demanding. Of the 206 cadets who went to France in the first two programs, only two failed the course.

Even if the young Saudi graduates from Saint Cyr serve only a few years in our armed services, they constitute a human resource of immense value to the country. They will be marked for life by their experience, and future generations will benefit. I was deeply moved when, on being invited to take the salute at Saint Cyr one year, I saw a large number of Saudi officers on parade, impeccably turned out and speaking perfect French.

I faced a good deal of opposition to this program from some of my colleagues. Why send young men abroad, I was asked, when we have our own military schools? But I believe there is nothing more important than to give our young officers international experience, opening their minds to the world and exposing them to the standards, achievements and working methods of other countries. In the United States, officers are regularly sent to attend courses at foreign academies, and I learned with interest that there are one or two places reserved for French officers at Egypt's Command and Staff College. If I had my way, I would send our cadets to West Point and Sandhurst as well as Saint Cyr, as there is no better way to gain an insight into other armies – and other nations.

❖⟫⟪❖

The first real step towards making air defense into a "Fourth Force" took place in 1982, shortly after my return from the United States. It was then agreed that we should have a separate budget – separate, that is, from the land forces of which we were still a part – and be accountable directly to the Chief of Staff.

"Don't call us a force yet," I pleaded. "But give us a two-year trial as a separate body. Give us time to experiment. If it doesn't work, shift us back again to the land forces or the air force with no harm done."

In those two years, 1982 and 1983, I worked very hard to create the instruments we needed: a finance department run by

Ali al-Hidaithi, one of the best men in the Kingdom in this field – he is there still; and a budgetary system so good that others were later to copy it. In fact the Finance Ministry wrote a letter to the other forces recommending them to adopt our system. Al-Hidaithi was, incidentally, the first person to institute payment of the troops by check, rather than cash.

Before the two years were up, Prince Sultan and others saw that air defense was just about the best organized branch of the armed services. I consider Ali al-Hidaithi one of the architects of the "Fourth Force" because finance and budgeting were among our biggest challenges. He created the finance department and picked the team to staff it. I am confident that his talents will carry him to still higher responsibilities.

In addition to my job as Director of the Projects and Planning Office, in early 1983 I was appointed assistant to the Air Defense Commander, Major General Munir al-Otaibi – a man with whom I worked very well – and was thus better able to pursue my campaign for a wholly separate air defense force.

To cut a long story short, in July 1984 I was appointed Deputy Commander of Air Defense and, shortly afterwards, my dream of seeing air defense as an independent Fourth Force was realized by a royal decree. It had taken me a decade of persuasion, lobbying, pressure and hard work to bring it about.

Looking back on that long struggle, I can say that my real dispute was not with the land forces: they did not really care whether air defense was attached to them or not. The real battle was with the air force, with its commander and its senior officers who, true to their belief in the Western school of air defense and supported in this by the American training mission, wanted our air defense assets to be under the command of the air force. Among them was my dear cousin, Prince Fahd bin Abdallah, head of Air Force Operations at the time, for whose intelligence and ideas I have the greatest respect. He engaged me in serious discussions on rival military concepts and doctrines, forcing me to develop and refine my own views, and thereby stimulated me to fight still harder to convince the various committees of the advantage, as I saw it, of a Fourth Force.

My advocacy for the Eastern as opposed to the Western school of air defense caused rumors to circulate that I was anti-

American. This is not true. I am neither pro- nor anti-American, or, for that matter, pro- or anti- any other country. I am pro-Saudi. But I believe that anyone who loves Saudi Arabia must recognize that it is very much in our interest to have extremely close and friendly relations with the United States. The relationship is vital to both of us. But I always add that it is better to have a strong friend than a weak one. I want Saudi Arabia to be a strong friend of the United States, not a friend that can be pushed around.

This attitude has governed my dealings with U.S. companies and the United States government. I should perhaps say a word here about the relative merits of contracting for weapons systems direct with U.S. companies or through the U.S. government – so called Foreign Military Sales (FMS). This is a subject of considerable concern to those responsible for weapons procurement in the Saudi armed services. Throughout my career at air defense, I developed a preference for direct contracting, on the basis that it gave us greater control over the contracts. This was true even when we were dealing with powerful companies like Raytheon and Litton. If things went wrong, you could ask a company to replace its local representative, you could delay payment until you received satisfaction, you could summon the chairman of the company for a project review – procedures which are not usually available in FMS contracting. However, in my experience, the balance of advantage in direct contracting versus FMS contracting depends very much on the type of item to be procured and its life cycle in the U.S. inventory.

With very high-tech items, FMS scores by providing access to the latest U.S. technical data, to U.S. government advice in defining technical requirements and to U.S. program management. However, the disadvantage lies in a loss to us of financial and management control because, in FMS cases, the U.S. government manages the contract and accepts the weapons system on our behalf. In direct contracting with U.S. companies, we ourselves have to define the technical product and assume management and financial responsibilities. However, in such cases we may find access to U.S. support and technical data more difficult to obtain. So, each case has to be examined on its merits and it is not always easy to decide which way to go. But I should add that I have no objection in principle to FMS contracting and, in the procurement of state-of-the-art systems, I fully recognize its advantages.

In the United States, arms procurement is also sometimes subject to domestic politics. In seeking approval for our U.S. arms purchases, I was unhappy about the whole bruising business of running the gauntlet of the American Congress. I did not appreciate paying large sums of money for American weapons, then facing insults from the Congress, and thanking the U.S. for the privilege. Our dignity needed protection from such humiliating procedures. Even worse were accusations in the press and in the Congress, which I read even today, that the American government *gives* us arms. Unlike Israel, Saudi Arabia pays, and pays dearly, for its American equipment and training. As is well known, U.S. hesitations in meeting our defense requirements caused us in 1985 to sign the large Al-Yamama contract with Britain for the Tornado aircraft, in both its air defense and strike versions, and for numerous training aircraft as well.

Air defense weapons were the only ones – with the exception of the Stinger – which went through Congress without insults to the Kingdom. I used to tell the companies and the U.S. government: "Is this sale in your national interest? Is it good for your company profits? Will it help your economy? If the answer is yes, then go and convince the Congress!" My view was that the companies and the U.S. government should do the lobbying, not ourselves. I did not relish spending time and effort in negotiations, only to be turned down by the Congress. "Once you get congressional approval," I used to tell my American interlocutors, "then we can talk terms."

❧⨯❧

On May 28, 1986 – or, according to our calendar, on 14 Ramadan 1406 – I was appointed Commander of the Royal Saudi Air Defense Forces.

I had worked my way to the top in seventeen years. I had attended and graduated from some of the most serious military schools Britain and the United States had to offer. I had taken no free rides. In our arduous dealings with foreign companies

I, and the many air defense officers who had served on various committees, had striven to equip the Kingdom with the best weapons systems possible and to train the men to run them. We had fought to make air defense a separate force. Now, when faced with the challenge of command, I wanted to prove myself worthy of the responsibility given to me. My troops had to know that a prince could also be a truly professional soldier.

As Commander, I reorganized the officer corps, recommended to Prince Sultan and the Higher Officers' Committee the removal of some officers, the promotion of others, and the sending of a good number to the United States and Europe for higher degrees. Aiming for the best, I sought to prevent any outside intervention in the personnel department and in the department of officers' affairs. I gave instructions that regulations were to be followed scrupulously and that outside interference in promotions or transfers of officers and men would not be tolerated. Any requests for transfers had to be made through me. My objective was to make air defense a closed entity, free from outside pressures.

I was very tough on discipline. Soldiers had to address their officers properly. There could be no sloppiness on parade. To create a smart, good-looking, effective force, I wanted everyone to know that good work would be rewarded and bad work punished. But, on matters to do with the personal problems of my troops, I was soft. In a small force of about 10,000 at that time, I was able to get to know many of the men personally, and liked to visit them in the field during the fast of Ramadan when some commanders succumbed to the temptation of relaxing at home. If any of my men were admitted to the hospital, I wanted to know about it and would telephone the doctor to see how they were getting on. If I heard a complaint on my tours of inspection, I would demand that every man be treated fairly, in the belief that the notion of soldiers' rights had not always been given adequate attention. "Give the man his rights!" I would say. In all this Prince Sultan was my model. His frequent visits to the troops and his preoccupation with their welfare put other commanders, myself included, to shame.

It had been my dream since 1974 to have a separate uniform for the air defense forces: if the truth be told, I dreamed of creating a perfect uniform for all the Saudi forces. I learned at Sandhurst that an officer should have a sharp, disciplined appearance in a well-pressed uniform and with a decent haircut. For soldiers too the uniform is all important, good appearance and show being necessary to impress others and instill pride in the men themselves. So I gave two of my officers, Muhammad al-Kayyal and Ali Mansur al-Shu'aybi, the task of devising new uniforms for our Fourth Force, and checked everything personally – the materials, the designs, the colors, the underwear, the socks. I was very drawn to red and at one stage tried out a specimen uniform with red jacket and a red stripe down the trouser, but it was over the top.

I eventually chose four uniforms, like the British army: No. 1 dress for special occasions; No. 2 dress of jacket and tie, in both winter and summer versions; No. 3 dress which was working dress; and No. 4 dress which was combat dress with boots. I wanted every soldier, even if he worked in an office, to have a combat uniform ready and gave orders that all ranks had to report for work in combat dress on the first day of each month, just to make sure they had one and that it was in good condition. It was a big day when we got an appointment with Prince Sultan to seek his approval for the new uniforms. I went to his office with men wearing the different uniforms we had designed, and he approved them on the spot.

One of the greatest technical achievements implemented under my command was the creation of a fiber-optics transmission network for our air defense and strategic missile forces. So successful was it that it was later expanded to serve all our armed services, linking military cities, bases and area headquarters around the country to the Ministry of Defense in Riyadh. Saudi Arabia is today the third country in the world – after the United States and Japan – to use fiber optics for internal and strategic communications stretching over thousands of miles.

My principal aide and adviser in this pioneering project was Brigadier General Engineer Daoud al-Bassam, a man of technical brilliance and great persuasive gifts. It was he who convinced me that the other options available to us – satellite, tropo-scatter, coaxial or microwave systems – were all of limited capacity and, worse still, were vulnerable to detection, jamming and destruction, and that fiber optics represented the way of the future.

In all this, my ambition as Air Defense Commander was to put into practice what I believed in – training, fitness, discipline, inspection and evaluation, technology transfer, professionalism – in order to create a combat-ready force. I wanted tactical exercises to simulate wartime conditions. Rather than simply busing to and from the range for practice firing, I wanted units to move location with their batteries and missiles. I wanted the troops to tear down their equipment, move, set it up again, fire, move again. I demanded night firings and ripple firings – that is when one missile goes off so many seconds after another.

I believed in preparing for war. "Put it into your heads," I used to tell my officers, "that war can break out at any moment."

CHAPTER X

Capturing the East Wind

I N MARCH 1988, the world learned that the Kingdom of Saudi Arabia had acquired strategic, medium-range, surface-to-surface missiles from the People's Republic of China. I believe the *Washington Post* was first with the news, quickly followed by other leading newspapers and specialist journals like *Flight International* and *Jane's Defence Weekly*. The outcry was considerable. The State Department spokesman, Charles E. Redman, declared that the acquisition of the missiles was "not in the interests of peace and stability in the region," while Claiborne Pell (D-R.I.), Chairman of the Senate Foreign Relations Committee, said the missiles were a threat to Israel. In fact, in a campaign similar to the ones we faced when we purchased F-15s and AWACS, Israel's friends in the United States accused us of acquiring offensive weapons, of upsetting the balance of power in the Middle East. Yosi Ben Aharon, an aide to Israel's Prime Minister Yitzhak Shamir, went so far as to threaten that Israel might launch a preemptive strike against our missiles! It was apparently legitimate for Israel to be able to threaten the Arab world with its weapons of mass destruction, but quite illegitimate for us to acquire any sort of deterrent or retaliatory capability.

The diplomatic row which followed resulted in the recall of the American ambassador who had angered King Fahd by his repeated and importunate protests at our Chinese purchase.

Although the Chinese missiles attracted a good deal of media attention at the time, the story has never been fully told. But, as this is a subject which touches on national security, the reader will understand that I can give no more than a brief anecdotal account of it.

I must acknowledge at once that the idea of purchasing the missiles came, not from our military commanders as one might expect, but from King Fahd himself. It was he who decided that we needed a weapon powerful enough to deter any potential enemy from attacking us. Although we had no diplomatic relations with China at that time, the King sent my brother Bandar, our ambassador in Washington, to Beijing with a message for the Chinese authorities. Would they sell us "East Wind" missiles? In due course the Chinese conveyed through Bandar their agreement in principle to the transaction. Bandar had done an excellent job, setting the stage for the mission which I was to perform.

The acquisition of strategic missiles represented a turning point in Saudi Arabia's defense strategy, and must be placed in the context of the proliferation of missile systems which has characterized the region in recent years. Besides reinforcing Saudi Arabia's defenses, the creation of a Saudi Strategic Missile Force reflected the Kingdom's growing responsibilities in the Middle East, in the Muslim world as a whole, and on the world stage.

Following the initial contacts, China sent Lieutenant General Cao Gangchuan, Deputy Chief of the General Staff of the People's Liberation Army, to Saudi Arabia to discuss the project in detail. To avoid unwelcome publicity, we arranged for him and his delegation to fly in to one of our air bases and hold his meetings with our people at night. I was not involved at this early stage but after some preliminary discussions Prince Sultan called me to say that King Fahd had agreed to put me in charge of the talks. Accordingly, a negotiating committee was formed chaired jointly by the Chinese general and myself. In a week of intense negotiations – December 16 to 23, 1986 – which sometimes lasted until 4 a.m. – we drafted an outline of the project.

I believe Prince Sultan recommended me to the King for the job because I had had previous experience of negotiating arms contracts with foreign states and companies; because as Commander of Air Defense Forces I had a suitable technical and professional background; and finally because missiles were, in a sense, my specialty. In any event the King, on the recommendation of Prince Sultan and the Higher Officers' Committee, had already decided that I was to command the projected strategic missile force, so I suppose I was an obvious choice to take charge of the negotiations and then implement the project.

The King's instructions were that we should purchase the missiles – known in China as DF-3As and in the West as CSS-2s – as soon as possible and that their acquisition be shrouded in secrecy. My task was to negotiate the deal, devise an appropriate deception plan, choose a team of Saudi officers and men and arrange for their training in both Saudi Arabia and China, build and defend operational bases and storage facilities in different parts of the Kingdom, arrange for the shipment of the missiles from China and, at every stage, be ready to defend the project against sabotage or any other form of attack.

Recalling that my grandfather, King Abd al-Aziz, was often referred to as the "Falcon of the Peninsula," I chose the word "falcon" – al-Saqr in Arabic – as the code name for this secret assignment, which was to preoccupy me for much of the late 1980s. My invaluable aide throughout this period was Lieutenant Colonel Abdallah al-Suwaylim, who had been my trusted adjutant since I assumed command of the air defense forces. I had known him since childhood as his father had been part of King Fahd's household. He accompanied me on all my journeys in connection with the Chinese project, taking notes and writing reports in longhand, sometimes over 100 pages long.

I made four trips to China – the first in February 1987 – traveling by way of another Asian country to put people off the scent. For instance, on the first occasion I arranged to pay an official visit to Malaysia before heading for China. Some members of my staff urged me to travel in disguise under a false name, but I felt it would be foolish to hide. If discovered, my disguise would only serve to arouse suspicion. I felt it best to give every appearance of normality. Accordingly, I flew in my own plane to China with my regular American crew. But I put about the story that, in the hope of dissuading the Chinese from selling arms to Iran, then engaged in its long war with Iraq, I had come to buy light weapons from China myself. The deception was simple but effective.

When planning my second visit to China, I decided to break my journey in the British colony of Hong Kong. Visas for me and my officers were requested from the British Embassy in Riyadh. Shortly before leaving the Kingdom, I attended a lunch in honor of a visiting British minister and was amused when the British ambassador wished me "Good shopping!" Clearly he assumed I was on my way to China.

In Hong Kong, I ran into the Amir of Bahrain who asked me the purpose of my visit. I replied that I was on vacation but, in view of the number of Saudi generals in my train, he may not have believed me. At any rate, he was polite enough not to inquire further.

As it happened, my negotiations with China ran into a hitch, and two Chinese envoys came over from the mainland to see me in Hong Kong. We decided to meet in my hotel suite to which they came by a roundabout route. We spoke in whispers but, to frustrate any eavesdroppers, I had taken the precaution of having my rooms swept for listening devices. The Chinese went one better. When the envoys arrived, I noticed they were both carrying heavy umbrellas, although the weather did not seem to warrant it. When one of them handed me a document to read, the other stepped forward, opened his umbrella and, to my surprise, held it over my head. Lined with what seemed like aluminum foil, it was intended to protect the document from any prying electronic eye! Not wanting to take part in this charade, I tucked the document away and perused it later in my bedroom – under the bedclothes!

On my travels, I needed from time to time to communicate with Prince Sultan in Riyadh. But how to do so without running the risk of my calls being intercepted and monitored? I hit on a simple expedient. Leaving the Hong Kong hotel where I was staying to stretch my legs, I would enter any hotel I chanced upon, check into a room, make my calls to Saudi Arabia on an open line using coded words, and then check out at once.

In China, my main contact was with Yang Shangkun, a member of the Politburo and First Vice Chairman of the Central Military Commission, a powerful body chaired by Deng Xiaoping himself. A chain smoker with a flawless memory for detail, Yang Shangkun was then responsible for overseeing major overseas arms sales. He was to become President of China in 1988.

Just as, in Saudi Arabia, we had taken pains to keep the visits of the Chinese negotiators confidential, so in Beijing the Chinese kept my own presence secret. Although I was beautifully housed (in a villa which, I learned, was to be occupied after me by the U.S. Secretary of State), I was never allowed to go out on foot, but was whisked by car to all my appointments, even when our meeting place was close by. The Chinese were at least as keen as we were to keep the whole project under wraps.

As our discussions advanced, Yang Shangkun arranged for me to visit a Chinese missile base to see the DF-3A missile, armed with a nuclear warhead and powered by a liquid-fuel rocket motor, in an operational setting. I was told I was the first foreigner to be so privileged, as the startled expression on the faces of officers and men at the base seemed to confirm. In addition to their military duties – which they performed with exemplary smartness – I noted that the Chinese soldiers sowed and reaped crops and shepherded livestock, as I understand they do on every military base. In a word, they feed themselves and are self-sufficient.

On those visits I learned a good deal about the Chinese and the way they conduct negotiations. They were extremely patriotic and strained every nerve in the service of their country. Before every session, they prepared themselves meticulously and were thus able to answer in detail any question we put to them. It seemed that nothing was left to chance. They never seemed to tire of discussion and could go on for hours. Their team was well disciplined: no one member would open his mouth unless the team leader called on him to speak in his own area of expertise. In fact, the Chinese were so well-drilled that it was not easy to identify any weak points in their presentation, or sense where they might be prepared to be flexible. They proved tough negotiators, only conceding a point if we managed to convince them of our utter commitment to our own positions. The main card in my favor was their evident eagerness that we should pay in cash – a card I used to my best advantage. The conclusion I reached was that the Chinese with whom I dealt were wise men who knew what they wanted and planned accordingly. I believe we earned each other's respect.

The deal we eventually signed was to our mutual benefit, paving the way (as I shall recount in due course) for political recognition and the establishment of diplomatic relations between China and Saudi Arabia. In the years that followed, I was able to retain my good relations with China, relations which, on both sides, are based on a sound and realistic appreciation of the other's merits. China has a remarkable weight of population and is emerging as a major economic power, while we are an important oil and financial power. We are both Asian nations. China sees itself as the leader of the Third World, while we occupy a central position in the Muslim world, and exert our influence for stability in the Arab and international arenas. We both subscribe to the famous five principles of coexistence (first enunciated at the Bandung Conference of 1955) which, in an ideal world, are meant to govern relations between countries of different social and political systems, and which may be summed up as mutual respect for each other's policies and the integrity of each other's territory, nonintervention in each other's internal affairs, equality in dealings with each other, preserving world peace, and coexistence itself – admirable principles which are, alas, more honored in the breach than in the observance.

After my retirement from the Saudi armed forces in the wake of the Gulf War, I was visited in Riyadh by a Chinese delegation and was touched to hear them say, "We will always remember you. We have for you the same regard we have for Dr. Henry Kissinger!" It will be recalled that, in the early 1970s, Dr. Kissinger, then President Nixon's National Security Advisor, negotiated the restoration of U.S. relations with the People's Republic of China after a twenty-year-long estrangement. Although the circumstances and the stakes were radically different, I too was happy and proud to have played a part in cementing relations between my country and China.

❦

I should say a word about the background to King Fahd's decision to acquire Chinese strategic missiles. In brief, the aim was to give us the capability to counterattack in the event of an attack on us by either Israel or Iran, both in their different ways hostile neighbors at that time.

Since the 1973 war – indeed since the 1967 war – Israel has attempted to impose its will on the region, brutally repressing the Palestinian population of the Occupied Territories and carrying out numerous acts of aggression against Arab states, of which the invasions of Lebanon in 1978 and 1982 and the raids on Beirut, Tunis and Baghdad were among the more flagrant. Moreover, it is no secret that Israel has acquired nuclear weapons, together with long-range strike aircraft and ballistic missiles (such as the Jericho) to deliver them, and is developing military satellites to improve its targeting and intelligence gathering in the Arab world. In spite of its clear military superiority, Israel raises a predictable uproar whenever we seek to upgrade our defenses by purchases of Western arms. Yet, our security and self-respect demand that we acquire some minimal deterrent capability. This, I assume, may have been one reason for the King's decision to seek Chinese weapons.

I also assume that another was the threat to us from the revolutionaries in Iran who, having overthrown the Shah, mounted a hostile propaganda campaign against us. Rebuffing King Fahd's friendly overtures, Iran's new leaders attempted to belittle our standing in the Muslim world and undermine our role as guardians of the Holy Places. The danger became more acute with the outbreak of the Iraq–Iran war in 1980, which from the start carried with it the threat that other Gulf states might be sucked into the conflict, ourselves included.

Throughout the eight-year war, King Fahd made repeated attempts to bring Iraq and Iran to the negotiating table but Iran, confident of victory, ignored his pleas. I am not alone in believing that Iran missed a historic opportunity for peace in 1982 when King Fahd, at an Arab summit in Morocco in September of that year, proposed a settlement on the basis of Iraq's complete withdrawal from Iranian territory and compensation payments to Iran, financed by Arab Gulf states. Iraq accepted the King's peace plan but Iran rejected it.

As is well known, in 1982 and 1983 Iran, using human-wave tactics, launched repeated offensives against Iraq in an attempt to capture the southern port of Basrah, cut the Basrah–Baghdad road and threaten Baghdad itself. In these offensives, tens of thousands of lives were sacrificed in vain. In February 1984,

Iran attacked again, this time seizing the Majnoon islands in the marshlands of the lower Euphrates. After this offensive, Iraq proposed a cease-fire, but Iran refused to consider it.

Then the Iranians launched the so-called "Tanker War," attacking Saudi and Kuwaiti tankers in the Gulf, allegedly in retaliation for Iraqi attacks on their own vessels. These attacks on our shipping were followed by verbal threats to bomb and shell our ports, oil pipelines and installations, facilities on which our prosperity depends. We were all too aware that our refineries and offshore wells close to the war zone, not to mention the desalination plants in the Eastern Province, were highly vulnerable to air attack and would not be easy to defend.

A particularly dangerous incident occurred on June 5, 1984, when an Iranian F-4 fighter crossed the "Fahd Line" – an imaginary line drawn in the Gulf during the Iraq–Iran war to increase our reaction time – and intruded into our airspace. It ignored two warnings to turn back, although we had told the Iranians that any aircraft overflying our territorial waters would be intercepted. The Iranian fighter was then engaged by one of our F-15s and shot down. As it happened I was in a helicopter over Jubail when the incident took place and heard the Iranian pilot talking to his base seconds before he was hit. In a test of wills, each side then sent up more planes ready to do battle and it looked as if a major air battle might ensue, but fortunately the Iranian authorities recalled their aircraft to base before further shots were fired.

A few months later, in 1985, Iraq and Iran widened the war by firing scores of long-range missiles at each other's population centers in the so-called "War of the Cities," and in May of that year the Amir of Kuwait narrowly escaped death when his motorcade was attacked by a pro-Iranian suicide bomber. Concerned by these developments, King Fahd renewed his peace diplomacy: he sent the Saudi Foreign Minister, Prince Saud al-Faisal, to Tehran to convey to Iran yet another Iraqi offer of a cease-fire. But once again these overtures were rebuffed.

The escalating conflict now seemed to pose an imminent threat to our security. But what form would the threat take? After a careful study of Iranian capabilities, we concluded that Iran was unlikely to launch a land offensive against us. To do so would have meant coming through southern Iraq and Kuwait or mounting a major amphibious operation. Sending an army across the Gulf would require a huge logistics effort which would dangerously extend and expose Iran's supply lines. Iran lacked the capability for such an adventure. Already locked in battle with Iraq, it was unlikely to contemplate opening a second front. Nor would it dare risk offending the whole Muslim world by invading our territory. It seemed more likely, therefore, that Tehran might launch a campaign of military and economic attrition against us. We thought it might seek to undermine our economy by means of air, naval and missile strikes against key coastal installations, and intimidate us by a campaign of sabotage.

It was against this background of Iranian violence and persistent belligcreuce that, I assume, King Fahd decided that we needed a weapon to improve the morale of our armed services and our people; a deterrent weapon not intended to be used, except as a last resort when it should be able to demoralize the enemy by delivering a painful and decisive blow; a weapon which, once launched, could not be jammed or intercepted; a weapon which would make an enemy think twice before attacking us. The challenge was to find a country able to supply such a weapon at speed and without constraining conditions. The King's choice fell on China, a decision which, not long afterwards, sent me on my travels to Beijing.

***

In Saudi Arabia, the project started in great secrecy with a single officer, Lieutenant Colonel Abdallah al-Suwaylim, working with me in a room no one was allowed to enter. Then, as our plans took shape, more people were drawn very discreetly into the project. I chose men I knew personally and with whom I had worked before, and whose family and military backgrounds we had carefully investigated. At the start, just a handful of them had to bear the burden of a huge workload. To allay suspicion, they continued to work the same hours they had worked before. All the paperwork regarding their appointment, transfer, pay and so forth, was handled by the Air Defense Forces of which they wore the uniform. With the expansion of our activities, some of the men had to work night shifts but, as they had been sworn to secrecy, they could not talk about their work. The funny thing was that, as a result, several of them got into marital difficulties because their wives became convinced that they had taken other wives. I myself became the victim of such rumors!

To design the storage and launch sites I assembled a team of military architects under a well-qualified engineer, Lieutenant Colonel Abd al-Aziz al-Namla, while much of the construction work was done by private Saudi companies, aided by Chinese technicians. To unload the missiles, explosive materials and related equipment at our ports I relied heavily on a trusted officer, Major Suleiman al-Namla (no relation of Abd al-Aziz above), an expert who so impressed the Chinese that they adopted his methods. Another officer, Lieutenant-Colonel Ali Shu'aybi was responsible for the management, organization and security of the project at our seaports (and was to play a similarly crucial role during the Gulf War as the ports liaison officer with friendly forces). He helped me survey our ports, choose the right berths and warehouses, place decoys, and devise deception strategies to outwit any surveillance. On one occasion, fearing that a cargo might be a target for sabotage, I berthed the incoming ship next to an American freighter. If someone was planning to blow it up, they would think twice before doing so! In spite of Ali Shu'aibi's attempts to keep me away, I once spent a whole night at the docks when liquid fuel was being unloaded – the first time our people had handled such a product. I went there to give them confidence but I must confess I was frightened.

In an accident at a construction site, a Chinese worker had an ear sliced off and was knocked unconscious. He was flown to the hospital and revived. But his ear was missing. "Please find us the ear!" the doctors requested. That night, I sent a convoy of cars with headlights blazing to sweep the desert around the construction site and, by some miracle, the ear was found before the sands had covered it. It was rushed to the hospital and sewn back on. Its owner recovered and soon returned to work as though nothing had befallen him.

To learn to handle the new weapon, some of our men were trained in China. But these courses had to be followed by months and even years of training in Saudi Arabia. We set up a secret training establishment in the desert but, once they had arrived there, the trainees could not be allowed to leave. They could call their families once in a while, but all calls were monitored to make sure no information about their whereabouts was leaked. Of course, when men disappeared for prolonged periods like this, their families became worried and suspicious. Wives would ring me up and plead with me to tell them if their husbands had gone off to fight in Afghanistan! Some would assume that their husbands had died and would beg me to notify them officially of their death so that they could mourn them formally, as is their right and duty under Shari'a law. I would have to swear an oath that their husbands were alive and well, but even then it was sometimes difficult to convince them.

One day my intelligence officer rushed into my office in a state of panic. He brought the startling news that an eighteen-year-old cadet, speaking to his father on the telephone, had divulged where he was stationed and what he was doing. I ordered my military intelligence people to place the boy in solitary confinement and bring his father to me as soon as possible – which they did early the next morning. He was an old man who, as I discovered, had himself served in air defense. In fact he was delighted that his son was now serving in the same force. A devout Muslim, he was anxious that his son should lead a pure and upright life and not fall in with the wrong companions. So, when the boy had telephoned him after a long absence, he had been anxious to know where he was and what he was doing. After persistent questioning by his father, the boy had finally admitted where he was calling from.

At this, the father had become angry.

"Don't lie to me! There are no camps or bases in that area. What are you really up to?"

So the boy had been forced to explain that he was on a secret mission to do with missiles. Realizing at once that his son was telling the truth, the old man had been very pleased that he had been chosen for such an important job.

I asked him which of his friends and relatives now knew the secret but he swore that he had told no one.

What was I to do? If the man returned to his village the news would soon be out. But I could not keep him with me against his will. So I made him an offer to become the *imam* – or prayer leader – at the mosque on the base at a handsome monthly salary. He agreed at once and summoned his family to join him. Today, he is still there and, every time I visit the area, he rushes out to greet me. He is fond of saying that the telephone call from his son was by far the best thing that ever happened to him.

One of the many lessons I learned from Prince Sultan was that, in setting up any military facility or establishment, one should always seek to benefit the surrounding civilian environment. For example, when Prince Sultan created military cities at Khamis Mushait in the south or Tabuk in the northwest, he was at pains to ensure that the presence of the military contributed to a general raising of living standards among the local population. I determined to do the same when it came to setting up yet another training establishment for the missile force in the oasis of al-Sulayyil, nearly 350 miles southwest of Riyadh on the edge of the Empty Quarter.

Al-Sulayyil was then a somewhat backward area and living conditions were difficult. I had been granted a budget to build housing for officers and men, roads, a hospital and an airstrip – and it was estimated that the whole development would take from three to five years to complete. But in line with Prince Sultan's philosophy, I issued instructions that we should not rush into building. Instead I reckoned that we could save money and spread the benefits by renting over 100 existing dwellings, which would give us time to put up new housing without resorting to an expensive crash building program. As my men needed clothes, shoes, household goods and many other things, I persuaded several Riyadh traders to open shops in al-Sulayyil in partnership with local people and in return I promised to buy our supplies from them. This brought business to the place and created employment. I was happy that Prince Sultan agreed with my suggestion to build a civilian airport there, which the local inhabitants had been requesting for two decades, and which was to help revitalize the region as a whole.

Some years earlier, a vocational training school had been built there but had not been put to much use. The air force, which was building a base in the area, wanted it, but I managed to secure it for my cadets and made it operational within three months.

The missiles and all the related equipment were shipped from China to Saudi Arabia and, in utter secrecy, were placed first in temporary and then in more permanent locations. At sea and at the various ports of call along the route, we were prepared to meet any possible threat to these cargoes. We were able to guard the launch sites and storage facilities during construction in various parts of the Kingdom, to provide the force with secure communications, and to train our people in China and Saudi Arabia to maintain and operate the missiles. By wide dispersion, camouflage and other means, we made it difficult for an enemy to take out our new deterrent weapon in a single strike.

All this meant that I would sometimes be away from my family in Riyadh for long periods and I would not be able to say where I was. Our Air Defense Forces did not suffer from my absence from headquarters because we had built systems for training, inspection, financial control, combat readiness, operations and so forth which more or less ran themselves. The strict secrecy surrounding our strategic missile force applied to me as much as to others.

I shall always be grateful to my wife, Abeer, for her incredible understanding during this period. She is the daughter of my uncle, Prince Turki bin Abd al-Aziz, and we married in 1981, on my return from my studies in the United States. She is an exemplary wife, a wonderful mother and a remarkable organizer and manager of our domestic arrangements, who has made our years of married life together a period of great personal happiness and contentment. We have been blessed with five children – Hala, Mishael, Fahd, Abdallah and Salman – who with Faisal and Sara, the two older children of my first marriage, are my enduring pride and joy.

Even when I was at home in Riyadh I would sometimes receive telephone calls from my officers very late at night and, sensing the sensitivity of the subject, my wife would immediately leave the room without hesitation, sometimes remaining outside for over half an hour. In fact, it was not until much later that my wife learned of my involvement in the project. Once at a family gathering, on the day the international media broke the news of our Chinese purchase, my uncle, Prince Salman, the Governor of Riyadh, turned to her and asked,

"How is the father of our missiles?"

"Missiles?" Abeer asked in some puzzlement. "Whom do you mean?"

"Why, your husband of course!"

✤✤✤

The effectiveness of a deterrent capability depends on a potential enemy knowing of its existence. When our Strategic Missile Force was close to being operational, I wrote an analysis for the high command suggesting that, if our acquisition of Chinese missiles were not detected by November 1988, this would be an advantage; if not by February 1989, this would be greatly in our favor; if, however, it was not detected by June 1989, we should consider leaking the news ourselves as the object of acquiring the weapon would not have been achieved. As it happened, we had no need to do so, because the Americans broke the news first.

We never learned with any exactness when our purchase was discovered. Certainly I was surprised that the secret was kept for so long. It was rumored that U.S. intelligence learned of the Chinese project early on but, not wanting to raise a hornet's nest, chose to keep silent until the project was almost completed.

Not wishing to venture into such quicksands, I can do no more than pass on an amusing anecdote. It is said that, when scanning satellite pictures of a secret Chinese missile base, a sharp-eyed American analyst noticed that some of the men in the pictures were wearing beards – which is not a Chinese habit! Alarm bells rang in Washington. Were the men Iranians? On closer probing of the site it was discovered that they were Saudis in training in China. Our secret was out.

As I mentioned earlier, the Americans made a big fuss about it. It was rumored that five CIA people had been fired for the intelligence failure, but this may have been bluff. Washington asked to inspect the missiles which had arrived in the Kingdom. We refused. But we did give an assurance that our warheads would only be conventional. In any event, and no doubt for reasons of American domestic politics, the American ambassador to the Kingdom at the time, Hume Horan, was instructed by the State Department to make representations to King Fahd. Horan was an Arabist who had spent a good deal of time in the Arab world and had, in fact, served in the Kingdom as deputy chief of mission. Having helped us acquire defensive weapons, the Americans might not have appreciated our acquiring what they took to be an offensive weapon without consulting them.

To make the point, Ambassador Philip Habib, a U.S. presidential envoy who had been much involved in Middle East diplomacy, notably in Lebanon, was sent to Riyadh and, accompanied by Hume Horan, was received by the King. I understand that during the meeting, Horan handed Habib a piece of paper, perhaps to remind him that time was short and that he should get to the point of his mission.

I am told that he did so forcefully, so much so that the Saudi translator toned it down considerably. Horan, whose Arabic is good, then corrected the translator and interpreted Habib's message more exactly. However, the King did not welcome what he considered undue interference in Saudi defense policy. Angered by the undiplomatic persistence of the American envoys, he replied sharply, singling out Horan for a special rebuke as he considered him the instigator of the *démarche*.

I understand that Horan informed the State Department of the whole incident, making clear that he could no longer work effectively in the Kingdom. He was withdrawn shortly afterwards.

On instructions from the King and the Crown Prince, and under the supervision of Prince Sultan, I laid the groundwork for the establishment of diplomatic relations between China and Saudi Arabia in discussions with China's deputy foreign minister. Seeing that our strategic links were so close, it made no sense to delay mutual recognition – and indeed it was something Beijing had insisted on from the start.

Once I had settled the details for the normalization of relations and the opening of embassies in our respective capitals, the matter was finalized by the two foreign ministries. My brother Bandar then went again to Beijing to convey to the Chinese the

King's formal approval of these arrangements. In due course, I recommended him and a number of senior officers to Prince Sultan and the King for medals – which were duly awarded.

As our first ambassador to China, Prince Sultan recommended Tawfiq Alamdar, a soldier turned diplomat who had served as ambassador to Pakistan and for whom I had the highest regard. I knew he would understand the importance of the deal, and if we were to do more business with the Chinese, he was the man we needed in Beijing. I was particularly proud and delighted at the choice because Alamdar had been Air Defense Commander when I first joined the force and had attended my passing-out parade at Sandhurst. In fact it was he who had determined my choice of career. Although I had been earmarked for the artillery, I had wanted to join the Special Forces. But he was then looking for young English-speaking Saudi officers for the Hawk missile which had just been introduced to the Kingdom. I was drafted to that program.

Twenty years later that decision had led me to Beijing in pursuit of the East Wind.

CHAPTER XI

Reading Saddam's Mind

WHY DID SADDAM HUSSEIN invade Kuwait? What were his calculations and miscalculations? Was he driven by political ambition or economic necessity? Was his move premeditated or spontaneous? Was he the victim of a conspiracy? Did he fall into a trap?

These puzzles, and many more, will occupy historians for years to come. They may never be fully solved, or perhaps we may have to wait for government archives to be opened, including those of the United States, Britain, Israel and, of course, Iraq itself. Will we ever know what exactly took place between Britain and the United States, let alone between the United States and other interested parties? And very little is known about the workings of Saddam's inner circle of colleagues and advisers. We must make do with partial information. Today, some four years after the conflict, it is my conviction that there are many secrets about the Gulf crisis which have still not been revealed.

It is possible that someone – we do not know who – persuaded Saddam that he could get away with the invasion of Kuwait. The source of this persuasion may have been internal to Iraq or external. Options were no doubt presented to him, as they are to most leaders. But, in the end, it was he who chose the wrong one. Saddam personally was responsible for the decision to invade. Of that there can be no doubt. The weakness of dictators is that they are surrounded by advisers who tell them only what they want to hear. I was very struck when I learned that my grandfather, King Abd al-Aziz, always made a point of choosing the best advisers, not only from Saudi Arabia but from neighboring countries as well – and encouraged them to speak their minds. If his example had been more widely followed, the Arab nation would not now be in the difficult situation in which it finds itself.

To try to understand the Gulf crisis – one of the greatest catastrophes in the modern history of our region – we need to explore the motives and state of mind of the Iraqi leader, the man most directly responsible. Why did he commit the criminal miscalculation of invading Kuwait? And why did he then commit a second strategic error by not withdrawing in time to save his country from destruction?

What follows is only one man's view and by no means an exhaustive analysis of the crisis.

❖≫⬥≪

In seeking to understand Saddam's actions, a starting point must be Iraq's long-standing reluctance to accept and respect Kuwait's independence. We know that Saddam Hussein, like many Iraqis, believed that Iraq had a "historical" claim to Kuwait, resting on Kuwait having been part of the province of Basrah in Ottoman times. This is no place for an examination of the evidence. Suffice it to say that independent scholars have carefully reviewed the case – and have concluded that Iraq's claim is baseless.*

Moreover, in reviving the claim in 1990, Saddam apparently forgot that his former colleague Major General Ahmad Hassan al-Bakr, B'athist Prime Minister and later President of Iraq, had in October 1963 formally renounced Iraq's claim, recognized Kuwait's independence and sovereignty, and approved its membership of the Arab League and in the United Nations. I might add that territorial claims, based on the situation which prevailed in Ottoman times, can no longer be realistically entertained. If they could, what would prevent Turkey, for example, from claiming much of the Arab world which the Ottoman sultans ruled for centuries?

Another source of Saddam's hostility to Kuwait appears to lie

---

* For a recent authoritative study of this subject, see David H. Finnie, *Shifting Lines in the Sand: Kuwait's Elusive Frontier with Iraq* (London, 1992).

in Iraq's limited access to the Gulf. The Iraqi–Kuwaiti border, drawn by Britain in the early 1920s, gave Iraq a narrow sea frontage of barely 35 miles, whereas Kuwait secured a shoreline four times as long. In addition, Iraq's route to the Gulf from its port of Umm Qasr is blocked by the two Kuwaiti islands of Warba and Bubiyan. The need for a better and safer opening to the Gulf, and therefore for control of these islands, has been a constant theme of Iraqi policy under successive regimes.

But this grievance, whatever substance there may be to it, cannot in any way justify Saddam's invasion of Kuwait. By resorting to force, Saddam destroyed whatever sympathy there might have been for his case.

Another of Saddam's claims was that he had not been properly rewarded for his long struggle against Ayatollah Khomeini. He argued that Iraq had shed its blood in the eight-year-long Iraq–Iran war to guard the eastern gateway of the Arab world, and therefore deserved political, strategic and financial rewards from its Arab neighbors. It was his contention that Iraq had not fought Iran on its own account alone but to protect the Arab Gulf as a whole. In advancing this argument, he did not appear to have considered that he had recklessly torn up the 1975 Algiers Agreement which he had signed with the Shah, and had then attacked Iran, plunging the region into war for almost a decade. He had exposed his Gulf neighbors to grave danger, while taking their support and their money for granted.

Yet, once the war was over, he wanted still more. He wanted his Arab neighbors to recognize Iraq's primacy in the Gulf, he wanted greater access to the Gulf for his navy – in defense, so he claimed, of Arab security as a whole – and he wanted his war debts to be forgiven and large new credits to be given him. In addition, he appears to have had ambitions beyond the Gulf: he hoped to become America's principal Arab interlocutor, the man with whom Washington could settle the problems of the region, including the Palestine problem. In other words, his ambition was to dominate the region and outdo Nasser, Egypt's charismatic former President, as an Arab leader and champion.

But these expectations and demands were not realistic or acceptable because they infringed on the interests of others. And they became still less acceptable when Saddam started to press his case with threats. The world had, to some extent, been happy to help Iraq contain Iran, but it was less happy when Saddam started to parade his own ambitions. And the more he pressured, agitated and threatened, the less inclined his neighbors were to accommodate him. In brief, one could say that Saddam ruined whatever case he had – and it was never a very good one – by the brutal and intolerable methods he adopted.

Saddam had not traveled much outside his country or gained much insight into the ways of the world by personal dealings with foreign heads of state. He had governed Iraq in an atmosphere of violence and conspiracy. And, as I have mentioned, no one around him seems to have dared give him candid advice. (The death of his relative, the Defense Minister Adnan Khairallah, in a helicopter accident in 1988 may have robbed him of the only member of his entourage who dared give him independent advice.)

In the year before the invasion of Kuwait, the growing apprehension about Saddam in the Gulf and in the West seems only to have sharpened his sense of grievance. He may have felt that, instead of rewarding him as he expected, the world was punishing him, driving him into a corner. Crippled by war debts, attacked in the Western media, his international arms and credit networks dismantled, he may also have felt that his country was exposed to the threat of a military attack by Israel. This, I suspect, is how the world looked to him in 1989–90.

Saddam did not seem to have grasped that the hostility being shown to him was a direct result of his own words and actions. Many people, and I was one of them, noticed a change in him at the time of the Arab Summit which he convened in Baghdad at the end of May 1990. I watched the proceedings on television. At the opening session, Saddam behaved as the master, addressing other Arab leaders as if they were his inferiors. He was condescending. You could see that he did not consider the assembled Kings and Presidents to be his equal. I could not help contrasting his appearance with the picture I had of him when he visited Jeddah after the Iranian capture of the Fao peninsula in the extreme south of Iraq in February 1986 – a strategic move which seemed to presage the capture of Basrah. Then, walking stooped and round-shouldered beside King Fahd, Saddam seemed dejected and humble as he pleaded for more help.

But at the 1990 Summit his haughty appearance gave a clue to his state of mind – bitter, vainglorious, intent on revenge, a man with a strong sense of being wronged who was no doubt preparing to take by force what he considered his due. No one could have predicted his later actions, but his behavior at the Summit gave cause for alarm. We all talked about it and worried about it at the time. In the Kingdom, our real worries about Saddam started with that Summit.

There had been some earlier reasons for concern. We had not been overjoyed at the formation in early 1989 of the Arab Cooperation Council, a regional grouping of Iraq, Jordan, Egypt and north Yemen. As I have mentioned, the ACC looked to us like a strategic riposte to our own Gulf Cooperation Council (GCC), which Saudi Arabia and its five Gulf neighbors had formed early in the Iraq–Iran war as a measure of self-defense and from which Iraq was excluded.

The ACC was formed without King Fahd being informed, still less consulted. On the day before its formation was announced, King Hussein of Jordan called on King Fahd at Dhahran, but failed even to mention it before he went on to Baghdad. At the start, the ACC was portrayed as an economic grouping, but we suspected there were other motives in its creation. A glance at the map will show why it seemed to us like an encirclement. However, we derived some comfort from Egypt's membership, as we were certain that Egypt would not act against our interests. Yemen was not at the start planning to be a member but, as we were to learn later, King Hussein played a major role in persuading it to join. Nevertheless, in spite of our misgivings, we did not criticize the ACC.

But our concern about the ACC grew when we learned that Iraq was pressing to give it a military dimension, which made it look even more like a hostile encirclement of Saudi Arabia. When the ACC leaders met in Amman in February 1990 to celebrate the first anniversary of their grouping, Saddam gave voice to some violently anti-American and anti-Israeli rhetoric. I remember he called in particular for the withdrawal of the U.S. Navy from the Gulf, although U.S. ships had played a crucial role on his side in the later stages of the Iraq–Iran War. (Indeed, the destruction by U.S. warships of two Iranian oil rigs, an Iranian frigate and a missile boat in April 1988 undoubtedly contributed to Iran's decision to give up the struggle in July.) My personal feeling was that Saddam's rhetoric was counterproductive and hollow seeing that it convinced no one and aroused Western opinion against the Arabs.

As I have suggested, our worries came into sharper focus as a result of Saddam's behavior at the Arab Summit in Baghdad in May 1990 – a Summit which he apparently saw as confirming his regional supremacy and from which his old enemy President Asad of Syria wisely stayed away. The Summit had been called to protest against the massive immigration of Russian Jews to Israel, but other quite different themes emerged which, with hindsight, signaled what was to come.

One was Saddam's accusation that some Arab countries – he was soon to name Kuwait and the United Arab Emirates – were waging economic warfare against Iraq by overproducing oil and thereby forcing down the price. Iraq, he charged, had lost billions of dollars as a result. This was the first clear indication that Saddam's prime worries were economic. In the first half of 1990, the price of oil had slumped by some 30 percent, from $21 a barrel in January to a mere $14 a barrel. Desperate for revenue to rebuild his war-ravaged economy, unable to raise fresh credit internationally, and burdened by some $70 billion of foreign debt, Saddam may have seen the collapse of the oil price as further evidence of a conspiracy against him.

In the spring of 1990, it must have dawned on Saddam that he was broke. Some observers believe that the event which brought it home to him at that time was, curiously enough, the visit of the Yugoslav Prime Minister to Baghdad. Saddam's deputy, Taha Yasin Ramadan, accompanied the Yugoslav to the airport and, on the way, pressed him for further loans. But the Prime Minister was not forthcoming. Quite the contrary. On arriving home, he issued a statement to Tanjug, the Yugoslav press agency, saying that he had told the Iraqis that Yugoslavia had done what it could to help them during the Iraq–Iran war, but now needed its loans repaid. This setback appears to have concentrated Saddam's mind on his financial crisis. He was not getting the fresh medium-term credits he wanted from the

Europeans, the Japanese and from the U.S. Export-Import Bank. He had several pet projects on the drawing board but no money to finance them. His many creditors were beginning to press for payment. It was then that he sent his Prime Minister, Sa'adun Hammadi, to Kuwait with a peremptory demand for $10 billion. I understand the Kuwaitis offered him a mere $500 million which he took as an insult.

The Iraqi army, swollen by the war with Iran, was also giving Saddam serious cause for concern. To demobilize large numbers of men risked stirring up grave social unrest, as had already occurred a year earlier when hundreds of Egyptian workers in Iraq had been killed by rampaging Iraqi soldiers who believed the Egyptians had taken their jobs. In the circumstances, it was perhaps tempting for Saddam to think of keeping his army busy with a foreign adventure.

Saddam's accusations against Kuwait and the United Arab Emirates were then repeated in mid-July in a memorandum to the Arab League, and by Saddam himself in a violent speech on July 17 – a speech which woke me up to the dangerous trend of events. Kuwait was the primary butt of his attack. He accused Kuwait of glutting the oil market, of stealing oil worth $2.4 billion from the North Rumaila field which straddles the Iraqi–Kuwait border, of conspiring with "Imperialism and Zionism" against Iraq's scientific and technological achievements. "Instead of rewarding Iraq, they have . . . thrust their poisoned dagger into our back," he declared, in a phrase which gave a clear indication of his mounting paranoia. These moves set alarm bells ringing in the Kingdom.

Saddam's increasingly intemperate statements against his Arab neighbors, and his threat in April 1990 to "burn half of Israel" if it attacked Iraq or any other Arab country, greatly heightened tension in the region. (Shortly after he made this inflammatory threat, a senior Arab official whom I know paid a visit to Baghdad and was surprised to hear Saddam say: "Tell the United States that our statement was for internal consumption only. We have no intention of harming Israel!" – a remark which would seem to provide further evidence of the incoherence of his thinking.) In the world at large, however, Saddam's warlike rhetoric was taken at face value. With good reason, the media began to regard him as dangerously unbalanced, while Israel and its supporters seized on the pretext to rouse international opinion against him. It could be argued that some part of the propaganda campaign which was then unleashed against Iraq was deliberately intended to provoke him into making a foolish move. To this extent, there may have been a conspiracy against him. But, despite these provocations, Saddam's freedom of action remained complete. It was he who took the fatal step of invading Kuwait. He was the victim of his own mistakes, and of his own rash and violent temperament.

⁂

Saddam's attitude towards the United States was ambivalent. While some of his rhetoric was anti-American – such as his demand in February 1990 that the U.S. withdraw its navy from the Gulf – he appears to have longed at the same time for a dialogue with the U.S., and wanted Washington to acknowledge his importance. He clearly underestimated the extent to which his words and actions had by this time turned opinion against him.

It is easily forgotten that during the Iraq–Iran war, Iraq had enjoyed very close relations with the United States. It had received weapons, precious intelligence about Iranian movements, as well as armed American support against the Iranian navy. In the final stages of the war, the U.S. in effect opened a "second front" in the Gulf against Iran. So close were U.S.–Iraqi relations that when an Iraqi Exocet missile hit an American warship, the U.S.S. *Stark*, by mistake, on May 17, 1987, killing 37 American sailors, the incident was quickly hushed up, and Iraq paid $27 million in compensation. Saddam's ambassador to the U.S., Nizar Hamdoun, was for a time the darling of Washington, and had access to the highest American officials.

Indeed, U.S.–Iraqi relations had been so close that Saddam may have been unable to adjust to the sudden change of sentiment towards him in the early months of 1990. Right up to the last moment, and perhaps beyond it, he evidently could not believe that the United States was truly hostile to him or that it would attack him. He seems to have thought the Coalition's military deployments were a bluff. He may have been encouraged to think so because the Bush administration had itself been ambivalent towards him in the run-up to the crisis. For example, it had played a part in helping to disrupt his international arms procurement networks, yet it had also bent over backwards to accommodate him in an attempt to moderate his behavior.

For example, on April 12, 1990, a delegation of five American senators, headed by Republican minority leader Robert Dole (and including James McClure, Alan Simpson, Frank Murkowski, and Howard Metzenbaum) spent two hours with Saddam in Mosul and assured him that President Bush wanted better relations with him.

The State Department's instructions to Miss April Glaspie, the American Ambassador in Baghdad, had been to woo Saddam, so as to bring him back to reasonable behavior. President Bush had himself intervened to make sure Iraq got some of the credits it wanted – all of which may have persuaded Saddam that Washington was still fundamentally well disposed towards him. When he conceived the invasion of Kuwait, he clearly did not think the U.S. would interfere with his plans. This was a grave misjudgment.

Saddam seems also to have misjudged the rapidly changing international situation. He was of course aware that the Soviet system was collapsing but, in planning his invasion of Kuwait, he might have thought this was to his advantage. In Iraqi thinking, U.S. interests in the region were limited to the defense of oil, the security of Israel, and holding in check any expansion of Soviet influence or threatened incursion from that quarter. On oil, Saddam was prepared to give the United States cast-iron assurances that he would not disturb the flow; he had no intention of threatening Israel; while the possibility of any sort of Soviet menace was fast disappearing. The conclusion he seems to have reached was that he had little to fear from the United States – at most token resistance – and that the end of the Cold War gave him more, rather than less, freedom of maneuver. He seems to have thought that the great powers would disengage from Middle East conflicts – such as his quarrel with Kuwait – much as they seemed at that time to be disengaging from regional conflicts all over the world. He expected to be given a

free hand. He seems not to have realized that Kuwait was different – different from Angola or Cambodia, for instance. With its
$100 billion of external assets, its oil reserves, its stake in key
Western industries, Kuwait was not a prize the West would
allow him to swallow.

It must be said that the U.S. never explicitly warned Saddam
against the use of force in his dispute with Kuwait. In my view,
this was a major diplomatic error due perhaps to America's fasci-
nated preoccupation at the time with the collapse of communism
in Eastern Europe. Curiously enough, it was an error which the
U.S. repeated a number of times, and which led some people to
speculate that it had set a trap for Saddam.

For example, when John Kelly, the U.S. Assistant Secretary
of State for Near Eastern Affairs, visited Baghdad in February
1990, he expressed American indifference to Iraq's border dispute with Kuwait. Similarly, U.S. Ambassador Glaspie told Saddam, in their fateful late-night interview on July 24, that "We
have no opinion on the Arab–Arab conflicts, like your border
disagreement with Kuwait." Clearly, she must have been obeying official instructions and Saddam took her at her word. In
the days immediately before the invasion, a number of U.S.
officials – notably the State Department spokeswoman Margaret
Tutwiler on July 24 and John Kelly himself again on July 31 –
stressed that the U.S. had no defense treaty with Kuwait and
no special defense commitment to it. Whether they were deliberate or not, these wrong diplomatic signals must undoubtedly
have encouraged Saddam to make his move.

After her interview with Saddam, Ambassador Glaspie did not
leave Baghdad to go on vacation as is generally supposed. I
understand on good authority that Saddam asked her to deliver
a message to President Bush – and to come right back to Baghdad
with the President's reply. Saddam's message ran something like
this: "As you know, I have successfully fought off Iran. But,
instead of rewarding me, the British and the Kuwaitis are driving
me into a corner. Please note that my record on oil is absolutely
clean. I have never acted irresponsibly over oil, and never will.
I want our dialogue to continue. I am the man with whom you
should do business in this region."

To me this message to the U.S. – which on good authority I

believe to be accurate – suggests that Saddam anticipated getting away with his takeover of Kuwait and looked forward to future negotiations and to a future relationship with the United States which would have confirmed his regional primacy.

However, no one in the West – or in the Arab world, for that matter – predicted that Iraq would seize the whole of Kuwait. At most, some Western intelligence agencies believed that Saddam might occupy Bubiyan and Warba, the islands opposite Umm Qasr, and perhaps the North Rumaila oil field on the Iraqi–Kuwaiti border – and that, if he did so, there was not much that outsiders could do about it.

If Saddam misjudged the reaction of the international community, he also gravely misjudged the reaction of Saudi Arabia – a mistake of equal, if not greater, importance. He appears to have gambled that the Kingdom would never dare invite foreign forces on to its territory and that, if it came to a fight, the worst he might have to face would be a bombardment by the U.S. Navy and, at the outside, a limited amphibious attack by the U.S. Marine Corps which, he might have calculated, his army could cope with, as it had with Iran's repeated attacks during the Iraq–Iran war. He seems to have thought that, after the traumas of Vietnam, and the further setback the U.S. Marines suffered in Lebanon in the early 1980s, no American president would be likely to commit troops to prolonged ground combat in the Gulf.

If such indeed was Saddam's thinking, it was further evidence that he had not grasped how profoundly the U.S. armed forces had been reformed and revitalized during the Reagan years. The architect of the rebirth of the American military after the post-Vietnam build-down was Caspar Weinberger, Defense Secretary in both Reagan administrations from 1981 to 1988. As I see it, three changes may be cited to sum up Weinberger's achievement. First, he introduced higher salaries and better benefits for military personnel, making it more attractive to be a soldier and thereby attracting a higher caliber recruit. For instance, I learned with interest during the war that almost every officer in the U.S. armed services was a college graduate, and many had a postgraduate degree. Secondly, he accelerated the purchase of hardware, greatly increasing the numbers of aircraft, ships, tanks and other items in the armed forces inventory. And thirdly, he opened the door to the funding of new military technologies, leading to the introduction of "smart" weapons and many other revolutionary weapons systems first seen in combat in the Gulf War.

So, Saddam appears not to have realized that the U.S. armed services had achieved a high degree of combat readiness. Nor did he read correctly the many signals that came out of Washington from August 1990 onwards, of which the following might usefully be recalled.

In an address from the Oval Office on August 8, President Bush said, "First, we seek the immediate, unconditional and complete withdrawal of all Iraqi forces from Kuwait. Second, Kuwait's legitimate government must be restored . . . Let me be clear, the sovereign independence of Saudi Arabia is of vital interest to the United States. This decision, which I shared with the congressional leadership, grows out of the long-standing friendship and security relationship between the United States and Saudi Arabia."

On November 8, 1990, President Bush announced a massive reinforcement of American forces in the region to give the Coalition what he described as an "offensive military option." On January 9, 1991, he wrote Saddam a letter – which James Baker handed to Tariq Aziz in Geneva – which left no room for doubt about U.S. intentions. "Unless you withdraw from Kuwait completely and without condition, you will lose more than Kuwait. What is at issue here is not the future of Kuwait – it will be free, its Government will be restored – but rather the future of Iraq. This choice is yours to make . . . Should war come, it will be a far greater tragedy for you and your country."

Finally, on January 12, 1991, four days before the outbreak of war, a joint resolution of both houses of Congress authorized the President to use force in the Gulf. The vote in the Senate was 52–47, in the House it was 250–183. Saddam chose to ignore these many signals.

To sum up, Saddam's dreams and illusions stemmed from a potent mix of motives and a large measure of wishful thinking. He was broke and required immediate, large-scale financial relief. But, as he saw it, Kuwait had refused to write off his war loans, was denying him fresh credits, and was bankrupting him

by swamping the market with oil. Moreover, it persisted in denying him access to Bubiyan and Warba islands. So, he decided to
grab what he wanted and confound the world! He must have
calculated that he would face no serious military challenge from
the Arabs or the West and that, once he was master of the Gulf,
his financial problems would be solved and Washington would
have to recognize his new importance.

This, at least, is my reading of Saddam's calculations and miscalculations.

There remains an unresolved puzzle about Saddam's invasion
of Kuwait: was it done on impulse or was it premeditated and
carefully planned?

Clearly Saddam's anger at the world in general and the
Kuwaitis in particular had been building up over several months.
Pressures on him were so severe and his mood was so explosive
that it probably required only some small incident to tip him
over the brink. The truth is that we do not know what the
immediate trigger was, and we will remain in the dark until
Saddam himself enlightens us. For my part, as there is little
public evidence of careful Iraqi planning, I tend to think
Saddam's decision to use force took shape gradually in his mind
in the five or six months before the invasion, so that by the end
of July he could restrain himself no longer.

One piece of evidence, however, does suggest an element of
preplanning. According to a senior official of the Kuwait Oil
Company, some six months before the invasion Iraq sent a
number of teams to Kuwait to study technological advances in
oil refining, power generation, telecommunications, banking
and the like – fields in which Iraq claimed it had fallen behind
owing to its long war with Iran. One team of four Iraqis was
assigned to the Kuwait oil industry and, in agreement with the
Kuwait government, spent nearly three months touring installations, acquainting itself with the working of the main control
panels and other equipment. However, two or three days after
the invasion these same Iraqis were spotted at the Company's
head office working under the direction of the Iraqi military.

The presumption is that their earlier visit had been a spying mission.

Yet, some features of the affair point to a distinct lack of planning. For example, it is striking that, before his invasion, Saddam did not bother to make contact with members of the Kuwaiti opposition whose relations with the Al Sabah were then very tense. It will be recalled that the Kuwaiti opposition was pressing for a restoration of parliament, suspended in 1986 during the Iraq–Iran war, and had rallied thousands of citizens in support of its demands at weekly *diwaniyas*, or gatherings in private homes, a unique Kuwaiti social institution where men get together in each other's houses to maintain contact and exchange views and which, at moments of crisis, assume political importance. Several opposition politicians, present at such *diwaniyas*, had been arrested after scuffles with the police.

Had Saddam drawn up a detailed plan to invade Kuwait, surely he would have devoted some time and effort to making contact with the opposition and to the preparation of a "provisional government" to head his new "province." During the Iraq–Iran war, Saddam was very worried that Tehran might encourage its supporters in southern Iraq to set up a "provisional government" in Basrah, and then "invite" the Iranians to come in. This was his great anxiety during the battle for Basrah. How could he not, therefore, have thought of doing the same thing himself in Kuwait, if indeed his attack had been long premeditated? Yet, as far as I know, he made no such preparations. He did not even seek the support of Kuwait's small faction of pro-Iraqi B'athists. When he needed a puppet government in Kuwait after his invasion, not a single Kuwaiti would collaborate with him.

It might be argued, however, that Saddam did not contact the Kuwaiti opposition because he wanted to protect the secrecy of his plans, and because he anticipated that the seizure of Kuwait would be a simple operation which would be accepted by most Kuwaitis.

Saddam's attitude to the Americans also suggests that he may have acted on impulse. As I have mentioned, Ambassador Glaspie was due to return to Iraq with President Bush's reply to Saddam's message. Stephen J. Solarz, who at the time was a Democratic Representative from New York with considerable clout in the American Congress, was also due in Baghdad for talks with Saddam on August 8. Saddam was anxious for a dialogue with Washington. That is what he wanted above all else. Yet he did not wait for the arrival of these envoys before making his fatal move. His anger and impatience evidently got the better of him – which again seems to rule out careful premeditation. But yet again, it is just possible that setting up appointments with the American envoys was a ruse to deceive the world and gain the benefit of surprise for his invasion.

To sum up, it seems to me that the most likely explanation is that Saddam may have been contemplating a move against Kuwait for several months, but that events in July blinded him with rage and precipitated the invasion. The scenario which took shape in Saddam's mind might have been the following: he would march in, execute the ruling family, encourage the opposition parties to proclaim their friendship with Baghdad, and then pull out – leaving a puppet government behind to do his bidding. An overwhelming show of force would deter any outside interference. He would have got what he wanted without having to fight for it.

Like President Gamal Abd al-Nasser of Egypt in 1967, this ambitious and impetuous ruler did not foresee that, once he had given the world a pretext to make war on him, his enemies would pounce on the chance to destroy him. They would not let him escape.

Although the circumstances were different, the parallel with Nasser in 1967 can be drawn. Once the Egyptian leader had made the mistake of asking United Nations forces to leave Sinai, Israel seized on the pretext to attack him – even though Israeli leaders knew well enough, as some of them have since confirmed, that his deployments in Sinai were defensive, not offensive. But they would not let him off the hook. Although Nasser proposed negotiations, and was about to send Vice President Zakaria Muhieddin to Washington to get them started, Israel struck before talks could get under way. In other words, Nasser was not allowed to save himself through negotiations.

Much the same thing happened in 1990–91. From the moment of the invasion of Kuwait, Saddam's enemies pressured the United States to act tough: there could be no retreat from the necessity to destroy Saddam's military machine. No "linkage" with other Middle East problems would be allowed.

Had Saddam been a strategic thinker, he would not have given his enemies this chance. On the contrary, he would have seized every opportunity to withdraw with dignity. The fact that he did not do so has led some Arabs to go so far as to suspect that he may be an agent of the West. Alternatively, my own view is that he is simply a dictator who made serious mistakes which his enemies exploited to weaken him and his country. They would not let him escape from a trap he himself had set.

At the start, the Arab members of the Coalition wished to contain Iraq rather than destroy it. They wished to restore legitimate government in Kuwait and remove the threat to themselves. They pleaded and urged Saddam to come to his senses and withdraw. No Arab state can lightly contemplate the physical punishment and the destruction of another. But the longer Saddam stayed in Kuwait, looting, sacking, torturing and defying the whole world, the more the war option seemed the only possible one. More and more people in the Gulf region began to worry that if Saddam withdrew from Kuwait with his arsenal intact he would threaten them again. Once again the trap into which Saddam fell was of his own making.

Saddam's blunder was to have threatened the vital interests of so many countries that he united against himself a formidable international coalition – the most powerful the world had seen since World War Two. His seizure of Kuwait posed an immediate threat to the independence of Saudi Arabia and its Gulf neighbors. He was known to be hostile to the rulers of the smaller Gulf states and seemed intent on destroying the basis of their traditional power. In the wider Middle East, Saddam's bid for hegemony was a grave challenge to Egypt, to Syria, to Israel, to Turkey and to Iran, Saddam's enemy-to-the-death for eight years. His challenge to such major Middle East states was also, of course, a challenge to the oil and strategic interests of the United States – interests which successive American presidents had pledged to defend – and beyond the U.S., to the oil-hungry industrialized world, including such economic giants as Japan and Germany. He showed that he knew very little about the way political and economic systems worked in the West and the way decisions were made, particularly in the United States. He seems to have thought that he could deal with foreign countries as he dealt with his own people.

It was Saddam's genius to unite much of the world against himself, including states that were usually opposed to each other. To have made such a gigantic mistake in August 1990 – and then to have failed to correct it over the succeeding months – confirms my impression of Saddam as a provincial dictator with little real understanding of the world, whose ruthlessness and brutality ensured that no one around him dared tell him the truth. There were no checks and balances in the Iraqi regime, no institutions to curb Saddam's absolute power, no one to dare say to him: "You have made a false move. Pull back!"

❖

During and after the Gulf crisis, some Arab intellectuals argued that it was a crime for Arab states, such as Saudi Arabia, Egypt and Syria, to ally themselves with the United States against another Arab state, and that by doing so we had subverted the principles of Arab nationalism and destroyed the Arab consensus. The real threat to the Arabs, they said, came not from Saddam Hussein but from the West. Others even went so far as to portray Saddam as a hero of Arab nationalism brought down by a Western or a Zionist conspiracy.

Such attitudes reflect the pain some Arabs feel at the West's colonial carve-up of the Arab world early this century, at its role in creating Israel after World War Two, and at the blind support the United States has given Israel ever since, even when this ran counter to America's own national interests. Many Arabs also feel an understandable nostalgia for the distant past when their civilization and power were unrivaled.

But views such as these offend against contemporary reality. Regrettable as it may be from an Arab perspective, "Arab nationalism," the credo of most Arabs, has not so far resulted in coherent political action, while an "Arab consensus" has been more often absent than present in most of the great events affecting our area.

My own view is that, by invading Kuwait, Saddam Hussein tried in a very crude and violent way to promote Iraqi interests and his own personal ambition at the expense of other Arabs. This had nothing whatsoever to do with Arab unity, Arab nationalism, or the Palestine cause. It could, of course, be argued in a general sense that all Arab dictators in recent times, Saddam included, have been products of the Palestine question: Israeli aggression has undoubtedly contributed to the rise of Arab militarism. But it was surely the greatest folly to believe, as some Palestinians did, that the road to the "liberation of Palestine" ran through Kuwait. There was no sense in which, by attacking an Arab state, Saddam could claim to have struck a blow for Palestine. On the contrary, the questions must be asked: did Saddam ever seek revenge for Israel's attack on his civilian nuclear facility in 1981? Did he arm his people to fight Israel? Did he conduct any successful battles against Israel? It could, in fact, be said that everything he did, both internally and externally, from the moment he rose to prominence in Iraq was ultimately to Israel's benefit. Certainly, his invasion of Kuwait has resulted in immense damage to the Arabs: quite apart from the tragic loss of life, it has caused material losses of hundreds of billions of dollars, forced hundreds of thousands of people from their homes, and created deep-seated divisions in the Arab world, marked at the popular level by mutual hate and suspicion. This is perhaps his most dangerous legacy.

We, in the Kingdom, were forced to fight Saddam but, throughout the crisis, I also sought to understand him. I tried to wear his hat and read his motivations. But I had to conclude that Saddam was an aggressor pure and simple – and an aggressor against the Arabs! It was necessary to stop him to safeguard ourselves. In our hour of need the nationality of the troops that came to our aid was our least concern. If your house is on fire, you are not too concerned about who helps you extinguish the flames.

I believe it was our duty as Arabs, and not just as Saudis,

Egyptians, Syrians or Moroccans, to oppose Saddam, because it would have been a cause of enduring shame and of countless future problems if our Arab world had come to be dominated by such a reckless and bloodstained man.

CHAPTER XII

The War Aims of the Arab Alliance

AT THE HEART OF the Arab opposition to Saddam Hussein was a Saudi–Egyptian–Syrian axis, which took shape immediately after the invasion of Kuwait and which, for the next six months, formed the backbone of the anti-Iraqi Coalition. Without this Arab axis, the war to liberate Kuwait could not have taken place. Some Arab and Western commentators have argued that the three Arab partners in this axis came together because of American pressure or because they hoped to gain something from Washington – in terms of money or weapons or political support. It has been said, for instance, that Saudi Arabia invited in friendly forces on American insistence, that Egypt joined the Coalition because it wanted its debts forgiven, that Syria joined to have a free hand in Lebanon or to secure American support in the peace process. In my view these arguments are wide of the mark.

The Arab axis was formed because each of its three members saw Saddam's move as a deadly threat to its own vital interests. Saudi Arabia, Egypt and Syria were united in a determination to defeat Iraq's bid for regional hegemony – a hegemony which would have undermined Saudi security and exposed it to extortion, marginalized Egypt in Arab affairs, and exposed the Syrian regime to extreme danger. Had Saddam not posed a deadly threat to the interests of these Arab states the Coalition would not have been formed and the war would not have been fought – or would have been fought very differently without Arab participation.

These "Arab" reasons for opposing Saddam are not well

On a secret mission to China to buy strategic surface-to-surface missiles, I inspected a Chinese guard of honor.

Pretending to be a tourist on the Great Wall of China.

Zhao Ziyang, Premier of the People's Republic of China from 1980 to 1987, was highly influential in military matters. When I met him in the late 1980s, he was serving as Vice Chairman of the Communist Party's Military Committee and of the State's Central Military Commission.

When negotiating the missile deal in Beijing in 1987, I met Yang Shangkun, a powerful figure on the Military Commissions of both the State and the Chinese Communist Party. A man with a remarkable memory for detail, he served as President of the People's Republic of China from 1988 to 1993.

ABOVE: Formed in February 1989, the short-lived Arab Cooperation Council brought together *(from left to right)* President Ali Abdallah Saleh of Yemen, President Saddam Hussein of Iraq, King Hussein of Jordan and President Husni Mubarak of Egypt. In Saudi Arabia, we saw it as a hostile encirclement.

RIGHT AND BELOW: Iraq's leader, Saddam Hussein, speaking on the telephone during the Iraq–Iran War, and addressing his troops in Kuwait after his invasion of August 2, 1990

With Dick Cheney, U.S. Defense Secretary, on one of his many visits to Riyadh in the run up to Desert Storm.

General Norman Schwarzkopf and I worked closely together in a "parallel command."

Lieutenant General Charles Horner, the Coalition's "Air Boss," was the architect of the air campaign against Iraq.

General Colin Powell, Chairman of the Joint Chiefs of Staff, was the principal directing mind of the campaign on the American side.

Lieutenant General John Yeosock, CENTCOM Army Commander, was my closest American associate in the early weeks of the crisis. Together we planned Desert Shield.

RIGHT: Lieutenant General Walter Boomer, Commander of Marine Forces MARCENT. His ground troops, side by side with my joint forces, fought through the most heavily defended obstacles in the Iraqi lines.

Inspecting a Challenger tank with Brigadier General
Patrick Cordingly, Commander of Britain's
7th Armored Brigade, the famous "Desert Rats."
Behind is Major General Salih al-Muhaya, the
Eastern Area Commander.

On a visit to British armored forces I was made an
honorary "Desert Rat."

ABOVE RIGHT: A briefing at British divisional head-
quarters with Lieutenant General Sir Peter de la
Billière and Brigadier General Patrick Cordingly.
Sir Peter secured a central role in the campaign for
British forces.

I introduced some of my generals to Tom King, Britain's Defense Minister. *From left to right:* Brigadier General Salem al-Uwaymer, Major General Attiyah al-Touri, Brigadier General Faisal al-Bali, and Major General Talal al-Otaibi.

Escorting Crown Prince Abdallah bin Abd al-Aziz, head of the Saudi Arabian National Guard, on a visit to front-line troops in August 1990.

Escorting Prince Sultan, Minister of Defense and Aviation, on a visit to troops in the field.

understood by Western opinion to whom Saddam has generally been portrayed as a maverick leader whose growing arsenal of unconventional weapons threatened Western interests and Israeli security.

Saddam's invasion of Kuwait in August 1990 posed the gravest threat to Saudi Arabia's security that I had yet encountered in my military career – and therefore the greatest challenge to our armed services and to me personally as Joint Forces Commander. Our vital, oil-producing Eastern Province – the principal source of our national wealth – lay open to his mechanized and armored divisions.

We had, of course, faced other crises in this turbulent region – the Yemen civil war of the 1960s, the June War of 1967, the overthrow of the Shah in 1979, Israel's invasion of Lebanon and its savage bombardment of Beirut in 1982 – but none to compare with this one in its immediate danger to the Kingdom.

For example, when Nasser intervened in Yemen in 1962, he did not possess the tremendous arsenal that Saddam had at his disposal. Moreover, everyone knew that Egypt would have a hard time pacifying the warlike tribes of the Yemen mountains before it could even think of venturing into Saudi Arabia itself. In any event, the Egyptian army in Yemen was a long way from our oil fields: in between lay the vast buffer zones of Asir, Najran and the open desert.

But this time the threat was in our backyard. Saddam's armies were in the Gulf itself, just a few days' march from Dhahran. The situation was far more dangerous than it had ever been.

Israel's aggressions against the Arabs, notably in 1967 and 1982, were also attempts by the Jewish state to impose its will on the Arabs by force of arms, and this could not fail to concern us acutely. Israel's frequent attacks spread destruction, displaced populations, resulted in illegal occupation of Arab territory and profoundly upset the politics of the Levant. The consequences are with us still and continue to preoccupy us intensely. But, on the many occasions that Israel assaulted Arab states and populations, it was mostly Syria or Egypt or Jordan that held the front line against Israel, not Saudi Arabia.

The same point could be made about Iran. When Iranian revolutionaries overthrew the Shah in 1979 and founded their

Islamic Republic, we faced a new security threat – from subversion, terrorism, sectarian incitement, and even possibly armed attack from the sea. The Islamic Republic of Iran across the Gulf has not been an easy neighbor to live with. But even throughout the eight years of the Iraq–Iran war, 1980–88, the threat to us was once again largely indirect, rather than direct. We provided Iraq with massive assistance in the conflict, but it was Iraq, not Saudi Arabia, that was in direct confrontation.

All this changed in August 1990 when Iraq attacked Kuwait. This time, the Kingdom itself was in the front line, with no buffer in between. That is why this crisis was so much more threatening than the others.

To safeguard our country and our people, we had no alternative but to call on friendly troops for help, notably from the United States, the one power with the will and the means to reverse Iraq's aggression. In defense of our independence, our foreign policy became more assertive and our alliance with the West more overt. Long-term dependence on the West for our security is, of course, not our objective. In an ideal world, we would prefer an Arab alliance. But so long as we and our Gulf neighbors are unable to defend ourselves against powerful predators like Saddam Hussein, an alliance with the West, with whom we share important economic interests, will in my view be necessary.

❖

On July 23, 1990, nine days before the invasion, our Higher Officers' Committee met at MODA, the Ministry of Defense and Aviation. Chaired by the Chief of Staff, General Muhammad al-Hammad, the Committee comprised the heads of the land forces, air force, navy, air defense forces – that is to say myself – and the Director of Officers' Affairs in the armed services. We had received a report the previous night from our military attaché in Baghdad that Iraqi armor was moving towards Kuwait.

To be candid, the mood of the Committee was still remarkably complacent. Saddam's inflammatory speech a few days earlier, on July 17, in which he violently attacked Kuwait and the United Arab Emirates had created considerable unease. But, if the truth be told, no one in the Arab world, or in the West for that matter, imagined that Saddam planned to attack and physically overrun the whole of Kuwait. No one was capable of that mental leap. There is something in the human mind which is attached to the familiar and which resists contemplating wholly new situations, which is no doubt why aggressors and revolutionaries often achieve an element of surprise.

Saddam's saber-rattling was seen as bluff. His heavy-handed tactics were well known. He had extracted a great deal of money from the Gulf states both during and after the Iraq–Iran war, and his latest accusations against Kuwait and the UAE were seen as another exercise in extortion. It was assumed that he would be bought off, and that things would then calm down – until his next cash crisis.

But there were several features of the situation which worried us, and which we debated at that meeting of the Higher Officers' Committee on July 23. Threats were developing all around the Kingdom – from Saddam's Iraq in the north; from Iran in the east (a large number of pilgrims had been killed in a tragic accident at the *hajj* earlier in the year, giving the Iranian media a pretext to attack us more violently than usual); from a harshly aggressive Israel in the northwest which seemed intent on attacking Iraq, with incalculable consequences for the peace of the region; and from Yemen in the south with which we had a border dispute.

We felt that, as a Committee, we should give more thought to the problems of how to confront these threats operationally and strategically. We thought there was a danger that Iraq and Iran might patch up their quarrel and unite in common hostility to us and to our moderate policy on oil prices. It was imperative that we improve our defense planning and devise medium-term strategies to confront these looming threats.

I argued that Saddam was potentially dangerous because he considered himself the victor in the war with Iran; because he saw himself as the next Nasser; because his temperament was overconfident and bellicose – and because he faced grave financial difficulties at home. He had huge armed forces which, following the cease-fire with Iran, no longer had a specific enemy. But he could not demobilize his armies without creating grave unemployment and risking social unrest. He evidently needed to keep his troops busy.

However, before the invasion of Kuwait, I did not think Iraq posed an immediate threat. I predicted that Iraq would emerge as a regional superpower within three to five years, and could then cause us considerable problems. That was the timespan I thought we had in which to prepare.

Our Committee was heartened when on July 24, the day after our meeting, President Mubarak returned to Kuwait from a short visit to Baghdad with assurances from Saddam that his troop movements were only routine maneuvers and that, while being deeply upset with the Kuwaitis, he had no intention of using force. This is what President Mubarak reported to King Fahd.

King Fahd had been working closely with President Mubarak to defuse the crisis with appeals for calm and efforts at mediation behind the scenes. After further consultations with King Fahd, President Mubarak proposed that Iraq and Kuwait hold a meeting of reconciliation in Jeddah under King Fahd's chairmanship. At the same time, I believe Mubarak privately advised the Kuwaitis to be conciliatory. A further move to conciliate Iraq took place at an OPEC meeting in Geneva on July 26–27 when, to ease Saddam's cash problem, it was agreed to raise the price of crude oil by $3 to $21 per barrel.

On July 30 King Hussein of Jordan, who had developed close ties to Iraq during the Iraq–Iran war, flew to Baghdad to see Saddam and then went on to Kuwait to brief the Al Sabah about what he had learned. According to my information, Crown Prince Saad asked him for his reading of Saddam's mood.

King Hussein: "He is very angry with you!"

Shaikh Saad: "But is there a military threat?"

King Hussein: "Oh no!"

Shaikh Saad: "Then why has he massed troops on our frontier?"

King Hussein did not believe the troops were there, to the point that Shaikh Saad offered to take him to the frontier to show him Iraq's advance positions which by then were clearly visible.

(I might add that, after the invasion, the Amir of Kuwait

was upset to read a statement by King Hussein in an American newspaper that he had warned the Kuwaitis about the military threat from Iraq but that the Amir had dismissed it, claiming American protection.)

Suffice it to say that, in that last week of July before the storm, there were enough pledges and assurances from Baghdad, even though accompanied by the usual huffing and puffing, and enough inter-Arab exchanges of the time-honored sort, for most people to believe that the Iraqi–Kuwait dispute was on the way to being resolved. No one anticipated a massive escalation of the crisis. Charles W. Freeman, the American Ambassador to Saudi Arabia, went home on vacation. In Baghdad, the British, French, Russian and Japanese ambassadors also left their posts to go on holiday, while in the United States, as I was later to learn, Secretary of Defense Dick Cheney and General Colin Powell, Chairman of the Joint Chiefs of Staff, were about to take a summer break.

What we then heard of the meeting King Fahd convened in Jeddah on July 31 between Shaikh Saad, Kuwait's Crown Prince, and Izzat Ibrahim, Vice Chairman of Iraq's Revolutionary Command Council, confirmed us in the view that, yet again, the King's wise counsel had managed to defuse a troublesome inter-Arab quarrel.

Contrary to some of the accounts which were subsequently published, the Jeddah meeting on August 1 was no shouting match. There were no explosions of anger. Nothing happened at it to justify or explain the invasion of Kuwait the following night. No doubt, after all the hectic Arab diplomacy of the previous few days, Izzat Ibrahim may have expected the Kuwaitis to be in a docile mood, ready to cancel Iraq's wartime debt, provide fresh subsidies, and sign away the North Rumaila oil field. But the Kuwaitis were not ready to make blanket concessions. They were determined to resist Saddam's underlying assumption that everything they possessed belonged in some sense to Iraq. In any event, when they did not give in immediately, Izzat Ibrahim appears to have lost interest.

After opening the meeting with the usual expression of brotherly greetings, King Fahd had left the two parties to talk alone. They then came to the Palace to report to him, traveling in the same car which flew both the Iraqi and Kuwaiti flags, and took dinner with him. Civilities were maintained. King Fahd placed Shaikh Saad on his right and Izzat Ibrahim on his left. Neither suggested relations had broken down or even that the meeting had ended in stalemate. It was agreed that discussions would resume shortly thereafter in Baghdad. But a few hours later, Saddam invaded.

❖❖❖

Having worked hard to defuse the Iraqi–Kuwaiti quarrel before the invasion, King Fahd and President Mubarak were outraged by Saddam's aggression and took the lead in opposing him. With their encouragement, the Arab League Council condemned Iraq's aggression on August 3, and demanded its immediate and unconditional withdrawal, a position echoed by the GCC Ministerial Council on August 7. As I explained in an earlier chapter, King Fahd was quick to see the threat to the Kingdom and the futility of a so-called "Arab solution." He immediately started to sound out the extent of U.S. and British commitment to the Kingdom's safety which, as I have related, led to Secretary Cheney's visit on August 6 and the arrival of the first American troops less than 48 hours later. Saddam's claim to have been assisted by a "provisional free Kuwait government" confirmed the King in his suspicion that the Iraqi leader would not withdraw until a puppet regime was in place.

President Mubarak, meanwhile, had his own reasons for being angered by Saddam's behavior. He believed that Saddam had lied to him in promising not to use force – and this had put the Egyptian leader in an embarrassing and humiliating position, because he had relayed Saddam's promise to the Kuwaitis, to the Americans, and to ourselves. Iraqi spokesmen tried to argue that Saddam's promise was valid only until the Jeddah meeting, but this was not what Mubarak had understood or what he had told others.

Moreover, Mubarak saw at once that Egyptian interests would be threatened if Iraq were allowed to dominate the Middle East scene. He could not run the risk of Egypt being shut out by Iraq from the Gulf, a region for which Egypt had expressed steady concern during the Iraq–Iran war and to whose protection it had contributed. An axiom taught at Egyptian military academies was that the security of the Gulf was an integral part of the security of Egypt.

But there was an additional reason for Mubarak's outrage. Egypt had made an enormous contribution to Iraq's war effort, sending military advisers, weapons, and some 1.5 million Egyptians, some to work the fields, others in every sector of the economy, freeing Iraqi manpower for the war effort. Saddam had never properly acknowledged this help. Worse still, he had allowed Egyptian workers to be severely ill-treated in Iraq.

In 1989–90, in the immediate run-up to the Gulf crisis, large numbers of Egyptians had been expelled from Iraq without their pay or possessions, and had been forced to make their long way home in very difficult conditions. Others had died in mysterious circumstances, at the hands of unknown Iraqi assailants, and their bodies had been shipped home, causing a great outcry in Egypt. One explanation for these brutalities was that Iraqi soldiers returning from the front were forcibly ejecting Egyptian workers who they thought had taken their jobs. The Iraqi government may have seen some advantage in seeking to stampede Egyptians into leaving.

The ill-treatment of these workers aroused Egyptian opinion against Iraq and made it politically easier for Mubarak to take Egypt into the anti-Saddam Coalition.

Of the three members of the Arab axis, Syria had perhaps the most to fear from a dominant and aggressive Iraq. Saddam was determined to punish his old rival, President Hafiz al-Asad, for siding with Iran during the Iraq–Iran war: there is little doubt that, had Saddam been allowed to digest Kuwait, the Syrian regime would have been an early target. In the year before the invasion of Kuwait, Saddam had already attempted to undermine Syria's position in Lebanon by sending money and arms to Syria's main Lebanese enemies, the Maronite leader General Michel Aoun and Samir Ja'ja's Lebanese Forces. In any event, Asad and Saddam had been engaged in a fight-to-the-finish for almost three decades, ever since a 1966 schism in the B'ath party of which they were both prominent members. So, although it may have caused some surprise in some Western quarters,

Asad's participation in the anti-Saddam Coalition was wholly predictable.

It was very welcome nonetheless, and this for two main reasons: first, because Asad's reputation as a stern Arab nationalist, dedicated to opposing Western and Israeli encroachments into the Arab homeland, helped legitimize the Coalition in the eyes of Arab opinion. Secondly, because Asad's close ties with Iran helped ensure Iranian neutrality during the Gulf crisis. This was particularly valuable when, following an offer by Saddam in mid-August 1990 to settle his conflict with Iran on Iran's terms, we feared that Iran and Iraq might unite against us. In a three-day visit to Tehran, on September 22–25, Asad apparently secured pledges from Iran that Saddam would find no comfort in that direction. When, during the war, Saddam sent much of his air force to safety in Iran, the planes were promptly impounded – and were not returned.

❧⚜❧

In an important speech on August 9, King Fahd described the invasion of Kuwait as "the most horrible aggression the Arab nation has known in its modern history." He outlined the efforts the Saudi Government had made to contain the dispute between Iraq and Kuwait. He reaffirmed the Kingdom's demand for a restoration of the situation before the Iraqi invasion and the return of the Kuwaiti ruling family. He explained the need to call on Arab and friendly forces to help us defend our territory, preserve our vital interests and enhance our military capability, and he stressed that the presence of these forces in the Kingdom would be temporary and that they would depart "immediately when requested to do so." He repeated that the moves he had taken were primarily defensive and not directed against anyone.

Certainly, Saddam's invasion allowed us to recognize our friends, and identify our enemies. Rightly or wrongly, we came to believe that Jordan, the PLO, Yemen and even Sudan had conspired with Saddam to control the Gulf. The reluctance of King Hussein, Chairman Yasser Arafat and President Ali Abdallah Salih to condemn Iraq's aggression aroused our deepest suspicions. Leaders who for years had benefited from Saudi generosity now sided with the aggressor and sought solutions to the crisis which would reward him. With Saddam's armies at the door, it was not far-fetched to fear that King Hussein dreamed of retaking the Hijaz, once ruled by his great-grandfather; that President Ali Abdallah Salih of Yemen dreamed of seizing our border province of Asir; that the Palestinians, present in Kuwait in large numbers, imagined that they might establish there a temporary homeland under Saddam's aegis, pending the recovery of Palestine from the Jews. Did these leaders have foreknowledge of Saddam's plans? Did they hope to benefit from his aggression? Or were they simply so dependent on him as to be unable to denounce him? We do not yet know the answer to these questions with any certainty.

It is rumored that some of Saddam's supporters, including Yasser Arafat himself, may have attempted to persuade the Iraqi leader to withdraw from Kuwait before it was too late. Others might have wanted to have a say in a policy from which all were to suffer, as the following anecdote suggests. I learned later from a reliable source that in early January 1991 Saddam entertained King Hussein, Yasser Arafat and the South Yemen socialist leader Ali Salim al-Bayd at lunch in Baghdad. As they discussed the gathering storm, with the UN deadline of January 15 only days away, Ali Salim al-Bayd had the guts to interject: "War now seems inevitable. But, although we are all in the same boat, you are running the show alone. The situation is so grave that no one person should handle it single handed. I believe we should be consulted at every stage and be allowed to participate in making decisions." The story does not record Saddam's reply.

No doubt the Palestinians believed that Saddam Hussein was strong enough to help them achieve their goals. The "street" in the Arab world, fed by his propaganda and longing for strong leadership, believed in him. He had managed by secret subsidies to influence the mass media in several Arab countries. He had given gifts of Mercedes cars to many top people and funded several political parties across the region. He had supplied weapons to hard-pressed governments in Mauritania, Sudan and Yemen. As a result of the Iraq–Iran war, the Jordanian economy had become heavily dependent on Iraq, and in any event the large Palestinian element in the Jordanian population, perhaps as much as 60 percent of the total, added to the pressures on King Hussein to side with Saddam.

While we understood the despair of the Palestinian people because of the injustices inflicted on them, the position adopted by their leadership during the Kuwait crisis caused us pain and disillusion. It was like a stab in the back, a poor reward for the very considerable help the Kingdom had given the Palestinians in their long struggle against Zionism. When King Abd al-Aziz met President Roosevelt in 1945, Palestine was his major preoccupation, and King Faisal, in his time, was no less concerned, repeatedly expressing his hope to pray at Al-Aqsa mosque in a liberated Jerusalem. King Fahd, in turn, has long campaigned for a just solution of the Palestine problem. As Crown Prince in 1977, he very nearly concluded a deal with President Carter whereby Carter would receive Arafat in the White House if the latter were to recognize Security Council Resolution 242. Arafat was about to agree but then backtracked under pressure from Palestinian "rejectionists," causing Crown Prince Fahd a great deal of embarrassment.

A high point of the King's efforts was the Fahd Plan of August 6, 1981, which a year later, on September 6, 1982, was unanimously endorsed by the Fez Summit of Arab heads of state in Morocco. The plan proposed an Israeli withdrawal to the pre-1967 frontiers; the dismantling of settlements in the occupied territories; the exercise of Palestinian self-determination under PLO leadership by the creation of a state on the West Bank and Gaza with its capital in East Jerusalem; and the right of Palestinian refugees to return home or be compensated. The Fahd Plan, as endorsed at Fez, implicitly recognized Israel's rights in a clause stating that "the Security Council will guarantee peace for all the states of the region."

Such were the principles of Saudi Arabia's Palestine policy when the Palestinian leadership sided with Saddam in his occupation of Kuwait. It seemed to us a colossal political blunder. How could a Palestinian leader condone the occupation of an Arab country when he was himself struggling to liberate his own homeland? In the event, the crisis and its aftermath led to the destruction and dispersal of the prosperous Palestinian community in Kuwait, numbering nearly 400,000 people, and to the isolation and virtual bankruptcy of the PLO. The terms of the Declaration of Principles which the Palestinians signed with Israel in Washington in September 1993 would surely have been substantially better had it not been for the mistakes of their leadership over the occupation of Kuwait.

For us in Saudi Arabia, the Palestinian cause has long been sacrosanct. Robbed of their homeland, forcibly uprooted and expelled, the Palestinians have been cruelly treated by Israel and by its American patron. I am not alone in believing that unless they secure a state of their own, no permanent peace will prevail in our area.

Gravely endangered by Saddam's aggression against Kuwait, we needed to secure a legal and political framework for the military measures we thought might be needed. If it were not immediately reversed, Saddam's move threatened to redraw the Middle East map to our grave disadvantage. Like Egypt, we had recommended flexibility to the Kuwaitis before the invasion, but we could tolerate no flexibility after it. Aggression had to be punished not rewarded, or the whole Arab system would fall to the law of the jungle.

Saudi diplomacy was quick to recognize that the emergency Arab Summit convened in Cairo on August 9, 1990 would be a decisive moment. The great split in the Arab family between those who condemned Saddam and those who excused him – a split which at the time of writing has still not completely healed – came into the open at that Summit, by all accounts one of the most shameful of such occasions because of the crude threats made by Saddam's supporters.

Saudi Arabia, Egypt, Syria and the Gulf states were determined that the Summit approve the dispatch of Arab troops to the Gulf to resist Saddam and also endorse the invitation to the West to come to Saudi Arabia's defense. Iraq and its friends were equally determined to prevent the passage of any such resolution, and resorted to wild personal abuse and threats. In the end, 12 Arab League members voted for the resolution: Bahrain, Djibouti, Egypt, Kuwait, Lebanon, Morocco, Oman, Qatar, Saudi Arabia, Somalia, Syria, and the United Arab Emirates; and only three – Iraq, Libya and the PLO – voted against; Algeria and Yemen abstained; Jordan, Sudan and Mauritania expressed reservations; while Tunisia was absent from the meeting. In our hour of need, we viewed abstentions, reservations and absences as hypocritical fence-sitting which did nothing to relieve our anger and hostility.

⬦⟩⟨⬦

To those of us who watched the Summit proceedings with close attention, because we suspected a conspiracy, it was interesting to note that Taha Yasin Ramadan, Iraq's number three who led the Iraqi delegation, assured us that the annexation of Kuwait – "returning the branch to the root," as he put it – posed no threat to the Kingdom. Iraq had no hostile intentions towards Saudi Arabia, he insisted. To us, these assurances made no sense. By seizing Kuwait, Saddam had already undermined our security, even if he went no further.

Nevertheless, Ramadan's remarks raised another great puzzle about Saddam. Did he ever intend to attack Saudi Arabia? And if he did, why did he not attack in the first month when the Coalition was weak? Why did he allow his enemies to build up their strength without attempting to stop them?

As I related in an earlier chapter, my anxiety in the first few weeks was that he would march into our Eastern Province and that, with the limited forces at my disposal, I would not be able to stop him. The Americans, too, feared that he would use chemical weapons against the lightly armed units of the 82nd Airborne Division which started to arrive in early August. This could have caused panic and paralysis – and heavy Coalition casualties – and might have undermined support in the United States for the American intervention. On August 15, in a move which took the world by surprise, Saddam suddenly offered peace to Iran: he agreed to all Iran's conditions; he was ready to pull back Iraqi forces from Iranian territory by the very next day; to release Iranian POWs; and to be bound by the terms of the 1975 Algiers Agreement which he had torn up at the start of the Iraq–Iran conflict. At a stroke, he seemed to declare vain and utterly pointless the eight-year war he had waged against Iran and the immense suffering and material loss it had inflicted on both countries. When there was clear evidence that he was

switching troops from the Iranian frontier to our front, I thought
an attack could be coming.

But, in fact, by early September, it became evident that, whatever had been Saddam's intentions, he could no longer realistically contemplate an attack on Saudi Arabia. Whether he had
ever intended to do so remains an open question. In April 1989,
King Fahd had visited Baghdad on Saddam's invitation. The Iraqi
leader had then said that his whole nation wished to express its
gratitude and appreciation to the Kingdom for its support during
the Iraq–Iran war. The two leaders had driven through the
streets in an open car to the acclamation of the crowd. On that
visit, Saddam had asked the King to sign a nonaggression pact
– "to show the world there is nothing between us," he had
explained. Saddam then signed a similar pact with Bahrain, but
he had shown no inclination to do so with Kuwait which he
evidently considered a special case.

A short while after the signature of the pact – and just two
months before the invasion of Kuwait – Saddam paid King Fahd
a friendly return visit to Hafr al-Batin. And when, on August 18,
I myself visited Hafr al-Batin on my field trip after the invasion, I
learned that pictures of Saddam had been taken down only that
very morning from the walls of the Officers' Club!

In the days immediately after the invasion, I was struck by
the behavior of Iraqi troops whenever they strayed into the old
"neutral zone" south of Kuwait. If they crossed into an area
which they thought might be ours, they would immediately
withdraw with apologies. They were obviously under orders not
to encroach on Saudi territory, even by one inch. Prince
Muhammad bin Fahd, Governor of the Eastern Province, also
reported that in the first four days after the invasion, the Iraqis
treated Saudis in Kuwait with great respect. Anyone with a
Saudi passport was waved through, to the extent that cars with
Saudi number plates were sent into occupied Kuwait to rescue
relatives of Kuwaitis who had already fled to the Kingdom.

Reflecting later on this good treatment of Saudis, I came to
the conclusion that Saddam probably hoped to digest Kuwait
without having to defend his conquest or proceed further.
He may have calculated that an attack on Saudi Arabia would
have posed formidable problems of logistics, that it would

undoubtedly trigger a Western armed response, and that it was in any event unnecessary, seeing that he could dominate the whole region, Saudi Arabia included, simply by holding Kuwait. He may also have been deterred from an armed attack on the Kingdom by the fear that this might turn the whole Muslim world against him.

If this analysis is correct, then Saddam was thrown off balance by the swift, vigorous and unexpected reaction of the international community to his invasion. By mid-September, over 100,000 American troops had arrived in the Kingdom. Saddam had, in any event, lost the initiative from the moment his forces began to dig in and take up defensive positions in Kuwait. With hindsight, it may be seen that he never regained the initiative. In the months between the August 1990 invasion and the war in January 1991, months during which the Coalition built up its strength and when he could have withdrawn to save himself and his country, he just sat tight as if robbed of the will to act.

This raises the question of the extent to which there was agreement among the allies about war aims. President Bush and Secretary Baker faced some criticism, I recall, from American and European commentators for declaring different war aims at different times. Was the prime object to defend Saudi Arabia? Or to undo the annexation of Kuwait? Or to guarantee Western access to Middle East oil? Or to protect American jobs? Or to destroy Saddam's war machine, especially his nuclear, biological and chemical capability? Or was it simply to punish an aggressor and uphold the authority of the United Nations? The fact that all these were advanced at one time or another led to charges of muddle, and even of lack of candor.

In defining their aims, President Bush and his colleagues had no doubt to provide reasons which the American public would accept and approve, and this may have led to some doctoring of the issues. But there was another factor, little understood by the public at the time, which was the Coalition's deception plan. This had two distinct aspects: the first was to keep Saddam guessing about our ultimate intentions, and this meant never stating clearly what our intentions were; the second was to exaggerate his strength in our public statements so as to lull him into a sense of false security. Hence the much-publicized slogan that we were taking on the world's "fourth largest army," which Secretary Cheney described as a "war-hardened" force of 1,500,000 men, 5,000 tanks and 1,000 aircraft. Among the military leaders of the Coalition, not all believed these inflated figures or were impressed by Iraq's fighting ability. It was largely a ruse of war.

But, equally, no one at that stage thought that victory over Iraq would prove so easy to achieve. There was always the fear that Saddam might, if driven to the wall, use chemical weapons and inflict large numbers of casualties, or that his air force might use kamikaze tactics against big targets like oil refineries or allied warships. Saddam was thought of as a dangerously unpredictable enemy who might spring an unpleasant surprise on the Coalition.

At the start, when the Coalition was weak and feared an Iraqi thrust into the Eastern Province, it was only sensible to say that our war aim was solely to defend the Kingdom. The line then was that the task of forcing Saddam out of Kuwait could be left to economic sanctions. We did not even say we would go into Kuwait. Then, from October onwards, when the Coalition was very much stronger and when he showed no sign of budging, our language became more aggressive: a clear indication was given that Kuwait would be liberated by force if necessary. But there was still no suggestion that this would involve attacking Iraq itself. This occurred later still, once the Coalition had been reinforced.

At the start at least, our Arab perspective was somewhat different from that of our American allies. We had no quarrel with the Iraqi people. They are our brothers, and it was with a heavy heart that we contemplated having to fight them. We never envisaged that Arab forces would fight inside Iraq. As the King had stated, our war aim was to force Saddam to withdraw within his borders so as to restore the rule of the legitimate government in Kuwait and remove the threat to the Kingdom's security. Immense efforts were deployed by the Arab League, by the Islamic Conference Organization, by the United Nations, by the

French and by the Soviets, by individual Arab leaders and numerous would-be Western mediators to persuade Saddam to withdraw peacefully, so that an offensive against him would not be necessary. But he refused.

As Saddam continued to threaten us, so our own attitude hardened. We had eventually to recognize that sanctions alone, and the pleas of the international community, would not bring him to his senses. Having designated Kuwait Iraq's 19th province on August 28, he went on to proclaim a *jihad* against us, calling for the overthrow of the Saudi monarchy, and threatening to destroy Kuwaiti and Saudi oil fields if sanctions against him were not lifted. The result of his threats and of his inflexibility was to cause us to align our war aims on those of our Western allies.

Regretfully, we came to see that Saddam would pose a long-term threat to us if his war machine emerged intact from the crisis. And once we had reached that conclusion, we had no alternative but to contemplate and prepare for war.

CHAPTER XIII

The Parallel Command

WHEN GENERAL H. NORMAN SCHWARZKOPF arrived in Saudi Arabia on August 26, 1990, I went to meet his plane and welcome him to the Kingdom. He had come to take command of the American forces then pouring in by air and sea. Breathing self-confidence, vigor and friendliness, Schwarzkopf looked and behaved like a commander. As I myself believe in doing things in style, I was impressed.

This was the man who was to be my closest associate for the next seven months. From the moment we met, we were both aware that the success of our relationship would to a large extent determine the success of the great mission we had been given: to defend Saudi Arabia, drive Saddam out of Kuwait, restore its legitimate government, and remove Iraq's threat to the Gulf. We represented the working end of the Saudi–American alliance which our political masters, King Fahd and President Bush, had forged. We knew we had to get on, and this provided the motivation for what was to be an effective partnership. If we were to quarrel, the alliance would suffer.

In late August, the threat of an Iraqi strike into our Eastern Province was still real, if not as acute as it had been early in the month. When, on August 28, I took Schwarzkopf to call on Prince Sultan in Jeddah, the American commander was reassuring:

"If Saddam attacks," he told Prince Sultan, "I promise you he will suffer the greatest losses in the history of warfare." Prince Sultan gave him a sad look and said, "That is not what I want to see. I have no wish to damage Iraq. But if Saddam persists in being stubborn, if he persists in being a disgrace to Islam" – that is the phrase he used — "then we will do everything in our power to stop him."

Hearing my father's humane words, I reflected that this was a statement of our basic dilemma: we needed American help to check Saddam, but we profoundly regretted having to take up arms against an Arab state. It was a dilemma not easily understood by our Western allies, still less by the Western media which were busy demonizing Iraq and its leader. Until the very end, there was a strong current on the Arab side of the Coalition that hoped and prayed Saddam would come to his senses, abandon his aggressive designs, save his country from destruction, and take his place once more in a reconstituted Arab system. But unfortunately, owing to the poor judgment and false pride of one man, it was not to be. I believe that, in that meeting with the American general who personified U.S. military power, my father had a sense of the tragedy that was to come. The decision to call for American help had not been an easy one.

After our meeting in Jeddah with Prince Sultan, Schwarzkopf and I flew back to Riyadh in my plane. I felt drained and wanted an hour to myself to collect my thoughts. My father's words about Saddam — "If he persists in being a disgrace to Islam" — were still ringing in my ears. I was too preoccupied to talk to Schwarzkopf, but how to keep him busy during the flight without seeming to ignore him? As it happened, someone had given me a tape of President Mubarak's latest speech about the crisis. Believing that Schwarzkopf might find it of interest, I asked my ADC, Colonel Ahmad Lafi, to translate it for him, sentence by sentence. They huddled together at one end of the plane for over an hour but, as they played the tape, I could tell from Schwarzkopf's face that he was not exactly overjoyed.

Even before he arrived, I already knew a good deal about General Schwarzkopf. He was a graduate of West Point, a military academy quite as tough as Sandhurst; he was a much decorated infantryman who had served twice in Vietnam; he had commanded a division and filled a top job at the Pentagon. For the previous eighteen months, since November 1988, he had headed the U.S. Central Command (CENTCOM) which, from its base at the MacDill Air Base near Tampa, Florida, was the expression of American readiness to defend its interests in the Gulf, if necessary by force.

Although Schwarzkopf was as charming as could be, I had been told he could be stubborn, and that his temper was sometimes explosive. His reputation for wanting his own way, and usually getting it, had preceded him. Among his own people, he was known as "The Bear." I had myself enough of the same characteristics not to be intimidated. I was soon to discover that we were alike in several other ways. We were both proud, prickly and somewhat domineering, but we were also – if the truth be told – more emotional and soft hearted than our appearance suggested. Physically, we were both over six feet tall, both heavily built, both left-handed. But he was 56 and I was only 42. He was a four-star general, I was only a three-star. He could draw on the resources of a great military establishment, while mine was still an embryo organization. He had experience of wars, while this was my first. I knew I would have to make a tremendous effort to establish a command which was parallel to his. There was one thing I had which he could not acquire: my princely title, and the prerogatives which went with it. I determined to play it for all it was worth.

Working in parallel, Schwarzkopf and I were often in close and instant agreement. Sometimes, however, we disagreed significantly, and at other times we were obliged to negotiate with each other to reach a compromise. He was not an easy man to deal with, but neither was I. We had our occasional disputes, although on most occasions they were quickly resolved. Once we got to know each other, we became friends and gave each other a good deal of warmth and support. No doubt on both sides was the realization that this would help us accomplish our respective missions. In the end, I felt we respected and liked each other, and enjoyed each other's company. Our relationship went beyond the needs of the job. He must sometimes have wished he had opposite him someone he could dominate. But as he got to know my personality, I believe he came to see that it was greatly to his advantage to have as co-commander someone with the authority to facilitate his mission in a thousand ways. To do his job, he needed the Kingdom to be strong and supportive, and that was my role.

I am, of course, aware that there may be considerable variance in our separate recollections of some of the events and incidents treated in this book. My object is to put the record straight as I saw it.

Right from the very beginning, on the first day we met, I politely suggested to Schwarzkopf that his staff get in touch with mine to arrange our future meetings. At the same time, I instructed my adjutant that my appointments with Schwarzkopf must always take place in my office: it was a nonnegotiable item. By insisting that he come to me, I was sending a signal about our parallel commands. If I went to his office, everyone would suppose I was under his command. But if he came to my office, no one would suppose for one moment that he was under my command. So it had to be that way around.

My brother Bandar, who as our Ambassador in Washington is a key player in the management of the Saudi–American relationship, called on me at my office at about this time. We reviewed the unfolding Gulf crisis together and our relations with the United States.

"Khaled," he then suggested, "why don't you have one meeting with Schwarzkopf in your office and the next meeting in his office?"

"Never!" I replied. "It has to be my office. Please don't interfere."

In his diplomatic way Bandar was trying to be helpful, but I wondered whether it was his idea or whether the Americans had asked him to mediate. I was grateful, however, to have a brother in such a sensitive position. I knew he understood my preoccupations. We had shared many experiences. We had, for example, been in England at the same time – he was at Cranwell learning to fly when I was at Sandhurst.

And so that was how the routine was established: throughout the crisis, Schwarzkopf came to my office every day at 4 p.m. for a meeting lasting between 45 minutes and one hour to review our war preparations and sort out problems as they came up. As we talked, we would often munch homemade Saudi cookies – kindly supplied by my aunt, Princess Nauf bint Abd al-Aziz – and sip Diet Coke, a small gesture towards our shared tendency to being overweight. When we had an outstanding problem to discuss, we would sometimes meet again around 11 p.m. for another chat and for a cup of what he called my "famous cappuccino" – an extra-strong brew calculated to keep one awake for an extra hour or two.

⁂

I should perhaps add a word of explanation here about the notion of a "parallel command." It did not, and could not, mean that my command and Schwarzkopf's were equivalent: there was no equivalence in the men, resources and equipment available to each of us. In view of its overwhelming military contribution to the Coalition, there was little doubt that the United States had to make the ultimate command decisions. Schwarzkopf's land forces were eventually three times as large as the forces under my command. In the air, the relative strength was at least of the order of five to one. At sea, U.S. power dwarfed that of the allies. Such was the unpromising background to the proposed structure of a parallel command. In American military history, there are few if any examples of such a parallel command being established. In World War Two, for example, or in Korea and Vietnam, there was always an American Supreme Commander. America's allies had their own commanders, some of great distinction, but they never equaled the status of the American supremo. Not so in the Gulf conflict.

In the early weeks, when our respective responsibilities were still being defined, there was a good deal of speculation in the international press about the question of command and control. The media wanted to know who was giving the orders. Evidently, the notion of a parallel command took some time to sink in. This was understandable because it was, after all, a unique arrangement. American troops could not serve under Saudi command; equally, Saudi troops – and other Arab forces, for that matter – could not serve under American command. A novel formula was required. The idea of a parallel command was sufficiently flexible to accommodate these difficulties. When asked about the command problem, I remember telling Georgie Anne Geyer of Universal Press Syndicate in early October that "the only two people who are not worried about it are General Schwarzkopf and me."

In endorsing the formula of a parallel command, I was not seeking to compete with Schwarzkopf or downgrade his importance. I knew well enough that having put some 550,000 servicemen and women into the theater, the United States was going to command these troops come what may. The Americans' preponderance was such that they swamped the Saudis, swamped the British, swamped the French and everybody else. In planning and running the war, Schwarzkopf – and General Colin Powell back in Washington – were going to have the prime roles. But I wanted Schwarzkopf to understand that it was necessary to assure Saudi and Arab opinion that we were exercising control over these Westerners arriving in the heart of Islam. Without such Saudi control, it would have been seen as an invasion by stealth, an occupation by the backdoor, an overturning of our most cherished values. Hence the need for people to see that I was up there with the American commander in a parallel command.

The "parallel command" structure defined relations between myself, as Joint Forces Commander, and Schwarzkopf as the commander of U.S. forces. For our partnership to be effective, we had to work closely together on a daily basis, but my powers were restricted to the area of responsibility of the Joint Forces Command inside Saudi Arabia. I had nothing to do with CENTCOM's wider responsibilities in the region, or indeed with the responsibilities it assumed in Iraq in the course of the war itself.

I was the principal point of contact between our Saudi national command authority and the incoming Arab and other friendly forces, including those of the United States. As such, I had to pay special attention to four areas of responsibility.

First, my main task was military, as in the early weeks of August 1990 my troops were the only ones in the field confronting Iraq. The American troops were busy disembarking from their ships and planes and moving to defensive positions almost 75 miles to the rear. We considered them the second defensive belt. At that stage, the only military assistance we anticipated receiving from the Americans was close air support.

Before the arrival of CENTCOM HQ, I was keenly aware of the danger of an imminent Iraqi attack and of my role as the principal military commander on the scene. Everything we had was up at the front facing the Iraqis. And that pattern was to endure. In the various defense plans, amended and refined with the passage of time, Saudi units, supported by Egyptian and Syrian forces and others, always manned the front line, with American units well to the rear.

When we faced the greatest danger from Saddam in those first three weeks of August, Schwarzkopf was not yet in the Kingdom. He arrived only at the end of August. A couple of weeks later, by mid-September, the threat of an Iraqi attack was rapidly fading, as was evident from Saddam's deployments. His posture had become defensive not offensive. Suicidally, he was digging in, in Kuwait.

In the first phase of the crisis, we in Saudi Arabia planned our own defense on the basis of the Saudi forces available, soon reinforced by Egyptian, Syrian and Moroccan contingents. Then, when American, British and other friendly forces started to arrive, we planned Desert Shield together. The concept of operations, the employment of forces, the areas of responsibility of the various national contingents, the rules of engagement, the training schedules and a host of other issues were all mutually agreed on. I was eventually to command 25 of the national contingents which came to our aid, while Schwarzkopf commanded a dozen. Militarily, my contingents, totaling about 200,000 men, were by no means as weighty as Schwarzkopf's, but this did not make them any easier to manage. I had the authority to deploy these troops, assign missions and take all other necessary military decisions within the framework of mutually agreed military plans, first for Desert Shield and then for Desert Storm.

When it came to planning Desert Storm, our contribution was essentially focused on the liberation of Kuwait, which was our primary war aim, although we were also able to vet the overall war plan and we did in fact make numerous changes to ensure its compatibility with our aims and resources. A possibility the joint planning group had to face was that Saddam might suddenly withdraw unconditionally from Kuwait before the start of the war. We played a major role in planning which vital locations and installations in Kuwait – such as airports, refineries and desalination plants – would have to be immediately secured and protected by our forces, before they were handed over to the Kuwaiti authorities, and what internal security measures would need to be taken.

If my prime task was military, my second area of responsibility was to cater for the local logistical needs of all the members of the Coalition – from serving hot hamburgers to friendly forces as they stepped off the plane to scouring the world for 10,000 heavy duty trucks, to equipping completely some of the smaller national contingents that arrived with hardly more than the clothes they had on.

Providing logistical support to our allies, as well as to my own forces, was indeed to be one of my major headaches in the first months of the crisis. This crucial area, in which we as the host nation played a central and predominant role, kept my Joint Forces Command extremely busy. Fearing a preemptive Iraqi attack on our ports and airfields at Jubail and Dhahran, Schwarz-kopf had concentrated on rushing in combat units like the 82nd Airborne Division and the 24th Mechanized Infantry Division. As a result, their own support units were held back – which meant that from the moment they arrived we had to supply them with food, water, accommodations and a great deal else. Deciding who should have priority was not always easy.

In these matters, my function was to solve problems as they arose – by intervening with the right authorities to speed up the decision-making process, by cutting through bureaucratic tangles, by issuing instructions myself. To do the job, I required and was given considerable authority as well as cooperation from several key ministries and government agencies. Of course, it took a little while for me to persuade everyone that I intended to exercise to the full the powers I had been given. But when the message sank in, people started to be truly responsive. I was then able to pick up the phone and make things happen – to the great relief and benefit of our Coalition partners. I will give a brief account in a later chapter of some of the engrossing logistical problems we faced.

My third task was to ensure the smooth political working of

the Coalition, as this was reflected in relations between the various national contingents present in Saudi Arabia. Let me be clear: my task was not to construct the political edifice of the Coalition. That was done at a higher level by the King, President Bush, and the respective national leaders. My task was to accommodate on the ground whatever political decisions these leaders made. Because of the large number of countries involved, politics were more important in this war than in any war since World War Two, and this applied particularly to the Arab members of the Coalition but also, as will be seen, to France.

Finally, to sum up my role, in addition to my specifically military command responsibilities, my special duty was to protect the sovereignty of the Kingdom, as well as our religion, culture and traditions, from any infringement by the forces which came to our aid. I was responsible to our leaders and to Saudi Arabia to see that it all came out right in the end. Therefore I had to make sure that Schwarzkopf understood the constraints within which I was working. If I had not exercised the greatest vigilance over what he and his troops did, if I had not stamped immediately on infringements, the whole relationship between Saudi Arabia and the United States – and between Saudi Arabia and Britain and France, for that matter – would have broken down because of pressures from within. I had enough direct experience of Westerners – and of Western armies – to be sympathetic to their needs and to the way they conducted their lives. But I had to lay down boundaries inspired by our faith and our traditions – "red lines," if you will – to preserve the integrity of the country.

❖⟫⟪❖

In early September, I discussed with Schwarzkopf how to perfect the hasty defense plan which I had put together with Lieutenant General Yeosock immediately after the invasion, before Schwarzkopf himself had arrived. Now, with more troops available and the danger of an Iraqi attack fading, this defense plan needed improving and developing into Desert Shield. I was anxious to draw Schwarzkopf and his staff into planning our defense, because I knew the Americans would soon start planning an offensive and I wanted to have a say in it. In any event, we made a considerable contribution.

In the same spirit, I also insisted on joint exercises with American forces. Schwarzkopf was preparing his troops for battle, and I wanted my forces to benefit from training as well. My staff were hesitant because we had never taken part in joint exercises with the United States, but I felt it was an opportunity not to be missed. In fact, I wanted to start the joint exercises not at platoon or company level but at battalion and brigade level.

The problem was that my Saudi forces, and most of the other forces under my command, had not had any experience of close air support. I felt the exercises should be as close to combat conditions as possible with real missiles and real bombs. I wanted my people to get used to the terrible sound of battle. But for exercises to be realistic, the possibility of incurring casualties had to be faced. I told Schwarzkopf that I was prepared to accept a small percentage risk that there might be casualties. But Schwarzkopf insisted on 100 percent safety procedures. He was anxious to avoid the hostile publicity which any casualties, on his side or ours, would attract, and he was probably right. Eventually, to reduce the risks and yet maintain combat realism, we agreed on a simple plan. U.S. air controllers would work with my units and the pilots were told to drop their bombs 300 to 400 yards from the front line of our forces. The exercises took place and went off beautifully

I then put a question to Schwarzkopf which surprised him.

"Why don't we announce our joint planning and joint exercises to the media?"

He looked at me and said, "You are sensitive about such matters. I am not."

"I'm not sensitive about it any longer," I replied. As I have said, I recognized the benefits of joint training with experienced American units and indeed welcomed such exercises.

Greater candor about our defense relationship with the United States was one of the inevitable consequences of the Gulf crisis. It was true that, unwilling to upset Arab opinion which was deeply resentful of America's close relationship with Israel, we had always been careful about seeming too closely involved with the U.S. in defense matters. However, leading American defense contractors and the U.S. Army Corps of Engineers had played a prime role in building our defense infrastructure. And, in the final stages of the Iraq–Iran war, in particular during the crisis over the reflagging of Kuwaiti tankers, when they were placed under U.S. flags to defend them from Iranian attack, our defense planning with the U.S. had grown closer. But, in spite of welcoming large numbers of American military advisers and technicians to the Kingdom, our official posture was still to keep American military power at arm's length – and preferably ''over the horizon.''

Now, with half a million American troops flooding into the Kingdom, this posture was no longer credible or tenable.

❖

Shortly after Schwarzkopf arrived with his CENTCOM headquarters staff, we discussed where to deploy the various American units as they arrived in the Kingdom. Strategic considerations were uppermost in our minds, but also the need to house, feed and otherwise support the troops. In the course of our discussion, Schwarzkopf casually mentioned that he would like to post an American brigade in Riyadh itself to deal with any problem he might encounter there.

My immediate thought was that Schwarzkopf was catering to a ''worst case'' scenario – that the brigade would be there to protect his command in the event of an internal disturbance. I reflected that it was only natural that he should feel insecure. Finding himself in a strange foreign country, he could not have the same sense of confidence that I had. I knew my people, he did not. But my second thought was that, if I were in his shoes, I would do the same. I too might need the comfort of a brigade close at hand in what was an uncertain situation, with Saddam's armies only a few days' march away. But my third thought was that, if Schwarzkopf insisted on having his brigade, I would have to find a way to conceal it. I was not going to allow his combat troops to become a highly visible presence in our capital city.

To gain a little time for reflection, I told Schwarzkopf we could discuss the matter further at our meeting the following day. Turning the problem over in my mind, I suddenly remembered that the late King Khaled used to have a farm, called al-Thamama, about 45 miles from Riyadh, which had since been turned into a public recreation area. There were several buildings on the farm and a small airstrip. It seemed the perfect location for Schwarzkopf's "fire brigade." His men would be a mere half hour away by road, but out of sight nevertheless. I put the proposal to Schwarzkopf and he readily agreed. His brigade sat there in considerable comfort for the duration of the crisis until the time came for it to fly home, not having fired a shot.

I was perhaps oversensitive in protecting my command from any semblance of American interference. I remember that on one occasion I received a call to say that Schwarzkopf was going north to inspect troops at Hafr al-Batin. This came as a surprise: the only American troops there were some helicopter crews and an intelligence unit. He was perfectly entitled to visit them if he wished. But then I heard he was going to visit the 10th Brigade, one of mine. I got mad. I had not been informed.

I instructed my staff to tell his staff that he could not inspect my troops. My staff came back with an assurance that Schwarzkopf had not initiated anything. What had happened was that, hearing that Schwarzkopf was coming to Hafr al-Batin, the Saudi area commander had called his office to invite him to lunch at Brigade headquarters and to visit some units in the field. He had done no more than apply the normal military courtesies towards an important guest. If it had been anyone else, or even him under normal circumstances, I would not have minded – but not Schwarzkopf at that time. Allowing him to inspect my troops would have signaled that he was the supreme commander, and that I could not accept.

"Get the area commander on the phone now!" I ordered.

When he came on the line I berated him.

"What can I do?" he asked.

"Cancel the visit to the troops. Let him visit his own forces. Give a lunch for him in the Officers' Club, and that's it."

I added, however, that if Schwarzkopf wanted to go up to the Kuwaiti border – as visitors to that area tended to do – then someone should escort him.

Schwarzkopf came to see me that evening. He was anxious to explain that he had had no intention of encroaching on my command. But he also had an interesting experience to relate. "I can't go to bed without telling you this story," he said. After lunch with the area commander, he had gone up to the border to view the sand berms which he had not seen before. He had called in at one of our coast guard posts.

"Look over there, General," the lieutenant in charge had said to him. "That truck is Iraqi!"

"Where?" Schwarzkopf exclaimed, scanning the distant horizon.

"Just there, in our post," the lieutenant said, pointing to a vehicle not ten yards away. Three hungry Iraqi soldiers had come in for a meal.

The American commander was taken aback. Seeing the enemy at such close quarters was a bit of a shock. I told Schwarzkopf that I had encouraged my people to maintain contact with Iraqi border troops. I wanted them to come to our posts and see the food my men were eating. I wanted them to fraternize. They were, after all, our brothers. I even told my men to send them back to their lines with a box of fruit or some other gift. I knew it would damage their morale and weaken their resolve to fight.

It was not until October 20 that, on Schwarzkopf's invitation, I paid my first visit to American troops in the field. He wished to show me the degree of combat readiness they had achieved. We met in Dhahran for a briefing by the commander of XVIIIth Corps. Accompanied by Schwarzkopf and the Corps commander, I then flew north for over an hour in a Black Hawk helicopter to the headquarters of the 24th Mechanized Infantry Division. I had a special feeling for this division. With its M1 tanks and Bradley fighting vehicles, it had been one of the first U.S. heavy units to arrive at Dammam in mid-September after a voyage from Savannah, Georgia, by fast sealift ship. We had had to support it for a while pending the arrival of its own supply units. Trained in desert warfare, it was a key unit in Schwarzkopf's mobile defense plan, able to block any Iraqi attack on the Tapline road, or to attack into the flank of any Iraqi advance down the east coast.

When the time came for me and my accompanying staff to perform the noon prayers, I was touched to notice that the division had prepared a place for us to make our ablutions and pray. A soldier was there with a jug of water.

❖

However close two allies might be, there is always a certain jockeying for advantage and always, in my experience, a measure of information which each side keeps to itself. With hindsight, I would say that most of my battles with Schwarzkopf were ultimately about securing information, about getting him to share what he knew. The Americans told us what they thought it was necessary for us to know, and little more than that. I did not entirely blame them, although I would have liked them to share more. I did not expect Schwarzkopf to reveal his sources, but I needed to assess the whole military intelligence picture in order to draw up my own plans and take my own military decisions. To command the Joint Forces, I demanded information. The view I took was that the Americans should either give us accurate information or no information at all. I did not want to be fobbed off with generalities.

In November, a couple of months before the war, I learned at my eight o'clock nightly briefing by my own staff that the Americans were planning an air exercise the following morning with fully armed planes. I had not been informed. I checked to make sure that our Air Force Commander had not given them clearance. It was obvious that the Americans had planned the exercise without informing the Saudi authorities. Doubts were aroused in my mind. Was this being done to test me? Were the Americans planning to attack Iraq without giving us prior notice? I had issued a directive that no one could carry out a major exercise without informing me. This seemed a clear infringement of my directive.

I decided to preempt. I issued an order banning all armed flights on the morrow. I then talked to Schwarzkopf and he cancelled the exercise. He may not have appreciated how important it was for me to know. The next day the U.S. Air Force explained that it had merely wanted to test takeoff and landing procedures for fully armed aircraft. A few days later my permission was requested and was granted. The incident delayed the exercise by five days – but an important point had been made.

On the subject of intelligence sources, I was struck by the fact that in their intelligence-gathering the Americans depended overwhelmingly on technology – satellite surveillance, radio intercepts and so forth – and very little on human sources. This was a strength and a weakness. I was sitting with Schwarzkopf one evening when he gave me a report of what Saddam had said at a meeting with his top commanders.

"Are you sure these are Saddam's words?" I asked. "How do you know? What is your source?"

"If Saddam utters a word, we know about it," Schwarzkopf replied with an air of mystery.

Was he trying to impress me or was the U.S. really able to keep Saddam under surveillance? I pondered the question for over an hour. I recalled that, for all their electronic wizardry, the Americans had apparently been unable to foresee Saddam's invasion of Kuwait. They could, if Schwarzkopf was to be believed, monitor his communications and watch his every move by satellite, but they did not have a human source in his inner circle to warn them of his intentions. Of course, nor did anyone else. All of us – Arabs and Westerners alike – had to take responsibility for that intelligence failure.

When I took over my command, one of my main concerns was to ensure that it embraced everything on the Saudi side: I wanted cooperation from every relevant ministry and government agency, including our General Intelligence Directorate. In this I discovered I was somewhat better off than Schwarzkopf, because I soon realized that the CIA was not entirely at his disposal.

At one point the CIA asked its Saudi opposite number, the General Intelligence Directorate, for permission to fly two spy planes from two of our air bases. The request was passed to Prince Sultan, who asked me for my views. He also asked me to check with Schwarzkopf. To my surprise, Schwarzkopf had no prior knowledge of the request. It seemed that his relations with the CIA were far from harmonious. There was evidently no love lost between them.

In fact, I got the strong feeling that Schwarzkopf was happy

I was in full coordination with our intelligence because, in this way, he could hope to learn through me what his spooks were up to! I am not suggesting that the CIA gave Schwarzkopf no information. Simply that from time to time, I was able to fill a gap. In any event, I told him that I would keep him informed of anything I learned, and Prince Sultan also assured me that nothing would be done except through the Joint Forces Command. In war you cannot have people playing around without the commander knowing what is going on. Schwarzkopf himself was fond of saying that we had to be careful not to repeat the mistakes of Vietnam, bedeviled as that war had been by independent agencies, politicians interfering in military matters and gross American insensitivity to local conditions.

In due course, the two spy planes the CIA had requested flew in. Schwarzkopf raised no objection and I gave my approval. We based one at Jubail and the other at Taif. Many more were to follow, but always after full consultation with all concerned.

❖⟩⟨❖

Never in my military career had I bothered much about personal security. In Riyadh I drove my own car and, when I traveled outside the city, I usually took one or at most two guards with me. But the fear of Iraqi-inspired terrorism heightened the sense of vulnerability. Schwarzkopf surrounded himself with a great deal of very visible security – a posse of soldiers and plain-clothesmen accompanied him everywhere, guns at the ready. And when he moved outside the Ministry of Defense, it was in a convoy of cars packed with sharpshooters. I felt obliged to do the same. If a Saudi on the street saw Schwarzkopf's armed escort and then saw me with just one or two guards, he would immediately conclude that Schwarzkopf was the supreme commander. That I could not allow. My public appearance as the Saudi commander had to be as impressive as his, down to the smallest detail. If he had men with guns, I had to have men with guns. So I formed a bodyguard to match Schwarzkopf's, and even sent a few men abroad for training. In copying him I was making a political not a security point. I had full confidence in our internal security. What I was actually doing was fighting for the image of the Kingdom.

When people saw my elaborate armed escort, they thought I was showing off. Working, eating and sleeping at the Defense Ministry, I was hardly in danger of attack. "My God!" people said, including some on my own staff, "What does he need ten men for – five in front and five in the rear, all carrying machine guns – when he goes from his office down to the Operations Room?" I did it because it was important for everyone, including allied officers and representatives of the media, to see that I was a commander of the same status as Schwarzkopf.

When he first established his headquarters at the Ministry of Defense, his staff wanted to post an American guard at every point in the building – outside, inside, in the elevators, everywhere. This was the message brought to me by Colonel Turki bin Abdallah, the commander of the military police battalion guarding the building. I gathered that the Americans were obsessed with the fear that Iraqi special forces might mount an attack on our headquarters and slaughter us all! I told Colonel Turki to go back with the message that an overprominent American presence was perhaps not the best way to ensure security. "We are not an occupied country!" I told him. We knew how to defend ourselves while keeping a low profile. However, to allay Schwarzkopf's fears, I agreed to reinforce the Saudi guards around the building and at all entrances. The one concession I was prepared to make was to allow the Americans to post one of their men at a back gate, so that he could recognize their vehicles as they approached.

In the War Room, a vast split-level complex known as "The Bunker," five floors below ground level in the Ministry basement, I insisted on joint teams of Saudi and American guards to underline the fact that it was a joint command. I used to laugh sometimes at how overprotected we were. Every twenty yards, there seemed to be six guards – three Saudis and three Americans. But even in such petty matters it was necessary to keep our end up.

I considered Schwarzkopf's safety my personal responsibility and assigned a military police platoon under Lieutenant Thamir al-Sabhan to look after him. But of course, Schwarzkopf had his own American guards as well protecting his bedroom and suite of offices. One morning, the commander of my military police battalion reported to me that Schwarzkopf had got up in the middle of the night, between 2 and 3 a.m., to check his guards and found them all snoring. He had raised hell. I never told Schwarzkopf that I knew about it. But, for the next night or two, I could not resist sneaking up in the early hours to see if my own guards were awake. They were.

Schwarzkopf's small, somewhat Spartan bedroom was next door to his office on the fourth floor of the Ministry. Believing that he might need something grander, I looked around for a suitable house for him. It so happened that one of our best guest villas was under my direct control. It was situated in the compound of the Saudi Officers' Club, and I had used it to put up visiting Chinese officers in connection with our strategic missile forces. I knew the villa was secure because I had personally seen to its defenses over the previous three years. Overcoming resistance from members of the Saudi high command, who wanted to reserve it for the many important visitors we expected, I allocated the villa to Schwarzkopf.

Despite my efforts, however, I do not think he spent more than a few nights there throughout the crisis, preferring to make do with his bedroom at headquarters just a step away from his office. Pressure of work, and the need to report every night by telephone to his superiors in Washington, were to give him little time to enjoy the more spacious accommodation of the villa.

As for me, at the start of the air campaign I moved from the fourth floor of the Ministry of Defense, where I had been living for several months, into a small bedroom in the basement close to the War Room. It was furnished with a narrow bed, a bank of telephones, a television set and video, and a shower cubicle in one corner. On the walls of this tiny room, I pinned up pictures by my children, crude drawings of tanks and guns. As my children blamed the Iraqi leader for keeping their father away from home, one of the pictures bore the inscription, "I don't like Saddam!" I stayed there throughout the war, paying only rare visits to my family. Pressure of work dictated my decision, but I also felt I owed it to my soldiers, many of whom were separated from their families.

The nights were the worst, especially around two or three in the morning. As I was so busy and wound up during the day, I found it difficult to sleep at night. I suffered from loneliness. The thought of a long confrontation with Saddam seemed like a nightmare. To calm myself and take my mind off the war, I developed a nighttime addiction to American TV comedies. After chortling over one of these for half an hour, I would fall peacefully to sleep.

I was comforted and deeply touched by the arrival from London of two of my best friends, Wafic Said and John Ind. I had known Wafic since my Sandhurst days and John had been my doctor since that time. Both had become my lifelong friends. Knowing I was busy with my military duties, they wanted to be on hand in Riyadh in case my family needed any help.

One of the first decisions I took at the Ministry was to build myself a gym – I believe the first fitness room ever built in a ministry in the whole history of Saudi Arabia. I needed it. I established a routine. After the day's work, I would nap from six to seven in the evening, work out in the gym from seven to seven forty-five, and be ready for my briefing at 8 p.m. I invited Schwarzkopf to use the gym, and he did so fairly regularly. We shared a powerfully built Egyptian trainer called Rushdi.

Apart from the fear of an Iraqi suicide raid on our headquarters, which seems to have been very much on Schwarzkopf's mind, there was always the possibility of a hostile reaction inside Saudi Arabia to the presence of foreign troops. It was an anxiety we shared. Early on, an incident occurred in Jeddah when a bus carrying American troops came under fire and one or two soldiers were slightly wounded. We caught the three men involved – two Yemenis and a Jordanian – and sentenced them to jail. No Saudis were involved in the attack, nor were there any other such incidents, although there were one or two false alarms.

On one occasion, shortly before the offensive, Schwarzkopf informed me that two Americans in the Eastern Province had been fired on at close range from a passing car and had suffered wounds. They claimed they were the victims of a terrorist attack. On investigation, however, it turned out that the wounds were self-inflicted: the two soldiers had shot themselves so as not to be sent to the front. I warned Schwarzkopf that if the media picked it up and started hinting that this was the first sign of the Saudi population rebelling against the presence of foreign troops, I would stand up and relate exactly what had happened. I could not have it said that terrorists were operating in the Kingdom. The Americans said no more about it, and I kept quiet. The story died.

✦➤←✦

Good soldier though he undoubtedly was, I discovered to my surprise that Schwarzkopf had little direct experience of the Middle East. In 1947, at the age of twelve, he had spent a year in Tehran where his father, an American major general, had the job of reorganizing the Iranian police force. Then in 1989–90, once he had been given the CENTCOM job, he had spent a few days in Riyadh, Kuwait, Cairo, Amman and Sanaa, but that, so far as I could gather, was the whole of his Middle East experience. CENTCOM's home base at Tampa, Florida, was 6,500 miles away from the region by air and some 10,000 miles by sea – and was as different from the Middle East as it is possible to imagine.

Schwarzkopf was of course well briefed on the strategic and military aspects of the area, but the people, the leading personalities of Arab politics, the families, customs, attitudes, language, history, religion, way of life – indeed all the complexities of our Arab world – were as foreign and unfamiliar to him as they are to the average American. It was my difficult task to fill him in. In contrast, Lieutenant Generals Horner and Yeosock had considerable Middle East experience, Horner because of his previous links with our air force and Yeosock because of his years with the Saudi National Guard. But Schwarzkopf, as a soldier, had a certain impatience for matters he did not understand or did not consider relevant to his immediate mission. This was to be the source of a number of misunderstandings.

I believe he never fully grasped my overriding concern to ensure that we did nothing during the war that might compromise our postwar future. It was my task to see that our conduct and that of our allies did not provoke unrest in our deeply conservative society and did not give potentially hostile elements inside or outside the country a vehicle for dissent. We had no interest in lending a hand to those who wished to destabilize our society.

We needed to keep a wary eye not just on the internal scene but also on the surrounding environment. For example, alarm bells rang in my mind when Schwarzkopf told me, one day early in the crisis, that he had received a message from President Ali Abdallah Salih of Yemen inviting him to visit Sanaa. I was furious with Yemen for the pro-Saddam stance it had adopted and interpreted President Salih's move as an attempt to ingratiate himself with the Americans and divide the Coalition.

"What do you intend to do?" I asked Schwarzkopf. "I hope you aren't thinking of going."

He promised he would not even consider it without first consulting us. "I am not here to play politics," he said. "I will keep you informed of my movements. We are one command."

"That is good enough for me," I replied.

But I sensed that Schwarzkopf's attitude towards Yemen was somewhat different from mine. He seemed to think that a visit from him might bring Yemen in on our side. He used to say that President Salih was not simply sitting on the fence: rather he had a foot in each camp, ready to jump one way or the other as circumstances dictated. But my own view was that President Ali Abdallah Salih was more committed to Saddam than that. I felt we should make clear to the Yemenis that they could not gamble with the security of the peninsula.

Because of the hostile position taken by the government in Sanaa, the Saudi government decided to end the favored treatment given to Yemenis in the Kingdom and decreed that henceforth they would be treated like other Arab nationals – in other words, they would need a Saudi sponsor if they wished to work in the Kingdom. Hundreds of thousands left for home, while others complied with the rules and are still happily residing in the Kingdom.

Reports of Yemeni troop movements contributed to our sense of unease. We suspected that, directly or indirectly, President Ali Abdallah Salih of Yemen, King Hussein of Jordan and PLO Chairman Yasser Arafat had encouraged Saddam to invade

Kuwait and were waiting to exploit the situation for their own gain. We had no firm proof of such a conspiracy but, in the heated climate of the time, suspicions were easily aroused. A month after the invasion of Kuwait, King Hussein in an address to a gathering of tribal and parliamentary leaders said, "Even if I were not a king, I would still be the Sharif, indeed you may call me Sharif." The term "Sharif" is an honorific title reserved for those who claim descent from the Prophet Muhammad. However, the King's words angered and alarmed our leadership because it seemed to signal Hussein's ambition, in the event of a great disturbance in the region, to seize territory in the Hijaz which had once been ruled by his great-grandfather, the Sharif Hussein of Makkah. What if Hussein allowed Iraqi troops through his territory to attack us? Might such a move incite Yemen to make a thrust at Najran or Jizan on our southern border? I had to consider a "worst case" scenario.

✦

As I have suggested, my job – or at least one of my jobs – was to ensure that the Coalition hung together by being its arbiter from the Saudi point of view. I had to make sure the Coalition partners worked smoothly together in Saudi Arabia within boundaries acceptable to Saudi, Arab and Muslim opinion – and, once that had been accomplished, then policymakers in Washington, Riyadh, London, Cairo, Paris, Damascus and at the UN could respond accordingly and agree on the broad lines of the campaign. In a way, my role was to be the cement of the Coalition. If, for one reason or another, Saudi Arabia had had reservations or had backed off, then Egypt, Syria and the other Islamic countries would have backed off as well, and the whole enterprise would have fallen apart. I think this is what General Sir Peter de la Billière meant when he said to a friend of mine, "Without Khaled there would not have been a Coalition, and without the Coalition the war could not have been fought."

It was my duty to lay down firm guidelines about what behavior by foreign troops could be tolerated – and what could not. In doing so, I was being neither fanatical, nor overzealous, nor even unreasonable. I was defending the traditions of my country.

One of my toughest problems was how to make American forces acceptable in a Saudi environment – that is, without causing offense to local opinion. As the center of the Muslim world, we could not afford to be as flexible as some other countries in matters of public behavior. For example, our tradition dictates that women wear long clothes in public and act demurely. Outside hospitals and schools, Saudi women are not much seen in the workplace, nor do they drive motor vehicles. How then were we to accommodate the tens of thousands of young women in the American forces?

These American women served as drivers, mechanics, logisticians, nurses, and indeed in every possible role short of combat – although I believe even that doubtful privilege has since January 1993 been accorded them. I discovered that, roughly speaking, one in every three American vehicles was driven by a female. To take them off the road – as I would have wished, to avoid any possible problem – would have brought the U.S. army grinding to a halt. This was not an issue on which I could stick. Off-duty driving out of uniform was the real knotty point. So I hammered out a compromise with Schwarzkopf. I agreed to women driving in combat uniform on military missions, but I drew the line at their driving in civilian clothes for civilian purposes, such as shopping. It worked.

These American women, and their British sisters – the French brought no women with them – did not rebel against these restrictions. In fact, to my agreeable surprise, they seemed eager to respect our customs, on occasion even more assiduously than some Arab women themselves.

However, the "cultural" guidelines I laid down sometimes resulted in comic misunderstandings – as occurred on one occasion over T-shirts. Schwarzkopf claimed that I objected to a T-shirt being sold to American troops because it showed a map of Saudi Arabia with some of the major cities marked. In his book, he quotes me as saying, "The location of our cities is classified." This is pure fantasy. In any bookshop in Riyadh, one can buy an atlas to Saudi Arabia in which every village is mapped, let alone the major cities. The only T-shirts I was enraged about, and quite legitimately, were the ones showing the Stars and Stripes in the middle of a map of Saudi Arabia. The implication was that the U.S. was an occupying power. I was mad about that, as was Prince Sultan who had insisted that I raise the matter.

Perhaps to suggest what a tough situation he found himself in, Schwarzkopf alleges in his book that Riyadh was practically closed to foreigners until the late 1970s – indeed almost until his own arrival! "When I'd taken over Central Command in 1988," he writes, "the two-star general in charge of our military training mission was permitted to enter Riyadh on official business, but always had to depart for his quarters in Dhahran before dark." In fact, members of the American military mission and their families, as well as representatives of numerous American companies, had lived in Riyadh since the 1960s – among some 200,000 other Americans and Europeans, not to mention a few hundred thousand non-Saudis from other parts of the world!

I feel I have to set the record straight on another relatively trivial matter. In his book, Schwarzkopf suggests that, having complained to me that Brooke Shields was denied a visa to Saudi Arabia, he then "cautioned Khaled not to allow the same type of thing to happen with the Bob Hope tour." The Saudis, he claims to have reminded me, ran the risk of "winning the war and losing the peace" with the U.S.

From the very start, I made crystal clear to Schwarzkopf that the King had laid down firm guidelines regarding the entertainment of the troops: there was to be no singing or dancing by entertainers. President Bush himself, I told him, could not make us bend on this issue.

Sometime later, however, Schwarzkopf came to me with the news that Bob Hope was planning to come to Saudi Arabia, accompanied by Brooke Shields and a troupe of cheerleaders from Texas.

"Bob Hope is very welcome," I told him, "but the others, no way. That is the clear answer I can give you. But please feel free to try another channel, if you like – either through James Baker in Washington or direct to Prince Sultan. But I can assure you the answer will be no."

The next day he raised the subject again. This time, he took the credit for the decision to exclude women entertainers:

"I warned Washington it was ridiculous to try and send Brooke Shields. I know it's against your customs. Believe me, Khaled, I put a stop to it!"

Then he added: "But can I ask you a favor? It's about Bob Hope. They've refused his daughter a visa. Khaled, I will show you her picture. She is fifty years old!"

I laughed. "Guarantee me she is fifty years old and I will guarantee you a visa!" That, to my recollection, was the sum of it.

❖

But, such misunderstandings apart, I must give credit where credit is due – and this on several counts.

First of all, the matter of alcohol. Most people are aware that Saudi Arabia is "dry": the sale and consumption of alcohol is prohibited. As I explained to Schwarzkopf, alcohol was one of a number of nonnegotiable items. If anyone were found drunk a yard beyond the camp perimeter or committed a crime under the influence of alcohol, he or she would be tried and punished according to Saudi law.

To my relief Schwarzkopf not only saw the point of it but decided to go one better. He agreed that alcohol would be banned everywhere, inside as well as outside the camps. When the British government asked Sir Peter de la Billière to issue two cans of beer to each member of the British forces at Christmas, the British commander was in a position to refuse.

As a result, it was on the Coalition side a very "healthy" war, if any war can be described as such. I used to tease Schwarzkopf that Saudi Arabia was the biggest health farm in the world and that we should charge his troops for the privilege of being there! More seriously, I think every commander in the war will attest that the number of problems he had to deal with – serious crimes or petty offenses – was far lower than in any previous military operation of comparable size. There could be no possible comparison between the health, bearing and discipline of the American, British and French armies in the desert and the squalor of Vietnam a generation earlier, when drink, drugs, prostitution and the rest of it dragged the Americans down and caused the local population to grow to resent them.

A second issue on which Schwarzkopf showed welcome sensitivity was that of Muslims in the American forces. During the months the crisis lasted, I learned with interest that quite a large number of American servicemen and women had converted to Islam, no doubt influenced by the contacts they had made with our civilian population. They would visit the religious authorities and declare themselves publicly as Muslims. Schwarzkopf would come to me at intervals and say, "Now you've got 150!" and a little while later, "Now you've got 175!" Eventually there were more than 2,000 of them.

Of course there were Muslims in the U.S. military long before the Gulf War. I was interested to read in the *Army Times* of October 25, 1993, that Muslims make up four percent of active-duty members in the U.S. armed services, and that the first Islamic clergyman was enrolled in the chaplains' course at Fort Monmouth, New Jersey, in January 1994.

Because religious issues loomed so large during the Gulf crisis, I consulted Major General Shaikh Abd al-Muhsin al-Shaikh, the highly respected head of our armed services' Department of Religious Affairs. He was of great assistance to me. As my adviser on religious affairs, he recommended Brigadier General Faisal Bali, a calm, open-minded and pious man who, apart from being a good air defense officer, had a master's degree in Shari'a studies. He organized a program of lectures for friendly forces with the aim of explaining the beliefs, rituals and practices of our religion. Understandably, we were happy when quite a number of U.S. servicemen and women embraced Islam. However, when some religious figures heard about it, they were anxious to make the news public, no doubt in the hope of bringing others into the fold.

I would not allow it. Not wanting to trigger a possibly hostile reaction from Christians in the West, I thought it best to delay the announcement of the conversions until after the war. I was afraid Christian missionary bodies might mount a counter-offensive against us – and, as I explained to Brigadier General Bali, they were far better equipped to do so than we were. Stirring up feelings of hostility to us in the West could not possibly benefit the war effort.

It was our policy, based on King Fahd's instructions, to send to Makkah any Muslim soldier who wished to perform the *umrah*, or smaller pilgrimage, from any of the countries that had come to our aid – Egypt, Syria, Morocco, Pakistan, Bangladesh, Niger, Senegal and so forth. I had instructed my staff to cater to these pilgrims, but it had not occurred to me to include the American converts.

At one of our evening sessions, Schwarzkopf said to me, "Khaled, I'm upset. I have a complaint to make. I hear you are sending all the Muslim troops to Makkah. I want the Muslims in my forces to go too!"

"Norm," I replied, "I take off my hat to you. Thank you very much." I appreciated his thought and, while he was still with me, I called in my staff to make sure that American Muslims, new converts for the most part, were included in the Makkah schedules. I must give Schwarzkopf the credit for reminding me to send them on the smaller pilgrimage.

I was also grateful to Schwarzkopf when, as we discussed plans for President Bush's visit to American forces for Thanksgiving in November 1990, he suggested that religious services on that occasion could be conducted on an American warship in international waters. I had suggested clearing one of our ports for the American President and his party, but Schwarzkopf went one better.

As a gesture of friendship to our Western allies, I told Schwarzkopf that I would like to send a message of greetings that Christmas to American forces, to be published in his daily news bulletin. He jumped for joy, thanked me profusely, asked me whether I was sure I wanted to do it, and so forth. I therefore wrote out a short message, signed it, added my title of Joint Forces Commander, and sent it in to Schwarzkopf.

Somewhat sheepishly, he came to my office holding the piece of paper.

"Khaled, you know and I know that American troops are not under your command. But with that title, my forces may get the impression that they were serving under you."

I laughed. "Write whatever you like," I said.

"Can we call you the Islamic Forces Commander?"

"You could, if it were true," I replied. "But how about the French, the Poles, the Czechs and the others under my command? They are not Muslims! Anyway, I can't change a single letter of a title given me by the King."

"May I tell you the truth . . . ?" he began, with a look of some embarrassment.

I interrupted him. "Let me make it easy for you. I wrote that letter out of courtesy. But if it's going to be a problem, just return it to me and we will assume I never sent it." So my Christmas message to the American forces was never published as I would have wished — just a tiny example of the mutual sensitivities of two generals fighting a war together.

In the months we spent working together, it was inevitable that Schwarzkopf and I should have a few squabbles, due to differences in our background, culture and responsibilities, but due essentially to differences in our respective missions. I will keep until later the one semiserious dispute we had over the planning of Desert Storm. But on the whole, as I have suggested, mutual respect and a certain similarity of temperament provided the basis for an effective partnership inside the strange hybrid of a "parallel command."

For me the stakes were high, higher perhaps than he understood — in terms of our national pride, our postwar stability, our need to justify our policies to Arab opinion. Saudi interest demanded that the Americans not be seen as an occupying force. As guardians of Islam's Holy Places, we had to be ultracareful that our Western allies did not cause offense to Muslim opinion, whether at home or abroad. Nothing that clashed with our Muslim customs, national traditions, religious practices and beliefs could be tolerated. To ensure this was an important part of my brief. I hope that history will record that, by insisting on certain rules of behavior from our powerful American ally, I helped preserve the honor and integrity of the Saudi armed forces, and indeed of the Kingdom. At no time were the Saudis treated as the Vietnamese had been during the Vietnam conflict, second-class citizens in their own country. However, I trust that history will also record that our relationship with the United States was strengthened and deepened by the respect and understanding we extended to each other throughout the crisis.

CHAPTER XIV

Managing the Coalition – 1

W HAT WAS THE NATURE of the international Coalition against Saddam Hussein? In my experience, there was a good deal of confusion about it. Most people supposed it was an American-sponsored Coalition bound together by a set of United Nations Resolutions or even by a single multilateral treaty. The Americans were, of course, active in stitching the Coalition together and UN resolutions were vital in defining and legitimizing our common aims, but the essential glue of the Coalition lay in the bilateral treaties which each of its thirty-seven members concluded with Saudi Arabia. Without Saudi Arabia, the Coalition could not have existed. Saudi Arabia was the host country of the Coalition, its pivot, its cement – and, by virtue of the powers conferred on me by Prince Sultan, who in turn received these powers from King Fahd, I was the man on the spot responsible for holding it together.

I hasten to add that, although the King gave me the job of "managing" the Coalition, I was a member of a Saudi royal family team, and by no means its most senior member. In the crisis, the royal family acted in unison, displaying a considerable variety of talents under the overall direction of the King. Prominent members of the family – such as Crown Prince Abdallah, the Ministers of Defense and Interior and their deputies, the Governor of Riyadh, the Minister of Foreign Affairs, and those members of the family serving as provincial governors, heads of Royal Commissions, ambassadors, members of national security committees, officers in the armed services, and so on – all had important roles to play in the crisis. The royal network proved flexible and effective and, with the support of many

non-members of the royal family in government, the professions
and business, the Kingdom looked more solid – internationally,
regionally and domestically – than any of its neighbors. In my
opinion, few countries, and none in the Arab Middle East, can
boast of a ruling elite to match that of the Kingdom. But, as
always, discretion was the family's watchword.

Inevitably, I was much concerned with the politics of the Arab
members of the Coalition. Ensuring that Arab armies remained
strongly within the Coalition meant spending countless hours
with their commanders – to make certain their troops were
happy and well positioned; that their political concerns were
addressed as to who was deployed to the left and right of them;
that their logistical needs were met; and that friction points
with other commands were avoided. All these things had to be
carefully worked out. To give orders to the Egyptians, or the
Syrians, or to any other contingent under my command required
political sensitivity and tact. In turn, it was not the easiest of
tasks to explain to Schwarzkopf how a fellow Arab might think.

To cite a single example, Syria was highly important to the
allies because of the imprimatur of Arab solidarity and Arab
nationalism it put on the Coalition. Syria, however, wished to
limit its participation to the defense of Saudi Arabia and the
liberation of Kuwait: it did not wish to attack into Iraq – a
sentiment shared by ourselves, Egypt and all the Arab partici-
pants – and it was somewhat wary of military cooperation with
the United States. Its wishes had to be accommodated. I understood this somewhat better than Schwarzkopf who throughout
the crisis seemed to me to display an insensitivity towards the
Syrians bordering on hostility, no doubt as a result of the long-
standing political differences between the U.S. and Syria. But
the fact that Schwarzkopf did not appear to like or understand
the Syrians was no concern of mine. My job was to keep them
on board and keep the Coalition together.

As I have suggested, the worst time of my life was the first
five or six weeks after Saddam's invasion when I had to scramble
together a hasty defense, enthuse my own troops, meet ministers and other envoys from around the world, give interviews
to reporters – and, throughout, smile and look relaxed although
I knew the situation was perilous.

As more and more emissaries came to see me, it dawned on me that we were going to receive troops from more countries than I had imagined. Were they to be under my command or under Schwarzkopf's? And what were the relative advantages and disadvantages? From the very start, I got the sense that the British had struck a deal with the Americans to fight together under American command. They were, after all, the closest of allies, with a long experience of working together in NATO. I would, of course, have loved to have the British under my command, but I thought it might even be to my advantage that they were not, as I had enough on my plate. My hopes rested on the French: I wanted history to record that they had served under Saudi command. No Arab or Muslim had ever commanded a European force. France is one of the greatest countries in the world, whose civilization attracts universal admiration. It is a permanent member of the Security Council; its armed forces have a glorious history and great combat experience. I felt it was a great honor for Saudi Arabia to welcome French forces on its soil and for me to command some French units.

Fortunately, the French proved as reluctant to serve under the Americans as I was anxious that they should serve under me! Only in January 1991, at the time of Desert Storm, did they move over from my command to Schwarzkopf's operational control.

From preliminary discussions, I knew that Egyptian and Syrian troops, as well as troops from other Muslim countries, would not serve under American command. So then it struck me: I would have to command the Egyptians and the Syrians. But these countries had never served under a Saudi commander in their entire history. Both were battle-hardened Arab countries which had fought in all the wars against Israel: I had not. I had had little contact with their armed services.

So in the weeks following my appointment in August 1990, and before the bulk of the friendly forces arrived in September and October, I worked hard to prepare myself, intellectually and psychologically, for the task ahead. I immersed myself in Soviet combat doctrine, knowing that it had been adopted by Egypt and Syria – and by Iraq as well – and I brushed up on what I had learned at Fort Leavenworth about Soviet tactics. I became a student again to comprehend Iraqi combat techniques, to determine the best way to use Egyptian and Syrian forces and understand their battle procedures.

A sobering thought was that previous experiences of joint Arab commands had not been successful. Fearing an Israeli attack, Egypt and Syria had signed a joint defense agreement at the end of 1966, although their relations with each other were marked by great mutual suspicion. With tension rising in the region, Jordan in turn signed a defense agreement with Egypt on May 30, 1967, and an Egyptian officer, Major General Abd al-Mun'im Riad, was given command of the Arab "eastern front." Two days later, on June 1, General Riad established his advanced headquarters in Jordan, but there was little he could do to regroup his forces before Israel struck on June 5. The absence of coordination between the Arabs allowed Israel to defeat Egypt, Jordan and Syria in turn. In the 1973 war, the Egyptian–Syrian command had not fared much better: each country had gone its own way. I thought, "My God! If these two or three Arab countries failed to work together at moments of great national crisis, how will I convince them to put their faith in me? But if I don't manage it, I will be a puppet in the hands of the Egyptian and Syrian commanders." I was determined that my own command would be more successful – and it was, but unfortunately against an Arab state! That was the tragedy we had to live with.

It was some weeks into the crisis before I heard that units were also joining us from Poland, Czechoslovakia and Hungary, former communist countries with whom we had had no contact. All were to be under my command. I was happy to accumulate these responsibilities, as I believed it was important that units from many nations should be seen to be serving under Saudi command to show the world that the whole international community had united in support of a just cause. But with East European countries we were in uncharted terrain.

My task was to integrate these different national contingents, speaking different languages, operating different and often incompatible equipment on land, sea and in the air, into an effective fighting force. By the adoption of equipment standards and constant training, NATO had solved the problems of "interoperability.'' Our Coalition had yet to do so. I had to set people the right tasks, assign them proper missions, arrange for their joint training. I had to worry about everything: not just about logistics, military deployments, weapons and tactics, but about political and religious differences, linguistic barriers, personal antipathies, customs and traditions which were precious to some and alien and incomprehensible to others.

The King, my supreme commander, Crown Prince Abdallah and Prince Sultan needed to be kept regularly informed of military developments. So special briefing rooms were set up for them. Whatever information I had was immediately available to them, although they wanted, of course, to be given a somewhat broader picture than the detailed briefing required by a field commander. In addition to briefings by the staff, throughout the crisis I personally gave Prince Sultan a complete briefing of developments twice a week and, on several occasions, I was able to present to the King a forward projection of what we expected to happen in the weeks and months ahead. During two of my meetings with King Fahd, Schwarzkopf was also present.

The biggest boost to my morale came from my meetings with Prince Sultan. I could see in his eyes the pride of a father. The minute I saw a certain look on his face, the moment I heard him utter certain words, my problems would fall away. Sometimes I had to seek his advice about certain urgent matters, but as soon as I sensed his anxiety that things might not turn out right, I would determine to solve every problem, however daunting it might be.

⇒⇐

Of all the Arab and Muslim countries that sent troops to the Kingdom, the most important was Egypt, a country which was our traditional ally and of which I personally was very fond. Before Saddam's rash invasion, King Fahd had worked closely with President Mubarak to defuse the Iraqi–Kuwaiti quarrel. Together they had then led the Arab opposition to Saddam's aggression. In fact, as I have already suggested, Saudi Arabia and Egypt, soon joined by Syria, constituted the Arab backbone of the Coalition, without which no Western military aid would have been feasible.

True to their commitment, the Egyptians immediately sent us advance units of a special forces regiment. Airlifted in, they were among the first foreign troops to arrive, but they were too lightly armed to serve as a blocking force. I felt they could only be used behind enemy lines. In due course, they were followed by the 3rd Mechanized Division, by two heavy artillery brigades, and then somewhat later by the 4th Armored Division – the best in Egypt's armed forces. I remember going down on September 22 to the docks at Yanbu, our new Red Sea port, to meet three ships carrying the first units of the mechanized division, with its tanks, APCs, artillery and missile launchers.

Some weeks earlier, I had had extensive discussions with a visiting team of senior Egyptian officers, and I had formed two committees, one to handle supplies for the Egyptian contingent and the other their operations, including arrangements for their journey to the Kingdom. The Egyptian team was led by Major General Hussein Tantawi, director of operations, a friendly and cooperative person. Throughout the crisis, he was my main link with Egypt's Chief of Staff, Lieutenant General Safieddine Abu Shnaf, an able officer of strong personality, and with Defense Minister General Yusuf Sabri Abu Talib. (Tantawi was to become Egypt's Defense Minister after the Gulf War.) Two other distinguished Egyptian officers with whom I had a lot to do were Major General Muhammad Omar Sulaiman, Head of Military Intelligence, one of the Egyptian officers I most admired (later promoted Head of General Intelligence), and Major General Muhammad Ali Bilal, the commander of Egyptian forces in Saudi Arabia during the preparatory Desert Shield phase. Major General Bilal was a good administrator who used his charm to get what he wanted. The Egyptians had done well to send him ahead to make all the arrangements for the reception of their troops. Prince Sultan was impressed.

I was, of course, concerned to discover whether the Egyptians would agree to serve under Saudi command, and was delighted when the answer was an unreserved yes. I also wanted to know whether they had any objections to joint planning with the Americans, and again discovered that, seeing they had trained with American forces for several years, that posed no problem either. Above all, I needed to know how many troops they were ready to send us and when we could expect them.

On this last subject, I had a curious private meeting with Major General Tantawi. Publicly, the Egyptians had committed themselves to sending one division only, but I had heard from Prince Sultan that President Mubarak had said two might be available – and two divisions is what I wanted. However, I did not know whether Tantawi knew about President Mubarak's suggestion and whether I could talk to him about it directly. So I dropped a hint, but he did not take it. Perhaps he knew about the two divisions, but thought I did not yet know, and that he therefore had to be discreet. We spent half an hour circling the question in a very courteous way, with neither of us coming out with it.

At last I said we would like to feel free to contact Egypt if we felt we needed more troops, to which he replied that the President had instructed him to say that Egypt was prepared to give its all – flowery language that I was not too happy with, seeing that I wanted to know whether or not I could count on two Egyptian divisions. I needed to draw up plans for their reception.

Unable to get a straight answer out of Tantawi, I called Prince Sultan to ask what exactly Mubarak had suggested. He advised me to plan for that second Egyptian division, but added: "We don't want to raise the matter now. We will come to it in due course." And that is how it happened. The second Egyptian division – the 4th Armored – was not too long in coming.

Egypt did not send any aircraft to accompany its ground forces – and this may have been due to a mistake of mine. Early on, Major General Salah Halabi (who eventually took over command of Egyptian forces from Major General Bilal) came to ask whether Egypt could send us a squadron of fighters, very probably F-16s. I told him we were expecting over 1,500 fighter planes from other countries, and this posed complex problems of command and control. I shared with him my worries about the possibility of midair collisions and other accidents. Halabi may have taken my remarks to be a polite hint that Egypt should not add to our problems by sending aircraft. In fact, we later sent them a message saying we were ready to receive their planes, and I made arrangements for them to train. It would

have been a good experience for them, but they never came –
perhaps as a result of my earlier remarks which I regret.

In due course, the Egyptians, and later the Syrians for that
matter, sent me word that their units were standing by ready
to move but, to my surprise, I learned that both looked to me
to provide the transport. I approached Schwarzkopf about
whether he could help with shipping. But the Americans were
themselves short of sealift capacity and had had to lease a great
deal of tonnage from European owners. So, after making some
urgent inquiries, I managed to find some Saudi ships to do the
job.

An unfortunate incident then took place which has not, to
my knowledge, been reported. The Egyptians and the Syrians
had requested that we undertake the protection of their forces
during the journey to our shores. I assumed they were concerned that the troopships might come under attack from Iraq
or from Jordan – the extent of whose commitment to the Iraqi
cause was then uncertain – or even from Israel. My own view
was that they asked for too much. I felt that they could have
assured their own protection, at least until they entered our
waters. But I suspected that they had made their request in the
expectation that, through the Joint Forces Command, I could
secure American protection for them. The Americans had two
carrier battle groups in the Red Sea and their Combat Air Patrols
were in action 24 hours a day.

So I passed the request on to Schwarzkopf. After a good deal
of discussion, we agreed that Saudi Arabia would provide transport for the Egyptian and Syrian forces, while the U.S. would
provide protection against hostile interference to both of them.
Schwarzkopf then secured his government's approval for this
arrangement and issued the necessary orders. We established
good communications on this subject and, the minute the Egyptians set sail, the Americans were informed so that they could
escort the troopships to the point where our own navy could
take over.

All seemed set. However, a day or so later I received a
heated and somewhat panic-stricken call from Cairo. Some 24
hours out of port, the vessels carrying an Egyptian brigade had
come under attack from two carrier-based American planes –

the very aircraft which were supposed to protect them! Evidently unable to identify the ships, the American pilots had opened fire. They may only have fired warning shots, but these were close enough to cause considerable alarm: the Egyptians thought it was a real attack. I could hardly believe my ears. Where were the ships now? I learned they had turned tail and headed back to their home port in Egypt. Someone on the American side had goofed.

The incident took a lot of sorting out and cost me a great deal of time and trouble. The reception party at our Red Sea port, the hundreds of vehicles I had rented to transport the Egyptians to their staging areas, all had to be stood down. I was on the telephone for about 24 hours. Schwarzkopf could not believe the attack had happened, but he finally admitted it and apologized. It seems a funny story in retrospect, but it was less amusing at the time. The Egyptians eventually set sail again and arrived without further incident.

On October 22, President Husni Mubarak came to the Kingdom to inspect his troops. He flew direct from Cairo to the civilian airport at al-Qaisuma, a town on the Tapline near Hafr al-Batin, and from there drove out to the troops. I flew up from Riyadh to join the reception party which included Prince Muhammad bin Fahd, the Governor of the Eastern Province, the Northern Area Commander, the Chief Administrator of Hafr al-Batin city, and many other dignitaries and officials. A vast tent was erected to house the VIPs, while several thousand Egyptian troops, all carrying their personal weapons, sat on the ground a few yards from the President to hear him speak.

After addressing the men, Mubarak called for questions. Were there any shortages? Did they have any special requests? At this point, there was a disturbance at the back of the gathering. A soldier carrying a rifle had got up and was trying to force his way forward towards the President through the sitting ranks of his comrades. Memories of President Sadat's assassination must have flashed through everyone's mind, because he was soon intercepted by the President's guards and pinned down.

"Release that man!" the President cried. "Let him come forward! Let him speak!"

"We've heard Saddam saying bad things on the radio about Egypt and about our President," was all he had to say. "What can be done about this crazy man?"

"Don't pay him any attention!" Mubarak exclaimed. "Forget what Saddam said. Don't listen to false rumors. We have full confidence in ourselves and in the justice of our cause . . ." And more words to that effect. I found the President's composure impressive.

One of the principles I adopted in managing the Coalition was never to ask from any national contingent more than I thought it could give. Before issuing an order, I always took the precaution of checking the political climate. My job was to get the best out of each contingent, not to create problems. But on one occasion my reading of the situation was faulty.

I had received an intelligence report that the Iraqis had sent some troops – including Special Forces – to reinforce their positions opposite our northwest town of Ar'ar, where the governor is a member of the royal family, my maternal uncle Prince Abdallah bin Musa'id al-Jiluwi. A reverse for us in that sector would have had bad psychological repercussions. Were the Iraqis planning to attack? I felt the need to reinforce my own troops. I increased Combat Air Patrols over the area and moved up a Saudi National Guard brigade. But I was still not wholly satisfied with the dispositions on the ground.

To match the Iraqi Special Forces, I wanted to strengthen my defenses with an Egyptian Special Forces battalion – a move which would have meant separating the battalion from the rest of the Egyptian regiment and from the close supervision of its Egyptian commander. I asked my planners whether they had consulted the Egyptians to secure their agreement, and they assured me they had. So I issued my orders. A short while later I received a call from Major General Salah Halabi (who by this time had taken over from Major General Bilal) who asked very politely whether I might reconsider my decision. I got the impression that he had consulted his government and was acting under instructions. Fortunately, he did not put his request in such a way as to force me to uphold my authority. On the contrary, he said he would immediately obey my orders to move if that was what I really wanted, but he begged leave to make one or two points . . . I realized at once that, whatever I might say, the Egyptian battalion was not going to move.

"Don't send me an official notification of your objections," I said to Halabi. "Just await my new instructions." I immediately rescinded my orders: instead of moving to the defense of Ar'ar, the Egyptian Special Forces stayed where they were.

If I were to attach blame to anyone for this incident, it would have to be my planners who had informed me that the Egyptians had agreed to the move. They earned a severe reprimand.

Late one night in my bedroom in the Ministry of Defense basement, unable to sleep, I flicked on the television and came by chance on an interview with an Egyptian woman whose son was serving with the Egyptian contingent in the Kingdom. She was proud her son was away in Saudi Arabia, fighting in a just cause. But then she burst into tears. "He never writes," she sobbed. "We never receive any letters from him." I was grateful for that reminder from an unknown mother. First thing the next morning, I sent a message to the Egyptian commander. He found the soldier, scolded him for not writing to his mother, and made sure he got off a letter to her the next day. I then did what I could to improve the collection and delivery of mail for the forces.

Shortly after Iraq's invasion of Kuwait, President Asad sent his Deputy Chief of Staff, Imad Ali Aslan, to discuss with me what contribution Syria could make to our defense. ("Imad" is a Syrian rank between Major General and Lieutenant General.) It was the first time I had met a senior Syrian officer. I found Imad Ali Aslan to be a suave and gentlemanly officer, with a soft voice and an air of quiet authority.

To put him at ease I began by saying, "I take off my hat to President Asad! He was right about Saddam and we were wrong. He was wise not to attend the Baghdad summit." This was the summit in May 1990 which, by conferring on Saddam the prestige he evidently wanted, may have encouraged him to invade Kuwait.

In praising Asad, I meant what I said. The Syrian leader is

widely considered to be one of the shrewdest in the region. But I also wanted to show Aslan that we, in Saudi Arabia, had some understanding of Syria's position, and that he could trust me to command Syrian troops in such a way as not to cause Damascus any political embarrassment.

Generally speaking, I felt it was my duty as Joint Forces Commander to protect the interests of every nation which had placed troops under my command. I thought I owed it to the political leaders of those nations. If they had agreed to let their troops serve under a Saudi commander, the least I could do was to keep their trust – regardless of whether I agreed with them or not.

That Asad hated Saddam even more intensely than we did was common knowledge. But I also knew that, as the standard-bearer of Arab nationalism, it was not easy for Syria to join the United States in making war on another Arab state. Moreover, the long contest with Israel had made the Syrians more than usually suspicious of Israel's American ally. Although there had been some recent improvement in U.S.–Syrian relations, a large backlog of bitterness and bad feeling remained. Just as Schwarz-kopf was wary of the Syrians and had little or no contact with them throughout the crisis, so the Syrians were anxious to keep the U.S. military at arm's length, no doubt fearing that anything the Americans might learn about them would be passed on at once to Israel. For all these reasons, I anticipated some problems between Syrian and U.S. troops in the Kingdom.

I was therefore prepared for what Aslan had to say. Very courteously, he made plain that he would prefer Syrian forces not to work too closely with U.S. forces. I was able to assure him that we would handle our relations with the U.S. quite separately and that Syrian planning, tactics, exercises, requirements and command structure would all remain confidential within the Saudi command.

But what, I asked, if Syrian and American soldiers were to meet by accident? It was important, he replied, to avoid embarrassment to either side. Syria was anxious to play its role in the defense of Saudi Arabia and – I recall his phrase well – to help in eliminating the threat from Saddam. But it could not contemplate a situation in which its forces might be seen to serve under

American command. Syrian troops would serve under a Saudi commander and none other. It was an arrangement which suited me well!

A unit of Syrian Special Forces was soon in the Kingdom. It was followed some weeks later by Syria's 9th Armored Division – that is, once I had had the time to organize the ships, the transport vehicles, the accommodation, the food and so forth which they required. They set sail under American aerial protection. It struck me that two countries which had not been on the best of terms could still cooperate effectively when confronting a common threat. I recall driving to the docks at Yanbu on November 4 to meet the advance units as they disembarked from a massive Saudi vessel, the *Saudi Qasim*. As they rolled ashore, I was a bit disappointed to see that their tanks were Russian T-62s, not the T-72s I had hoped for. But I knew that the Syrians had defense commitments on the Golan and in Lebanon and that, apart from confronting Israel, they had also felt it necessary to move two divisions towards the Iraqi frontier to deter Saddam from any adventures against themselves. The truth was that I would have been happy had they brought antique T-34s. I was in no position to be fussy. It was great to have the Syrians on board.

At the start, I put their armored division in the east next to the Americans, but I soon noticed the latter were not too comfortable. Syrian tanks and tank formations, of Soviet manufacture and inspiration, were identical to those of Iraq. I was afraid that any incident between their forces, however small, might blow up into a problem. So I replaced them with an Egyptian division. The Syrians were relieved, and the Americans in turn were far happier to have the Egyptians, with whom they had trained, on their left flank. Indeed, when at a later stage the Americans swung west to carry out their "left hook," I moved the Egyptians to their right flank.

One of my responsibilities was to make sure there were no serious problems between allies in the field. I knew Saddam was counting on the Coalition falling apart. He believed that if he could spin things out, problems would inevitably occur between its members: problems, say, between Syria and the United States; or inter-Arab problems between those who were for and against the war; or religious problems because of the impact of foreign troops on Saudi society; or violent incidents carried out by Arab or Muslim soldiers of fundamentalist persuasion. Saddam was evidently hoping that the soldiers would open fire on their officers. To fan the flames, the Iraqis invented a number of incidents which were carried by the media in Jordan and in some North African countries – for instance, that in a clash between Egyptian and American troops, sixteen Egyptians and four Americans had been killed. All this was hostile disinformation, but I was aware that if a single shot were fired, we would have a major crisis on our hands.

Much of Saddam's propaganda against the Coalition was couched in religious terms. There was, of course, something fraudulent about Saddam Hussein, the boss of a secular political party, attempting to assume the mantle of Islam. After his invasion, his propaganda services distributed a picture of him at prayer in Kuwait. He is seen praying alone, hemmed in closely by armed guards. He is wearing a military beret well down on his forehead, whereas prayer demands that the believer touch the ground with his bare forehead. An analysis of the picture, and of the shadows cast by the figures in it, shows that he was not even facing in the direction of Makkah, as he should have been. So much for Saddam Hussein as a model Muslim!

To my relief and satisfaction, the Syrian commander, Major General Ali Habib, displayed enthusiasm, discipline, and a willingness to cooperate without hesitation or reservation. He soon became one of my favorites among the commanders of national contingents. (In August 1994, he was promoted to head *al-wahdat al-khassa*, an elite unit of Syrian Special Forces.)

Some people have tried to say that the Syrians did not fight. This is neither fair nor accurate. As their reservations about attacking Iraq were known from the start, I positioned their armored division in JFC-North, some 35 miles behind the front line, where they proved extremely active in defense. Their well-trained and determined troops had clear orders to fight back if attacked. I placed them in reserve in case clearance for them to join the allied offensive into Kuwait did not reach me in time for the ground war. I did not wish to embarrass them by making a political issue of it. In any event clearance did come in time, and they joined in the liberation of Kuwait. I should add that the reserve position in which I placed the Syrians was itself an important one. Their mission was to reinforce the first echelon troops if necessary, to counterattack if the Iraqis broke through, and to guard the flanks and rear of our position as well as the gaps between the forward units. They were well prepared to perform all these tasks.

Moreover, well before the ground war, I had for political and tactical reasons made some attempts at integrating the various forces under my command. For example, two weeks before the start of the air campaign, I attached a battalion of Saudi para-troopers to the Egyptian Special Forces where they remained until the liberation of Kuwait, when I assigned them to the Rafha camp for Iraqi refugees. I thought the American-trained Egyptian rangers might have something to teach our men. I put Saudi artillery under Syrian command in JFC-North; and then, to balance things up, I put Syrian engineers up front under Saudi command where, once the ground war started, they were among the first units to breach Iraqi defenses. That is why, when critics object that the Syrians did not fight, I can rightly say, "nonsense!"

❖⟩⟨❖

Like the Egyptians, the Syrians did not bring aircraft with them – which was perhaps just as well as I had problems enough integrating Arab and Islamic land forces with the air forces of our other allies. A number of technical difficulties arose which I will attempt to describe in layman's language.

Most of the land forces which flooded into the country brought with them surface-to-air missiles and antiaircraft guns with which to defend themselves against the possibility of Iraqi air attack. But these organic air defenses – that is to say, air defenses attached to ground units – posed a real danger to the huge air forces of the Coalition. There was a conflict of interest: the land forces needed to be able to defend themselves, but the security of the air forces had also to be assured.

It was a dilemma which I had to arbitrate. I came down firmly on the side of the air forces. After the first few weeks, once the Coalition had established air supremacy – in fact total domination of the air – I did not see us facing any real danger from the Iraqi air force. Paradoxical as it may seem, the real risk to our planes was from our own ground forces. There were so many different national contingents fielding such a variety of air defense weapons – Soviet, French, American, Swiss, among others – that integrating them with the thousands of aircraft in our air space seemed an impossible nightmare. Simply within the Saudi forces, we had faced a problem, as other countries have done, of getting the air force and air defense to work together. Now the problem was magnified many times over. The Air Coordination Center was unable to provide Close Air Support to any of my units unless it was certain that Coalition aircraft would not be fired on. Someone had to control the ground defense.

To solve the air defense problems and ensure Close Air Support for my own forces, I called for a briefing by the air force. Among the senior officers taking part were Lieutenant General Horner, the Joint Force Air Component Commander, Lieutenant General Ahmad al-Buhairi, the Saudi Air Force commander, Major General Majid Tilhab al-Otaibi, the acting Air Defense Commander (a well-qualified officer with whom I had worked closely over many years and whom I had personally prepared for this command), Brigadier General Ahmad al-Sudairy, Chief of Air Operations, and Brigadier General Hussein Habter, Chief of Air Defense Operations, an exceptionally knowledgeable officer with a real gift for tactical thinking.

The U.S. XVIIIth Corps was then at Dhahran and its Air Support Operations Center was to provide Close Air Support to the Joint Forces in addition to its own units. I insisted on having Saudi liaison officers at that ASOC. But I was still not satisfied. It was evident that until we had a foolproof integrated system in operation, the organic air defenses of my units would simply have to be declared "tight" – that is to say, firing would be restricted to self-defense. I therefore ruled that the land forces under my command could not use their air defense weapons unless they came under direct attack from Iraqi aircraft, in which case they could fire back in self-defense. The danger of hitting

Coalition planes was too great to allow any more leeway than that.

But the longer term problem remained: how to integrate organic and regional air defenses into one system to meet operational as well as safety requirements.

These air defense issues had been extensively discussed during the drafting of the Desert Shield plan and a start had been made in linking the organic air defenses of Saudi and GCC units to our air defense group in the Eastern Province. But this was not sufficient to cope with the influx of Coalition forces. In the three months before the air offensive against Iraq, I directed my staff to survey the entire area of allied deployment to determine air defense requirements and work out how to meet them. It was essential to ensure adequate cover for our own units in JFC-East and JFC-North, as well as for the main maneuver of the ground war: the movement by two U.S. Army corps from east to west as they enveloped and got behind the main Iraqi forces.

Our air defense network had now to be extended to protect the vast allied force that was going to surge into Iraq and Kuwait. As a result of the survey by my staff and the Americans, we decided that an additional air defense subsector had to be created – in effect a separate northern area of responsibility – under the control of eastern air defense in Dhahran. This would require a Combat Reporting Center (CRC), a Message Processing Center to pick up information from the AWACS and elsewhere, and an Air Support Operations Center (ASOC) – in fact a whole new mobile air defense system. Additional Hawk batteries were brought in as well as Patriots to cope with Scuds. My staff briefed all the Coalition commanders on this new air defense concept, and all agreed to it. The equipment was flown in from the U.S. by C5 and located at KKMC. With information flowing in from ground radars and AWACS, the new CRC could pick up the whole air picture and automatically pass on early warning to the Patriot and Hawk units in the field to which it was linked by voice and data. A Hawk interface system was brought in from Jeddah to integrate Saudi with U.S. batteries, both controlled by the CRC. Top Saudi air defense officers, as well as air defense representatives from Britain, France, Egypt and Syria, were selected to work with their American counterparts in the CRC.

Thus was solved the problems of integrating different national air defense systems, operating in different languages over often incompatible communications networks, according to different doctrines and procedures and deploying different weapons systems.

So, to sum up, the solution adopted was a) to restrict firing by organic air defense weapons; b) to ensure that such weapons received early-warning information enabling them to distinguish friend from foe; and c) to introduce an additional regional air defense capability in the form of the new CRC. It took three months' intense work to set up the new system and to train people to use it – from November 1990 to January 1991. But by the launch of the air campaign against Iraq, it was working well.

To test the system, we generated our own intruders, picked them up by the AWACS, passed the information to someone in front of a screen at the CRC who would then issue orders to missiles at regional centers, to organic air defense artillery with the land forces, or to aircraft to scramble and intercept the intruders. As I knew from experience, this sort of thing is fairly complicated when you are dealing with a single force, speaking one language. It becomes a real mind-boggling puzzle when you are dealing with a multinational Coalition.

In the end, the Coalition's air defenses were outstanding. No mistakes were made by ground air defenses, because they were tightly controlled and well-trained for nearly six months. No friendly aircraft was hit by friendly fire, either during training or during the war.

So much, in brief, for ground-to-air problems. But what about air-to-ground? If they were to go into battle, my forces needed Close Air Support (CAS). We had to establish suitable procedures for the ground to talk to the air, and in particular for my ground forces to talk to the American air forces. This was another complicated puzzle to be resolved – and resolved it had to be before we went to war. If air strikes are not accurate and are not properly coordinated with the ground, you risk hitting your own forces.

I asked the Americans for help and they agreed to supply our forces, down to battalion level, with Tactical Air Control Parties

(TACPs) – that is to say two- or three-man teams equipped with the necessary communications to enable them to talk to the air force and call in air support when needed.

In Saudi Arabia we had not as yet attempted to provide immediate Close Air Support to our land forces. We had, however, carried out some exercise missions to provide preplanned Close Air Support. An urgent effort was required to upgrade our capabilities in this field, and this meant developing the right concept, devising adequate operating procedures, forming Saudi Tactical Air Control Parties and training them. I attached a Saudi to every American TACP so that he could learn the job, and arranged for the Americans to give our people more systematic training at KKMC. Using American resources, we developed a CAS concept in both English and Arabic for use by the Joint Forces, and I issued signed orders for training to proceed on this basis. Before long, six of our own Saudi TACPs, each consisting of two officers and four warrant officers, were organized, trained and attached to Joint Forces brigades. They were the first operational Close Air Support teams in the Kingdom. In due course, the Saudi Air Force set about building its own school at Khamis Mushait based on this model.

Coordination between American TACPs and the Joint Forces went smoothly, especially with the Egyptians who already had the experience of joint annual maneuvers with the Americans. The only problem was that the Syrians showed no interest in working with an American Tactical Air Control Party! I am not blaming them. They simply had never had any contact with the American military, and no doubt needed clearance from above to do so. I recalled the preference expressed by Imad Ali Aslan, but I reckoned this was a problem diplomacy might be able to solve.

I first approached Schwarzkopf. "Norm, before you hear it from someone else, I want to tell you about the Syrians. They are showing some reluctance to work with your air controllers."

Schwarzkopf was evidently annoyed. "Khaled," he said, "I'm only doing what you asked me. If they don't want them, fine. I'll take them back. I have no problem with that."

"No, no, Norm. I still want your air control parties, and I think we can persuade the Syrians to cooperate. Please ask your people to be patient. But don't let them go to the Syrians just yet. Let them stay as our guests at Hafr al-Batin for a few days while I sort things out."

I then turned my attention to the Syrian side of the equation. I sent my deputy, Major General Abd al-Aziz al-Shaikh, to sound out the Syrians and find out whether we were facing a purely local problem or whether they were obeying an order from Damascus. If it were the latter, I would have to respect it. Major General Abd al-Aziz reported back that the Syrians had no formal instructions forbidding them to work with the Americans. Finding himself in uncharted territory, the Syrian divisional commander, Major General Nadim Faris Abbas, was simply playing safe. He was a good and amiable soldier who always greeted me with a warm smile (and with whom I shared an enjoyment of food).

But the time had come for me to intervene with the Syrian forces commander, Major General Ali Habib. Not wanting to make a big issue of it, or force him to take up a position he might later regret, I decided to call a meeting of all the commanders – the Egyptian, the Syrian, the Kuwaiti, the French and so forth – for a review of our campaign plans. It had been my deliberate policy to keep these commanders out with their troops in the Northern Area Command, a long way from politics in Riyadh, which was my business. Had I allowed them to attend the daily briefings with me and Schwarzkopf, as the latter had first suggested, I would have had no end of problems. Each one of them would have wanted to have a say in the deployment of the forces. They would have wanted to work on the campaign plans. There might have been leaks and interference from governments. It would have greatly complicated my decision-making, so I kept them out of town. I wanted to avoid the Tower of Babel effect, in which important issues would be lost in a tumult of voices, grievances and details. Not until the ground war was almost upon us did I agree to the Joint Forces commanders attending our meetings on a regular basis.

However, on this occasion, I thought that bringing them in for a general discussion would provide cover for the meeting I wanted to have with Major General Ali Habib. As the others were leaving, I asked him to stay behind for a moment.

"If you have orders not to work with the American air controllers, please let me know," I said. "I will defend you."

"No, on the contrary," he replied. "We have no problem with
them. There must have been a misunderstanding. We would
like to have a TACP with us."

But Lieutenant Colonel Ayedh al-Ja'id, my air force representative, had confirmed to me that, at a lower level, the Syrians
had refused to accept an American team. It took a few days to
straighten things out.

In the event, the Syrians agreed to work with the Americans
and gradually became involved in training. They even treated
the Americans very hospitably. When I went to visit the Syrian
contingent and had lunch with their officers, the American air
control team was there as well. The relationship eventually went
more smoothly than I could have imagined.

Once all the new air defense equipment was in place and
working, my multinational units felt confident and secure, and
serious training could begin. I had had to smooth some ruffled
feathers, but the cohesion of the Coalition – my number one
objective – had been assured.

❦

On being appointed Joint Forces Commander on August 10, my
first task had been to build a team. This I did by personally
interviewing and selecting senior men in every field – whether
it was the land forces, air force, navy, air defense, logistics, intelligence, communications, planning, chemical warfare, and so
forth. I then delegated authority to these men to pick their
own assistants. Within a week I had a staff to fill the command
structure I had devised.

The first officer I appointed was Colonel Abdallah al-
Suwaylim, a clever, active and loyal officer who had been my
office director at the Air Defense Command and my trusted aide
in the Chinese missile project. He now became the director of
my office at the Joint Forces Command. A graduate of Saudi
Arabia's Command and Staff College, he also had a degree in
management from Oregon State University. He was joined by
Captain Zaki Marzuk, head of my security team, a well-trained

officer who had completed several courses in the U.S. and whose efficiency was matched only by his charm and discretion. As my ADC, I chose Colonel Ahmad Lafi whose personality and talent for leadership I had grown to appreciate at air defense. He accompanied me everywhere throughout the crisis and kept a record of my meetings and activities in a series of hand written notebooks.

As I have already mentioned, I chose as my deputy commander Major General Abd al-Aziz al-Shaikh, a man whose complete frankness was hard to take in peacetime but was invaluable in war. As Chief of Staff I eventually chose a distinguished officer, Major General Talal al-Otaibi of the armored corps, then the commandant of our Command and Staff College. He did a very good job.

In the field, my two key officers were Major General Salih al-Muhaya, the Eastern Area Commander based at the King Fahd Military City, Dhahran, and Major General Abd al-Rahman al-Alkami, the Northern Area Commander based at the King Khaled Military City, Hafr al-Batin. Somewhat later in the crisis, when it was evident that we might have to move quickly against the Iraqis and that these two area commanders would be too far back and too busy at base to command forward troops, I created two forward command posts, Joint Forces Command-East and Joint Forces Command-North, linked directly to my command in Riyadh. JFC-East, 350 miles north of Dhahran, was under Major General Sultan 'Adi al-Mutairi – who was later to lead the Arab forces into Kuwait City – while JFC-North was under Major General Sulaiman al-Wuhayyib. Operational responsibility over maneuver units was vested in these forward commanders, while logistical and administrative support remained in the hands of the area commanders. These changes had the advantage of freeing the area commanders from tactical and operational responsibilities in order to devote themselves fully to the crucial problems of logistics, essential for the effectiveness of our own forces and central to our host nation responsibilities towards others. Separating operational from logistical responsibility was an innovation. The fundamental military rule of unity of command was maintained, although it was stretched. But it worked.

I chose two logistics supremos who, in my opinion, were the unsung heroes of the war – Brigadier General Abd al-Aziz al-Hussein was director of the support unit responsible for the logistics of the Western forces, while Brigadier General Salem al-Uwaymer was the logistics chief for the Saudis and for the other Arab and Islamic friendly forces. A strict, highly devout Muslim, Brigadier General Uwaymer wore a long untrimmed beard. He was dedicated to his work and proved himself to be a top-notch logistician. With thousands of contracts to be negotiated and implemented at speed, I needed someone of scrupulous honesty.

The Air Force Commander submitted to me a list of four officers for me to choose one as the air force representative on the Joint Forces Command. But I rejected all four, and instead personally chose Lieutenant Colonel Ayedh al-Ja'id, an F-15 pilot, a superb administrator and one of the finest air force officers I have ever met. He and his team of air force officers relieved me of enormous burdens by playing a useful coordinating role. As will be recalled, the Coalition was to deploy almost 5,000 aircraft, a vast and complex operation which demanded the closest cooperation – in fact nothing less than integration – between U.S. and Saudi air force personnel, who were soon joined at Saudi air force headquarters by British, French and other representatives. All these allied aircraft needed support – in the form of bases, hangars, control towers, radars, clean runways, working lights, maintenance workshops, accommodation for the pilots and crew, food – and aviation fuel and still more fuel of all varieties and in unimaginable quantities. Much of this support was provided superbly by the Royal Saudi Air Force through the Joint Forces Command.

Until their air defenses were ready, allied aircraft needed to be dispersed to make them less vulnerable to attack. As Prince Sultan had allowed me to use some of the facilities of the Presidency of Civil Aviation, I was able to arrange to disperse many military aircraft to civilian airports. There were inevitable hiccups and moments of sheer panic, but thanks to Lieutenant Colonel Ayedh and his colleagues – and of course to the many air operations officers at headquarters and at air bases around the country – the whole air operation ran as smoothly as clockwork and, as is well-attested, there was not a single midair collision.

Special tribute should be paid to four commanders: the Chief of the Air Operations Directorate, Brigadier General Ahmad al-Sudairy, who made a great contribution to the success of the air campaign but who regrettably died shortly after the war; Brigadier General Prince Turki bin Nasser, Commander of the King Abd al-Aziz Air Base, Dhahran, the largest in the Middle East and situated in the most vitally important region of the Kingdom; Brigadier General Prince Mansur bin Bandar, Commander of the Prince Abdallah Air Base at Jeddah; and Brigadier General Prince Abd al-Rahman bin Fahd al-Faisal, Commander of the King Fahd Air Base, Taif, whose military qualities I have admired over many years. The task of ensuring the closest operational relationship with the air forces of all Coalition members, and especially with the U.S., rested largely on the shoulders of all the base commanders.

Providing and installing our field communications – sometimes requiring miracles of improvisation – was the responsibility of Brigadier General Daoud al-Bassam, the founder and head of the Air Defense Forces communications department. He is one of the most untidy officers I have known but also one of the most brilliant, indeed something of a genius in his field.

Allied naval forces at sea required far less support from us than the air forces. Nevertheless, the man the Saudi Navy sent me, Rear Admiral Shami al-Zahri, did a most competent job.

Major General Salih al-Ghufayli (now our Ambassador to the United Arab Emirates) is a wise man whom Prince Sultan nominated as Chairman of a War Media Committee responsible for controlling all information questions relating to the military, and for working throughout the crisis in coordination with the Ministry of Information. I was able to ask him to secure all the permissions and authorizations which my command needed from Prince Sultan's office. I should add that he also had to correct my mistakes. I would sometimes jump the gun and do something without authorization, leaving him to put it all in writing and tidy things up.

To negotiate and sign treaties, protocols, memoranda of understanding and Host Nation Agreements with more than thirty Coalition members, I needed the help of a skilled diplomat. The Foreign Ministry, under the able direction of my cousin, Prince Saud al-Faisal, sent me the names of half a dozen candidates, from which I selected Dr. Muhammad Omar al-Madani, a veteran ambassador and specialist in international law whom I had first met on the Improved Hawk committee in 1974. He proved an outstanding representative of his ministry. To cut through red tape and speed the flow of information, a special operations room was set up at the Foreign Ministry. All information relating to members of the Coalition was channeled to that operations room and then, through Ambassador Madani, to me.

In choosing a representative from the Ministry of Interior I sought the advice of the Minister, Prince Naif bin Abd al-Aziz, who was kind enough to send me one of his senior officials, Major General Muhammad al-Suhaili. He and his staff kept me informed of any warlike incident − coastal incursions, Scud impacts, casualties, major accidents, terrorist threats, and the like − which might have had an impact on the activities of my command. Internal security officers played a most valuable role in helping the military police direct the huge volume of military traffic on our roads, especially in the great move west, when Coalition forces moved from defense to attack positions.

Senior security officers, assigned by Prince Naif, also joined the team to organize the screening of the thousands of refugees which poured into the Kingdom from Kuwait at the two main crossing points of al-Khafji and al-Ruq'i. After the chaos of the first few days, the screening became both more effective and less obtrusive. Suspected of harboring Iraqi agents, certain refugee families were kept under discreet surveillance for weeks. In fact, the Iraqis sent quite a few people over the border with weapons and money, posing as refugees but, so far as I know, they were all detected. The absence of terrorist incidents throughout the crisis must be attributed to the excellence of the Saudi internal security organization. I cannot mention this subject without paying tribute to the extraordinary efforts of Prince Naif who, as

Minister of Interior for the past 20 years, is in truth the architect of the Kingdom's internal security. His presence in that role throughout the crisis relieved us all of a great deal of anxiety.

Our intelligence team, headed by Major General Muhammad 'Id al-Otaibi, a daring and resourceful officer who is now our Ambassador in Afghanistan, also took in hand a campaign of psychological warfare against Iraq. In this task, they were helped by an Egyptian officer, Major General Amin Husni, who in my opinion is one of the most expert officers in this field in the Arab world. Major General Husni was one of four Egyptian liaison officers whom I attached to my headquarters.

To head my financial team, an obvious choice was Ali al-Hidaithi, the principal financial controller of the Air Defense Forces, where he had demonstrated his ability over several years.

In charge of personnel was Brigadier General Ghazi Muflih al-Harbi, an excellent man, a strict disciplinarian devoted to duty, and an old colleague who now commands the Air Defense Forces Institute.

Two months before the war started, it became apparent to me that we would have to give a daily briefing to the press, similar to that of the Americans. But who was to be our spokesman? I needed to find a suitable person and make sure he was properly briefed. My choice fell on a one-star general who had trained for many years in the United States. He spoke fluent English and seemed tailor-made for the job. Without consulting anyone, I appointed him. He gave the first two briefings of the war – but they proved unsuccessful. In every other way he was an excellent officer, but he just did not have a gift for handling the media. I had to get him off the job, and pondered how to do it tactfully. But when I broke the news to him, I was relieved to hear him exclaim: "That's the best news ever! May I say something as a friend? I was dreading having to give those briefings. I couldn't sleep from worry. Thank you, sir, very, very much!"

I called Prince Sultan and admitted my mistake. He recommended another good English speaker, Colonel Ahmad Muhammad Rubayan, who after being well briefed and well coached did a very creditable job as our spokesman throughout the war.

My instructions to our spokesmen throughout the crisis were

not to exaggerate or minimize our achievements, but to stick to the facts. I was anxious not to repeat the mistake the Arabs had made in 1967. They were not to suppress information unless it jeopardized our national security or that of our allies. However, I barred the spokesmen from access to the planning team to restrict their knowledge of future operations, and so protect them from any inadvertent slip of the tongue in their dealings with the media.

Last but far from least, to look after my public relations I was fortunate to have the services of Colonel Shakir Idris. He handled the press, arranged all my trips, both inside and outside the Kingdom, handled questions of protocol like a born diplomat, and took in hand many other matters with which he had become familiar over the previous six years as my public relations director at Air Defense Forces headquarters.

What all armies need – and few Arab armies have – is a sound system for evaluating officers. In all too many cases, sympathy, friendship and family ties tend to intrude into the writing of officers' confidential reports, so that accurate grading and assessment become impossible. When I was putting my team together I chose a number of officers from other arms on the basis of favorable reports, only to find them hopeless when it came to work. I was forced to get rid of them. Six months before the crisis, I had proposed a system for evaluating officers to my colleagues on the Higher Officers' Committee. I am a diehard proponent of discipline and training, believing that it is pointless matching top-notch, high-tech equipment with low-grade, or only average soldiers. To get the best out of men and equipment one has to shake old habits and tread on toes, because most people hate change and will resist it. But in forcing through reforms at Air Defense Forces Command, I always tried not to offend. I might punish someone in the morning, and play cards with him in the evening. I did not want him to believe I was against him personally; simply that he had to do his job. These were the principles I sought to apply at the Joint Forces Command.

ORGANIZATION OF JOINT FORCES AND THEATER OF OPERATIONS COMMAND

As of October, 1990

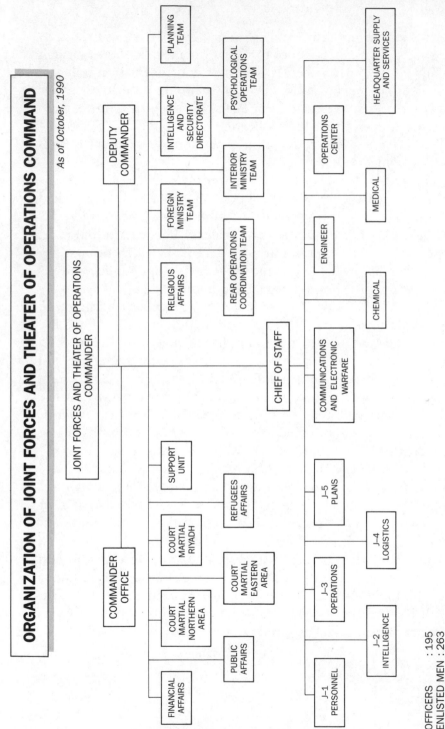

OFFICERS : 195
ENLISTED MEN : 263
CIVILIANS : 79
TOTAL 537

DESERT SHIELD
OPERATIONAL THEATER COMMAND RELATIONS

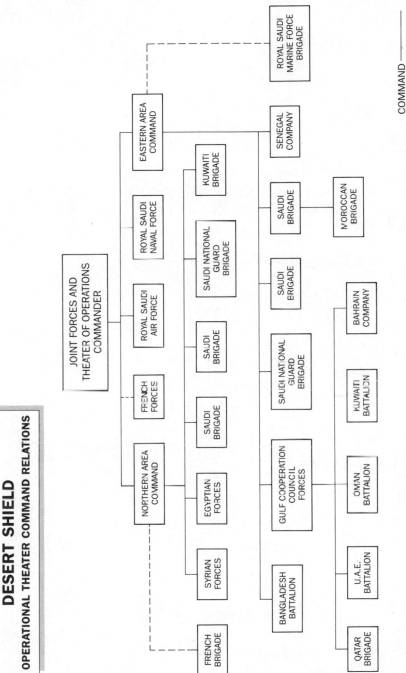

Operation plan for defense of Saudi Arabia (unclassified)

COMMAND ——————
OPERATIONAL CONTROL — — —

JOINT FORCES AND THEATER OF OPERATIONS COMMANDER

NORTHERN AREA COMMAND

FRENCH FORCES

ROYAL SAUDI AIR FORCE

ROYAL SAUDI NAVAL FORCE

EASTERN AREA COMMAND

ROYAL SAUDI MARINE FORCE BRIGADE

FRENCH BRIGADE

SYRIAN FORCES

EGYPTIAN FORCES

SAUDI BRIGADE

SAUDI BRIGADE

SAUDI NATIONAL GUARD BRIGADE

KUWAITI BRIGADE

SENEGAL COMPANY

BANGLADESH BATTALION

GULF COOPERATION COUNCIL FORCES

SAUDI NATIONAL GUARD BRIGADE

SAUDI BRIGADE

SAUDI BRIGADE

MOROCCAN BRIGADE

QATAR BRIGADE

U.A.E. BATTALION

OMAN BATTALION

KUWAITI BATTALION

BAHRAIN COMPANY

DESERT STORM
OPERATIONAL THEATER COMMAND RELATIONS

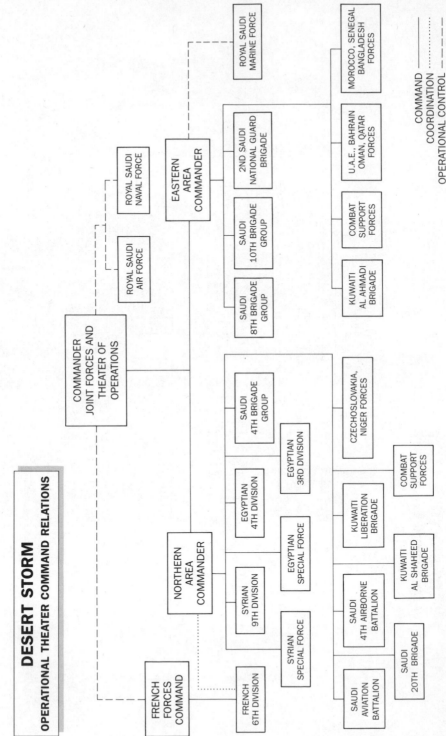

Operation Desert Storm (unclassified)

COALITION COMMAND RELATIONSHIPS DURING DESERT SHIELD

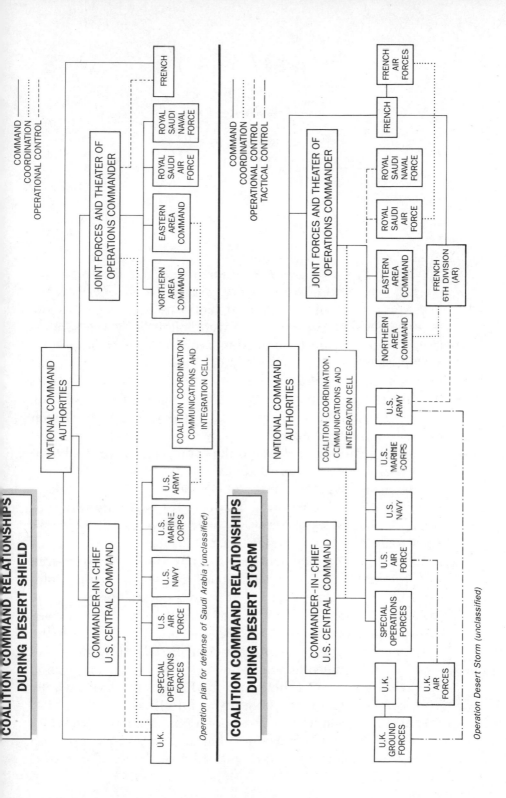

Operation plan for defense of Saudi Arabia (unclassified)

COALITION COMMAND RELATIONSHIPS DURING DESERT STORM

Operation Desert Storm (unclassified)

CHAPTER XV

Managing the Coalition – 2

W HEN SADDAM THREATENED US, the allies that came to our aid were a very diverse lot. At one extreme, the big old U.S.A. sent half a million troops; at the other, Niger sent 481 men, who were followed by 496 Senegalese, a medical team from Poland, a few dozen *mujahedin* from Afghanistan and quite a few others – most of them militarily insignificant, but politically important. The number of countries that made a significant military contribution to the Coalition was very small, but we needed the others just as badly. It was my job to combine all the contingents into one overall effort and give everyone a purpose in the campaign, for that surely is what coalition warfare is all about.

Among our allies the closest, both geographically and ideologically, were our five partners in the Gulf Cooperation Council (GCC) – that is to say Kuwait itself, the victim of Saddam's aggression, together with our other Gulf neighbors, the United Arab Emirates, Bahrain, Oman and Qatar. During the Iraq–Iran war, the rulers of the six GCC states had set up a small joint force known as Peninsula Shield to respond to threats to the Gulf region. It was based in Saudi Arabia under a Saudi commander, in recognition of the fact that the Kingdom was the biggest participant. Saudi Arabia contributed a brigade group while each of the others a battalion or less. One of the first disagreeable lessons of the crisis was that this force was wholly inadequate to handle the Iraqi thrust into Kuwait.

Peninsula Shield fell under my Joint Forces Command. When I inspected it, I realized at once that its structure and strength were not adapted to the present crisis. As each of our GCC partners was sending us more troops, it seemed logical to attach the Peninsula Shield units to their mother units, or assign them to the task forces I was then forming on the basis of their armament and capability, and of our immediate defensive needs. Thus, I issued orders attaching the Omani battalion and the Bahraini company to the 8th Saudi Mechanized Brigade, and the Emirates and Qatari battalions to the 10th Saudi Mechanized Brigade, both brigades constituting in those early days our thin defense line against a possible Iraqi thrust towards our Eastern Province.

As for the 25 officers which made up the headquarters staff of Peninsula Shield, I proposed that they rejoin their home units, seeing they no longer had a separate body of troops to command. The Saudi commander of Peninsula Shield, Major General Turki Hedaijan, resumed his command of a Saudi brigade under the Northern Area Commander.

Early in the crisis, Prince Sultan instructed me to visit the Gulf states to brief their rulers on the steps we were taking to confront the threat from Saddam. Not unnaturally, they wished to be informed of the role we envisaged for their troops. I would be reporting to them as the commander of their forces in exactly the same way as I reported to my own King. I intended to give each ruler a military and intelligence briefing showing the extent of the Iraqi threat, the deployment of our forces, and the thinking behind our defense plan. The Gulf rulers wanted me to come in September, but I deliberately delayed my trip until early October as I was busy amending and improving the hasty defense plan which I had put together in the first panic-stricken days after the invasion. I was reluctant to make public the details of my new deployments until they had been implemented. This was secret information which I feared Iraq might exploit if it were revealed prematurely.

It was eventually decided that I would start my briefing sessions in our summer resort of Taif on October 8 by calling on the ruler of Kuwait, Shaikh Jaber, at his quarters at the Sheraton Hotel which had been put at his disposal, and then visit the other Gulf rulers between October 11 and 17.

As it happened, the day I flew to Taif was the day on which the Crown Prince of Kuwait, Shaikh Saad, was heading for Dubai in

the United Arab Emirates to offer his condolences to Shaikh
Maktoum on the death of his father, Shaikh Rashid, the shrewd
architect of Dubai's prosperity. We met at the airport. Although
we had no maps, I was able to give Shaikh Saad a broad view
of the military preparations we were making on the border.

I was struck by his calm. He was proud, he said, that a son of
the Arabs was in command. Then, taking my hand, he looked
at me earnestly and added: "I want you to promise that when
the time comes to free Kuwait, Kuwaiti troops will be in the
front line." I replied that I was honored to command units from
his country and that I would do everything in my power to
make sure they played a leading role.

In what was for me one of the most touching encounters of
the crisis, I then went to see Shaikh Jaber in the hotel which
had become his headquarters. I could see in his eyes a poignant,
yet unspoken question: "When are you going to liberate
Kuwait?" It was hard for me to explain that the build-up of
forces would take time and that, in spite of the terrible things
the Iraqis were doing to Kuwait, we had to plan carefully and
cooperate with the forces of many nations to eject the Iraqis
with the minimum of casualties. He listened very quietly, but I
could see the grief in his face.

On a subsequent visit a little later, I was able to explain our
strategy in greater detail to Shaikh Nawwaf, the Kuwaiti Minister of Defense. In response to my exposition, he conveyed to
me a word of encouragement from Shaikh Jaber which touched
me deeply: "Tell our son, Khaled," the Amir of Kuwait had said,
"you design [the clothes] and we will wear [them]" – *ent tfassil
w-hinna nilbas*. His message brought home to me the heavy responsibility I bore. I swore to him that in every move I made,
the fate of Kuwait would be my prime concern. It is a pledge
which I trust I have kept. We, in Saudi Arabia, feel that Kuwait
is our second home, and for me personally, after the experience
of the crisis, it will always have a large place in my heart.

I was extremely well received in the Gulf states. Several of
the rulers were kind enough to say they were glad I was in
charge. I was especially touched by words of encouragement
from men who had known me since my youth, like the Crown
Prince of Qatar, Shaikh Hamad bin Khalifa al-Thani, or the

Crown Prince of Bahrain, Shaikh Hamad bin Isa al-Khalifa, and his cousin the Minister of Defense, Shaikh Khalifa bin Ahmad al-Khalifa, who nearly 25 years earlier had endured with me the rigors and joys of Sandhurst.

The infantry company the Bahrainis sent us performed well, but it was understandable that they should want to keep the bulk of their small army at home to defend their islands in the event of an Iraqi attack. Bahrain's Shaikh Isa Air Base played a valuable role in the conflict, which is no doubt why Iraq launched three Scuds at it. They missed the base and caused no damage or casualties.

Bahrain made another little-known contribution to the Kuwaiti cause. Computer disks containing details of Kuwait's population were smuggled out of Kuwait to Bahrain where Bahraini experts, with the help of Dutch and French technicians, managed to break the computer codes and recover the material which was then handed over to the Kuwait government in exile. Although the manner by which they were obtained was kept secret, these population statistics became a United Nations document and allowed the Kuwait government to defend itself against Iraqi claims.

When I briefed Shaikh Isa, the ruler of Bahrain, about the military situation, I found him robustly hawkish. Believing that time was running against us, he wanted the Coalition to take immediate action in the form of a massive air strike to dislodge Saddam from Kuwait. As with Shaikh Jaber of Kuwait, it was not easy for me to explain the Coalition's need for time in which to build up its strength.

Our Ambassador in Bahrain at that time was Dr. Ghazi al-Gosaibi, a distinguished poet and writer (who had been Saudi Minister for Industry and is today our Ambassador to the United Kingdom). As I was about to board my aircraft after my visit, he thrust a package into my hands with the words, "Please open this on the plane." Inside I found two tapes of his poems, a handsome Mont Blanc pen, and a note which read, "I'm sending you this pen in the hope that you will use it to sign the order for the liberation of Kuwait, but please make haste for the ink will soon run dry . . ." When, in January 1991, the time came for Schwarzkopf and me to sign the combined campaign plan for Desert Storm, I remembered Gosaibi's words and used his pen. Regrettably, it was not as soon as he and my Bahraini hosts had hoped.

I knew I could count on a warm welcome in Qatar where the Crown Prince, Shaikh Hamad bin Khalifa al-Thani, had been my friend since 1964 when, as boys, we had gone to London together for a two-month language course. After I had briefed the ruler, Shaikh Khalifa, I was delighted to learn that Qatar had decided to double its military contribution to the Coalition almost to brigade strength. Qatari tanks were to play a notable role in the battle for al-Khafji. In Salala, I was privileged to have a private talk with the ruler of Oman, Sultan Qabus, a man so disciplined, enlightened and well informed that one cannot help but respect him. The fact that he was also a Sandhurst graduate like myself contributed to my warm feelings towards him.

In Abu Dhabi, I was received in his palace by Shaikh Zayid, President of the United Arab Emirates, surrounded by his ministers. After an exchange of greetings and formalities, he expressed the wish to speak to me alone, retaining by his side only his son Muhammad bin Zayid, then Deputy Chief of Staff for Operations, who had already earned a high reputation for professionalism (which he was later to confirm as UAE Chief of Staff).

At one point in our discussion of the military situation, Shaikh Zayid put a point to me which I felt I needed to contest. I said to him:

"Sir, may I speak to you as I would to King Fahd? Would you permit me to talk to you as to a father? I consider myself your son – like Muhammad here."

Shaikh Zayid's kindly face took on a serious expression:

"You? Like Muhammad? Never!"

Thinking I had offended him, I prepared myself for a rebuke, only to hear him say:

"In this crisis, you are more precious to me than Muhammad himself!"

One of my headaches during the crisis was what to do with small national contingents of a few hundred men each. What mission could I entrust to them? How could I deploy them most effectively? Pondering the problem, an idea came to me which was encapsulated in the term "strongpoint." We had a great number of vital locations to defend, such as the oil facilities at al-Safaniya, not far from the Kuwaiti border, and the major oil terminal at Ras Tannura, to cite two examples among many.

I determined to use the small national contingents to establish defensive strongpoints at such key locations. This gave me added flexibility as it removed the need to disperse or split up major units. The strongpoints were designed to be self-sufficient. Well dug in, they could hold their ground and threaten the flank of any Iraqi advance. Each force had to be deployed according to its capability, to fulfill the mission assigned to it. However, in appraising each national contingent, I did not wish to change their concept of employment or place them in a situation where language differences would create problems of communication. I wanted everyone to feel welcome and be comfortable. Above all, I wanted to avoid clashes between the different contingents. In order to maintain the cohesion of the Coalition and respect the political sensitivities of each member, I tried to be fair to everyone and to greet every commander personally, whether he was a general or a major. All commanders of national contingents deserved equal treatment, regardless of rank. (I must confess, however, that I paid special attention to the Egyptian and Syrian contingents, well aware that the Saudi–Egyptian–Syrian axis was vital to the stability of the Coalition and of the region as a whole.)

My insistence on strongpoints led to a minor disagreement with Schwarzkopf. I recall a meeting we held on September 13 when we reviewed our defense plans with our staffs and at which our different perspectives emerged. At the start, because he had very few troops available, he could only contemplate the defense of enclaves around Jubail and Dhahran, the major ports and airports of our Eastern Province which were vital for the build-up and deployment of American forces. Beyond that, he preferred a mobile defense able to engage whatever the Iraqis threw at us. Wedded to enclave defense, he did not like my forward strongpoints, no doubt fearing they might be overrun or bypassed by advancing Iraqi forces. He wanted to trade space for time. But I had to look at the situation from a political as much as a military standpoint. Right at the start, as I have already recounted, once I had realized that our border town of al-Khafji, within range of Iraqi artillery, was indefensible, I had pulled back my forces a few dozen miles to create a "killing zone." But I intended to hold a line north of our seaport of Ras Mish'ab. It must also be said that the two forward areas close to the border were at that time my responsibility, not Schwarz-kopf's. American troops were still far to the rear and were not yet ready to fight.

My defensive strategy in the event of an Iraqi attack into the Kingdom could be summed up as follows: first, draw them into the "killing zone" so as to expose their extended lines of com-munication to air attack; secondly, effect a fighting withdrawal towards the east so as to reinforce the coastal strongpoints. Such a coastal belt would have several advantages: it would benefit from supporting gunfire from Coalition ships in the Gulf and, in addition, if the Iraqis attacked south, our strongpoints would be a thorn in their side and they would have to divert forces to deal with them.

Fortunately, my differences with Schwarzkopf over these defense questions, which provided for some lively discussions in the early months, never blew up into anything more serious because Saddam did not move. Had Saddam chosen to attack us, it might have been a different story.

The 1,200 Moroccan rangers were among the first foreign troops to arrive. They were the best desert fighters I had ever seen, but they also constituted the smallest force to reach us from a major Arab state. I installed them in a "strongpoint" at al-Safaniya, near Ras Mish'ab, guarding the approaches to an offshore oil field. As it was my duty to improve the living con-ditions of all the forces that had come to our aid, I sent the Moroccans tents, good sleeping bags, mobile kitchens and supplies of food. But when I went to see how they were getting on, their commander, Colonel Ahmad Binyas, a quiet, well-disciplined officer, asked to speak to me privately.

"My God," I confided to my Area Commander, "I must have forgotten to send them something they need." I was used to getting requests for more of everything when I visited field units. People would ask and ask.

So, when I was alone with the Moroccan commander, I inquired what I could do for him.

"I really don't know how to put it," he began. "But I must tell you. You are sending us too much! Your supplies are so lavish that I am afraid they will spoil my troops. I would like you to reduce everything. We don't need this, or this, or that . . ." And he reeled off a list of items.

I looked at him and said, "I only wish all the commanders were like you!" The Moroccans were the least demanding of all the forces that I had to deal with.

When they first arrived they said to me: "We are under your command. Do with us as you please!" But, seeing that they had put their trust in me, I sensed that I had to protect the interests of their country and of their supreme commander, King Hassan, a monarch whom I know personally and for whom I have the greatest admiration. From the start of the crisis, he had tried to mediate the dispute between Iraq and Kuwait. Rather than condemning Saddam out of hand, he had used soft words to persuade him of the disaster which war would bring. In adopting this stance, King Hassan was no doubt taking into account the powerful current of opposition in Morocco to an American-led war against Iraq, and to the even greater opposition in neighboring Algeria, a fellow member of the Arab Maghreb Union with whom he was then seeking better relations.

It was my duty, therefore, not to do anything with the Moroccan contingent that might embarrass him. I had to play it by ear. I asked Colonel Ahmad Binyas whether he had received any instructions from King Hassan on the crucial question of whether his men were ready to fight Iraq. He said he had received none. "I am under your command," he repeated, "and will do whatever you ask."

I told him I was anxious to abide by the wishes of the Moroccan government on this question. But he declared, "I am a military commander, at your orders. My instructions are that you will assess what mission you wish to give us."

I decided to ponder the matter for 24 hours. I had two options. Either to refer the question to higher authority at the risk of causing embarrassment, or to assume the political burden myself. I decided to adopt the latter course. If it turned out to be the wrong decision, I would take the blame. As it happened, we had planned to leave some troops in defensive positions in the rear once we attacked into Kuwait. Some Saudi National Guard units had been given this mission. I decided to put the Moroccans in a defensive position also, where they would not be called upon to enter Kuwait. They participated fully in Desert Shield, and were ready to fight back if the Iraqis had attempted to outflank their positions, but I left them out of Desert Storm.

Niger and Senegal also sent us well-disciplined contingents under well-trained officers. In absolute terms, their numbers were very small, but in percentage terms, the few hundred men that came, amounting to a substantial proportion of their army, represented a remarkable effort unmatched by any other state. Niger, for example, sent 481 men out of an army of 3,200. They offered to send more but, as they expected us to equip and supply them fully, I contented myself with this token force. The support of Egyptian and Syrian forces – and of American, British and French forces as well – was already straining my resources. So, while we were anxious to have as many countries as possible in the Coalition, I had a preference for small contingents. I established the Niger contingent in a strongpoint near the city of Hafr al-Batin.

In early September, I received a visit from the Senegalese Chief of Staff who conveyed to me a pledge of solidarity from President Abdou Diouf, a distinguished figure well respected in Saudi Arabia who had assumed the presidency in 1981 following the retirement of Leopold Sedar Senghor. His largely Muslim country was anxious to participate in the defense of the Holy Places. But Senegal was engaged in a bloody conflict of its own with its northern neighbor, Mauritania – which, in turn, was apparently backed by Iraq. This caused the Chief of Staff to declare that the security of Saudi Arabia could not be separated from that of Senegal, and that they were prepared to give their all! I thanked him for his support and responded with similar courtesies.

The Chief of Staff was anxious for me to tell him what mission I had in mind for his troops. I had to explain that in a large theater of operations, it was sometimes difficult to define the mission of a force as large as a brigade, let alone a smaller unit. He proposed sending us 1,100 officers and men, and more if required. But when I inquired whether they would come with their own vehicles and supplies, he mentioned Senegal's limited resources and their struggle with Mauritania, adding that their weapons, uniforms and equipment were more suited to jungle than desert warfare. I got the point. I said it would be best if they sent a single battalion of 400 or 500 men, carrying their personal weapons only.

Requesting an hour's break in our meeting, I telephoned the man in charge of our weapons and ammunition directorate, Muhammad al-Hidaithi, whom I had got to know and appreciate during the Chinese missile project. There seemed to be no problem he could not solve. I recalled we were phasing out of our armed forces over 200 French-built AML-90 Panhard armored fighting vehicles of a type with which the Senegalese were familiar.

"How many can you make operational?" I asked.

"As many as you want."

"Fine. Hold on to them."

In due course, we issued these vehicles to the Senegalese, and also to the contingents from Niger and Morocco, and at the end of the war, on Prince Sultan's instructions, we gave the armored cars to them in gratitude for their help.

"I have to be honest with you," I told the Senegalese Chief of Staff. "Hold your forces at home until we are ready for them." Within a month I sent two Boeing 747s to fly them in. It was the easiest way to do it. I put the Senegalese at the Ras Mish'ab strongpoint, next to the Moroccans. As they both spoke French, this solved a communication problem.

The Senegalese commander, Colonel Mohamadou Keita (now Chief of Staff), was naturally concerned about the possibility of casualties. For a reason which I cannot explain, I told him I would swear on the Quran that the life of every soldier under my command, whatever the country he came from, was as precious to me as the life of a Saudi. I would endeavor to minimize casualties, but if there were to be any, Saudi Arabia would take the biggest share. However, two tragic events, which were to move me more deeply than I can say, were to prevent me from keeping my promise.

On February 21, 1991, shortly before the end of the war, an Iraqi Frog missile hit the Senegalese strongpoint as the men were lining up in the morning for food from a truck. Eight were wounded. A month later, on March 21, a Saudi C-130 Hercules transport plane, carrying a party of Senegalese soldiers on a return flight from Makkah, where they had gone to perform the *umrah*, crashed on attempting to land at Ras Mish'ab. To my great distress, 91 Senegalese were killed – a fifth of their contingent – as well as the six-man Saudi crew. Senegal suffered proportionately more than any other member of the Coalition.

We were ready to repatriate the bodies, but the families of the dead men said they preferred them to be buried in Saudi Arabia. So we buried them at al-Nu'ayriyah, in the Eastern Province, on March 22. I spent a day there and joined in digging their graves and carrying their shrouded bodies. Their Minister of Defense and their Chief of Staff came and we prayed together. For me, it was one of the most painful moments of the war, which to this day remains a subject of immense sadness.

I recommended – and Prince Sultan endorsed my suggestion at once – that all the families of the dead, from whatever Muslim country, should be invited to perform the pilgrimage. Special planes were provided for them.

A more cheerful and a more unusual duty for me was to welcome contingents from countries which, until recently, had been in the Soviet orbit. I believe I was the first person ever to sign a treaty between Saudi Arabia on the one hand and Czechoslovakia, Hungary, and Poland on the other. Early in the crisis, all three had declared their willingness to help us by sending medical assistance or other noncombatant units. When I heard they were coming, I felt a special thrill. It was our first opportunity to work closely with former members of the Warsaw Pact. And when I met them, I found the enthusiasm of their men and women remarkable.

Czechoslovakia sent us a 180-strong chemical defense unit – a capability I truly needed, because no one knew whether or not Saddam would use his chemical weapons. After the first few weeks, it seemed highly improbable that Saddam would dare launch a conventional attack: the Coalition was far too strong. But the possibility of his using unconventional weapons remained a persistent worry right up to the end. He had used chemical weapons before against the Iranians and the Kurds, and many believed he would do so again if hard-pressed. In the area north of Hafr al-Batin, I was totally dependent on the Czechoslovaks to monitor the possible use of poisonous chemicals and to wash down or otherwise decontaminate any affected personnel, equipment and terrain. They set up a small chemical laboratory of their own.

When the Czechoslovaks first arrived at Jeddah in early November 1990, I went to meet their delegation. Our task was to draw up an agreement covering the various aspects of their participation. As it happened, I had not yet been given the necessary authorization by Prince Sultan to sign an agreement with them, but I knew the authorization was on its way to me. Not wishing to pass up the chance of being the first Saudi to put his name to an agreement with Czechoslovakia, I decided to sign nevertheless.

Poland dispatched a hospital ship, a rescue ship, and a medical team of 152 doctors and nurses who came in very useful at the King Khaled Military Hospital at Hafr al-Batin. Many of the foreign nurses employed at our forward hospitals had left for home, frightened by reports of what the Iraqis did to nurses in Kuwait. Some packed their bags even though they were working in Riyadh and Jeddah. So we were glad to have the Poles and also a 38-strong medical team from Hungary (which included several top specialists) which we attached to our forces.

Bangladesh made a most valuable contribution to our logistics, sending us some of their best support units which, at that stage, I needed more urgently than combat troops. Antiwar disturbances in Dacca may have put a constraint on the type of help they could offer us. I developed a great respect for their army Chief of Staff, Lieutenant General Muhammad Nurreddin Khan, a powerful figure in his own country, who came to see me to make the necessary arrangements. After my retirement, I paid a visit to Bangladesh and was very touched to see that the military authorities in Dacca had assembled to meet me, not only the commander of their forces but also all the officers who had

served under my command. Many had traveled a long way in
spite of the floods, the refugees from Burma and other difficulties
then affecting that brave country.

Pakistan was also a great help to us, although its troops were
not directly involved in the main theater of operations. Since
the 1970s, Pakistan had helped ease our manpower shortage.
Its fine, well-trained men were usually stationed at Tabuk in
the northwest and at Khamis Mushait in the south. When the
crisis broke out, our Chief of Staff, General Hammad, sent one
Pakistani brigade to reinforce our defensive positions facing
Yemen. Because of our fear that the Yemenis might seek to
exploit the crisis with adventures of their own, we could not
leave the south undefended. At that time, however, the
southern front was outside my theater of operations. Then,
when I learned that an Iraqi Special Forces brigade, supported
in the rear by a division, had moved into positions opposite
Ar'ar, a town in the extreme north of the Kingdom on the main
pilgrimage route from Iraq to Makkah, I brought up the 7th
Pakistani Armored Brigade to reinforce our National Guard
brigade already in place there.

❧❦

Although the 45,000-strong British expeditionary force served
under Schwarzkopf, I saw a great deal of its commanders, not
only Lieutenant General Sir Peter de la Billière, who commanded the force in theater, but also Air Chief Marshal Sir
Patrick Hine, in overall command back in the UK, who paid
frequent visits to Saudi Arabia during the crisis and with whom
I had long and most interesting talks. We both enjoyed making
forecasts and trying them out on each other. In calling on me,
both men were often accompanied by the excellent British
Ambassador, Sir Alan Munro.

I see from my diary that almost every week I received a high-
level visit from a British representative, including the Chief of
the Defense Staff, Sir David Craig, in late October and the Minister of Defense, Tom King, in mid-November. On his way out,
via Riyadh, to visit British troops in Dhahran, Mr. King suggested
a meeting but I was unfortunately unable to see him as I was

struck down by a sinus infection and a bout of severe flu, which affected my vocal cords. On his return, however, he kindly suggested rerouting his journey through Riyadh once more, and we managed to spend a useful hour together at the airport, although I was still very sick. I was impressed by his grasp of detail and was glad he had insisted on seeing me.

In early December, a Saudi physician, Dr. Rashid al-Kohaimi, and Dr. Sayyid Ayyoub (my father's doctor for a quarter of a century), together with a team of British doctors, led by an ear, nose and throat specialist, Dr. Richard Maw of Bristol University, drained the infected fluid from my sinuses and passed a fine fiber-optic telescope into my lungs to take a look at what was causing the trouble. On coming to an hour or two later from a general anesthetic, I made my way to a meeting with the French Chief of Staff who, judging from my battered appearance, must have wondered what I had been up to.

Mrs. Margaret Thatcher, who had been with President George Bush at Aspen, Colorado, on the day Saddam invaded, also paid a visit to the Kingdom on September 17–19, 1991, after she had left office and after the war, when most Coalition troops had already gone home. "George had been a bit wobbly," she told Prince Fahd bin Salman, then Deputy Governor of the Eastern Province, with whom she had a long talk. But, she added, she had fortunately been able to stiffen his resolve! Prince Fahd later recounted to me that, gazing at a great assembly of tanks and guns in the Eastern Province, she had exclaimed (with some hyperbole), "All of this because of me!"

Permanent members of the Security Council such as Britain and France were important members of the anti-Saddam Coalition because of their long involvement with the Middle East. Had it been up to me, I would have liked to have the Russians in as well. We did not want to be left alone with the Americans, and nor did the Americans wish to be left alone with us. Just as Saudi Arabia, Egypt and Syria were the principal members on the Arab side of the Coalition, so on the Western side the leading roles were played by the U.S., Britain and France.

When, at one of our early meetings on August 25, Sir Alan Munro, the British Ambassador, asked me whether I would like our forces to exchange intelligence about Iraq, I readily agreed.

I needed all the intelligence I could get. Accordingly, a British officer was attached to our intelligence department and provided a two-way channel for a flow of information. What the British provided turned out to be similar to what we were getting from the Americans, but it was reassuring nonetheless to receive intelligence from more than one source.

I developed a close relationship with Sir Peter de la Billière. Trust was established between us at our very first meeting when he declared, "Although I am under General Schwarzkopf's command, my government has instructed me to keep you fully informed of everything we do." I appreciated his remarks and invited him to come to see me every week, which he did. Indeed, he sometimes came more frequently. I was thus able to help resolve some of the difficulties the British forces encountered. But quite apart from day-to-day working problems, I sensed that he was anxious to enhance the wider Saudi–British relationship.

Later in the crisis, when Sir Peter sent British SAS teams into Western Iraq to hunt for Scud launchers – and thereby rob Israel of any pretext to enter the war – I was able to smooth their secret passage across our borders.

Because of his long experience of the Middle East, I found that Sir Peter had a good understanding of the constraints I found it necessary to impose on Western forces in the Kingdom, so as not to offend against local custom, tradition and above all religious practice. In managing the Coalition, one of my main responsibilities was to make sure all would be well at home once the war was over – a concern for which Sir Peter expressed a good deal of support. It was refreshing to be able to talk things over with him in a perfectly straightforward and frank way.

Knowing my views he could not agree to London's request that he issue two cans of beer to each man at Christmas, but at least he appreciated my reasons. In fact he once told me that if the troops had been allowed alcohol, there would probably have been fights between British regiments or between the British and the Americans, quite apart from unacceptable tensions with the Saudi population. Given the chance, he said, he would certainly prefer to have another "dry" war!

I, in turn, understood his reasons for wanting his main strike force – the 1st UK Armored Division – to take part in the main allied thrust into Iraq. Originally the British had been given only a supporting role in the attack which the U.S. Marine Corps was to conduct up the east coast towards Kuwait. This did not satisfy Sir Peter and resulted, as I understand it, in some sharp differences between him and Schwarzkopf.

Sir Peter believed that the British people would not be satisfied with a supporting role for their troops. In this, Britain's biggest overseas deployment since World War Two, British forces had to be seen to be part of the main thrust. There were other more technical reasons. British tank formations had been trained in long-range reconnaissance in Europe. To show off their mobility and firepower, they needed to participate in a longer, wider-ranging assault. The route up the east coast was too short for their liking and too encumbered with oil installations and pipelines.

I also suspect that though the British got on well with the American Marines, and trained successfully with them, Sir Peter was reluctant to risk his men in what might turn out to be gung-ho operations. Anxious to prove their worth in the continual Pentagon battle for budgets, the Marines might, he feared, take risks which he was not prepared to take with British soldiers. In any event, Sir Peter won his argument with Schwarzkopf and his armored division moved west, eventually taking part in the main attack into Iraq under the tactical control of the U.S. VIIth Corps.

❧⟫⟪❧

Accommodating Coalition aircraft was a complex problem in itself, made manageable by our extensive infrastructure and the high quality of our air force personnel. With several thousand allied aircraft expected in the Kingdom – excluding helicopters, carrier-based planes or long-range bombers flying in from afar – the pressure on our bases was intense. The Royal Saudi Air Force had been ordered to bring all its bases up to a maximum state of readiness. As these were still not sufficient, my staff scoured around looking for airports which were no longer in use, such as the one at al-Ahsa, east of Riyadh, which was upgraded relatively quickly and which, as I will relate in the next chapter, we allocated to the French. At al-Kharj, south of Riyadh, we were able to use a new air base still under construction to accommodate U.S. aircraft coming in from Oman and from the U.S. itself. At Tabuk, British Tornados joined U.S. F-15Cs and some of our own planes. I had no worries there because the Governor, my brother Prince Fahd, was on hand to deal admirably with all the problems which the friendly forces in his province encountered.

Qasim and Hail airports were used by our own air force; Jeddah airport was used by U.S. air tankers and B-52s; King Khalid airport at Riyadh was used by the U.S. and the French; Riyadh air base was used by American, British, French and Saudi aircraft – tankers, AWACS, transport planes; at KKMC, there were French helicopters as well as U.S. aircraft for Close Air Support missions and training; U.S. A-10 tank-killers were to be found at al-Qaisuma airport. And this was not the end of it. Air strips were provided for helicopters in forward operating areas and my staff surveyed the desert to locate suitable areas for C-130 strips to support our forces during the ground war.

Lieutenant General Horner wanted a base for his B-52s in Saudi Arabia, but both he and I were well aware of the negative image these big Cold War bombers had with the public. The U.S. was flying them out of Diego Garcia in the Indian Ocean, out of Moron in Spain and out of bases in the United Kingdom. In fact the first airplane to take off in the Gulf War was a B-52 from Louisiana: it got to the war the next day! It dropped Cruise missiles, part of the immense degradation of Iraq's air defense system. But such distant bases were hours away from Iraq. Horner argued that he could get twice the utilization rate out of the planes if they were based in Saudi Arabia. So we reached an agreement whereby the first B-52 raid would recover at Jeddah and fly the rest of the war out of Jeddah. The day the war was over, the planes would take off and fly home immediately. And that is what happened. The agreement was put in writing and I signed it.

If the truth be told, the task we faced during the crisis was not winning the war against Saddam. Considering the Coalition's overwhelming strength, that was the easiest part of it. This was one of the few wars in history in which we were absolutely certain of the outcome before we started. (Indeed I was interested to see that a book on the Gulf War, written by a team of U.S. officers and published in 1993 by the Office of the Chief of Staff, U.S. Army, was entitled *Certain Victory*.)

In my view, the greatest challenge we faced – and our failure was what Saddam was counting on – was to make sure that the members of the Coalition worked together without friction or dispute. Every time a difficulty arose, I would say, "Don't try to solve it. Just come and report it to me." I feel my main contribution was to keep all those nations in place with no problems between them. That is what my brief to "manage" the Coalition was all about.

CHAPTER XVI

Duel with Chevènement

FROM WHAT I HAVE OBSERVED of the French character, I would say that the French cherish their independence above all things and hate to be subordinate to anyone. Accordingly, they strive to achieve a position of superiority – an attitude I fully understand and respect. Yet these very characteristics were to create a few problems for me during the Gulf crisis, problems which, I hasten to add, were by no means unusual in the circumstances.

There was hardly an aspect of the French expeditionary force, known as *Les Forces Daguet*, which did not become a subject of argument – whether it was the matter of where French ground troops and combat aircraft were to be deployed, who was to control them, the adventures of their reconnaissance patrols, the entertainment of their forces, or indeed the distinctly ambivalent attitude towards the war of the French Defense Minister in Paris, Jean-Pierre Chevènement.

However, I must add in the same breath that the French trained harder and longer than any troops I had ever seen; that French suppliers went out of their way to deliver the spare parts we needed for the French-built weapons in our armed services; and that once we had settled our various disagreements the French performed faultlessly. I discovered that dealing with French generals was not so very different from dealing with French industrialists, as I had done when negotiating air defense contracts: they were extremely tough and difficult negotiators, but once they had agreed on terms they carried out their obligations to the letter.

France's military contribution to the Coalition consisted of some 54 combat aircraft, Jaguars, Mirage F1s and Mirage 2000s; 60 attack helicopters; several naval vessels; and a light armored division, equipped with AMX 10 RC tanks (wheeled not tracked), a superb highly mobile force of which any commander would be proud. It was not fashioned for static defense, still less for breaching operations, such as we eventually needed in the liberation of Kuwait. But it could travel great distances at high speed and deliver a punch where the enemy least expected it. Mobility and surprise were its watchwords. The commander of all French troops in theater – and there were some 16,500 in all – was Lieutenant General Michel Roquejeoffre, a small, seasoned and extremely tough soldier, whom my staff called "Napoleon the Second."

I attended a rapid-response exercise involving armored vehicles and helicopters by a French Foreign Legion regiment, part of the light armored division, and was hugely impressed by the toughness and combat readiness of the troops. After the exercise I was invited to join the officers in a light meal.

There, in the dust and howling wind of the desert, a guard of honor turned out in white capes and drawn sabers. Even the steward who served us tea wore his combat medals!

Before I recount some of the details of my local difficulties with the French, I should perhaps say a word about French political attitudes towards the crisis, as these provided the backdrop to my own negotiations with French commanders and the Defense Minister.

France had been a principal arms supplier to Iraq since 1974: it had been Iraq's ally for 16 years before the invasion of Kuwait. Defense Minister Chevènement, a far-left member of the Socialist Party and a leading light of the Franco–Iraqi Friendship Society, had campaigned publicly in favor of a key role for Iraq in the Middle East, seeing in Saddam's secular B'athist regime a bulwark against the forces of Islamic radicalism. There was nothing new about France's close relations with Baghdad: it had concluded major arms contracts with Iraq in 1974, and then again in 1977, 1982, 1985 and 1987. When Iraq was hardpressed by Iran in 1983, France had even lent the Iraqi air force Exocet-armed Super-Etandard warplanes from its own fleet air arm. The intimate Franco–Iraqi relationship, built up over several years and involving contracts worth billions of dollars, was a political fact of life in the region, to be compared for example to the close ties Britain maintained with a number of Gulf states or indeed to our own relationship with the United States. Needless to say, we in the Kingdom also have close relations with Britain and France.

Ideologically sympathetic to Saddam, opposed to cooperation with the United States and having no great love for traditional rulers in the Gulf, Chevènement found it difficult to follow Washington's lead and switch to outright hostility to Iraq after Saddam's invasion of Kuwait. His inclination was to give Saddam the benefit of the doubt, as was confirmed in a book he published after the crisis. In it, he went so far as to argue that the United States may have deliberately encouraged Iraq to invade Kuwait, so as to purge what it imagined to be the "Saddam Hussein abscess" threatening the oil market, Israel's security and regional stability. In other words, Chevènement believed that, far from being an aggressor, Saddam was perhaps the victim of a conspiracy!*

Holding views such as these, Chevènement opposed offensive action against Iraq, pressed for negotiations with Baghdad until the very last moment, and insisted that the Coalition's sole war aim should be the defense of Saudi Arabia. He eventually came round to the view that Kuwait had to be liberated, but he would not accept that this entailed the destruction of Iraq's military potential. When the Coalition's war plans were taking shape, the French minister objected both to the proposed strategic air campaign against Iraqi targets and to the "left hook" maneuver aimed at enveloping and destroying Iraq's Republican Guard divisions outside Kuwait. In contrast, President Mitterrand appears to have accepted from the start that a military solution might be required. Four days after Saddam's invasion, he was the first Western leader to say that the crisis had entered a phase that could lead to war — "Une logique de guerre," as he put it. He gave a similar signal when he sent the aircraft carrier *Clémenceau* to the region with a regiment of combat helicopters able to

---

* Jean-Pierre Chevènement, *Une certaine idée de la République m'amène à . . .*, Paris, 1992, p. 39.

support French ground troops if their deployment were to prove necessary. The sack by the Iraqis of the French ambassador's residence in Kuwait in September led to a hardening of Mitterrand's position.

When French troops were deployed on the ground, further strains emerged between Defense Minister Chevènement and the President. Chevènement was anxious that French forces should not be located too close to American forces, should not share bases with them nor be dependent on them, as he seemed to fear that they might be swept by the Americans into offensive action against Iraq, without the French government having its say. As I was to learn, there was to be nothing "automatic" about French participation in the Coalition: Chevènement wanted the terms and conditions of any joint action to be carefully negotiated and agreed in advance.

From the start of the crisis in August 1990, I began a long and sometimes difficult dialogue with the French Ambassador, Jacques Bernière, his military attaché and a general from the French military mission, a dialogue which I continued with the French Chief of Staff, General Maurice Schmitt, and indeed with Lieutenant General Michel Roquejeoffre when he arrived in the Kingdom on September 19, 1990, to take command of French forces. Three days later, on September 22, we met at Yanbu, on the Red Sea, to inspect an advance party of the *Daguet* Division and French helicopter crews, some of whom had come with their machines from the *Clémenceau*, then in the Red Sea. (I learned, incidentally, that *Daguet*, the randomly chosen code name of the force, is French for a young stag or yearling deer whose antlers have not yet grown.)

Lieutenant General Roquejeoffre hitched a lift in my plane back to Riyadh, during which he impressed on me the special characteristics of his ultramobile force. He was reluctant to occupy a fixed sector. He seemed to want a roving role, able to strike to the left or right of the wide front, wherever danger threatened – a point of view for which I had considerable sympathy. If the Iraqis attacked, his strategy would be to let them come in, check them with a blocking force, then hit them hard in the flank.

My discussions with the French centered on a number of

closely interlinked subjects, of which perhaps the most contentious was the command structure. Unlike the British, the French did not want to serve under American command. But nor did they want to join the Egyptians, Syrians, Moroccans, Czechoslovaks and the rest of them under my Joint Forces Command. They wanted their own independent command on the same level as Schwarzkopf's and my own.

I told the French envoys that they had to choose: it had to be either Schwarzkopf or me – and I did not think they would choose Schwarzkopf. I explained that we needed a clear-cut command structure that would simplify matters on the battlefield and protect the lives of our soldiers. We could not put lives at risk because of command disputes.

"I would like you to know," the French Ambassador told me, "that French forces can serve only under the authority of the French national command, that is to say the French government."

"But that is a principle which applies to every national contingent," I responded. "However, once your government has given its agreement for you to help defend Saudi Arabia, and once you enter my theater of operations, then you become part of a local command structure that has nothing to do with politics. This applies not only to the French force but to every force that has come to our aid."

What complicated matters was that Chevènement insisted on every local move being cleared through him in Paris. The British Commander, Sir Peter de la Billière, had London's authority to delegate command over British servicemen to the Americans, if he thought it appropriate. But Roquejeoffre had no such authority from Paris. Whatever we asked him to do, he had to clear with his high command before responding. Questions would fly back and forth, delaying any decision.

On instructions from Paris, Roquejeoffre wanted to place strict limits on French participation. He wanted us to draw up and sign a sort of contract, defining the mission of his force within strict space/time parameters. Only then could the force be placed under my operational control. Paris would retain the right to withdraw the force at any time, if it considered the "contract" had been breached. It looked as if the French wanted to retain the right not to fight! Their formula suggested a lack of confidence in us, but it also seemed far too rigid to cope with the uncertainties of war. What if the Iraqis attacked? There would be no time for such legal niceties. "You say you want to help with our defense but you won't operate under our command," I protested.

I explained to Lieutenant General Roquejeoffre and to the French ambassador that if they insisted on an independent command, they were free to stay outside the theater of operations and to take no part in the conflict. The question of command was, therefore, intimately connected with where French troops would be deployed.

They first asked if they could base their division and its helicopters at Tabuk, our major base in northwestern Arabia. But there was little room at Tabuk, as I had already earmarked it for the British who, at that stage, were more committed to the conflict than the French, and who were planning to provide a major strike force of Tornados. The Americans also had a presence at Tabuk. I suspected that it would be asking for trouble if the French were accommodated there as well. And I was afraid that if I put them there temporarily, they would be reluctant to leave. So I refused them Tabuk. They then asked if their helicopters could be based at Wajh, on the Red Sea coast, close to their carrier. But I felt that, if the planes were meant to support their ground forces, they would be better placed closer to the front.

My preference was to position the French contingent at the center of the theater, somewhere near King Khaled Military City and Hafr al-Batin, where I promised them a sector of their own if they agreed to fit in to my command structure – but this they refused to do. The impasse seemed total.

As the argument raged back and forth, I suggested to the ambassador almost as a joke that French forces could use the Red Sea port of Yanbu as their main base until we agreed where they were to go. Of course, in military terms it made no sense. I might as well have said, "Stay in Cairo." They would be miles away from the war. But as they would be outside the theater of operations, the thorny problem of command would not arise.

To my surprise, the ambassador took up my suggestion. In

fact, he jumped at it. He was obviously not a military man. Yes, he said, the French would like to base themselves at Yanbu.

"Are you coming to fight the Iraqis," I asked him, "or are you coming here for political reasons?"

I urged him to consult his military planners. They would tell him that, at Yanbu, French forces could play no part in the war. They could be given no military mission. I assured him I would support his force in every way I could, but France's contribution would have to be considered as purely political.

"What concerns us most at present," he replied, "is to let others understand" – he did not say whom he meant by "others" – "that France is not distant from this region but has a presence here. If Saudi Arabia is attacked, then we will take other steps."

"I would like you to assure your government," I told him, "that I am here to solve problems, not to create them. But I have a mission to perform. I know, and I am sure you know too, that one cannot fight a war with two commanders, let alone three!"

So, as a result of the stalemate, the small French advance party stayed at Yanbu by themselves for six long weeks, no doubt awaiting a clear directive from Paris.

Even Schwarzkopf was surprised.

"Oh my God!" he said. "Why did you put them at Yanbu?"

"Leave it to me," I said. "It will be all right in the end."

Although French opinion was hardening against Iraq, Chevènement had evidently not yet decided how far he wished to fall in with Coalition war plans.

It was at this time, in late September 1990, that I received a visit from a score of French senators led by Jean Lecanuet, then Chairman of the Senate's Foreign Affairs, Defense and Armed Services Committee. From their probing questions, I got the impression that they were testing the ability of the Kingdom and of me personally to command French troops. Seeing I was in dispute with the French military commander, I made an attempt to be extremely polite to them. I was anxious to stress the importance we attached to French participation. I explained that Iraq's invasion of Kuwait had put at risk not only Saudi Arabia's Eastern Province, but all the Gulf states which, on the domino theory, might fall to Saddam one after the other.

This was not strictly true as, by mid-September, the danger

of an Iraqi attack, which had been extreme at the start, was receding day by day as our own strength grew. I had learned that the Iraqis were beginning to lay mines and improve their Kuwaiti defenses – hardly the prelude to an attack. But I did not pass this on to Lecanuet as I did not want him to think that the threat was over and that we therefore had no need of the French. In any event, even if our own security from attack was probably assured, the problem of how to get Iraq out of Kuwait was still unresolved.

Moreover, Saddam had a record of unpredictability. In spite of mounting evidence of his defensive posture, we could not rule out a sudden attack or even a resort to kamikaze tactics. In his war against Iran, he had retaken the Fao peninsula by a surprise assault. Having dug in and given every appearance of looking to his defenses, he had suddenly thrown his second echelon Republican Guards into the fray. It had been a great plan. It was a precedent, I told the senators, which we had to bear in mind.

No sooner had the party of French senators left me than I was visited by the French Chief of Staff, General Maurice Schmitt, a tall, gray-haired man who spoke slowly and with deliberation. It seemed that the internal French debate had been resolved. He informed me that France was prepared to base its light armored division at a desert location north of the Tapline road, some 50 miles from KKMC, in the Joint Forces Command theater of operations – in effect under my command. The dispute was over.

In due course, the French division, with its equipment and supplies, landed at Yanbu and traveled some 1,200 miles across the desert to their location near KKMC, supported by us all the way.

The search for a suitable base for French combat aircraft proved if anything more difficult. We wanted them to go to the well-equipped base at Dhahran where we were prepared to give them some space next to the Americans. We understood that President Mitterrand was not opposed to the French air force going to Dhahran. But Chevènement, for reasons already mentioned, did not want French aircraft to bed down with American aircraft. After much searching, we found them a small civilian airport for their exclusive use at al-Ahsa, east of Riyadh and south of Dhahran. There was a control tower, but the runway was not long enough and there were not enough taxiways and aircraft parking. At great speed and considerable cost, we converted the airport into a fully equipped military air base. The French themselves brought in from France the air defense, radars and military infrastructure they needed, as well as the engineers, armorers and munitions. We financed it all. The French were happy. They were independent. They started flying Combat Air Patrols with the Saudis and the Americans, and training for the air campaign.

Mind you, they wanted to operate their own rules of engagement and they had a different concept of Close Air Support from the Americans. They wrote to me twice saying that they wished to use their air force separately to support and defend their own troops. And twice I had to write back officially to General Schmitt urging him to use the same rules of engagement and Close Air Support employment as the other Coalition air forces. The French were not used to American Air Tasking Orders.

To ensure operational safety and enhance air defense procedures, and because their Mirage F1s were also in use by Iraq, these had to be explained to them. All this took several weeks to sort out, and a U.S. Tactical Air Control Party was eventually provided to liaise with the French.

Once these teething problems were resolved, the French went out of their way to be helpful. Lieutenant General Roquejeoffre proved to be an excellent commander. He called on me frequently and made a point of keeping me fully informed of everything he was doing. This was the pattern throughout Desert Shield until the transfer of the French force to Schwarzkopf's operational control for Desert Storm.

≫≪

I had read accounts of the difficulties Winston Churchill, Britain's war leader, had faced with the Free French leader, General de Gaulle, during World War Two, and I was aware of France's independent posture within NATO. But reading about such things or seeing a movie about them was one thing: facing such a problem myself was quite another.

For this was not the end of my problems with the French. There were a number of troublesome incidents which took up a good deal of time. On one occasion a French soldier was reported missing at Yanbu, and the French thought he might have been kidnapped by elements hostile to the war. I immediately instituted a search and the man was found, not long afterwards, hiding away in one of the hangars. It turned out that he was a pacifist: he did not want to fight. He was shipped back to France and court-martialed. Such incidents are not uncommon in most armies.

A far more serious incident occurred on October 29 when a French reconnaissance patrol, comprising an officer and two NCOs, lost its way in our northern desert, strayed across the border, was captured by the Iraqis and taken to Baghdad. No doubt eager to ingratiate themselves with their former allies, the Iraqis – some say it was Saddam Hussein himself – contacted the French ambassador to say they were holding three of their men. Saddam was shrewd. He could have had the men killed. Instead, he proposed returning them to Paris in the hope of driving a wedge between the allies.

Lieutenant General Roquejeoffre had been unaware that three of his men were missing until he heard the news a day or so later from General Schmitt in France. He called on me to say that General Schmitt had instructed him to report the incident to me. In fact I later learned he had been told to keep it quiet for another day until the French had had a chance to question their men about the incident. I was angry at not having been told sooner, but I was also incensed that the French had disobeyed my orders in sending out a long-range patrol.

For some weeks I had been concerned about the long-range patrols which the French division, commanded by Major General Jean-Charles Mouscardès, was sending up north to our border posts. The French argued that their highly trained reconnaissance patrols – manned by members of the 13th *Régiment de dragons parachutistes* – were specialized in collecting intelligence behind enemy lines. They claimed that the security of their mobile force depended on having full intelligence of what lay in front of them. But I was worried that such active patrolling might lead us inadvertently into war and I had put a stop to it. Major General Mouscardès evidently found my restriction irksome.

In spite of my ban, a two-vehicle patrol had gone out. It had then split up, agreeing to rendezvous in 24 hours. When one of the teams did not turn up as arranged, the other sounded the alarm. But by this time the three men were in Baghdad.

I was of course concerned about how the incident would be reported. I knew the press would pick up the story soon enough and wanted to ensure that whatever announcement was made was jointly agreed on between the French and ourselves. To my irritation, however, I learned from Roquejeoffre that the French government was planning to issue a statement without consulting us. I demanded to see their statement first.

When I read the text, I thought it was just about the worst press release I had ever seen. The French were intending to say that their men had come under Iraqi fire and had been captured by the Iraqis inside Saudi Arabia!

I was aghast and gave Roquejeoffre a piece of my mind.

"First of all," I exclaimed, "this report is like a declaration of war. It suggests hostilities between us and the Iraqis have already begun. Secondly, what you say is not true. It is an insult to my command. How could the Iraqis have entered the Kingdom, opened fire, and captured soldiers under my command without my knowing about it? Everyone will conclude that we cannot defend our own territory, that our screening force and our border guards are ineffective. We will look weak and defeated. I'm sorry, I cannot accept this statement. You will have to revise it."

In Paris, Defense Minister Chevènement, perhaps swayed by his former friendship for Iraq, insisted that the men had been captured by the Iraqis on the Saudi side of the border.

"Make Prince Khaled understand," he ordered Roquejeoffre, "that that is how it happened and not any other way!"

"Yes, minister," Roquejeoffre replied, "but we are in Saudi Arabia and we cannot impose . . ."

Roquejeoffre found himself uncomfortably placed between his government and myself. The poor man was embarrassed. But the French Minister of Defense would not budge. He was not prepared to reveal to the French people that three of his soldiers had got lost.

"What's wrong in admitting it?" I asked. "Even the Bedouin who live in the desert sometimes get lost." For my part, I wanted to establish the truth, but I was also understandably anxious to get a wording which did not give the Iraqis any credit.

Late in the evening, in the presence of Roquejeoffre, I decided to call General Schmitt in Paris. Chevènement was beside him. We had a long talk. I explained to them that I had sent troops to the area and they had seen the tracks of the patrol's truck heading for the border. The border is marked by sand berms, except for a 30-mile gap. We presumed that, believing they were still in Saudi Arabia, they had ventured through that gap. There was no doubt in my mind that their men had got lost.

But both Chevènement and Schmitt were determined to publish their version of the affair.

I asked Prince Sultan to intervene and he called them again. We also sent our Ambassador in Paris, Jamil al-Hujailan – one of our best envoys and a close friend – to make representations at the Quai d'Orsay, but he failed to make headway. It was a horrible night.

For several hours on the evening of November 2, Roquejeoffre and I worked on a draft text, trying to agree to a wording which would satisfy us both. We were still at it long after midnight when a French officer came in to my office with a piece of paper which was passed round. Acting unilaterally, Chevènement in Paris had released his own statement to the press!

At that, I lost my temper. I demanded an explanation. I reached General Schmitt on the telephone and, to the evident alarm of my staff who sat there quaking, I decided to get tough: "Allow me, *mon général*, to ask you a question. Whose side are you on? Are you our friend or our enemy? That is the first thing I would like you to make clear. Why have you released a statement which shows a lack of confidence in our troops and in our Joint Forces Command?"

The row went on and on. We had spent four days and nights arguing about it. Roquejeoffre later called it a four-day war!

The French statement no longer said the Iraqis had opened fire inside Saudi Arabia, but it did say that their men had been surprised and captured by an Iraqi patrol. It left vague the question of *where* this had occurred which was at the heart of the dispute. We issued our own statement which was broadcast on our television. It made clear that the French had got lost in the desert inside Iraq and had then fallen into Iraqi hands. There was a clear difference between the French statement and ours but, to my surprise, neither the American, nor the British, nor even the French media, made much of it. This was just as well as I was keen to see the matter settled.

After this incident, I withdrew the French division south of the Tapline road. To express my disapproval, I pulled the French out of the controversial border area. Curiously enough, I later learned that Chevènement himself had thought that their previous location was too close to the border. He had asked General Schmitt to submit a proposal to me for moving the division closer to KKMC. So my directive actually fitted into their plan. Tactically, they were now better placed to intervene either to the left or to the right, as circumstances dictated.

At the same time, however, I also banned patrolling by the French north of the Tapline road. They lost their long-range reconnaissance ability. I was determined to express my unhappiness at French behavior so, despite their pleas, I kept this prohibition in force for several weeks. I did not want another incident of the same nature. It was, in a sense, for their own protection. They did not like it but, in all fairness, I must admit they obeyed. From then on, discipline was tighter and the French performed splendidly.

On November 6, a few days after the row, Prince Sultan expressed the wish to visit the French air base at al-Ahsa. Lieutenant General Roquejeoffre and the French ambassador were there to receive the Prince, and I was there as Joint Forces Commander. Prince Sultan gave a speech praising France as a friendly nation which had come to our aid – of which the best proof, he added, was the friendship between General Roquejeoffre and General Khaled! The orchestration of this event was a characteristic example of Prince Sultan's gift for mediating quarrels and reconciling opponents. The chief had spoken and the incident was closed.

I had no further problems with the French – except for a slightly comical one.

Shortly before Christmas 1990, I received a call from the Northern Area Commander, Major General al-Alkami, to say that a French male singer, Eddy Mitchell, had arrived to entertain the French troops, accompanied by his band and two women. It was the first I had heard about it. I told him to hold them at the military hotel where they were staying while I made inquiries.

Lieutenant General Roquejeoffre claimed to have notified us a month earlier about their arrival and to have received approval from someone on my staff, on condition that the visit was not given any publicity. But they could not produce any piece of paper to support their claim, neither their written request nor any letter of authorization from us. They said the two women accompanying the singer were his wife and a make-up artist, but we suspected they were go-go dancers. As singing and dancing girls were not permitted in the Kingdom, I knew this was an affair which could backfire badly. I was always accessible. Why had the French not raised the matter at one of my weekly meetings with their commanders?

Contradictory statements were being made on all sides. I did not want another incident nor did I want to make an issue of it. I learned that a French TV channel had sponsored Eddy Mitchell's trip, was planning to film his concerts live, and that publicity about the visit had already been splashed across the pages of the French popular press. So much for the French pledge not to publicize the visit!

I had to report the affair to the King and Prince Sultan. They were displeased and took the view that if a Saudi officer had given the French permission, he should be court-martialed.

There was no way the concert could take place. But Eddy Mitchell and his troupe were already in the Kingdom. They had arrived on December 21 with the evident intention of putting on Christmas concerts for the *Daguet* Division in the desert, for the airmen at al-Ahsa, and even for the French headquarters staff in Riyadh.

Perhaps egged on by the French press, Defense Minister Chevènement decided to challenge our ban. He telephoned Lieutenant General Roquejeoffre with the order that "Eddy Mitchell must sing!" Once again, as in the incident of the three lost soldiers, the unfortunate Roquejeoffre found himself in an impossible situation. As he later related to me, he had two options, both of which looked like stripping him of his command and returning him to France. If he disobeyed the Minister's orders, he could expect to be recalled. But, if he obeyed the Minister and flouted our ban, we were likely to say that he was no longer welcome in the Kingdom.

Roquejeoffre decided to put his dilemma to his superior officer, Chief of Staff Schmitt in Paris. In turn, General Schmitt went for guidance to Admiral Jacques Lanxade (France's current Chief of Staff) who was then serving at the Elysée Palace as chief military adviser to President Mitterrand. After consultations with the French Foreign Ministry, the matter was then put before the President himself.

In his wisdom, President Mitterrand overruled his Minister of Defense and issued a directive that Eddy Mitchell must not perform in Saudi Arabia. France did not want problems with the Kingdom. The singer had to return home. As it happened, while this drama was unfolding Chevènement was due in Riyadh where Prince Sultan had invited him to lunch. I had been asked to join them afterwards to review arrangements for the French forces.

In fact, Chevènement was in the air on his way to Riyadh when President Mitterrand decided that Eddy Mitchell was not to sing. The presidential directive was very probably conveyed to him during the flight. At any rate, General Schmitt in Paris instructed Lieutenant General Roquejeoffre in Riyadh to meet Chevènement's plane and confirm to him the President's directive: there were to be no concerts. This must have angered Chevènement because on landing he decided, on his own initiative, not to attend Prince Sultan's lunch.

So instead of being taken to the Guest Palace, Chevènement

was taken to Roquejeoffre's command post. Meanwhile Prince Sultan, stung by Chevènement's lack of courtesy in declining his invitation, decided that he did not want to see him at all.

By this time, the French press was up in arms over the cancellation of Eddy Mitchell's performances. Fearing that the incident might blow up into a diplomatic crisis and that we might lose the French, I rang Prince Sultan to ask if he would allow me to call on Chevènement at the French embassy to try to smooth things over. Somewhat reluctantly, he gave me his permission, so I swallowed my pride and went.

As gracefully as I could, I tried to explain that as we both had public opinion to contend with it was best if we drew a line under the incident and allowed it to fade away.

Until then, Chevènement had been calm and polite. But then, with an impatient gesture – as if to say, "I've made up my mind about this: don't confuse me with the facts" – he turned to me and exclaimed:

"But music is not *haram!* [an Arabic word meaning forbidden by Islamic law] Singing is not *haram!* You have music on your television. The Egyptians, who are also Muslims, allow music and singing."

"Monsieur le ministre," I replied, "I cannot engage in a discussion with you about what is *haram* (forbidden) and what is *halal* (permitted). If you want to go more deeply into the matter, we would have to keep you here for several days. I myself listen to music and enjoy it. But what is now at stake is the protection of our national customs and traditions – in effect our national security. About this we cannot compromise. I will be blunt with you. We have no interest in winning a war against Saddam if we endanger our country in the process." I told him that we had had a similar problem with the Americans who wanted to send some female entertainers with Bob Hope. But the Americans had seen the point and reacted sensibly.

"If you want to send someone of that sort, please go ahead," I said. "But no girls, please!"

By this time, Chevènement's mood was frosty. I tried to warm up the atmosphere as best I could by saying that we had probably both made a mistake and that I was sorry the incident had happened. But I left the embassy in an angry mood.

The air campaign against Iraq started in the early hours of January 17 and, contrary to some later reports, French aircraft participated from the very first day – but only against Iraqi targets in Kuwait. There was a debate on the crisis in the French National Assembly on the evening of the 16th and President Mitterrand had declared that he would not decide on French participation until after the debate. In any event, I learned that General Schmitt telephoned Lieutenant-General Roquejeoffre during the night of January 16–17 with the news that he could go ahead. French tanker planes were already in the air, ready to refuel their combat aircraft, which followed shortly before dawn. The first French raids took place at about 7 a.m. local time.

On January 19, Chevènement returned to the Kingdom to review the situation with the Saudi authorities. He had a meeting with Prince Sultan. With the air campaign raging, the Eddy Mitchell incident was forgotten. The Minister visited French air crews but, as a sandstorm was blowing, he could not visit the *Daguet* Division. I was glad I did not have to see him. He returned to France.

Chevènement had from the start opposed offensive action against Iraq, believing that political and diplomatic options had not been fully explored. He believed France had been dragged into it by the Americans who, he suspected, had wanted to go to war from the very beginning. But his ideas were unsound. He appears not to have considered the long-term threat Saddam would have posed to the region and to interests farther afield had Kuwait been left in his hands. As Chevènement's views could no longer be reconciled with those of France's allies and indeed of his French government colleagues, he resigned shortly afterwards. A major obstacle to our cooperation with the French had been removed. Some ten days after the start of the air campaign, French aircraft joined Coalition aircraft in attacks on targets in Iraq itself.

Chevènement was replaced as Defense Minister by Interior Minister Pierre Joxe who visited the Kingdom on February 4. From then on, we had no further problems with the French. My only regret was that their admirable, highly mobile, light armored division passed from my operational control to that of

General Schwarzkopf. Knowing the capability of this division, Schwarzkopf and I agreed, after further discussion, to assign it the mission of protecting the western flank of the Coalition and seizing al-Salman, an important road and air junction inside Iraq.

The irony was that the final outcome was very different, indeed the opposite, of what Chevènement would have liked. He had not wanted French troops to attack into Iraq or get mixed up with the Americans. In the event, placing the French on the Americans' far left made it inevitable that they would be among the very first Coalition troops to enter Iraq and would penetrate most deeply into Iraqi territory.

Lieutenant General Roquejeoffre, the excellent soldier with whom I regrettably had to clash on a number of occasions, was after the war promoted to command France's *Force d'action rapide* (FAR), a rapid deployment force of some 47,000 men, many of whom later saw action in Somalia, Cambodia, different parts of Africa and in the territories of former Yugoslavia. Roquejeoffre retired in December 1993 after a distinguished military career.

After the war was over, I paid a visit to the United States and called on Schwarzkopf and his wife at their home where I was warmly received. He had assembled his son and two daughters to meet the man with whom he had fought the war. They showered me with gifts for my own children. As generals tend to do, we talked over some of our campaign experiences, continuing our conversation in the car as he accompanied me to the airport.

"How did you get on with the French," I asked, "once they were attached to XVIIIth Corps? Did you get along with them?"

"Fine," he replied. "They were just fine. I had no problems with them at all."

"Yes," I said jokingly, "because I drew their fire!"

I don't think he liked that particularly.

Needless to say, I meant no disrespect to the French for whose military prowess I continue to have, despite our Gulf War disagreements, the greatest admiration.

CHAPTER XVII

An Army Marches on Its Stomach

WHEN ROMMEL AND MONTGOMERY slogged it out in North Africa during World War Two, it used to be said that the desert was a tactician's paradise and a quartermaster's hell – paradise because the open desert was ideal for the great tank battles between the Afrika Korps and the Eighth Army, and hell because of the lack of water, the trucks lost in the moving sands, the huge distances the supply columns had to travel under the constant threat of air attack.

The Gulf War was a paradise all right for the Coalition's tacticians – Iraq was "blind," the allies all-powerful – but it was far from being a quartermaster's hell. If anything, it was a quartermaster's heaven. Supplies were abundant. Support was lavish. It must have been the first war in history in which the troops never missed a meal. And the enemy proved so ineffective – or at least so inadequate to confront the formidable power of the Coalition – that the war turned out in the end to be more of an elaborate exercise than a real conflict. The picture which summed it all up was that of a happy GI pouring a bottle of mineral water down the throat of an equally happy camel.

This fortunate situation was not achieved without the most tremendous logistical effort by the host nation, Saudi Arabia. Not only did we mobilize all our resources, from both the public and private sectors, but we also paid the bill for what we could not ourselves supply.

The food and fuel bills were massive. On King Fahd's instructions, over 750,000 troops were fed each day at our expense. American forces alone were supplied with 2,000,000 gallons of drinking water each day. And the fuel consumption by the two

American corps approached 4,500,000 gallons – that is 880 truckloads – each day. To quote Lieutenant General William "Gus" Pagonis, the American logistics chief with whom his Saudi counterpart, Brigadier General Abd al-Aziz al-Hussein, worked closely, "We would have been in a very difficult situation if our host nation had been either 1) poor, 2) hostile, or 3) both."*

Of Greek origin, Gus Pagonis was a live wire. I used to tell a funny story about him during the crisis. If anyone mentioned President Bush or General Schwarzkopf to me, it meant the Coalition was in place and functioning. But if Pagonis was mentioned, I would start to worry: it would mean a bill for millions of dollars was on its way to me. Every time his name came up, it would cost the Kingdom money! But Pagonis was a good manager who could probably have done well in a large corporation. His merits were recognized when he was promoted to three-star general while still in Saudi Arabia.

But, with us, he started out on the wrong foot. He had not been long in the Kingdom when he issued an order to his subordinates to confiscate anything useful to the war effort – commercial vehicles, cars, equipment, and so forth. The Eastern Area Commander, Major General Salih al-Muhaya, reported this to me and sent me a copy of Pagonis's order. It reached me when I was with Schwarzkopf in the War Room. Angrily, I raised the matter with him and showed him the order. I told him it was quite unacceptable. Saudi Arabia was not occupied territory! I demanded that he do something about it at once. To calm me down, Schwarzkopf called Pagonis, scolded him and said, "Gus, your third star is coming. Don't blow it!" Pagonis apologized to Salih al-Muhaya and duly issued a counterorder.

For the successful logistics operation, Pagonis must share the credit with my own team of logisticians, led by Brigadier General Abd al-Aziz al-Hussein who handled logistics for the Western forces and Brigadier General Salem al-Uwaymer who looked after the needs of the Saudi forces and the other Arab and Islamic troops. The job these two Saudi officers did deserves the highest praise. We started with a support unit of six officers under

* Lieutenant General William G. Pagonis, *Moving Mountains*, Harvard, 1992, p. 205.

Brigadier General Uwaymer, and ended up with a logistics staff of 130, drawn from all branches of the Saudi armed services. The pressure of work was such that they spent many a sleepless night. They probably worked harder that year than in the whole of their military careers. I certainly did.

I can say, in all modesty, that without Saudi Arabia, the Gulf War could not have been waged, or only with the greatest difficulty. The Western allies would have had to build power plants, desalination plants, air bases, and a thousand other things. To meet their fuel needs, they would have had to mobilize the world's tanker fleets. Thanks to our magnificent port facilities at Jubail and Yanbu, at Dammam and Jeddah, they were able to offload 15 ships a day, over 600 ships in six months carrying American men and supplies, not to mention the many ships from other countries – a record few countries, even the most industrialized, could have matched. Without Saudi Arabia's domestic resources and infrastructure, it really would have been a quartermaster's hell. Coalition troops would have died of thirst in the desert. It may be that no host country has ever given such vast and unstinting support to allied troops fighting on its soil.

It might be objected that we acted from self-interest, seeing that no one had a greater stake than Saudi Arabia in the success of the Coalition. That may be true, although of course every member of the Coalition, the U.S. included, acted from self-interest. But it leaves something out. Hospitality is an Arab virtue of which we are proud.

Every military commander knows that no army can fight without supplies, in the volume and place where they are needed. The Gulf War put logistics on the map. It was a "logisticians' war" – as the timetable demonstrates: Desert Shield, the defensive build-up, lasted six months; the air campaign lasted 38 days; while the ground war was over in a mere 100 hours; Desert Farewell, the withdrawal of foreign troops from the Kingdom, ran to seven or eight months. So for a few weeks of fighting, the logisticians had to labor for well over a year!

Opening my diary at random, I see that on September 7, 1990, Lieutenant General John Yeosock, CENTCOM's army commander, came running to me. He was expecting 15,000 men within 48 hours and needed accommodation for them. We had to create a staging post for the incoming forces before they could move on to their destinations in the field. Fortunately, a brand new military city had been built at Umm al-Sahik in the Eastern Province for my air defense forces which they had still not occupied. I postponed their move and turned the city over to the incoming Americans.

Over half a million foreign troops were to pour in through our ports and airports over the next few months. The Kingdom would have been overwhelmed by this tremendous influx had we not had the annual experience of managing over 1,000,000 pilgrims from overseas for the *hajj*, without counting the hundreds of thousands of Saudis who perform the pilgrimage at the same time. Feeding, transporting and accommodating vast numbers of visitors are, in fact, something of a Saudi specialty.

From the moment the first ship docked and the first airplane landed, we had to provide full support – food, water, fuel, transport and accommodation. We not only had to have the resources, we also had to have the men to administer them – men like Colonel Khalaf al Shammari who received the 82nd Airborne Division at Dhahran, facilitated its mission in very many ways, and continued to support the flow of U.S. troops into the Eastern Province throughout the crisis. At the same time, we were wrestling with the problem of finding homes for some 360,000 Kuwaitis who had flooded into the Kingdom after Iraq's invasion. It was a worrying time which would have strained the resources of any nation. Fortunately, the Kingdom also had large housing complexes, built in the late 1970s and early 1980s, but never fully occupied. Kuwaiti refugees and U.S. troops were found accommodation there.

In the first three months of the crisis, August to October 1990, a good deal of my time was spent on logistics. I had to keep a very close eye on the logistics situation as it was one of my main responsibilities. I demanded daily briefings, sometimes twice a day. The King had delegated to Prince Sultan the immense financial power to buy what was required for the support operation to which we were committed, and Prince Sultan, in turn, gave me some of his powers. I had to report to him regularly about the financial position. He gave me control of the funds which, through a number of committees, were disbursed to over 600 Saudi contractors and subcontractors. To head these committees, I appointed my logistics chiefs and, for greater rigor, I also brought in Ali al-Hidaithi, the head of the financial directorate of the air defense forces.

To control the flow of supplies and the suppliers, we built a system covering direct order purchases, contracts put out to tender, rentals of vehicles and equipment and much else besides. For greater fairness and efficiency in awarding contracts, Brigadier General Uwaymer adopted a system somewhat different from regular competitive tendering. He allowed bidders to sit together with him and his staff and open the bids together. The full contract was not always awarded exclusively to the lowest bidder. In order to spread the benefits and eliminate the risk of defaults, Uwaymer divided big contracts between several bidders, provided they were prepared to match the lowest price and meet the specifications laid down by the Joint Forces Command. If they were not, the full contract went to the lowest bidder.

Brigadier General Uwaymer also went to great pains to check that the local prices we were charged were in line with international prices. For example, he went himself to Pakistan to buy the large number of tents we required, and sent logisticians to the United States to buy rubber fuel tanks because the prices of such items were far more competitive than anything available in the Kingdom.

As I have said, I acted under the authority of the King and Prince Sultan and briefed them regularly to secure their approval. I was in a position to call up any minister or any official to speed things along. Cutting corners became my trademark. I found, for example, that a call to the Port Authority or the Royal Commission of Jubail and Yanbu could work wonders. I could not have done the job without the backing and cooperation of the various agencies and departments of government.

Both Schwarzkopf and I realized that, quite apart from the problem of deploying combat troops in the field as quickly as possible to check any Iraqi attack, the real challenge was to be able to sustain them for as long as the campaign lasted. That is where the logisticians came in. I know that Pagonis saw Schwarzkopf far more frequently than did the U.S. corps commanders. Schwarzkopf first thought he needed enough supplies to sustain the armies for 30 days. Then, as war approached, this was doubled to 60 days. Clearly, it was not foreseen that the Iraqis would collapse so quickly, and Schwarzkopf – a highly cautious commander – did not want to be caught short.

With hindsight, it could be said that two of Schwarzkopf's decisions – no doubt justified in their time, but perhaps questionable in retrospect – put the logistics system under great strain. The first decision was to rush U.S. combat troops to the Kingdom without adequate support units, which meant that we had to support them in the early months of the crisis. Quite apart from food, water, ice, and fuel, they needed shelter, kitchen equipment, sanitation and hygiene facilities, water purification units, telephone communications, buses, trucks and heavy equipment transporters, storage facilities, civilian labor support such as drivers, stevedores and porters, indeed everything that they were used to finding in permanent camps.

Yet, once Saddam had failed to push down the coast in the first few weeks following his invasion of Kuwait, it was increasingly obvious that he had neither the will nor the means to exploit his initial success. By late August allied air power would have played havoc with his supply columns had he attempted to do so. Against this background, Schwarzkopf's decision to give priority for several weeks to the deployment of combat units and defer the deployment of combat service support (CSS) units may have been overly prudent. It certainly placed enormous demands on our funds and material resources.

His second decision, taken later in the crisis when war preparations were gathering pace, was to stock for 60 rather than 30 days, a decision which put additional heavy burdens on supply facilities and cost us billions of dollars. Once again it pointed to excessive caution and may have stemmed from a mistaken intelligence assessment of Iraq's strength and its capacity to withstand the strategic air campaign.

One of my roles was to be the single point of contact between all Coalition forces and the Saudi government. In any endeavor there is confusion and less than optimal performance if it is not clear who is in charge. I had to create a staff to enable the insatiable American logisticians to work closely with my logisticians so as to tap the tremendous resources of the Kingdom. The relationship worked smoothly, although not without some moments of tension, which was hardly surprising considering the herculean efforts deployed and the vast sums of money disbursed.

At the start, we did not have a logistics structure to cope with the size of the operation -- very few countries do – and we had to build one from scratch. We welcomed help from friendly countries. Two Egyptian support battalions, each numbering about 500 men, came to help us run the forward supply points at al-Nu'ayriya and al-Qaisuma. They were skilled in the handling of ammunition and fuel. We also had the services of two supply companies from Bangladesh, which we based in Dammam. These Egyptian and Bangladeshi logisticians were paid as if they were Saudis.

The different languages of the various national contingents posed problems of liaison. Not every Saudi in our logistics outfit spoke English, let alone French. Another problem was that troops hundreds of miles out in the desert expected to get what they wanted in a very short time. They did not always appreciate the distances the supply trucks had to travel. An allied officer might request 1,000 tents – and expect to receive them the next day. Another, later in the campaign, might ask for hundreds of transistor radios and TV sets for his troops – and this would send my staff on a frantic search of the local market.

❖≫≪❖

In early September 1990, King Fahd gave the Americans an undertaking that the Kingdom would provide U.S. forces in Saudi Arabia with all the food, fuel, water, accommodation, local transport and other facilities they needed – at no cost to themselves. No formal agreement was signed at that time. It was not until October 17 that the U.S. Department of Defense sent a team to discuss with us how the King's undertaking could be formalized in a Host Nation Support agreement between Saudi Arabia and the United States. Negotiations continued for a month and an agreement was finally signed in mid-November, retroactive to the beginning of the U.S. deployment. It was called the "Implementation Plan for Logistics Support of the United States Forces in Defense of the Kingdom of Saudi Arabia."

While the talks were in progress, Schwarzkopf appeared to be getting more and more restive and impatient. He seems to have worried that our word might not be as good as our bond. In his book *It Doesn't Take a Hero* he fusses over having troops to feed and supplies to transport without knowing where the money was coming from. He quotes Major General Dane Starling, his director of logistics, as saying "for what seemed like the one hundredth time . . . 'The Saudis still aren't paying any of our bills.'" The clear implication of his account is that the Saudis were poor payers – an astonishing comment about one of the most open-handed nations in the world from a general whose task in the Gulf campaign was made vastly easier by Saudi munificence.

The main reason for the delay in signing the Host Nation Support agreement was that the bill for $2.6 billion presented to us was far too large. I suggested that both sides should form a committee to look into it in detail. It was then discovered that the U.S. Department of Defense had tried to inflate the bill by a cool $1.9 billion to include the Pentagon's expenses in airlifting and sealifting men and supplies *to* the Kingdom – costs which King Fahd had not agreed to pay. He had agreed to pay U.S. transport and other costs only *within* the Kingdom. Although Schwarzkopf claimed he had nothing to do with finance, he sent his two-star generals to my people almost on a daily basis to press for the money. I recall him telling me, however, that he had advised the Department of Defense not to inflate the bill. But, he added, the Department had in effect replied, "Let's try it on. If it works, so much the better. If it doesn't, we'll take it out."

And take it out they eventually did. Thanks to my staff, the error was corrected and the agreement was signed in mid-November. From then on, we agreed to pay new bills as they came in. But Schwarzkopf was evidently still not satisfied! He writes: "I . . . felt as reassured as you can when someone says the check is in the mail."*

Fortunately, I was soon able to lay his anxieties to rest by handing him a check from our Ministry of Finance for $760 million, to reimburse the U.S. government for its expenses in the Kingdom between August and October 1990.

In those first three months, the U.S. government – in the person of Lieutenant General Pagonis – went on a spending spree. The overriding aim was to get the troops fed, sheltered and transported. As we were footing the bill, Pagonis asked for everything but never asked the price of anything. It was said of Pagonis that he always asked for more than he needed, which was no doubt a good negotiating tactic. He always wanted more of this and more of the other, especially when he realized what was available in the Kingdom. Local contractors who supplied the voracious demands of the U.S. military were of course over-joyed. It was a once-in-a-lifetime opportunity.

At the start we had a tough time with Pagonis, because he wanted to deal direct with Saudi suppliers, with little regard for price. We decided that, once he had selected the product he wanted, the support unit of my Joint Forces Command was better placed than he was to negotiate with local businessmen. We knew the country, we knew how to write the contracts, and we could get a much better price. Eventually, after a bit of a tussle, my command took over the negotiation and adminis-tration of contracts from November 1, 1990, and we were able to reduce prices substantially.

From then on, the procedure we followed was for Pagonis to put out a statement of work for what he needed. He would then review the dozen or so Saudi bidders, and select the two or three whom he thought were competent to do the job. My staff would then take over, negotiate the price and decide which bidder should have the contract. We would then pay the bill. In the case of food and transportation, we paid the contractors on a monthly basis. In the case of equipment, payment was made on delivery.

For the record, supporting friendly military forces in the King-

---

* Norman Schwarzkopf, op. cit., p. 365.

dom throughout the crisis cost us some $10 billion. In addition, the Saudi Ministry of Finance made a direct contribution to the U.S. Treasury of about $14 billion, while a further $3.5 billion was paid direct to the treasuries of other countries that came to our aid, such as Britain, France, Egypt, Syria, Morocco, Senegal, Niger and the rest of them. These figures do not include the considerable sums spent by other Saudi ministries and government agencies in connection with the war effort.

In meeting the supply requirements of the Coalition, the Kingdom had two options. As it was an unprecedented national emergency, the King could have commandeered or expropriated the buildings, vehicles, engineering equipment, food and the rest of it needed for the war effort, as other countries have done in similar circumstances. The alternative was to let the Saudi private sector participate by supplying the Coalition's needs on a commercial basis. Very sensibly and admirably, King Fahd chose the latter course, incidentally providing a great stimulus to the Saudi economy which had been in the doldrums before the war. Hundreds of Saudi businesses were able to flourish. And many foreign suppliers also did well, especially those who already had business ties with Saudi importers.

It was my task to ensure that no one contractor was favored over the others. I believed that everyone who was able to contribute to the war effort should have the opportunity to do so. Big contracts for such items as uniforms and camouflage nets were sometimes divided up among several companies. I used to tell my staff, "I want to see different names, different companies. I don't always want to see the same people. We must give everyone a chance." By such cooperative work, we were able to give as many firms as possible a chance to work, and our allies were able to draw on Saudi Arabia's remarkable privately owned assets. Because of their wide shareholding, we made a special effort to direct business to public companies dealing with road and maritime transport and with vehicle leasing and maintenance.

The whole Saudi business community was mobilized for the emergency, as were relevant Saudi ministries, like the ministries of Commerce, of Petroleum and Mineral Resources, of

Health . . . Representatives of various ministries came to work
with our logistics team.

It was discovered to everyone's surprise that the Saudi private
sector could provide just about everything that was needed –
the trucks, the buses, the bulldozers, the accommodation, the
food, the fuel. Saudi Arabia had become one of the most industrialized countries in the region, without local or Arab opinion
taking full notice.

✦≫≪✦

In spending my procurement budget, my policy was twofold: to
promote the war effort but also to pump money into the Saudi
economy. Before the war, some 400 companies were in financial
difficulties. But luckily, King Fahd's decision to put so much
business through Saudi companies changed the whole picture
radically. A total of 592 Saudi companies secured contracts to
do with the war – and this was quite apart from the thousands
of individuals who benefited by renting out their houses,
vehicles, and other items of equipment we required. The King
was anxious to stimulate the economy and rally support for the
war. We managed to do both. Firmness and flexibility became
my watchwords. I found they worked wonders when I had to
make sure that everyone's interests were addressed and that all
pulled together.

For water supplies, we brought into use more than 3,000 water
tankers to carry drinking water from our large desalination
plants at Jubail, al-Khobar, Hafr al-Batin and elsewhere. Saudi
desalination plants are among the best and biggest in the world.
In 1970, the capacity of our plants was a mere 5 million gallons
per day (mgd), but by 1990, capacity had grown to over 500
mgd. The largest single plant, with a capacity of 240 mgd, is at
Jubail, our new industrial city on the Gulf coast. Not only was
there enough water for everyone, but it was supplied in plastic
containers which allowed for easy distribution to the hundreds
of thousands of troops in the field, and which were designed to
keep water cool for several hours. We contracted for water at
several water-bottling plants. We also dug many wells at different sites in the desert. We installed small desalination units on

the well heads themselves. We supplied ice-making machines to many units in the field. Each battalion-sized unit had more than 10 refrigerator trucks to ensure a steady supply of fresh food and cold water.

On August 6, before my appointment as Joint Forces Commander, Major General Abd al-Aziz al-Shaikh, the Deputy Land Forces Commander, contacted Astra, one of the largest food producers in the Kingdom and a major supplier to the Saudi land forces since 1967.

"We need hot meals for some visitors expected at Dhahran within 48 hours," he told the company. "Can you manage?"

Astra promptly took over the local fast-food chains in the Eastern Province and started supplying hamburgers to men of the 82nd Airborne Division as they stepped off the plane. It did so well that, within a few days, Major General Abd al-Aziz al-Shaikh gave Astra a contract to supply the incoming U.S. forces at the Saudi government's expense.

This was the situation I found when I took over as Joint Forces Commander. Before the crisis, Astra had supplied food to the land forces but not to my air defense forces. I had employed another contractor whom I thought was better. In fact, when I learned that Astra was to be the main contractor I was worried as I wanted allied troops to be well fed. But as Astra was the only company which could deliver in the bulk required, and as I was anxious to ensure a steady flow of supplies, I agreed that it should continue in the job. Despite my prior misgivings, Astra did the job so well that I recommended a medal for its company president.

But I instructed Astra to spread the work as much as possible to Saudi subcontractors all over the Kingdom. With this in mind, my logistics chiefs then renegotiated the contracts with Astra. In the end, more than 125 Saudi companies were involved in supplying food to the Coalition.

I discovered that Saudi Arabia had a great infrastructure of food suppliers. There was actually an overcapacity of hamburgers, bread and other items. There was also an overcapacity of juice. Juice factories had been producing at only 20 percent of capacity. When the troops arrived, they went into full production. The same applied to milk. The facilities were unbelievable and every subcontractor was able to fulfill his obligations.

Mobile kitchens, manufactured by Saudi Arabia's National Metal Industry (NMI), delivered fast-food to soldiers in the most isolated locations while, in addition, front-line troops cooked for themselves on hundreds of huge gas barbecue kits. So much fresh food was delivered right up to the front that most MREs (Meals Ready to Eat) were not used. But we also bought emergency rations by the million and distributed them to units just in case the dislocation of war made it impossible to distribute fresh supplies. These emergency rations were prepared and packed locally. To give a boost to local industry, we insisted that the ration packs include locally produced items like dates and biscuits. The troops did not expect to be pampered, but they were. It was very probably the most luxurious war ever fought.

At the start, we had thought we might have a shortage of food and that we would have to appeal for help to the Ministry of Trade and the Chambers of Commerce. We had an emergency plan to ration certain items. But we never had to implement it. There was plenty of everything: flour, sugar, rice, pasta, meat, fresh fruit and vegetables, bottled water, fruit juice and so forth. It emerged that the Kingdom's business community was well able to cope with the emergency, and that their productive and import capacity was even greater than was needed. They had stockpiled enough supplies to cope with a year-long conflict without replenishment from outside. In many cases, the forces that came to our aid found the Kingdom more lavishly and abundantly supplied than their own countries. For some items, this was true even when compared with the United States, let alone Third World countries. Food in the field was better than in most restaurants.

What undoubtedly helped was that the heavy influx of troops did not occur until November/December giving contractors time to make their arrangements. It was a smooth operation, with first-, second- and third-line supplies distributed to all areas. Not one day passed during the crisis without Saudi Arabia supplying the troops with the full requirement of fresh locally baked bread, fresh milk and juice. Meat and ketchup were the main food items imported from such countries as Australia, New Zealand,

Ireland and Brazil. None of the forces that came to our help had to worry about supplies. We pushed supplies forward so that everyone could get what he wanted. We attached our own supply trucks to the various units. So much stuff was carried forward that, when Kuwait was liberated after the brief war, a lot of it had to be carried back again. Some suppliers were stuck with large surpluses, of which some perishable items like meat were distributed to needy countries. Because of the ritual slaughter of great numbers of sheep during the *Hajj*, we have become experienced in the processing and distribution of large quantities of mutton.

Catering for the troops during the Gulf crisis was a remarkable management success. By insisting on the recruitment of an army of subcontractors, we managed to spread the profits and the risks, while demonstrating to our visitors and to the Saudis themselves the great industrial and agricultural advances made by the Kingdom in recent years.

❖⟩⟨❖

Although our food caterers did a fine job, tribute must also be paid to the men who ran Saudi Arabia's oil industry – from the top production and refinery managers to oil field workers and tanker drivers.

The Kingdom was the Coalition's primary source of fuel. Without the millions of gallons of fuel a day we supplied, it is doubtful that Kuwait could have been liberated. Coalition armies would have remained encamped at their ports and airports of disembarkation, and Coalition aircraft would have been grounded. U.S. forces shipped in some fuel from the United States and other regions, but without Saudi Arabia's massive contribution there could have been no war – or at least not a war on the scale it was waged.

My logistics team gave me a daily briefing on the picture in the entire theater of operations, both north and east. But they also gave me a separate daily briefing on the fuel situation. Because fuel was such a major headache, a Fuel Operations Center was set up to monitor the availability of all types of fuel on a day-to-day, almost on an hour-to-hour, basis, to track the movement of oil shipments at sea, and allocate supplies.

Working at the Center were representatives from the Saudi armed services, from our Ministry of Petroleum, from Saudi ARAMCO (our oil production company), from Samarec (then the Kingdom's refining and marketing arm) and from U.S., British and French forces. These latter representatives brought their demands to us on a daily basis and we set them against what we had available. We would determine what we had in stock; we would establish how many gallons had been consumed the previous day; how many would be needed tomorrow; how many might be needed in one, five, 10, 15 weeks ahead.

I set the planners a gloomy scenario: suppose that two of our oil refineries were put out of action by enemy or terrorist action. How would we cope? Our refineries, indeed all our vital installations, were heavily protected from air attack by my beloved air defense forces, and from sabotage or terrorism by the Saudi Arabian National Guard, but we still had to work on the assumption that they would be attacked, and that some attacks might get through. (During the strategic air campaign, the Iraqis did strike back by firing Frog missiles at our refineries, but failed to score a hit.) Creating back-up facilities cost us a great deal of money, but it was a precaution we had to take. In examining such a scenario, we faced the paradox that Saudi Arabia might have to buy oil from outside! In fact, we bought some $700 million worth of petroleum products, mainly jet fuel, and stockpiled it at sea, and we increased our own refinery output. We were worried that, if the war were prolonged, we would not be able to meet the Coalition's vast fuel demands. I have criticized Schwarzkopf for exaggerating the supply needs of the Coalition, but perhaps I was guilty of the same mistake myself.

Supplying the fuel was our responsibility. To guarantee the flow to storage bladders, we contracted with American companies to build a pipeline from the refinery at al-Safaniya to the new King Fahd bin Abd al-Aziz airport in the Eastern Province, a distance of more than 150 miles, and another pipeline from al-Safaniya to the bladder farm at al-Qaisuma, a distance of over 400 miles. Fleets of fuel trucks – we used more than 2,500 such trucks in all – moved daily from our refineries at Ras Tannura, Riyadh, Jeddah, Yanbu and Jubail to forward petroleum terminals along the supply routes where fuel bladders of different sizes, from 10,000 gallons to 250,000 gallons, were placed. But taking fuel forward to units in the various battle areas was the responsibility of the various national contingents. Drivers could simply fill up and go. In addition we set up a number of bladder farms, each holding some 200 to 300 fuel bladders, where units could come to draw their supplies. All in all, we supplied fuel to the Coalition worth $1.9 billion!

❖⟩✕⟨❖

I do not want to bore the reader with a recital of the Kingdom's achievements in building a modern infrastructure, but it needs to be said that without these facilities – airports, ports, roads, telecommunications and the like – the Coalition would have faced a daunting, and even an impossible, task. Our 21 major airports played an indispensable role in bedding down thousands of Coalition aircraft. A great many additional air strips were built – in the Eastern Province, at KKMC and elsewhere – and runways added or extended at existing airports, to take the big C5 transport planes. Our seven major ports also played a vital role in the campaign and tribute should be paid to Lieutenant Colonel Ali Mansur al-Shu'aybi, the Kingdom's ports liaison officer, for his dedication throughout the crisis.

The Americans shipped much of their equipment to the huge King Abd al-Aziz port at Dammam, one of the most modern and best equipped in the world. They used three-quarters of its 39 berths, leaving berths 1 to 10 free for commercial traffic. Fifteen ships arrived daily carrying vehicles and war materiel. The troops flew in by plane – to Dhahran airport or to the splendid facilities of the new King Fahd airport which had just been completed north of Dhahran – and were bused to the ports to pick up their equipment, usually staying a couple of days before moving on. At the very beginning the incoming troops had to sleep in warehouses, but soon a new compound at Dammam, built to house 3,500 stevedores, was turned over to the Americans.

Expecting to face difficulties in unloading their supplies, the Americans brought handling equipment with them, but it was not used. In the event, 28,000 containers were unloaded smoothly, together with 114,000 wheeled vehicles, 12,000 tracked vehicles – both tanks and APCs – 1,500 helicopters and 360,000 tons of ammunition. A Saudi officer was assigned permanently to Dammam to help clear goods through the port. Every 15 minutes, a convoy left the port. From a helicopter, the sight was of vehicles as far as the eye could see. The Dhahran–Riyadh railway was used to carry passengers and cargo so as to relieve congestion on roads going north.

The American Marines came in at the Jubail commercial port which they shared, somewhat reluctantly, with the British armored division. (We had to intervene with the Marine Commander, Lieutenant General Walter Boomer, to give the British some space in which to land their armored vehicles.) Eight or nine blocks of new buildings were turned over to the British to house their incoming troops. The Jubail commercial port was closed altogether to civilian traffic. The industrial port at Jubail which is a maze of pipelines for transporting petrochemicals was considered too delicate for military use.

Across the peninsula on the Red Sea coast, the French came in at Yanbu's industrial port while the Egyptians and the Syrians came in at Yanbu's commercial port. As a standby facility, we used al-Qadhima, a little-known military port near Jeddah. As it happened, these Red Sea ports had been under my control during the Chinese missile project, when we had had to resort to a good deal of deception to prevent the weapons being detected. In the course of it, I had got to know the ports and the people running them, which stood me in good stead during the Gulf crisis.

When the new ports were being planned at Jeddah and Dammam, at Jubail and Yanbu, the Kingdom had the funds, the space and the access to modern technology to build world-class facilities which will probably be good for the next century. Big and well designed, they are unlikely to be saturated or outdated for many decades to come. They certainly served us well during the conflict.

ABOVE: A few weeks before the assault, President Mubarak flew in to inspect front-line Egyptian troops. He was met by Prince Muhammad bin Fahd, Governor of the Eastern Province, and myself.

LEFT: On a visit to Egyptian headquarters with the Commander of Egyptian forces, Major General Salah Halabi.

BELOW: On a visit to Syrian troops with their Commander, Major General Ali Habib.

The Egyptian and Syrian contribution to the Coalition was militarily significant and politically essential.

ABOVE: With Bahrain's Minister of Defense, Lieutenant General Shaikh Khalifa bin Ahmad al-Khalifa, my Sandhurst companion and friend.

RIGHT: The sun was setting at the end of a long day when I met with Colonel Amadou Seyni, commander of troops from Niger, at their desert strongpoint.

BELOW: Visiting the strongpoint manned by troops from Senegal, with their commander, Colonel Mohamadou Keita, now General and Chief of Staff.

ABOVE: A farewell meeting with Czechoslovakia's 180-strong chemical unit which, throughout the war, monitored any possible use by Iraq of chemical weapons against my troops.

LEFT: At a tent in the desert, I met with Colonel Ahmad Binyas, commander of a unit of elite Moroccan special forces.

My clashes with France's Defense Minister, Jean-Pierre Chevènement *(left)*, sometimes made life difficult for Lieutenant General Michel Roquejeoffre, the French commander on the spot, a seasoned and extremely tough soldier *(on my left with his arm raised).*

BELOW: Supplies in the desert war were so abundant that there was bottled water to spare for a thirsty camel.

Captain Ayedh al-Shamrani, a pilot in the Royal Saudi Air Force, shot down two Iraqi Mirages in a single engagement: a double kill in less than one minute.

At prayer in the desert. Immediately to my right are Colonel Ahmad Lafi, my ADC, and Lieutenant Colonel Abdallah al-Suwaylim, my office director at the Joint Forces Command. To my left are Major General Abd al-Rahman al-Alkami, Northern Area Commander, and Major General Sulaiman al-Wuhayyib, Commander JFC-North.

Directing the battle for al Khafji – a pivotal battle of the Gulf War – at Major General Sultan al-Mutairi's underground forward command post. On the telephone is Brigadier General Suhail Abu Samh, a member of the forward command staff.

Saudi infantry in al-Khafji after driving out the Iraqi invaders.

One of the saddest moments of the war was the
burial of 91 Senegalese troops killed when their
transport aircraft crashed on a return flight
from Makkah. After the war I visited Senegal to
convey our thanks to President Abdou Diouf
(*right*), a distinguished figure well respected in
Saudi Arabia.

BELOW: The debris of one of the 43 Scud
missiles launched by Iraq against the Kingdom
during the war. One Scud hit the school which
my son attended and another killed 28
American soldiers – the heaviest blow Saddam
managed to inflict on the Coalition in the
whole conflict.

بطاقة مرور أمن

يسمح لحامل هذه البطاقة بعبور اخطوط القوات المشتركة والصديقةوالشقيقة
ويلقى معاملة حسنة من الجميع حتى يصل إلى أقرب قيادة للقوات المشتركة . .
كما يسمح لكل من يحمل هذه البطاقة من الأشقاء في القوات العراقية بأن ينضم
إلى القوات المشتركة التي تضمن سلامته وحسن يعامل طبقاً لاتفاقية
جنيف .

قائد

القوات المشتركة ومسرح العمليات

In a vast "psyops" operation, millions of leaflets were dropped over Iraqi lines. Among the most effective was one designed as a "pass" promising the holder a warm welcome in the Kingdom, and signed by me as Joint Forces Commander. Waving this pass, thousands of Iraqi troops crossed our line to surrender.

My favorite leaflet showed an Iraqi soldier and a Saudi soldier holding hands fraternally.

RIGHT: The caption on the bomb reads: "Warning! This place will now be bombed. Leave your equipment and save yourselves."

تحذير !

سيجري قصف
هذا الموقع !

اتركوا معداتكم
وانقذوا انفسكم

تحذير !

ABOVE: Arriving in Kuwait immediately after its liberation with Major General Salih al-Muhaya, the Eastern Area Commander, now the Land Forces Commander *(behind my right shoulder)*. On my left is Colonel Prince Turki bin Abdallah, commander of a Military Police battalion.

LEFT: With Major General Sultan 'Adi al-Mutairi, Commander of JFC-East, at his forward headquarters. Standing behind us are Captain Zaki, head of my personal security team, and Colonel Shakir Idris, in charge of Public Affairs.

BELOW: Kuwaiti children celebrate the liberation of their country.

In supporting the Coalition forces, the biggest single problem we faced was a shortage of transport. None of the allies brought enough vehicles with them; some brought none at all. Without our help, it would not have been possible to deploy men and supplies at speed across the vast distances from the ports and airports to the forward areas. The U.S. alone unloaded 600 shiploads of equipment and over 10,000 aircraft loads: this gives some indication of the magnitude of the transportation challenge posed by the American forces alone. As our own armed services had limited transport capabilities, commercial vehicles belonging to the Saudi private sector came to the rescue. I believe my support unit contracted altogether for no fewer than 22,000 vehicles and more than 4,000 civilian drivers.

The vehicles were of every conceivable type – giant Heavy Equipment Transporters able to carry tanks; refrigeration vehicles to deliver ice to troops sweltering in the desert; water and petrol tankers, flatbeds, bulldozers, trailers, buses, mobile homes for headquarters' staffs, jeeps, ordinary automobiles and all-purpose 4x4 trucks by the thousand. To flush out commercial vehicles which I knew were in the Kingdom, I had a bright idea. I made an appeal to individual owners, not companies: I announced that we would pay the new price for any used vehicles they were prepared to sell us. This was no time to bargain or be unduly fussy. My logistics department was immediately swamped by offers of vehicles from all over the country. That simple ploy netted us several hundred trucks. Of course, we insisted that they were well serviced and in good condition.

The Egyptian and Syrian forces came fast but traveled light. They brought their weapons and ammunition with them, but few vehicles. I needed an immediate 3,000 trucks to give them some mobility. We launched a vast, worldwide purchasing program to support the Egyptian and Syrian divisions – not just trucks, but tents, generators, tractors, mobile kitchens, food, latrines, shower units, engineering equipment and a thousand other items needed to turn them into a combat-ready force. Procuring what they needed was both costly and time-consuming. We eventually supplied the Syrians with some 2,800 vehicles and, as there were twice as many Egyptians as Syrians, the Egyptian need for vehicles was correspondingly greater. I wanted the Egyptian and Syrian commanders to know that I was giving them top priority, even if I had to strip my own forces of support to meet their needs. In appreciation of their contribution to the war effort, Prince Sultan instructed me to give the Syrians and the Egyptians thousands of vehicles and many different types of equipment to take home with them.

The different national contingents that came to the Kingdom had different requirements. For example, the first American units to arrive were wholly dependent on us for transportation, housing, water – a dependency which lasted throughout the crisis – and just about everything else (including black robes for women soldiers to wear over their uniforms during off-duty hours to make their presence more acceptable to our population). In due course, the Americans built up their own support, although they continued to need fuel and transportation in vast quantities, as did the British and French.

Some national contingents were heavily dependent on us for practically everything for the duration of the crisis. We had to feed them from the moment they arrived. Some forces came with no capability at all. In some cases, we even had to supply them with rifles. The 300 Afghan *mujahedin* came with what they stood up in.

Heavy Equipment Transporters (HETs) were a particular nightmare, because even the Americans were very short of them, bringing in only 500 out of a requirement three times as large. The Kingdom managed to supply the Americans with more than 1,000 HETs – mainly leased by us from the oil and construction industries – and more were found in Europe. The Pentagon negotiated most of the overseas deals, but we paid. We also supplied the British with 250 HETs and the Egyptian and Syrian forces with 500 HETs. Buses we supplied to take troops to their deployment areas made more than 3,000 journeys.

I extended our maintenance infrastructure to the east and north of the country to cope with the huge number of vehicles, and arranged for some 200 Egyptian mechanics and maintenance men to enhance our capability at KKMC and Taif. Such was the volume of traffic that most of the roads heading north were clogged with supply vehicles traveling only seconds apart.

Lieutenant General Pagonis told me that on one occasion he went up to check a movement-control point on the northern route. Eighteen trucks were roaring past every minute. The traffic was so dense that he could not cross the road. He was finally forced to crank up his helicopter and fly to the other side!

Many drivers were killed in traffic accidents, especially on the narrow Tapline road which has no hard shoulders. Among the casualties were several dozen American drivers, out of total American casualties (both battle and nonbattle deaths) of 293.

In preparation for the ground war, two huge American formations, VIIth Corps and XVIIIth Corps, crossed each other – one traveling 400 miles and the other 650 miles – to take up offensive positions on the battlefield. With other Coalition troops, this involved a movement of 300,000 troops, 60,000 wheeled vehicles, 6,000 tanks and tracks and over 20,000 containers. An immense effort by us was required to support this vast movement by the American and other forces. We had to shift a large part of our support infrastructure from the north and east to the west, and build new logistics bases and distribution points.

In view of our great contribution to the Coalition and the devoted work of my logisticians, I was sorry not to see due credit given us in the many Western accounts of the war I have read. It is probably true to say that never in the whole of its military history had the United States received such support in war as it received from Saudi Arabia during the Gulf conflict, as my co-commander, General Schwarzkopf, recognized at the small ceremony in Riyadh at which we exchanged medals after the war. "From the minute the first American arrived on the ground in Saudi Arabia," he said,

> we were supported 100 percent by the Saudis. We received our food, our water, our fuel, our transportation and on and on and on from the Saudis. Let there be no mistake about it, what we have accomplished together has been a great military accomplishment, but it simply could not have been done without the 100 percent cooperation of Saudi Arabia.
>
> The ports we brought our equipment into were Saudi ports, the airfields from which we all launched our air strikes were, for the large part, Saudi airfields.

The host nation support we received over here we never could have mustered anywhere else, and without that host nation support, any offensive operation we would have conducted would have taken literally months longer, if not years longer, to accomplish. So I think it is at this time very appropriate for us to recognize the contribution of the Kingdom of Saudi Arabia to this very, very great victory.

I appreciated Schwarzkopf's private tribute, but I wish he had repeated it publicly in his book.

In the end, there was probably too much of everything for the job at hand – not just supplies but combat troops, tanks and aircraft as well. I could not help being struck by the wastefulness of the operation. The American command had so built up Saddam's forces as "the fourth largest army in the world," no doubt for purposes of deception and to lull Saddam into a sense of false security, that in the end it may even have come to believe it. Of course, it took the Coalition some time to realize that many of Saddam's divisions were understrength. On a simple divisional count, the army facing us was enormous; but when the true numbers of each division were established more accurately, much of this army melted away.

At one point, no doubt on an intelligence assessment of Iraq's strength, Schwarzkopf decided that his M1 tanks were not good enough to take on Saddam's T-72s. It was decided to replace them with the latest Abrams tank, the M1A1. But these had to be modified. They had come green from Germany and had to be painted desert colors. They had to be fitted with an extra shield, and we provided the warehouses where the modifications were made. The new tanks were sent to all the armored units and the M1s were returned. At one point, 700 M1s were at the port on standby. The 105mm rounds of the M1s were exchanged for 120mm rounds for the M1A1s. I later read that 220,000 120mm tank rounds had been shipped in for the U.S. armored forces, but that only 3,600 had needed to be expended in defeating the world's "fourth largest army." Was the immensely costly decision to bring in the more powerful tank and huge amounts of its ammunition based on a wrong estimate of Iraq's strength? Was it an intelligence failure? Or was it, I wondered, another example of Schwarzkopf's caution?

In December 1990, I issued a directive that our whole logistics infrastructure had to be in place by January 15 (which was the deadline fixed by the UN Security Council Resolution 678 of November 29, 1990, authorizing the use of "all necessary means" if Iraq failed to obey the will of the international community by that date). But a switch of focus had already taken place. The logisticians had done their heroic work and war planning had long since taken precedence.

CHAPTER XVIII

War Planning with a Superpower

I F ONE HAS TO GO TO WAR, it is best to do so with a super-power ally. To have overwhelming strength on one's side is both reassuring and exhilarating. But it is also somewhat alarming: there is a downside to such an alliance. Because of the disproportion of forces, the relationship is inevitably unequal. A superpower will want to lead and will insist that others follow. It will want to make decisions alone. It will not wish to share its intelligence. It will want full control over its diplomacy, its strategy, and its high-tech weapons. And as war approaches, these tendencies will become more pronounced. The junior partner will have to run to keep abreast.

In the Gulf conflict I represented the junior partner – and I had to do a great deal of running. I could not afford to be left behind. Neither could I merely rubber stamp the wishes, decisions and strategic choices of our superpower ally. As the host country, Saudi Arabia was indispensable to the Coalition. Without us – without our facilities, finance and political backing – no war could be waged. We therefore had some leverage and we used it. It was agreed that we had the right to participate in the overall planning of the campaign, and that no military operation could take place without our approval. But theory is one thing, practice quite another. Making the arrangement stick was my difficult task.

If one thing characterized my relationship with Schwarzkopf it was my constant quest for information on matters that concerned my mission. To get him to reveal what he knew I had to resort to a variety of methods: I could surprise him with information of my own and seek to draw him out; I could question his moves and persuade him to explain them; on occasion, I could demand to know. We spent hours together in friendly probing and jousting. One way or another, I needed to be fully abreast of what our superpower ally was thinking to make sure that Saudi interests were protected.

Schwarzkopf, in turn, had to report to his own political masters and military superiors, and take instructions from them. He was by no means the principal decision-maker on the American side, which complicated my search for information. In fact, his superiors in Washington had a large hand in almost every aspect of the campaign. The strategic concepts, the overall plan, the timetables – all these were shaped in the Pentagon by General Colin Powell and his 1,600-strong staff, with input from Defense Secretary Dick Cheney and from Brent Scowcroft, the National Security Advisor and his staff, with the President, of course, establishing the overall objectives and giving his ultimate approval to the plans. Of all these, General Powell was clearly a key player.

More than one observer has remarked that a striking feature of the Gulf War was the authority General Powell exercised as Chairman of the U.S. Joint Chiefs of Staff – an authority which owed much to the reforms and the provisions of the 1986 Goldwater-Nichols Defense Reorganization Act. The Act, which set in motion the most thorough reorganization of the Pentagon since World War Two, streamlined the chain of command, reducing the powers of the various service chiefs and increasing those of the Chairman. For the first time, the Chairman of the Joint Chiefs of Staff was given complete authority over the whole military apparatus, thus putting an end to, or at least reducing, the congressional lobbying and horse-trading between the services which had earlier hampered joint command decisions.

A veteran of Washington politics, Powell made full use of the powers he thus acquired. Under the Act, he was the President's chief military adviser. His large staff was accountable only to him. He had the power to override the rival service chiefs and to speak independently of them. All the reports reaching us from the United States confirmed that the Bush–Cheney–Powell team worked well together. I soon grasped that grand strategy was decided in Washington, tactics in Riyadh, a division of tasks which limited my access to information and restricted my input to the planning process, while reducing Schwarzkopf's own role to that of a field commander.

In any conflict, intelligence is of prime importance. Without it, one blunders about in the dark, uncertain about the enemy's capabilities and, perhaps more relevantly, his intentions. War plans are based on intelligence – and inevitably the United States provided most of it. I had some independent sources of information, notably from our General Intelligence Directorate, Military Intelligence and the Ministry of Interior. But, of the many reports that reached me, quite a few were fanciful and had to be ignored. There were so many of them that I assigned a member of my staff to sift through and summarize them, with instructions to pass on to me only the most significant – and the funniest. One of these was that Saddam was planning to load caravans of camels with high explosives and send them into our ranks! I remember passing on this intelligence gem to Schwarzkopf – as a joke.

Some of the agents we sent inside Iraq and Kuwait brought back useful material but, until deserters (whom I preferred to call "military refugees") started coming over in large numbers after the beginning of the air campaign, and until POWs were taken and interrogated, I had to rely largely on what the Americans were able to glean about Iraq's capabilities and intentions from their satellites, spy planes, cryptanalysts and Special Forces.

Our Western allies regretted that I did not give them permission to interrogate Iraqi POWs. But I had good reasons not to do so. POWs were my best and most valuable source of intelligence: it was a card I wanted to hold. More important, I did not want Arab prisoners to be in the hands of non-Saudis in my own country: my own Saudi troops – and of course the Iraqis as well – would believe we were controlled by Westerners. In any event, I did not want Iraqi prisoners to be turned by harsh interrogation into long-term enemies of the Kingdom. However, I had to be realistic. I knew that whoever captured the prisoners, whether it was the Americans, British, French or Egyptians, would question them at once, but I insisted that prisoners be handed over to us within a very few days of their capture. The Americans wanted to listen in to our interrogations, but even that I refused.

I was sorry not to have my own Saudi teams of Special Forces to match those which the Americans – and the British – sent in to gather intelligence behind Iraqi lines. I thought many times of ordering into Iraq men from Egypt's Special Forces regiment. In an ideal world, I would have used them. That is what they were trained for. But I hesitated to do so for political reasons. I did not want to give them an assignment that might have aroused resistance from the Egyptian Commander, Major General Halabi, causing him perhaps to refer back to his national command. I did not want to cause embarrassment to the Egyptians or indeed to ourselves, or to make any move which might put at risk the political cooperation we were receiving.

Had the Egyptian commander refused to send in his rangers – which was a distinct possibility – I would have been upset. But, had he accepted such a dangerous and sensitive mission, Egypt's political leaders might, in turn, have been upset. I did not want to face the charge that I had sent in Egyptians rather than expose Saudi troops to danger. In such a "no win" situation, I preferred not to issue the order.

In Saudi Arabia, we had not put much effort into gathering intelligence about Iraq, because we had not considered it a serious threat, especially during the 1980s when it was engaged in its war with Iran. We had to learn the lesson that today's friend could become tomorrow's enemy. But there was a price to pay for our poor information about Iraq: our heavy dependence on the Americans robbed us of effective leverage over war planning.

Throughout the crisis, I detected a paradox in the Coalition's intelligence posture. The U.S. and its allies deployed tremendous intelligence assets, probably more than in any previous war. They enjoyed the advantage of excellent airborne observation. Allied satellites and aircraft could look deep into Iraq (except on those days when visibility was obstructed by sandstorms or low cloud). Some of the electronics were remarkable, such as the imagery reconnaissance systems which allowed for the precise targeting of Cruise missiles. The desert also provided unrivaled opportunities for air-delivered fire. Ground and air weapons systems could engage their targets at maximum range.

Vast intelligence staffs labored diligently away in such bodies as CENTCOM's Joint Intelligence Center, the Combat Assessment Center and the Joint Reconnaissance Center which collected airborne intelligence. Our own photo-reconnaissance aircraft patrolled the Kuwaiti and Iraqi borders.

But, despite these considerable efforts and advantages, there was a great deal that the Coalition did not know. I remain of the opinion that intelligence about Iraq was one of the Coalition's biggest weaknesses. U.S. space-based monitoring devices had apparently been unable to predict Iraq's invasion of Kuwait by more than a few hours. There were also great short-falls in post-invasion intelligence. Was Saddam massively re-inforcing his armies in Kuwait as he claimed? How strong were the much-vaunted Republican Guard divisions and how did he intend to use them? How would his air force perform in battle? It was supposed to be very good, but it had not exactly distin-guished itself in the war against Iran. How far advanced was Iraq's nuclear, biological and chemical (NBC) weapons program? Did he ever intend to use the unconventional weapons in his arsenal? Would he dare do so? Would he use fuel air explosives? Would he use his Frogs, Scuds and other short-range missiles? Could he mount a terrorist campaign against us? The areas of uncertainty were vast. Above all, uncertainty about Saddam's intentions remained a persistent source of anxiety throughout.

If the U.S. knew the answers to these questions, it did not share them with us. Either they had poor intelligence in these areas, or they wanted to give us just enough to ensure our cooperation, but not so much as to reveal their sources. The problem lay more with Washington than with the Americans in Riyadh. In fact some senior American officers told me that, in some cases, information was withheld from U.S. forces in the Kingdom because it was known in Washington that the Ameri-cans in Riyadh were attempting to be open and honest with their allies.

I suspect, however, that in most cases the U.S. was as much in the dark as we were. As Dick Cheney himself conceded in his report to Congress on the conduct of the war, "The morale

and intentions of Iraqi forces and leaders were obscure to us."
So there was a paradox: the Coalition was, at one and the same
time, all-seeing and yet extraordinarily ignorant.

What we and the Americans most evidently lacked was
human intelligence: that is to say, well-placed agents inside
Iraq's military and political apparatus. In theater, the best results
in terms of "humint" were probably provided by the brave
members of the Kuwait underground who fed us information
about Iraqi force levels, about where Iraqi commanders were
meeting and where people were being tortured. Out of theater,
the most useful information about Iraq's arms industries, including its nuclear facilities, came from the Western firms that had
helped build them.

My own view, and that of most knowledgeable Arabs, was
that Iraq was not nearly as strong as the Americans chose to bill
it. During the anxious years of the Iraq–Iran war, when our
own security was threatened, it was clear that Iraq had had the
greatest difficulty in holding Iran, even though it was lavishly
supplied with modern weapons from both East and West, while
the Iranians were starved of them. The Iraqis could field a lot
of men but, with the exception of some elite units, they had little
mobility or fighting spirit, a fact confirmed to my satisfaction by
the 100 or so defectors who came over to us even before the
start of the air campaign, when the stream turned into a flood.
I did not believe Saddam's claim to have mobilized an additional
19 divisions in a month. He might have given each man a rifle,
but that was no way to create a credible fighting force. In sheer
numbers, Iraq might have had the "world's fourth largest army,"
but in efficiency and combat readiness it probably ranked about
twentieth.

I am not for one moment suggesting that Saddam Hussein's
Iraq was a "paper tiger." He had put together a vast military
machine. But I was, nevertheless, somewhat puzzled by high
Western estimates of Iraq's fighting ability, particularly in view
of the devastating air campaign which was being planned against
it. Was it Saddam's bluster which caused so many foreign
observers to think that his power to resist the Coalition was
greater than it was? My own feeling is that it was essentially
the fear of Iraq's chemical weapons – an unknown quantity to

the very end of the campaign – which made many Coalition commanders think Iraq was a formidably dangerous enemy. In any event, when the crunch came, the 100-hour rout of the Iraqi army made it abundantly clear that the Coalition had over-estimated Iraqi strength and, more significantly, had under-estimated the impact of the long air campaign which preceded the ground war.

There was also a specifically American reason why the U.S. felt it necessary to deploy immense military resources against Iraq, which was after all no more than a medium-sized Third World power. This was America's traumatic experience in Vietnam. After that defeat, there was, as I learned, a revulsion among the U.S. military against the notion, when confronting an enemy, of "gradual escalation," of an incremental build-up of U.S. strength. Generals Colin Powell, Chuck Horner and John Yeosock, who were all at the National War College together, class of 1976, were all profoundly marked by the Vietnam War, as was Schwarzkopf himself. As Lieutenant General Horner put it to me,

> The problem in Vietnam was that it went on and on and on. We thought we could mix diplomacy with war fighting. And you can't. Perhaps the reason we used so much force in the Gulf was that we had come to expect that we were going to fail. Before the war, we started believing the news-papers which said we were incompetent. They said that our equipment didn't work, that our people were no good, that our generals were stupid. We had to prove them wrong.

The new American doctrine was to guarantee victory by applying massive, overwhelming combat power against the enemy, in the air, at sea and on the ground, at night and during the day. To give him no respite. The AirLand battle doctrine, developed in the U.S. armed forces in the 1980s, called for the deployment of ultra-mobile, hard-hitting, integrated air and land forces, able to seize and hold the initiative and dictate terms to the enemy by striking at his heartland deep behind his lines. From this point of view, the Gulf War was to prove a model campaign – even though the enemy in question hardly put up a fight.

In General Horner's words, "The new reality of war is to use overwhelming force and get it over fast."

✖

Most published accounts of the Gulf War – and there have been a great many – relate that the crisis unfolded in two distinct phases: first, a defensive phase from August to November 1990, when the main concern was the defense of Saudi Arabia; then an offensive phase to free Kuwait, signaled by President Bush's announcement on November 8 that he was doubling the number of U.S. troops in the Gulf.

There is a lot wrong with this categorization. In war, there is seldom a clear distinction between defense and offense. The record shows that, from the moment Saddam invaded Kuwait, U.S. military planners at the Pentagon and at CENTCOM head-quarters prepared an offensive strategy – and from the very beginning this envisaged a wide-ranging air attack on Iraq itself, and not just on Iraqi troops in Kuwait. Instead of attacking Iraq's occupation forces in Kuwait, the plan called for the use of massed air power against Iraq's political and military leadership in Baghdad; its command, control and communications net-works; its air defenses; its elite Republican Guard forces; its military industries; its power grids, oil refineries, roads, bridges, railways and other transportation infrastructures; indeed, in the term used widely at the time, its "centers of gravity."

We were not involved in the making of this plan, nor were we officially informed about it. It was only in September that I began to get a sense of it. Indeed, the whole world was soon alerted to American thinking when, on a long flight back home from Riyadh in mid-September, the U.S. Air Force Chief of Staff, General Michael J. Dugan, let the cat out of the bag by telling the press that the aim of the air campaign was to decapitate the Iraqi leadership in Baghdad! His dismissal for this indiscretion served only to give added weight to his remarks.

It was, of course, only prudent for the U.S. to plan an offensive against Iraq from the very beginning. Militarily, it made good sense. The making of such plans did not mean that the U.S. necessarily meant to go to war from the very beginning. Indeed some well-placed Americans maintain that one reason the plan was kept secret – and why Dugan was sacked – was precisely because the U.S. hoped for a political settlement of the crisis, and did not want to spoil the chances of such a settlement by unveiling its war plans.

In any event, in Saudi Arabia our concerns were somewhat different. When we were faced with the real likelihood of an Iraqi attack on the Kingdom, we had to defend ourselves. Our immediate dispositions were wholly defensive. I described in an earlier chapter how vulnerable we felt and what hasty measures we took to protect ourselves. Before the arrival of the Americans, the Royal Saudi Air Force was the only serious weapon we had. Although it had not trained to face Iraq, it was at once placed on full alert. Our aircraft – Tornados, F-5s, F-15s – were armed and ready to take off. Our air refueling tankers were waiting at their bases and our AWACS were in the air almost 24 hours a day. Within hours of the invasion, our air force was ready to counter any threat from Saddam. Could we have halted and turned back an Iraqi attack? No one can be certain of the answer to that question. But we would certainly have given a good account of ourselves and made Saddam pay dearly for any aggression against us.

Rather than an attack from Iraq, however, the first challenge our air force faced was the sudden arrival of fleeing Kuwaiti aircraft. Some planes escaped on the first day from Kuwait's northern air base, but most flew in on the second day from the southern base, a clear indication that Iraq was slow to gain full control of Kuwait. We received most of the planes at Dhahran, and then moved them on to Taif and Khamis Mushait, because we needed to use the Dhahran base ourselves. Some Kuwaiti helicopters landed safely at nearby Saudi airports like Ras Mish'ab, but others crashed or got lost in the desert in the scramble to get out.

I mention these details to illustrate the difference between ourselves and the United States at that time. While we struggled to put together our defenses and welcome the remnants of the Kuwait armed forces, as well as a huge flood of civilian refugees, the United States had, by August 25, already planned a four-phase offensive campaign, which envisaged a strategic air campaign against Iraq; an air campaign against Iraqi air forces in Kuwait; the neutralization of Iraq's Republican Guard forces by a process of attrition and the isolation of the Kuwaiti battlefield; and finally a ground attack to eject Iraqi forces from Kuwait. This was, in fact, an early blueprint of the plan finally adopted.*

According to my personal reading of the situation, the difference between ourselves and the Americans in those early weeks reflected a difference in war aims. Our immediate objectives, shared with our Arab allies, were to roll back Iraqi power, remove the threat to our security, and restore the status quo ante in Kuwait and the Gulf. No doubt we would have welcomed Saddam's overthrow, as we had come to see him as a dangerous man, but we had no wish to see Iraq itself devastated. Despite our quarrel with its leader, Iraq was a brotherly country whom we had helped in its war against Iran, and whose regional role we valued as a counterweight to both Iran and Israel.

In contrast, America's war aims, in so far as we understood them, were to defend U.S. access to Arabian oil – a vital strategic resource for the West; protect Israel's security; remove Saddam's threat to the political order in the Gulf; and more generally affirm America's global supremacy. To be fair, President Bush and the American people were also concerned about the injustice of the invasion of Kuwait and mobilized themselves in what they saw as a "just cause."

While there was some overlap between our aims and those of our superpower friend they were by no means identical. At the start, we wished to contain Iraq, while the U.S. wished to destroy its military power. Only gradually, as Saddam's threats against us grew more violent, and as it became clear that he had no intention of relinquishing Kuwait peacefully, were we persuaded that his war-making capability in Iraq itself would have to be reduced.

High on the list of targets was Iraq's nuclear, biological and chemical (NBC) plants and its ballistic-missile production facilities – that is to say, its capability to manufacture and deliver weapons of mass destruction. Israel had for some time been

---

* U.S. Department of Defense, *Conduct of the Persian Gulf War*, Final Report to Congress, p. 84.

pressing its American ally to destroy Iraq's facilities – threatening
to do so itself if the United States failed to act. It is a remarkable
achievement of Israeli diplomacy to have persuaded the United
States and much of the Western world that Israel's own nuclear
bombs, chemical weapons and long-range missiles in whose
grim shadow the Arabs have had to live for decades are legitimate weapons of self-defense, whereas any Arab attempt, however feeble, to achieve a modicum of deterrence must be
considered a threat to the "civilized world." The extensive U.S.
targeting of Iraq's NBC plants, and the alarm raised over Iraq's
nuclear program, strongly suggested that Washington, in
defense of its own interests as the dominant world power, was
anxious to keep a lid on a potentially explosive region and
prevent the proliferation of weapons of mass destruction.

The fact remains, however, that once Saddam had invaded
Kuwait and his aggressive, expansionist nature had been
revealed, we too were anxious to see his NBC plants destroyed.
His nuclear program became a direct threat to us too. We were
extremely vulnerable to weapons of mass destruction: we had
no effective deterrence; our major economic assets were concentrated in the Eastern Province; and our population was
concentrated in a small number of centers. As an Arab, it is sad
for me to have to admit that Saddam's move into Kuwait and
his bellicose rhetoric made him seem as dangerous as Israel to
us. The war provided a chance to remove the threat Saddam
posed. Such was the painful course which the adventurism of
the Iraqi leader forced upon us.

✦➤✦

The truth is that others saw the potential dangers from Saddam
before we did. I have since learned that, in the late summer of
1989, a year or so after the end of the Iraq–Iran war, U.S.
defense analysts came to the conclusion that Saddam Hussein
posed a greater threat to the stability of the region than the
radicals in Iran. Once Iran had given up the struggle and agreed
to a cease-fire, the Iraqi leader began to lean on his neighbors,
demanding fresh credits, the forgiveness of Iraq's war loans, and
other far-reaching concessions.

Growing concern about Saddam's large war machine led to a flurry of activity in the Pentagon and at CENTCOM headquarters in Tampa, Florida, as defense planners switched the focus of their contingency plans from Iran to Iraq. The result of this activity was that by mid-1990, CENTCOM had produced a secret plan to counter any possible Iraqi aggression against Saudi Arabia or the Gulf. Titled *Defense of the Arabian Peninsula*, it was known as *Operations Plan 1002–90*; and in July 1990, just a month before Saddam's invasion of Kuwait, CENTCOM conducted a headquarters war game, called Internal Look, based on a scenario which turned out to be astonishingly similar to the events which were soon to unfold. (To my considerable amusement, Schwarzkopf told me early in the crisis that, in the first run-through of the war game, his headquarters had lost the "war" – an experience which might have had some bearing on the vast force levels the U.S. later deployed when it came to face the real thing.) At any rate, once Saddam invaded Kuwait, the prewar contingency plans "gave CENTCOM a head start" (as Defense Secretary Dick Cheney was later to report to Congress) and contributed to the speed with which American forces – fighter wings, ground troops, carrier battle groups – arrived on the scene.

From my perspective in Saudi Arabia, the very first plans we Saudis put together in the first anxious weeks were day-to-day ground and air defensive plans. These were later refined and expanded, in cooperation with our allies, to become the overall defense plan known as Desert Shield. In fact, especially in terms of planning for land operations, Desert Shield was very much of a cooperative effort, with Lieutenant General John Yeosock and myself as its first architects. When Schwarzkopf came on the scene in late August, the main dispositions had already been taken.

As the prime instrument for integrating our land forces and concerting our defense plans, Yeosock and I invented the C3I cell, as I have already related. That was the body which tied together the Western, Arab and Islamic forces of the Coalition. Meanwhile, Chuck Horner and his air staff were, in great secrecy, building their plan for the strategic air campaign against Iraq. The plan for the ground campaign was separate and came later. In the whole of the planning process, it must be said that the Americans played their cards close to their chest. We were not brought in fully until late November – after the passing of UN Security Council Resolution 678 authorizing the use of "all necessary means" against Iraq. It was then that a Military Planning Group was set up in Riyadh in which the principal Coalition partners were represented, the Saudi representative being Major General Yusuf Madani, who had served as my deputy during the Chinese missile project. Major General Madani was a capable and ambitious officer, with a dry, tenacious manner not unlike that of his American opposite number on the planning group, Rear Admiral Grant Sharp. But by the time the group was set up, the Americans had already determined the main lines of Desert Storm.

As is now well known, the plan provided for a campaign in four separate but overlapping phases:

PHASE ONE: Waging a strategic air and missile war against the Iraqi heartland to neutralize the Iraqi leadership and the country's principal "centers of gravity."

PHASE TWO: Securing air supremacy over the Kuwait Theater of Operations by destroying Iraq's air defenses and command and control systems.

PHASE THREE: Reducing the combat effectiveness of Iraqi ground forces and their supporting rocket, missile and artillery units by at least 50 percent, cutting their supply lines and destroying their C3 systems by intense air and naval fire.

PHASE FOUR: Liberating Kuwait by a ground offensive.

As the plan went back and forth between me and the Americans, we were able to make several changes, especially to the last two phases. I was concerned that, prior to the ground attack, we should achieve the required attrition rate of Iraqi forces. Another area of intense concern was the allocation of supply routes for the units under my command. Under the original plan, the U.S. had taken over the main arteries, the best roads, forcing our convoys to zigzag back and forth. I insisted that each sector had to have its own supply routes. I wanted to protect my supply routes by ensuring that they did not cross those of the United States and would not therefore be controlled by them. After some discussion, the routes to all our sectors were straightened out. We were also able to determine with greater precision the sectors of responsibility of the various national contingents under my command and define where exactly my forces were to breach Iraqi defense lines around Kuwait. In such breaching operations, I was anxious to establish that Saudi forces would lead the attack.

Although we were not involved in the early planning, I could not help being aware that, throughout October 1990, a debate was raging in the American camp about how best to mount the attack on Iraqi positions. I was later able to fill in some of the details. As I understand it, early in October Schwarzkopf's original concept for the ground offensive was presented by CENTCOM's Chief of Staff to Secretary Cheney and Paul Wolfowitz at the Pentagon and to President Bush, Vice President Dan Quayle, the CIA's Robert Gates and the National Security Advisor, Brent Scowcroft, at the White House. This first plan provided for a frontal assault at night on Iraqi positions by a single corps with the aim of seizing high ground northwest of Kuwait City. But, as it soon became clear, this plan was dismissed. The risk of casualties from such a frontal attack was considered too high, and there was the real possibility of an Iraqi counterattack or preemptive strike which might have caught the Coalition off balance. "Why straight up the middle?" Scowcroft is reported to have asked CENTCOM's representatives. "Why don't you go around?" The "indirect approach" was after all a tactic as old as war itself.

It was as a result of these objections that Cheney ordered the planners to explore the option of a flanking and enveloping attack through Iraq's Western desert – a maneuver which, as everyone now knows, was eventually adopted with devastating success. But it was generally agreed at the time that, if this strategy were adopted, more than one American corps would be needed. General Powell came to Riyadh on October 21–22 to find out what forces Schwarzkopf thought he would require to do the job. It was then that Schwarzkopf persuaded him that two corps would be necessary, and on October 31, President Bush approved the new American deployments. At a news conference on November 8, he informed the public of these large reinforcements, thereby giving notice that America was serious about going to war. "After consultation with King Fahd and our allies," the President declared, "I have today directed the Secretary of Defense to increase the size of U.S. forces committed to Desert Shield to insure that the coalition has an adequate offensive military option should that be necessary to achieve our common goals." This was a clear signal which, by some accounts, Saddam failed to heed. A contrary suggestion is that the Iraqi leader knew that war was coming but considered that he would be putting his own position at risk if he withdrew from Kuwait at this stage. In other words, he was prepared to sacrifice his country to save himself.

The American reinforcements were spectacular in their scope. They included the entire VIIth Corps, shipped to the Gulf from Europe and, in the war plan, given the prime task of mounting the main attack into the heart of Iraq's defenses and destroying the Republican Guard forces. In addition, the Americans brought in the 1st Infantry Division, together with another Marine Division, three more aircraft carrier battle groups and an extra 400 war planes.

I remember Schwarzkopf saying to me at the time, "I can't believe it. They are giving me much more than I asked for!"

The ground armies facing Saddam were thus swollen to two complete U.S. army corps (the XVIIIth Airborne Corps and the VIIth Corps); one corps of American Marines; a British armored division and a French light division; one Arab corps made up of one Syrian and two Egyptian divisions; and several Saudi and GCC brigades. An invincible combination, if ever there was one!

As I saw it, Schwarzkopf's contribution to the conceptual basis of the campaign was a reluctance to take risks. As a military commander he was careful rather than bold. Right up to the end, he persisted in believing – and declaring – that Iraq was a formidable opponent which should not be underestimated. He seemed particularly apprehensive about Saddam's armored Republican Guard divisions. Hence his pressure for more and more troops, planes and supplies, and for the Abrams M1A1 battle tank which in his estimation alone could take on Iraq's T-72s.

As with the air campaign, so with the ground war: the new doctrine was one of guaranteeing victory by the use of overwhelming force. In the event, devastated by the air campaign – the most remarkable campaign of battlefield preparation since World War Two – Saddam's Iraq proved to be highly vulnerable, and it must be left to future military historians to determine whether Schwarzkopf's caution was prudent or excessive.

As I recall, Dick Cheney and General Powell paid a visit to Riyadh on December 19–20 for a final review of the plan for Desert Storm. I remember driving out to meet them at Riyadh air base with Schwarzkopf and U.S. Ambassador Charles Freeman. It was a solemn moment because we all knew that there could be no turning back. The Coalition's great war machine was being primed for action.

Although the operational plan was a complex one, the basic concept was simple enough, and has by now been much written about. In essence, Iraq was to be led to believe that the main attack was coming from the east, while in fact it would come from the west, a flank which Saddam had left virtually unprotected. Feints and deception operations would fix the Iraqis in southeastern Iraq in fear of a Marine amphibious attack on the Kuwaiti coast, which the Americans had well advertised by conducting rehearsals for the landings in Oman – filmed by CNN! Plans for the amphibious attack had been leaked as far afield as Japan, in the expectation that the Iraqi ambassador in Tokyo would pick them up. Meanwhile, under cover of the strategic air campaign, the Coalition's ground forces would race to their offensive positions in the west. The main punch would be delivered by VIIth Corps, one of the world's most powerful armored units, together with Britain's First Armored Division. They would be assisted by supporting attacks on both their flanks. Far to the west, the air mobile XVIIIth Corps with the French light armored division on its left flank would, in a wide envelopment, bottle up Iraqi forces in the Kuwait Theater of Operations; while in the east, three further supporting attacks would be launched by JFC-East, by the First Marine Expeditionary Force and by JFC-North to penetrate Iraqi defenses, destroy Iraqi forces and block their retreat. It was planned that the first and third of these supporting attacks, conducted by my forces in JFC-East and JFC-North, would take Kuwait City.

❧❦

I was not entirely happy with these arrangements. For one thing, sending the main U.S. strike forces in a "left hook" flanking attack through Iraq's western desert meant that my forces would have the difficult task of going into Kuwait. I had always insisted that Arab troops under my command should be the first into Kuwait, but now that we were given the job I needed to be sure that we had adequate air and artillery support. I knew that Iraq's artillery was superior to mine, and I wanted to be sure it would be suppressed. In my view, field guns were the best weapons the Iraqis possessed. These were the weapons with which they had gained most experience in the Iraq–Iran war. Soviet doctrine, which the Iraqis had adopted, prescribed a massive concentration of field artillery. Not surprisingly, I thought it was very important that these guns be neutralized before we attacked.

More specifically, to secure a satisfactory ratio between attacking and defending forces, I wanted a guarantee that Iraqi tanks and guns opposite my sector would be degraded by 50 percent. I told Schwarzkopf very clearly that I would not move one inch until that had been done. Inside the Coalition, there was inevitably a prolonged debate over how to determine when the desired attrition rate had been achieved and where to put the various national contingents.

There was also the worrying possibility that Saddam might attack my forces just as American, British and French units were on the move heading for their attack positions. The roads would be clogged as hundreds of thousands of men and tens of thousands of vehicles moved from east to west. It seemed to me a moment of vulnerability which Saddam might exploit if he were to get wind of the "left hook" maneuver. The American plan provided for only one heavy infantry division to remain as a theater reserve, and I was not sure that that would be sufficient if a significant rear area threat were to develop. But with air supremacy firmly in Coalition hands, there was really not much that Saddam could do.

Taking Kuwait itself was problematic enough. Since occupying the state, the Iraqis had created a great many obstacles for any attacking force attempting to dislodge them. There were antitank ditches, field fortifications, mixed antitank and antipersonnel minefields, trenches flooded with oil. Along the Kuwaiti coast, the beaches were mined and protected by fire and other obstacles. Buildings, exposed underground pipelines and industrial infrastructure presented further major obstacles to movement by combat troops, as indeed did the large numbers of people still living in Kuwait City. There was minimal cover from direct or indirect fire. I reflected that if the Iraqis were to stand and fight, the city would have to be recaptured in hand-to-hand fighting, street-by-street and house-by-house. It was a daunting prospect. In fact, had the Iraqis chosen to stay in Kuwait, I was prepared to surround the city and lay siege to the Iraqi force for weeks, rather than attempt an assault which could have resulted in thousands of military casualties and great loss of civilian life.

In the event, of course, taking Kuwait City proved very easy because the Iraqis fled. More men were lost in accidents than in fighting the enemy. But we were not to know that.

Another of my worries was about logistics. By doubling the number of troops in the theater and insisting on stocks for 60 days instead of 30, Schwarzkopf had put the whole logistical system under enormous strain. It would also cost us several more billion dollars. But enough has been said about logistics in the previous chapter not to need further elaboration here.

A third source of anxiety was that the Coalition was not ready to fight a ground war until February 1991. I knew that my own units would not be combat ready before the end of January. But the longer the delay, the more anxious I became. The month-long fast of Ramadan, which that year was due to begin in mid-March, was approaching. The Coalition's confrontation with Iraq had stirred up passions in several Arab and Muslim countries, raising two alarming possibilities. If the crisis were prolonged, violent demonstrations could take place in a number of countries. My fear was that they might cause disruption in some cities. One might see disturbances in Sudan, in North Africa (where, far away from the conflict, there was a current of support for Saddam, seen as a victim of Western imperialism), in the cities of Pakistan and Bangladesh, in Malaysia and Indonesia. War is a time when worst-case scenarios have to be contemplated and addressed.

Another concern was that, if the crisis were to drag on for a year and the Iraqis held out, there was a strong chance that other fronts might open up, posing a grave challenge to the Coalition. The Yemenis, for example, might seize the opportunity to cross our frontier and attempt to seize our border province of Asir. Jordan, too, might be tempted to exploit the situation. As I suggested earlier, when King Hussein indicated to his own people that he would like to be called "Sharif," he seemed to be reviving the claims to the Hijaz of his great-grandfather, the Sharif Hussein of Makkah.

I also had to face the possibility that the invasion of Kuwait was part of a well-planned, long-range campaign, and that Saddam might have already planted Iraqi agents inside the Kingdom. A report reached me that Iraq had recruited men in the Egyptian and Syrian contingents with the specific mission of killing me. The report was almost certainly disinformation, calculated to disrupt the Coalition, but it posed a sensitive problem. I did not want the Saudis to have doubts about the Arab forces that had come to our aid, nor did I want the Egyptians and Syrians to take offense as they would do if they heard that they were being accused of harboring agents. Mistrust would be created. To demonstrate my contempt for the report and for those circulating it, I set off on a visit to Egyptian troops in the field, addressing them as they gathered around me in a vast semicircle, and then, ignoring my worried security men, plunging into their midst to shake hands. I was heartened by the smiling faces and the warmth of the welcome I received. The event was well covered by the Western and Arabic news media, and in this way I laid the seditious reports to rest.

But, even if all these fears proved vain, I could not pretend that the presence of nearly 750,000 foreign troops in the Kingdom – including over half a million Americans – was not a cause for concern. I was uncertain about their impact on our local

Saudi population, and this was a major reason why I regretted the long delay in resolving the crisis.

❧❦

The debate over the plan for Desert Storm was to lead to one of my more serious disagreements with Schwarzkopf. It was our habit to meet every evening to sort out problems as they arose. On one occasion, rather than wait for our daily meeting, I thought I would put a few points on paper to give him the chance to ponder them. My memo – which was in Arabic – was headed "Points of discussion relating to operation Desert Storm." In other words it was a discussion paper.

I put into it several of the points which had been worrying me over the previous weeks and which I felt had not been properly covered in our regular discussions. But the truth was that I was also seeking information. I was dealing with a super-power. There was no way I could get access to the full range of its information. Initiating discussion – even raising controversial questions – was the only way I had of getting at the truth. At the back of my mind was the worry that I might have been fed a dud plan which concealed quite different operational intentions.

I raised several points in my memo, of which one had to do with the priority to be given to different targets in the strategic air campaign. Put simply, I wanted to know which targets were to be destroyed first. (I had earlier demanded a complete briefing about the air campaign, and had been given one in the operations room by General Horner, ably assisted by a woman major in U.S. air force intelligence. But I was still not satisfied.) I did not feel the matter had been sufficiently clarified in the combined operations plan. I recognized that the air campaign was very nearly an all-American show, but I wanted to be sure that I knew 100 percent what was going on. To receive detailed information, I had to show a grasp of detail.

My main concern was to make sure that Iraq's ballistic missiles – its Scuds – would be among the very first targets to be attacked. I knew that these weapons could have a considerable psychological impact. I feared they would cause panic in Saudi Arabia if launched against our cities whose inhabitants had never experienced war. There was also the risk that any Scud attacks on Israel would boost Saddam's popularity in the Muslim world – as indeed happened – although they would have little military significance.

In my memo, I therefore listed what I considered the right order of priorities in target selection: first, ballistic missiles; then, the Iraqi air force, airfields and air facilities; command, control and communications, and jamming and surveillance centers; the air defense system; field artillery and multiple rocket launchers located close to our borders; ammunition dumps and fuel supply points in Kuwait and south of Basrah. I argued that these targets represented a direct threat to my forces and hitting them was important to guaranteeing a successful attack.

Another point I raised in my memo concerned the role of Special Forces. In several campaigns I had studied, intelligence gathered by Special Forces behind enemy lines had resulted in changes in the operational plans. I queried whether it was wise during the first and second phase of the campaign to rely solely on air power. Should the Coalition not mount raids by Special Forces behind Iraqi lines even before the start of the air campaign? They could gather intelligence, take POWs and create panic by attacking isolated positions. As this was a highly sensitive subject, I did not press too hard for information, but I did want to be kept generally informed. I wanted to know if I could get help from U.S. Special Forces if any of our pilots were shot down over Iraqi territory. If I was told which broad sector they were operating in, I might in turn be able to give them some help. But it was only later that I learned that U.S. Special Forces entered Iraq about a week before the start of the air campaign. The British, in contrast, took us into their confidence. British SAS teams entered Iraq through my sector several weeks earlier, and with support from ourselves.

On a quite different topic, I queried whether the Desert Storm plan made full use of the unique capabilities of the 82nd Airborne Division and the 101 Air Assault Division, fast-moving, highly mobile American formations, able to control critical targets behind enemy lines. It seemed to me that Schwarzkopf proposed using these two extraordinarily versatile units like standard infantry divisions. I argued that if used deep inside

Iraq, they would cause such panic and chaos as to bring about the collapse of the entire Iraqi front. The reason I queried the use of these formations was that, as already mentioned, I suspected I was not being given the full facts about the plan. My suspicions were fueled by what seemed to me an inappropriate use of these divisions. I knew that Schwarzkopf would resent my question, but I reckoned I would judge from his reaction whether the plan was genuine or not.

As for my own eastern and northern sectors, I inquired whether in positioning our units the joint planning group had properly considered the strength of the enemy opposite, the sector of penetration of his front, the objectives to be secured, and whether there was supposed to be a tactical pause after each day's fighting. I felt that while the plan defined in general terms the mission of the Joint Forces, it did not spell out the what, who, where, when and how. My units needed to be clear what role they were expected to perform. Nor did the plan spell out which units would remain in defensive positions.

My anxiety about Yemen and Jordan, Sudan and Iran, also found expression in the memo. I recommended greater monitoring and surveillance of these countries. If they were to launch a surprise missile attack on us, it might not be easy in the heat of battle to detect the source of such an attack.

But the most controversial point in my memo concerned Turkey. Would it not be wise, I suggested, to make a contingency plan to launch the main attack on Iraq from Turkey? Of course I meant the air attack which (as I explain in the next chapter) was meant to cripple Iraq. This would lead Saddam to think that a ground attack might follow from that direction. The advantages were many. By opening a second front in the north we would expose a weak flank in Saddam's defenses; disrupt his logistics by forcing him to rush men and supplies north; expedite his surrender by raising the specter of the dismemberment of Iraq. A success on the northern front would, I argued, greatly boost the morale of Coalition forces.

On a number of occasions I had raised with Schwarzkopf the possibility of opening a second front from Turkey, but I had always been told it was still under discussion with the Turks. By raising the matter again in my memo, I wanted him to know I was following the situation. Although the Desert Storm plan made no mention of an attack from Turkey, the air campaign made it plain that neighboring NATO air bases would be used, no doubt including the Turkish air base at Incirlik. What was going on?

It was common knowledge that Turkish opinion was divided on the question of Turkish participation in the war. President Ozal was a staunch supporter of the Coalition, but the majority of his countrymen seemed to prefer a neutral stance. Perhaps fearing that Iraq would strike back at Turkey, the Turkish military opposed sending ground troops to the Kingdom. Fortunately we did not need them. The question had already brought about the resignation of the Turkish Defense Minister, Safat Giray, in November, followed by that of the powerful Chief of Staff, General Necip Toruntay. But both we and the Americans had hoped that Turkey might send a token force.

Some weeks before the start of the air campaign, and perhaps in the hope of persuading the Turks to join in, CENTCOM in Riyadh asked our permission to invite some senior Turkish officers to the Kingdom for a briefing. My immediate response was that the invitation should come from us. Accordingly, an invitation was sent and a Turkish delegation arrived. We gave them a brief outline of the plan and showed them the War Room, but without arousing their enthusiasm for the war.

I also had a number of meetings with the Turkish ambassador who stressed that his country considered itself a partner in the conflict, with close historic ties with the Islamic world. He indicated, however, that there were constraints on what Turkey could do. He reminded me that his country had already incurred Iraq's anger by closing the pipeline carrying Iraqi oil through its territory.

For Schwarzkopf, the query about Turkey in my memo appears to have touched a raw nerve, perhaps because of the political sensitivities surrounding the issue. I was at a meeting with the Higher Officers' Committee when my ADC, Colonel Ahmad Lafi, brought me word that Schwarzkopf wished to see me in my office as soon as possible. I sent word back that I would finish my meeting first and then – breaking my usual rule – I would drop in at his office on my way back to mine.

From the moment I entered his room, I sensed that he was not his normal self. He had not stepped outside the door to escort me in as protocol demanded. He did not invite me to sit down. He was standing, his face flushed with anger. This caused my own temper to start rising.

He waved a paper at me.

"You disagree with my plans for the attack?" he asked in a tone I did not appreciate. "What's this about Turkey? King Fahd himself agreed that the attack would be launched from Saudi Arabia."

"Have you read my memo?" I retorted angrily.

"I never interfered with your forces," he complained. "Why did you ask about my forces?"

As I suspected, Schwarzkopf had not appreciated my remarks about his use of the 82nd Airborne and the 101 Air Assault Division.

"Cheney knows about your paper, and so does the President," he snarled. He had apparently sent my memo up the chain of command to the Chairman of the Joint Chiefs, to Secretary Cheney and even to President Bush.

"Norm, it's only a discussion paper. Your translator must have made a mistake."

But I could see immediately that a clash was coming.

Then he said, "What about the Syrians? I've heard rumors that they don't want to fight."

"We haven't had their answer yet," I replied.

"Oh my God!" he screamed. "What do you mean?"

We had asked the Syrians for their position, and they had replied that their only mission was to defend Saudi Arabia. We still did not know whether they would join in the attack to free Kuwait.

"Norm, it's my problem!" I said. "Nothing to do with you. Saud al-Faisal [our Foreign Minister] has gone to Damascus to see Asad. We should know more on his return."

Cursing the Syrians, Schwarzkopf brushed aside my explanations and turned again to the memo. He may have thought I was challenging his authority.

"Is this your position?" he cried, his voice rising by the instant. "We want to know! Are you insisting on a certain plan of action?"

At that we started shouting at each other.

"Don't raise your voice," I cried. "I think it's better to stop now before we really open fire on each other."

And with that I marched out of the room.

After the row, we both retreated to our quarters. Only our private staffs knew what had happened. Anxious to avoid him, I did not attend the briefing that night. Nor did he.

Prince Sultan called me that evening with a problem he wished me to discuss with Schwarzkopf. I had to tell him we were not talking and that it would have to wait for a day or two.

He was perturbed. "What can I do?" he asked. "You have to work with him. You can't . . ."

"Please, sir," I said. "I beg you to let me handle this. If I think we have reached a point of no return, I will report it to you. But for the moment, it's just a tiff between two mad generals."

Prince Sultan telephoned again. "Shall I call you both in?" he asked. But I could not agree. I wanted Schwarzkopf to come himself.

The next day, I didn't see him. I conducted my meetings as usual. But in the afternoon, I sent my adjutant to confirm with his adjutant that our evening meeting would take place as usual.

So he came, tense and watchful as I was. Contrary to my habit, I did not welcome him at the door of my office.

"General," I said, "let me invite you to sit down – something you forgot to do with me!"

We apologized to each other after I explained that I was not seeking to dictate strategy to him.

"I had a rough day," he said.

"By the way," I remarked, "next time please remember that when I come to your office, you should step outside to greet me, and you should then invite me to sit down."

"Did I insult you?" he cried.

"Of course you did," I said. We had a good laugh over it.

The misunderstanding was soon cleared up and in a few moments we were back to our cordial relationship.

"Khaled," he said as he was leaving my office, "have you ever seen your face when you are mad? It turns *black!*" Then he added, "I'm really mixed up about how to treat you, Khaled. Should I treat you as a general or as a prince?"

"Both!" I replied.

That was the end of it, so far as I was concerned.

Schwarzkopf's account of this incident in his book *It Doesn't Take a Hero* is to my recollection not entirely accurate. He claims that I "had stated publicly that . . . the best approach to war would be an offensive launched out of Turkey." This is mistaken as I made no public statement on this subject, but only conveyed my views to him in a private message. Had I made a public statement – to attack from Turkey rather than from Saudi Arabia – it would have made front-page news around the world. Worse still, he writes that I was "voicing the old Saudi unease at attacking fellow Arabs," thereby insinuating that I had suggested Turkey because I was reluctant for the attack to be launched from Saudi soil. This is quite misleading.

In suggesting that Iraq might be attacked from Turkey as well as from Saudi Arabia I anticipated what in fact happened. American aircraft went into action against Iraq from Incirlik on January 18. In making my suggestion, I was really saying that I knew they would have to do it that way. As with so many of my communications with Schwarzkopf, my memo was something of a ploy to get him to take me more fully into his confidence. I was insisting on my right to know. I had not expected my discussion paper to lead to a row, but perhaps our moment of anger reflected some underlying tensions which, rising to the surface, were safely defused.

❖

Early in January, in the immediate run-up to the war, King Fahd expressed the wish to visit the troops in the field. I felt it was too late. Knowing that the air campaign was coming very soon, I feared for the King's safety, and pleaded with Prince Sultan to persuade him to defer his visit until after the war. But the King would not hear of any delay. He wanted to be close to his troops. And he wanted to go on January 6, so that was that. As it turned out, he was right because his visit proved to be a great morale booster for us all.

I immediately ordered intense "capping" of the entire area by fighter aircraft, much as we had done when President Bush visited American troops in the field for Thanksgiving the previous November. I wanted to put on something extra for my King – and thought of a grand parade in which all the different national forces would be represented.

I told Schwarzkopf that the King wished to review a standing formation and that it would be good if an American contingent were present. He said it would be an honor. I envisaged all the troops – Saudi, American, British, French, Egyptian, Syrian, Moroccan, Senegalese and the rest of them – lined up together, ready for the King's inspection.

"Hold it!" Schwarzkopf said. "Let me think. If I put American soldiers among the troops under your command, and if the King inspects them with you, it will look as if my men are being commanded by you. My people will never accept that. Americans cannot be commanded by other nations. It's against the law."

"There's no question of commanding them," I protested.

"I'm sorry," he said. "If King Fahd and you drive in a jeep up and down our ranks on a tour of inspection, it can mean only one thing. I have the greatest respect for the King, but I can't accept it."

The problem seemed to have the makings of a diplomatic incident.

Schwarzkopf and I racked our brains for a way out. Eventually, we came up with the suggestion that the American troops would parade separately. I would escort the King to the American location and hand him over to Schwarzkopf, who would then accompany him on a tour of inspection. Schwarzkopf would then escort the King back to me and I would take him to inspect the other national contingents.

"I don't even have to ask Washington about it," Schwarzkopf said. "I know it will be all right."

We agreed to go ahead on that basis, and I was happy that the problem had been solved. I knew the forces under my command would agree to this formula. When I explained it to Sir Peter de la Billière, he said it would be an honor for the British to parade with me. The French, in turn, raised no objections.

It was agreed to hold the parade at Hafr al-Batin, flying in thousands of troops from different locations. I wanted the King to have the finest parade conceivable and to create an occasion such as we had never witnessed before. We had less than a week to organize it, but we worked day and night.

Then, thinking it over in bed that night, a nightmarish thought struck me. I had planned for the Americans to parade separately at the airport. This meant that they would be the first troops the King inspected!

But how could I even conceive that my King would inspect Americans before his own Saudi troops? The very thought of it drove me crazy.

I summoned my staff in the morning. "Whatever we do," I said to them, "I will not allow my King to inspect Schwarzkopf's forces before mine. Don't leave this room until you come up with a solution!"

Lots of ridiculous ideas were put forward. But at last someone said, "Why don't we draw up a Saudi guard of honor for the King to inspect first as he comes off the plane?" That was it! I recalled that our land forces had a helicopter air wing. I would line up the planes on the tarmac and take the King by jeep on a tour of them. Only after finishing with them would I hand him over to Schwarzkopf. And when the King had finished with the Americans, I would drive over and escort him to our own parade. The problem had been cracked and I was as happy as can be.

Some Americans may have realized what I was up to. Among my own staff I noticed a few knowing grins. It meant I had inflicted three parades on the King, but I felt I owed it to him. He had to be met by his own commander first! It was, after all, the first time in the history of Islam that an Arab and Muslim leader had inspected troops from more than 24 nations. It was an occasion of which I was very proud.

In a most moving speech, the King outlined the history of the crisis and of his repeated efforts to bring about a peaceful settlement. He explained how he had hosted the meeting in Jeddah on August 1 between Shaikh Saad, the Crown Prince of Kuwait, and Izzat Ibrahim, the Iraqi Vice President, and that both men had agreed that talks should be resumed in Baghdad three days later, followed by a further meeting in Kuwait. It was, therefore, with surprise and shock that the King had learned of Iraq's invasion of Kuwait just seven hours after the Jeddah meeting.

"There can be no peaceful settlement," the King declared, "without Iraq's unconditional withdrawal from Kuwait and the restoration of the legitimate Kuwaiti government.

"Who is the wrongdoer?" the King asked. "The wrongdoer is the man who has defied the whole world.

"I think we have reached deadlock," he continued. "But the door to end this tragedy can be opened – either by peaceful means or by other means.

"No one is keen on the other means, but no one can say that self-defense is not a legitimate right."

It was a sentiment fully shared by the troops from many nations drawn up for the King's inspection.

CHAPTER XIX

The Air War and the Scuds

ONE OF THE MOST THRILLING and yet shocking spectacles of the late twentieth century was the destruction of Iraq's military power by the Coalition's strategic air campaign of January–February 1991.

The technological marvels of this "first space-age war" excited my mind as never before, even while my heart bled for the punishment inflicted on an Arab state through the criminal folly of its leader. For me the dilemma was acute because, as early as November 1990, I knew that unless Saddam withdrew unconditionally from Kuwait there could be no escape for his war machine. The danger he posed to the peace of the region had to be removed, and his sickening behavior in Kuwait – the torture of civilians, the execution of children in front of their parents – had made war against him not only necessary but legitimate.

By invading Kuwait and then by refusing to withdraw – the second mistake as grave as the first – Saddam Hussein set in motion a chain of events which was to bring destruction on his country and change the lives and ways of thinking of countless people in the Middle East. Quite apart from the devastation of war and the uprooting of hundreds of thousands from their homes, the crisis opened up a great chasm in the Arab world, casting doubt on one of the key principles of Arab politics since World War Two, namely that whatever their quarrels the Arabs form a single family, inspired by the same nationalist ideas, aspiring if not to political union at least to solidarity in times of danger. Saddam shattered this ideal, introducing into inter-Arab relations unprecedented hostility and distrust.

For soldiers such as myself, there was a further dimension to the crisis. The conflict opened our eyes to the revolution in warfare that had taken place, throwing a harsh light on the widening gap between our own capability and that of advanced countries, in spite of the great efforts we were making to keep abreast.

Thus, Arab political fragmentation and military vulnerability are among the consequences of the war which, four years later, we are still struggling to absorb and rectify.

The 1991 Gulf War has been much discussed and analyzed, but how many understand its real nature? Even those who were directly involved on a day-to-day basis did not immediately grasp a simple fact: the war against Saddam was, at the start at least, to be an air war. That is how it was planned. Air power, used in new, massive and revolutionary ways, was to paralyze the Iraqi leadership's ability to command and control its forces – either for offense or defense. Once Saddam and his high command had been blinded and crippled, Iraq's conventional military strength and its weapons of mass destruction were to be systematically degraded by the most ferocious air campaign the world had ever seen.

Saddam had intended to fight a slow, old-fashioned sort of war, on the pattern of his war with Iran, in which ground armies would be locked in hand-to-hand combat for months, if not years, on end. No doubt he hoped to inflict heavy casualties on the Coalition, undermining support for the war in the West, and thereby winning if not a military victory then political prestige. But the Coalition was determined to fight a fast-moving, high-tech, ultramodern war, waged from a distance with stand-off weapons – essentially an air war. The crucial battle in the first few hours would be for air supremacy. Once the Coalition had achieved mastery of the air, Iraq would be at its mercy. Modern, high-precision weapons would then be used to destroy Saddam's capability to fight on.

It was recognized, of course, that air power alone could not win the war. A ground campaign was necessary to liberate Kuwait – our major war aim – and to complete the process of attrition designed to strip Saddam of the capability to threaten the future security and stability of the region. Coalition ground armies – infantry, tanks and artillery – were necessary for the last phase of the military plan. They were also an essential insurance policy in case the air campaign, for one reason or another, failed to deliver the expected results.

Air Assets D-Day and Missions Flown as of February 28, 1991

Countries Sharing in Air Campaign	Air to Air	Air to Ground	Dual	Attack Helicopter	Support	Totals	Accumulated Missions
Bahrain	0	0	24	0	16	40	294
Canada	0	0	24	0	0	24	1,308
France	12	24	18	60	83	197	2,326
Italy	0	0	9	0	0	9	240
Kuwait	0	24	15	12	16	67	802
New Zealand	0	0	0	0	2	2	32
Qatar	0	9	12	0	29	50	63
Saudi Arabia	106	54	87	9	187	443	7,018
UAE	14	51	25	0	97	187	102
UK	18	48	0	0	31	97	5,546
U.S.A.	196	500	423	385	2,134	3,637	90,312
Totals	345	710	637	466	2,595	4,753	108,043

Beginning in late August, a special planning group started working on the air campaign in the basement of the Royal Saudi Air Force headquarters in Riyadh. Because of the strict secrecy surrounding the planning group, the heavily guarded basement where they worked became known as the "Black Hole." Their task was to collate all known information about Iraq's military capability and devise how best to use air power to cripple its ability to fight in the first 48 hours of the war. At their disposal was a dazzling array of airborne weapons, many of them never used in combat before.

Security had to be stringent to ensure that Iraq was taken by surprise. But there were a number of other good reasons. The United States insisted on strict secrecy because this was to be an overwhelmingly American effort. Of the 108,043 sorties eventually flown during Desert Storm, 83.6 percent were flown by the U.S. Air Force, Navy and Marine Corps; 6.5 percent by the Royal Saudi Air Force; 5.1 percent by Britain's Royal Air Force; and 2.1 percent by the French. Several other countries, including Belgium, Germany, the Netherlands and Oman also contributed, in one way or another, to the air campaign. The Royal Saudi Air Force was able to join in and integrate easily with the major Coalition air forces because its doctrine, training, weapons and state of combat readiness were comparable to those of the U.S. and the UK.

Another reason for secrecy was that the U.S. was planning to deploy the latest products of its military R&D, such as the F-117 Stealth fighter, invisible to radar; precision-guided munitions (PGMs), such as Tomahawk Cruise missiles as well as numerous types of laser-guided and TV-guided bombs and missiles; night-vision devices, principally infrared detectors; and a wide range of electronic systems for communications, surveillance and combat, which would jam Saddam's radars, disrupt his communications, and generally suppress his defenses.

Information from space satellites was an integral part of the preparations for and the conduct of the air campaign. Satellites provided targeting data, communications facilities, weather information, warning on Iraqi Scud launches and much else besides. They also provided the basis for the Global Positioning System (GPS), a small device which allowed ground forces to navigate through the featureless desert or through Iraqi mine-fields with extraordinary accuracy.

These American high-technology systems acted as "force multipliers" vastly enhancing the Coalition's military capability – indeed putting the Coalition in a totally different league from Iraq. From a strictly military point of view, Saddam's biggest mistake was to have failed to understand the vast gap that had opened up between his armed forces and the sophisticated arsenal of a superpower.

It was inevitable that the command structure of the air campaign should reflect American supremacy. For greater coherence in the conduct of air operations, Coalition members agreed that Lieutenant General Charles Horner should control all Coalition aircraft. He was to be the single "air boss" with the title of Joint Force Air Component Commander (JFACC). However, as became apparent during the campaign, he faced some challenges to his authority from the U.S. Navy and Marine Corps, who each wanted to reserve some air assets for their own use.

Horner's Director of Plans, Brigadier General Buster Glosson, had the difficult job of overseeing the production of the daily Air Tasking Order (ATO), a document the size of a telephone book. Among many other details, it spelled out the flight call signs, radio frequencies, take-off times, inflight refueling instructions, primary and alternate targets to be hit, and preferred munitions to be used for more than 1,000 sorties a day, rising at times during the campaign to more than 3,000 a day. Without the use of powerful computers, the job could not have been done.

Among Saddam's many errors was that he gave General Horner and his colleagues nearly six months in which to train their forces, refine every detail of the air campaign, and bring in highly specialized aircraft for specific missions.

The air campaign of January–February 1991 was a truly awesome event. As the American superpower flexed its muscles, what I found particularly chilling was the combination of space-age technology with the political will to use overwhelming force. Anxious to lay the ghosts of Vietnam, U.S. military commanders wanted to show off to the world the weapons and skills which they had acquired during the revitalizing decade of the 1980s. Saddam had doubted America's readiness to fight. Horner and his team were determined to prove him wrong.

❖〜❖

Although the Coalition was all-powerful, there were moments when it seemed less so. One of these, which occurred before the start of the air campaign, preoccupied us for a couple of days. We received a report from American intelligence that several helicopters had been detected entering Saudi air space. I was doubly embarrassed: first as a former Air Defense Commander, and secondly because my own people had not confirmed the sighting. We spent 24 hours hunting for the mysterious helicopters. Information I received suggested that they were Iraqi and that the Americans had seized them and were holding them on board an aircraft carrier without informing us. I decided to confront Schwarzkopf.

"Norm," I said to him, "what have you done with those

helicopters? Your intelligence reported them entering our air space. Where are they? We simply have to know." Schwarzkopf gave me a sharp look.

"I've received a report that your people hid the helicopters at al-Khafji," he said.

Each of us thought the other was playing games. We spent fifteen minutes taunting each other:

"Where have you hidden them?"

"No, where have *you* hidden them?"

After further inquiries, the conclusion was reached that a radar screen had malfunctioned and that the phantom helicopters were indeed no more than phantoms.

On January 13, 1991, four days before the start of the air campaign, I needed to fly up to Ras Mish'ab to inspect the 10th Saudi Brigade which was deployed in the desert some 30 miles inland from the Gulf coast. I drove to the Riyadh air base and boarded the Air Defense Commander's G4 Gulfstream, taking with me John Sweeney of CNN who was itching to get into the field.

Eventually we reached Ras Mish'ab, circled the strip and, in the absence of a control tower or guidance from the ground, landed with some difficulty. We then drove out along a muddy track to the headquarters of the 10th Brigade, where I had a series of meetings and inspections, and lunched with the troops. I returned to the plane at about 8 p.m., well after dark, with John Sweeney of CNN still in tow.

I had to attend a meeting that night at the Ministry of Defense in Riyadh, but the pilot looked doubtful. There were no runway lights.

"Can't you take off without lights?" I asked.

"Risky," he replied.

Half a dozen navy police cars had escorted us to the air strip, so I sent them off down the dark runway and asked the drivers to switch on their headlights. With these points of light to guide him, the pilot took off safely.

The weather was terrible – a foretaste of the sandstorms, low cloud and bursts of thunder that were to disrupt some sorties of the air war. Throughout the noisy and bumpy ride, Sweeney kept hammering at me with his questions. He was anxious to know whether or not the Syrians would commit their troops to battle. Perhaps he may have hoped that the bad weather would weaken my defenses and cause me, by a slip of the tongue, to give something away. Although he seemed rather pale, he evidently wanted to prove that his nerves could stand the severe turbulence. As the plane bounced about, our friendly duel continued for much of the flight. We reached Riyadh in time for my meeting.

Little more than 24 hours after the expiration of the UN ultimatum to Iraq of January 15, the air campaign was unleashed in the early hours of January 17. H-hour was set at 0300 hours. In fact the opening shot was fired 21 minutes earlier, at 0239 precisely, when three AH-64 Apache attack helicopters, versatile all-weather machines armed with Hellfire missiles and Hydra rockets, destroyed two early warning stations on Iraq's frontier, ripping open a breach in Iraq's air defenses through which Coalition strike aircraft – F-15E Eagles and F-14 Tomcats – were soon to roar.

In the next 25 minutes, waves of F-117 Nighthawk Stealth fighters, Lockheed's revolutionary radar-foxing plane armed with laser-guided bombs, attacked Saddam's Presidential Palace, command bunkers at air force and air defense headquarters, telephone exchanges, microwave towers, relay stations and transmission lines, air defense radars and integrated air defense operations centers in different parts of the country. The F-117 was able to penetrate Iraq's defenses by surprise and at will, and deliver its bombs at key targets with pinpoint accuracy. Not a single F-117 was hit by Iraqi fire during the war.

The Iraqis could not see the Stealth aircraft coming. The first indication they had that the war had started was when bombs started falling on their own capital, hitting headquarters buildings and command and control networks. The shock, confusion and carnage must have been tremendous. Although the Iraqis had no defenses against such an advanced weapon, the battle to secure control of the air was bitterly fought during the opening minutes.

Very shortly after the Stealth fighters came the turn of the Tomahawks — stand-off, deep-strike Cruise missiles also able to deliver pinpoint attacks against targets in heavily defended areas. Launched from 16 U.S. Navy ships and two submarines, they started slamming into the Taji chemical weapons complex, the Ba'th Party headquarters, the Presidential Palace, and Iraqi power plants, largely shutting down the national grid. Six Tomahawks hit the Iraqi Ministry of Defense between 1010 and 1017 hours on the first day of the war, out of about 180 Cruise missiles launched in the first 48 hours of the war against high-value Iraqi targets.

Then took place one of the major deception operations of the air campaign. The first wave of Coalition attacks had prompted into full alert what was left of Iraq's air defenses. Seeing massed targets coming over again, Iraqi radar operators took them to be a second wave of Coalition aircraft. In a desperate bid to isolate targets for their surface-to-air missiles, the Iraqis switched on their radars to full power, thus betraying their locations. But the "second wave" was not aircraft at all: only drones and decoys, dropping chaff to simulate an attack. And behind the drones and decoys came F-4G Wild Weasels and F-18 Hornets whose specific mission was the suppression of enemy air defenses (SEAD). Once Iraqi radars had been switched on, formations of these SEAD aircraft then blew up dozens of Iraqi air defense sites with High-speed Antiradiation Missiles (HARMs). The same destructive pattern was repeated that night around Basrah and Kuwait.

It was soon clear that Iraq's rigid, highly centralized air defense system had been surprised by stealth and overwhelmed by electronic warfare and massive air attack.

The Iraqis tried to send up some MiG-29s and Mirage F-1s to intercept the Coalition attackers, but they did not stand a chance: unable to communicate with the ground, they were quickly shot down with air-to-air missiles or flew into the ground. On paper, the Iraqi Air Force was large and powerful, but it was wholly outclassed by the Coalition and, from the very start, hardly attempted to fight back. In the first three days, the Iraqis flew little more than 100 sorties a day.

The first morning of the war brought the Iraqis no respite.

B-52 intercontinental bombers, which had taken off from Louisiana 17 hours earlier, arrived over Saudi Arabia to fire 35 air-launched Cruise missiles at Iraqi power plants, forward operating airfields and other key targets.

As I learned, there was some dispute between Schwarzkopf and Horner regarding the use of the big B-52s – a dispute which reflected their different strategic perceptions. Schwarzkopf, whose mind was focused on the coming ground war, had a healthy respect for Saddam's Republican Guard divisions and wanted them degraded from the start by heavy B-52 strikes. Horner, however, wished to give priority to the task of seizing control of the air and of hitting Iraqi leadership targets. In his view, the Republican Guards could be dealt with at a later stage.

On the night before the start of the air campaign, Schwarzkopf went over to Horner's command center in the basement of Royal Saudi Air Force headquarters. But when he saw that the B-52 attacks on Republican Guard divisions were not to be as numerous or as heavy as he expected, he threw one of his celebrated tantrums and threatened to fire Horner. The latter replied that that was his privilege. I gathered that Horner had seen Schwarzkopf's explosions of temper before and was not unduly bothered.

Eventually they went upstairs to Horner's office where Buster Glosson, the Director of Plans, showed Schwarzkopf the briefings he had been giving him all along. There had been no change in the number of B-52 sorties planned. Schwarzkopf apologized and the war unfolded according to Horner's strategy.

Of all the many systems deployed by the Coalition, perhaps the two most vital were the AWACS (Airborne Warning and Control Systems), a battle-management platform which provided Coalition commanders with a comprehensive long-range air picture, and the multi-role F-16, the backbone of the USAF fighter force. A total of 251 F-16s took part in Desert Storm, attacking Iraqi oil refineries and petroleum stocks, transportation facilities, SAM and Scud sites, airfields and aircraft bunkers, Republican Guard divisions, and much else besides. In the largest single raid of the war, 56 F-16s attacked the Nuclear Research Center in Baghdad on January 19.

The flat desert terrain, the ability of Stealth aircraft to

penetrate Iraq's defenses, the ability of modern airplanes to fly five sorties a day, the use of precision-guided munitions to destroy thousands of tanks, artillery pieces, bunkers, hardened aircraft shelters, bridges and many other individual point targets – all these factors favored the attackers. The Coalition put more sorties in the air each day than Saddam Hussein had seen in eight years of war with Iran. He could have had no concept of what was hitting him. On the first day of the campaign – some would say in the first hour – Iraq's ability to wage war was gravely damaged.

Much of Baghdad was without electricity. Several "centers of gravity" were attacked and demolished. Numerous Iraqi radars and SAM sites were knocked out. Only small isolated parts of the highly centralized air defense system still operated autonomously – although, on occasions, with lethal efficiency. However, the Coalition soon enjoyed absolute air superiority, allowing its aircraft to roam over Iraq, seeking out and destroying strategic targets and military and civilian infrastructure. Two hundred attack missions were launched against Iraq in the first hour of the air campaign, 900 in the first day and 4,000 in the first week. The pounding continued for 38 days, until Iraq's will to fight was extinguished.

❖❖❖

As commander of Saudi Arabia's Air Defense Forces, I had over the years watched the development of Iraqi air defenses with admiration and even a touch of envy. With help from the Soviets and the French, the Iraqis had built up a dense network which some experts considered even more formidable than Warsaw Pact defenses in Eastern Europe. It was certainly one of the strongest in the Middle East and was said to consist of 16,000 surface-to-air missiles, 10,000 antiaircraft guns and 700 aircraft. The French, who played a big role in building up Iraq's armed strength, had tied the network together with a sophisticated command and control system named Kari. Before the start of the air campaign, U.S. navy and air force intelligence had made a detailed study of Kari, identifying the key early-warning and control centers. These were targeted first. It was widely recognized that neutralizing the Kari system would be vital to Coalition success.

Iraq was strong by any standards, yet most of its defenses were neutralized within minutes. Some low-altitude weapons, with optical sights, continued to be effective for a while because they were impervious to U.S. electronic warfare. They scored some striking successes, notably in shooting down six Tornados of Britain's Royal Air Force as they dropped JP233 airfield-denial bombs in low-level attacks on heavily defended Iraqi air bases. But, as an integrated system, Iraq's air defenses soon collapsed. In the early days of the war, over 800 sorties destroyed 29 Iraqi air defense centers, a blow from which Kari never recovered.

I could not help being aware of the implications of the air campaign for our own security and for my efforts in air defense over the preceding years. As I recounted in an earlier chapter, the October War of 1973 had been an inspiration to me. In the crossing of the Suez Canal and the storming of Israel's Bar Lev line, Egypt's surface-to-air missiles had performed well against the Israeli air force. The contest between them had seemed even. Missiles had even acquired an edge, managing to hold air power in check. I felt then that the October War had reversed the harsh verdict of the 1967 June War. Impressed by the lessons of 1973, I had sought to build Saudi air defenses as a "Fourth Force," and after years of effort I had succeeded in doing so. But now, the pendulum had swung back to the pre-1973 era.

For me, one of the main lessons of the Gulf War was the triumph of air power — not just of modern warplanes but of the electronic, night-warfare and space systems which served as formidable "force multipliers" of air power. Air defense was once again lagging behind.

Stealth aircraft, Cruise missiles, precision-guided munitions, AWACS, and the rest of the U.S. space-age arsenal had made fixed air defense installations extremely vulnerable. Integrated systems were especially at risk since national and sector operations centers could be knocked out with apparent ease, as I had witnessed in the fireworks over Iraq. It was evident that, more than ever before in modern military history, control of the air was crucial: it was virtually impossible to fight without it.

Pondering these questions, I watched the unfolding of the

campaign sitting side-by-side with Schwarzkopf in a small underground war room in the basement of the Ministry of Defense. One floor up was a commanders' briefing room with angled-glass windows through which generals could look down into the C3IC a floor below where hundreds of American, Saudi and other allied officers worked and coordinated their endeavors on huge wall maps. I had made sure that every element of the Saudi armed services was represented there – National Guard, land forces, air force, air defense forces, navy, Ministry of Interior forces, intelligence, and so on – in parallel with the Americans.

In the first two weeks of the war, all the chairs in the small war room had been of the same size. Then, quite suddenly one day, new seating was brought in. Schwarzkopf's chair was now bigger and at least a foot or two higher than anyone else's, while I had been given a chair on the same level as his staff. It seemed that he wanted to look down on the rest of us for the duration of the war! I did not want a chair like Schwarzkopf's, but I did want one which was different from those of his subordinates. So I came up with a stratagem. It was the first time I had put my back problem to work.

"My God," I exclaimed, looking at the chair I had been given. "I can't sit in that. My back won't stand it."

I called for a selection of chairs to choose one that suited me better. Moving back and forth, I tried one after the other. Eventually, my choice fell on a great chair, different from any other in the room. Whatever Schwarzkopf may have thought of my antics, I had to be on an equal footing in that war room. But I made sure I did not crowd him. I knew he had private briefings every day and I made sure I left the war room before they were due to take place. He needed to talk privately to his staff, as I did to mine. In the end we sat next to each other in the small war room and it worked satisfactorily.

❧⟩✕⟨❧

Of all the weapons in Saddam's arsenal, the only one to give the Coalition a headache was the Scud, an inaccurate, Soviet-built surface-to-surface ballistic missile. It was one of the ironies of the war that all the Coalition's high-tech wizardry was unable fully to suppress this old-fashioned weapon.

The basic Scud has an effective range of 200 miles. However, during the Iraq–Iran war, Saddam's military engineers had modified it to produce two home-grown versions with a longer reach: the al-Husayn with a range of 450 miles and the al-Abbas with a range of 600 miles. These stretched missiles, which carried more fuel but a smaller payload, had a CEP (circular error probable) of over 3,000 yards so they were, in effect, more of a terror weapon to be used against population centers than a counterforce weapon of strictly military use.

During the Iraq–Iran war, Saddam had fired about 200 al-Husayn missiles at Iranian cities, driving a large part of Tehran's population into the countryside. Iran, in turn, had fired Scuds back at Baghdad, but in smaller numbers and without the same long range. The Arab world had watched this "War of the Cities" with apprehension in the final phase of the Iraq–Iran war and, as air defense commander, I could not help wondering how our own population, which had had no direct experience of war, would respond to such random attacks.

As early as 1976, I had paid a visit to a Raytheon plant in the U.S. where the SAM-D, precursor of the Patriot, was being developed as an answer to medium-to-high-altitude aircraft and to tactical ballistic missiles such as the Scud. In due course, more than a decade later during the Iraq–Iran war, we contacted Raytheon again to learn more about the development of the Patriot system. But it was only when Saddam invaded Kuwait that the U.S. rushed Patriot batteries into the Kingdom between August and December 1990 to protect our vital facilities such as refineries, airfields, ports and command centers.

However, I was not unduly worried about Saddam's Scuds. I knew that they could not cause large material losses since they were highly inaccurate and carried only a small payload of high explosives. I had a gut feeling that Saddam would not dare fit chemical or biological warheads to his missiles for fear of exposing himself to devastating retaliation. It was one thing to use chemical weapons against defenseless Kurds, quite another to use them against American troops.

Our specific concern was that, once the war started, Saddam

might use Scuds to attack Israel – it was probably the only weapon he had which could penetrate Israel's air defenses – in order to transform his aggression against an Arab neighbor into a general Arab–Israeli war. As it was an obvious and predictable strategy, it was a problem to which we gave a good deal of anxious thought. We had to plan for the worst case. On the Saudi side, a decision was reached that, whatever Saddam did, we would not allow the liberation of Kuwait to be derailed. This was our prime war aim. If Saddam tried to distract attention by attacking Israel, we would simply carry on with our campaign. Wars cannot be switched on and off. Once you commit your forces to war, you have to follow through. If you stop, you get killed.

In the early hours of January 18, 1991, Day 2 of the air campaign, Iraq fired seven Scuds at Tel Aviv and Haifa, slightly injuring seven people. The next day, four more Scuds launched from western Iraq landed in or near Tel Aviv. Then it was Saudi Arabia's turn with a total of 20 Scuds launched against Riyadh and Dhahran from southern Iraq on January 20, 21, 22 and 23. Further firings followed against both Israel and Saudi Arabia but with declining intensity, with the last one reported on February 26. By the end of the war, Iraq had fired 88 Scuds – 42 at Israel, 43 at Saudi Arabia and three at Bahrain.

Although the Scuds themselves had been anticipated, their enormous psychological impact had not. The Scud was actually an old weapon. It had first made its appearance in the Middle East in 1973 when the Soviets deployed it in Egypt just before the October War. However, it played no role in that war except to add a footnote to military history. At the precise moment that President Sadat announced a cease-fire, three Scuds were being made ready for launching. The firing procedure could not be reversed, and the Scuds hit Israeli positions in the Deversoir area west of the Canal five minutes after the cease-fire came into effect.

Over the years, Israel has bombed, shelled and raided countless Arab towns and villages – in Egypt, Syria, Jordan, in Lebanon untold times, in Tunisia, Iraq and in what remains of Palestine but, except for an occasional Katyusha rocket on a border settlement, its own population centers have never come under attack. But the Scud attacks showed that Israel had no active defense against ballistic missiles. Fearing a gas attack, its population took refuge in sealed rooms. Its military leaders itched to strike back at Iraq, but American pressure forbade it.

Israel then put great pressure on Washington to deal with the Scud threat. This in turn caused Washington to demand action from Schwarzkopf and Horner. So began a vast diversion of air assets – between 25 and 30 percent of all sorties – to the "Great Scud Hunt" in western Iraq, disrupting Horner's plans for the strategic air campaign and providing the most frustrating and least successful aspect of the Coalition's war against Iraq.

Thus a handful of primitive Iraqi Scuds, more of an irritant than a significant threat, managed to precipitate a political and military crisis and cause considerable tension between Washington and American field commanders on the ground. Until then, and in deliberate contrast to what had happened in Vietnam, American political leaders had adopted a "hands off" policy towards the war, leaving operational decisions to the military commanders. But now, overriding the judgment of General Horner who considered the Scuds little more than a "nuisance," Washington insisted on giving the Scud hunt top priority.

I, too, had wanted the Coalition to give priority to dealing with Iraq's Scuds, not so much because of their military significance but because of their possible impact on civilian morale. But Washington's urgent insistence on diverting vast air assets to the great Scud hunt was of a quite different order. I was not alone in suspecting that the U.S. was reacting to Israeli threats to use nuclear weapons against Iraq.

Indeed, I believe the Scuds caused Israel to take its nuclear bomb "out of the basement" and use it to pressure its superpower ally, as it was said to have done nearly 20 years earlier when Egypt and Syria overran its defenses at the start of the 1973 October War. Evidently, nuclear weapons are as useful to pressure allies as they are to frighten enemies.

Before the start of Desert Storm, Saudi Arabia and the United States had made massive preparations for the defense of the Kingdom. Twenty-one U.S. Patriot batteries, comprising no fewer than 132 launchers, were deployed at key sites. The first significant test of the system in combat occurred on the nights of January 20 to 23 when, as I have mentioned, 20 Scuds were fired at us.

Not surprisingly, these attacks prompted us to think of retaliation. We made ready our Strategic Missile Force under Brigadier General Ibrahim al-Dakhil, a well-disciplined, hard-working officer who had been my deputy, and targeted our weapons on major Iraqi cities. If ever there was a right moment to unleash our Chinese-built surface-to-surface missiles, this seemed to be it. We felt we needed to hit back in self-defense so as to deter further Iraqi Scud attacks. Accordingly, I gave orders to assemble in the right locations all the various elements of our missiles — save for the liquid fuel, which is pumped in at the very last stage, following which a launch cannot be reversed. I then waited for Prince Sultan to transmit to me the King's order to fire. But, after some anxious hours, King Fahd decided not to escalate the conflict. He made a rational decision to reserve the missiles as a weapon of last resort, thereby demonstrating the Kingdom's sense of responsibility. He did not want to cause casualties among innocent Iraqi civilians and he no doubt judged that the Coalition's air campaign being waged against Iraq was sufficient retaliation.

I will not pretend that the Saudis behaved with exemplary calm when faced with the Scud attacks, but I was pleased to see that, after a few firings, curiosity seemed to get the better of fear. Many Saudis enjoyed watching the contest of Patriot against Scud. Opposite the Ministry of Defense in Riyadh is the Hyatt Regency Hotel, home of the international press corps during the war. Many journalists and cameramen camped out at night on the flat roof of the hotel, from where they had a fine view of the old airport where the Patriots were deployed. I am told that when the sirens sounded on the first night, the correspondents climbed hastily into their chemical suits and stumbled down to the basement. No one knew for sure what the Scuds were carrying — high explosives, or perhaps chemical, biological or even nuclear warheads. But they were soon back upstairs to watch the noisy and colorful duels in the sky.

The Patriot had originally been developed as an antiaircraft defense system. Its antiballistic missile capability was added later and was just about ready for testing when Saddam invaded

Kuwait. At that time only a handful of Patriot PAC-2 missiles had been produced for flight tests. But in the months between the invasion of Kuwait and the start of the war, Raytheon went into round-the-clock production.

Although the Patriot was a new weapon, still suffering from a good many teething problems, its overall performance in Saudi Arabia must be judged successful. However, an unexpected problem with which it had to contend was that Scuds, modified by Iraq to give them longer range, would often fly in erratic patterns and break up in flight, making them difficult to intercept. Falling debris from these Scuds triggered automatic Patriot launches, I believe as many as 33 in Riyadh on the first night. Paradoxically, better engineered Scuds which the Russians had modified proved easier to shoot down. One Scud – or part of one – slipped through the barrage and destroyed a school a few hundred yards from the Riyadh Sheraton: it happened to be the school my son attended. Fortunately, the attack took place at night and there were no casualties.

Since the war there has been much debate about the success rate of the Patriot. In Israel, it does not appear to have performed well. Appearing on television, General Dan Shomron, Israeli Chief of Staff during the war, went so far as to say that the Patriot's success was "a myth." But I understand that the reason the weapon did not work well in Israel was because the Israelis wanted to be in complete control of it. They wanted to align the batteries themselves, and they wanted to operate the Patriot manually. They might have been better off letting it run automatically under the control of the skilled American crews which Washington provided.

Another reason for the relative failure in Israel was that the Patriot was not designed to protect large population centers. The Patriot system was designed for point defense – to protect air bases, oil installations, command centers – and that is how we deployed it. Had Saddam's Scuds been carrying chemical warheads they might have posed a serious problem as interception would have caused them to disperse their poison over a large area. In any event, if you manage to shoot down a Scud, or part of one, over a populated area, the wreckage is likely to fall on you and can cause extensive damage. Displaying great faith in the Patriot, General Horner kept the entire fleet of precious AWACS at Riyadh airport, within range of Iraq's Scuds, whereas he could have deployed them farther south.

However, an unfortunate incident occurred towards the end of the war which demonstrated the Scud's lethality. On February 25, an Iraqi missile landed on a U.S. barracks in Dhahran, killing 28 personnel and wounding 100 more. It was the heaviest blow Iraq managed to inflict on the Coalition in the whole conflict. The 26 men and two women killed were American reserve logisticians called up to staff water-purification units. They had arrived in the Kingdom a week earlier and were due to go into Iraq behind the Coalition armies to drill wells and purify the water. But, as it happened, trucks carrying bottled water were sufficient to meet Coalition needs, so the purification units were not required. By a grisly coincidence, all 28 of the dead were from small towns in Pennsylvania, very near to Charleroi, home town of General Pagonis, the U.S. logistics chief.

Despite this tragic event, the presence of the Patriot in Saudi Arabia provided considerable reassurance to civilians and military alike. Quite apart from its ability to bring down the Scuds, its impact was as much psychological as military. Just as the Scud was a weapon of terror, so the Patriot proved to be a weapon of comfort.

⤜⧽⧼⤛

From the start of the Scud attacks it was realized that the key to stopping them was not to destroy the missile in flight but to destroy its launcher on the ground. But first you had to find the launcher. Two U.S. missile-warning satellites were able to detect the plume from a Scud firing and transmit warning data about it within two minutes of the launch. However, after a firing, mobile launchers raced away from the launch site to pre-arranged hiding places. Unless Coalition planes could reach the launch site swiftly, the launcher would have escaped.

This basic conundrum was to cause the Coalition more frustration and sheer annoyance than any of Saddam's other moves. Each day hundreds of fighter-bomber sorties were diverted to western Iraq to look for launch sites and mobile launchers.

Whole squadrons of airplanes, equipped with the latest night detection systems, orbited overhead waiting to hit them. But in spite of bold claims, few if any mobile Scud launchers were hit.

On January 18, 1991, in his first press briefing of the war, Schwarzkopf confidently declared that,

> This morning, the United States Air Force found three mobile erected launchers with missiles on board inside Iraq ... Those three mobile erected launchers have been destroyed.
>
> In addition to that, at the same time we found eight more mobile erected launchers in the same location. We are currently attacking those launchers, and we have confirmed – confirmed – the destruction of three more of those mobile erected launchers and we are continuing to attack the others ...

A member of my staff, who had had considerable experience with Scuds, sent me a report expressing skepticism at Schwarzkopf's statement. It was most unlikely, he wrote, that the Iraqis would move their launchers during the day and expose such a highly valuable asset to air attack. In his view, the American pilot probably destroyed decoys, rather than launchers. Or, if they were not decoys, they could have been long-bed vehicles used to carry missiles (and which are similar in shape to launchers). He thought that Schwarzkopf's statement might have been intended to reassure Israel that the U.S. was doing all it could. However, he conceded that there was just a chance – one in a thousand – that the pilot had destroyed real launchers and that the Iraqis had simply lost their heads.

I discussed the report with Schwarzkopf, but he assured me that there was no doubt that the USAF pilot had destroyed the launchers, as he had announced. U.S. intelligence had confirmed it. However, it was not long before it was generally acknowledged that the targets destroyed had in fact been decoys.

I was therefore surprised to read in Schwarzkopf's book his claim that "our bombers had obliterated every known Scud site in western Iraq, destroying thirty-six fixed launchers and ten mobile ones." This is not accurate and betrays a certain confusion of thinking. For one thing, there is no such thing as a "fixed launcher." All Scud launchers are mobile, mounted on long-wheeled vehicles. Some fire their missiles from roads or open country, and then race for a hiding place after firing; others fire from prepared sites, reinforced with sandbags and equipped with fortified shelters for the crew and battery commander. Several of Iraq's prepared sites were attacked by Coalition bombing in the first few days, but the mobile launchers escaped and survived to play cat-and-mouse with the Coalition until the end of the war. Some postwar analysts concluded that, contrary to wartime claims, U.S. forces did not destroy a single mobile launcher.*

In the "Great Scud Hunt," the Coalition was defeated by the ingenuity of Iraqi Scud crews – but also by the weather. Iraq launched Scuds only in bad weather, when the cloud ceiling was 3,000 feet or below. We noticed there was a strict correlation between Scud launches and bad weather at the launch site. Many pilots on Combat Air Patrols actually saw the Scuds come out of the weather. But the U.S. missile-warning satellites monitoring the launches were Cold War systems built to preclude surprise attacks on the United States by Soviet intercontinental missiles. They did not have the accuracy needed to detect the exact launch point through the cloud cover and transmit it to the pilots waiting above.

Several attempts were made to overcome these limitations, namely by small teams of Special Forces from Britain's elite SAS which, roaming around western Iraq, raided launch sites, destroyed some launchers and drove others deeper into Iraq.

But it was soon clear to us that the difficulty of locating mobile Scud launchers had been seriously underestimated. Although the United States knew the weapon's specifications, U.S. forces had had no practical experience with it. They did not understand its employment. Only by using the Scud oneself could one know its strength and weaknesses.

As it happened, an officer on my staff had commanded an Egyptian Scud unit for two years. By a process of logical deduction, he set about trying to solve the puzzle of how to locate

---

* See Mark Crispin Miller, "Desert Scam: Not One Mobile Scud Launcher Was Destroyed," *International Herald Tribune*, January 25, 1992.

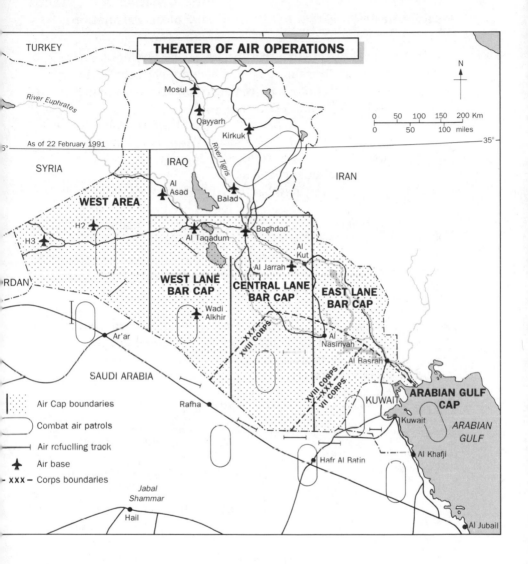

THEATER OF AIR OPERATIONS

TURKEY

River Euphrates

As of 22 February 1991

SYRIA

IRAQ

IRAN

Mosul

Qayyarh

Kirkuk

River Tigris

Al Asad

Balad

WEST AREA

H2

H3

Boghdad

Al Taqadum

Al Kut

Al Jarrah

WEST LANE
BAR CAP

CENTRAL LANE
BAR CAP

EAST LANE
BAR CAP

RDAN

Wadi
Alkhir

XVIII CORPS

Ar'ar

Al
Nasiriyah

Al Basrah

SAUDI ARABIA

Rafha

XVIII CORPS

VII CORPS

KUWAIT

ARABIAN GULF
CAP

Kuwait

ARABIAN
GULF

Air Cap boundaries

Combat air patrols

Air refuelling track

Air base

xxx — Corps boundaries

Jabal
Shammar

Hafr Al Batin

Al Khafji

Hail

Al Jubail

N

0   50   100 150   200 Km
0   50   100 miles

35°

and bomb Scud launch sites in the few minutes available between the firing of a missile and the evacuation of the launch site. What follows is a rough summary of his calculations:

1. On the assumption that the Iraqis were trying to hit targets in Riyadh, he drew a diagram placing the city at the center of an arc of which the radius was equal to the maximum range of a Scud.

2. A careful study of the map around the circumference of the arc then served to identify probable launch sites, based on such factors as proximity to roads and to potential hiding places.

3. On the assumption that the Iraqis would not move their mobile launchers during daylight, he deduced that the most likely firing time would be between nightfall (1800 hours) and first light (0600 hours).

   However, if one took into account the time needed, under cover of darkness, to move the launcher and its missile from its hiding place to the launch site and prepare for the launch, and then, after firing the missile, the time needed to evacuate the launch site and return the launcher to its hiding place, one could deduce that the most likely firing time would be between 1910 and 0520 hours.

4. From his own experience, he knew that it took between seven and ten minutes for a Scud launcher to evacuate a launch site, while the orbiting U.S. missile-warning satellite took two minutes to report a launch. This meant that, from the moment warning data was received, the Coalition had from five to eight minutes in which to bomb a launch site.

5. In turn, this meant that Coalition fighter-bombers would have to be on patrol, waiting for that warning, some 35 to 70 miles from the launch site if they were to stand a chance of getting there in time to detect and destroy the launcher.

I passed these ingenious calculations on to Schwarzkopf, and the Americans acknowledged their usefulness. They were helpful in determining where our Combat Air Patrols should be stationed. But all these efforts were not able to overcome the limitations of the satellites in pinpointing launch sites and the protection which the weather gave the Iraqi missile crews.

One of the striking paradoxes of Desert Storm was that it took the clumsy outdated Scud to stimulate fresh thinking about the nature of warfare and the need for Middle East peace. It spurred the United States into making fresh efforts to check missile proliferation, and it gave a great boost to the development of anti-missile defenses; but it may also have helped convince some Israelis that their long-term security lay less in acquiring still more weapons than in seeking peace with their neighbors, and in preparing themselves to pay the necessary price for peace, namely the return of Arab territory seized in 1967.

⊱⊰

Apart from the Scuds, another surprise which Saddam sprang on the Coalition was the flight of 135 aircraft to Iran. The first exodus of about 80 planes took place on January 26 and on the next three days, followed by another mass flight between February 6 and 10. Among the planes that escaped were brand new MiG-29 fighters, low-level "Fencers" – a Soviet bomber in the same class as the Tornado or the F-111 – some transport planes, but also a lot of older MiGs which were hardly worth maintaining. Nevertheless the whole package made a handsome addition to Iran's air force which, after the war, Tehran made clear it had no intention of returning.

After the first three days of the air campaign, the Iraqi air force had more or less quit flying. The few planes which took off were shot down. Realizing he was outclassed, and perhaps wishing to preserve his air force for a mass break-out later in the war, Saddam then parked his aircraft in hardened shelters of which about 600 had been built, some of them reputed to be the strongest in the world. The Coalition then attacked the shelters with 2,000-lb. case-hardened laser-guided bombs, gutting over 150 of them.

Watching these developments on the screens in his headquarters, Horner guessed that what remained of the Iraqi air force would try to flee to another country. He thought the destination would be Jordan because of the close relationship between Saddam and King Hussein. So he positioned extra air patrols of U.S., British and Saudi interceptors south and west of Baghdad. But he had guessed wrong. The Iraqi planes sped across the border to the safety of Iran.

My first thought was that the pilots were defectors, fleeing Saddam's dictatorship. This was Schwarzkopf's view, too. He even told me we should protect the defecting planes. We expected to hear that other pilots had been executed in Iraq. But then came another mass exodus to Iran, and it seemed clear that Saddam had done a deal with Tehran to provide safe haven for his planes. By this time, Horner had moved his air patrols east of Baghdad and some Iraqi planes were shot down. But large numbers still got through to Iran.

I was surprised at the time at the Coalition's inability or unwillingness to prevent this mass escape. Air movements in the whole area from the Gulf to the Red Sea, and from Saudi Arabia to Turkey were monitored at all altitudes by AWACS, by U.S. Navy E-2C Hawkeyes and other platforms, by surface radars on carrier battle groups, all linked together by satellite communications and data links to produce a near real-time "air picture." The movement of any enemy aircraft would be immediately transmitted to Coalition Combat Air Patrols flying from land bases and carriers. Not a single aircraft in the whole region could take off without being detected, and every plane was tracked from the moment it was airborne.

I asked my staff to investigate how the Iraqi planes had slipped through the net, and they came up with three main reasons. First, as I have mentioned, the Iraqi planes were expected to flee to Jordan not Iran, and the Combat Air Patrols had been waiting for them south and west of Baghdad. Secondly, the distance from Iraqi airfields to the Iranian frontier is very short: interception was not easy without intruding into Iranian air space. Thirdly, the Iraqis were flying very low. To shoot them down, Coalition planes would have had to fly as low, and this would have made them vulnerable to ground fire. But, in spite of these explanations, I remained skeptical. The episode of the mass exodus of Iraqi planes to Iran — one of the most curious of the war — remains something of an aberration to this day. I also wondered what had become of the Iraqi pilots who flew

THE AIR WAR AND THE SCUDS

the planes to Iran. They seemed to have disappeared without trace.

The incident made me wonder whether the Iraqis could have managed to penetrate our air space had they been bolder. Did the incident show up a gap in the Coalition's capability? If the Iraqis were able to fly to Iran without being stopped, might they not have been able to fly at least some way into the Kingdom? The extraordinary fact remains that, for all his warlike bluster, Saddam made no effective use of his air force. Nor did he make good use of his long-range artillery, nor thankfully of his arsenal of chemical weapons. He invited attack, but then did not fight back.

The Iraqi air force did make one attempt to attack us. On January 24, in a complex and well-executed operation, two Iraqi Mirage F-1s took off and came south. There were a lot of other planes in the air at the time – Iraqi planes flying north along the Iranian border, U.S. Air Force patrols chasing them, and other Coalition aircraft returning over the Gulf from missions over Basrah – so perhaps the Mirage F-1s were hoping to be lost in the radar clutter. The fighter bombers seemed to be heading for our port of Jubail.

In spite of their clever maneuver underneath the other airplanes, the minute they were airborne they were picked up by a U.S. Navy controller in an AWACS. He first contacted a U.S. Navy F18 over the Gulf whose mission was to protect an American cruiser. But the cruiser's captain would not release the plane – an example of a challenge to the Joint Air Command. The AWACS controller then alerted a Saudi Combat Air Patrol orbiting just south of Kuwait. Captain Ayedh Salah al-Shamrani of the 13th Fighter Squadron, Royal Saudi Air Force, piloting an F-15C, rolled up behind the two Mirages.

"Clear to kill," the AWACS controller instructed him.

At that instant, Captain Shamrani saw a flare of flame beneath one of the Iraqi planes. Its pilot had dropped his weapons to give himself greater maneuverability and perhaps in the hope that falling fragments would affect any attacking aircraft. He broke left then sharply swung right, but Shamrani, in a split-second decision, downed him with a supersonic AIM-9 Sidewinder missile. A moment later, as he saw the first plane explode, his radar locked on to the second Iraqi Mirage which had now turned towards him. A second Sidewinder destroyed the incoming Iraqi. The double kill, in less than a minute, was an impressive display of skill.

I wanted to decorate Captain Shamrani soon after his exploit, and was about to fly to Dhahran to do so when word reached me on January 30 that Iraqi forces had the previous night slipped into our undefended border town of al-Khafji.

So I flew north instead – to face my own personal test of courage and competence.

CHAPTER XX

The Battle of Al-Khafji

T HE KEY TO VICTORY in battle does not lie only in the weapons, equipment and supplies of one's men, still less in their numbers. As every commander knows, it lies also in something less tangible called morale: the perception in every soldier's breast that he is on the winning – or on the losing – side. There is a celebrated passage in Leo Tolstoy's *War and Peace* in which he declares: "The strength of an army depends on its spirit."

In his great classic, Tolstoy relates how Napoleon captured Moscow in 1812 with his 600,000-strong imperial army – and then, as the tide of war turned, how the scattered remnants of this great army fled home across the icy wastes of Russia. "The success of a military action," Tolstoy writes, "depends not on the commanding general but on the man in the ranks who first shouts 'We are lost!' or 'Hurrah!'" If there is "a brave, spirited lad who leads the way with shouts of 'Hurrah,' a division of five thousand is as good as thirty thousand."

The Coalition against Saddam knew that it must eventually triumph: its superior manpower, resources and technology more or less guaranteed victory. Yet nagging doubts remained. What was the impact of the air campaign on Iraq's ability to fight? Would Saddam use chemical weapons? Would he manage to draw the Coalition into a ground war at a time of his choosing? Would he manage to inflict heavy casualties and turn a military defeat into a political victory, as Nasser, the Egyptian leader, had done at Suez in 1956? No one could be certain of the answers to these questions. (The fear, even the expectation, of heavy casualties was reflected in the Coalition's provision of 18,000 hospital beds in the theater of operations.)

The battle of al-Khafji cleared the air by providing some answers. It taught us a great deal about the real state of Iraq's armies. But, for me, its importance lay primarily in what it did for morale, ours and Iraq's. Our troops shouted "Hurrah!" while Saddam's cried "We are lost!" After al-Khafji, every man on our side knew that we were going to win the war, and every man on his side knew that they were going to lose it.

In every conflict there is a moment when the tide is seen to turn. In the Gulf War, the battle of al-Khafji was such a moment.

❧❦

During the night of January 29–30, an Iraqi battle group crossed the Saudi–Kuwaiti border, moved down the coastal corridor and occupied the undefended town of al-Khafji, some eight miles inside Saudi Arabia. It was an easy prize: anyone could have walked in. There was no Coalition military presence there whatsoever. But Baghdad radio, and the media of two or three Arab countries sympathetic to Iraq, immediately trumpeted the capture of al-Khafji as a great victory, and it was true that Saddam had achieved a tactical surprise. It was only the second time in the entire crisis that he had seized the initiative, the first being his use of Scuds.

The timing of the attack on al-Khafji was significant. The air campaign against Iraq had been raging for 12 days, and had provoked a heated debate inside the Coalition on a number of related issues: how long should it continue? What did we know about Battle Damage Assessment? Were the air planners giving too much attention to hitting strategic targets inside Iraq and too little to degrading Iraqi forces immediately opposite our front? I, for one, certainly wanted priority to be given to military targets close to our borders rather than to Iraq's civilian infrastructure. I was particularly worried about Iraq's massed artillery, the effectiveness of which had been proved during the Iraq–Iran war.

While this debate was in progress, preparations for the ground campaign continued apace. Under cover of the air campaign, hundreds of thousands of troops from the American VIIth and

XVIIIth Corps were moving into attack position. On the east–west Tapline road, trucks roared past 24 hours a day virtually nose to tail. The French 6th Light Armored Division was moving to the extreme left flank, while keeping open its supply lines from Yanbu. Closer to my own positions east and south of Kuwait, two U.S. Marine divisions were leapfrogging past each other, and relocating their supply points from the Gulf coast to new bases about 70 miles inland at al-Kibrit and al-Khanjar. C-130s, flying night and day, were busy ferrying men and supplies to hastily built dirt strips deep in the desert.

The Iraqis appeared to be totally unaware of the giant war machine which was about to roll over them. The Coalition was preparing to deliver the coup de grâce. The endgame was approaching.

It was at this moment that the Iraqi attack on al-Khafji came like a bolt from the blue, threatening to disrupt the Coalition's preparations and raising fears that, even at this eleventh hour, Saddam might succeed in preempting our plans.

What was he trying to achieve? Some Coalition analysts believed this was a prelude to a larger attack down the Wadi al-Batin, the wide dry valley which runs along Kuwait's western frontier with Iraq, although Iraq's total lack of air cover made this scenario highly implausible. Pessimists predicted that he would try to push down the coast as far as Jubail in the hope that a psychological shock to the Kingdom might bring about an internal collapse. Was Saddam perhaps seeking to impress Arab and international opinion by discrediting Arab armies and regimes?

The coastal highway which passes through al-Khafji is of great strategic importance. It links Kuwait with Saudi Arabia, with Bahrain (via the causeway from Dammam to Bahrain Island), with Qatar, the Emirates and then Oman. The coastal plain and its adjacent territorial waters, with their oil wells, pipeline terminals, loading ports and main harbors, are the region from which the Gulf states derive their wealth. By occupying al-Khafji, Saddam seemed to threaten the whole of this vital coastal corridor, causing considerable disquiet in Riyadh and other Gulf capitals.

A less alarmist explanation of Saddam's move into al-Khafji

was that this was a desperate attempt to seize the initiative and force the Coalition to respond to him. As interrogations of prisoners of war later revealed, the Iraqis were anxious to capture as many soldiers as possible to use as bargaining counters. Saddam's only hope of inflicting substantial casualties on the Coalition – and therefore of claiming a political victory – was to draw the allies into ground combat while his defense lines around Kuwait were still more or less intact. If he waited until his defenses were completely destroyed, he would lose all freedom of maneuver and would have no option but to give up the fight. On this argument, the attack on al-Khafji was an attempt to trigger a Coalition ground attack and draw allied forces into Iraq's killing zones around Kuwait, a tactic which Iraq had perfected in its long struggle against Iran. Although this seems a plausible explanation, to this day no one is quite sure what Saddam had in mind.

❖

Early on January 30, I flew from Riyadh to the King Abd al-Aziz Naval Base at Jubail to decorate some Saudi naval officers and men who had sunk the biggest ship in the Iraqi navy. Before leaving Riyadh that morning I had received a report of an overnight Iraqi border incursion in the direction of al-Khafji. My reaction had been that we were well able to handle it. If the Iraqis were rash enough to venture across the border and into the no-man's-land beyond, they would be destroyed from the air.

Then, just before the ceremony at the naval base, which was to be followed by a press conference, I received another more troubling report that the Iraqis had crossed our frontier in strength. I felt a great deal of anxiety, and wanted to get away as soon as possible to deal with the problem. The minutes ticking by seemed like hours. But, not wanting to disrupt the proceedings or alert the press, I forced myself to keep smiling.

I had been due to fly on to Dhahran by helicopter to decorate Captain Shamrani, the Royal Saudi Air Force pilot who had single-handedly shot down two Iraqi Mirage F-1s. But the news I received made clear that the Iraqi incursion had developed into something bigger than a cross-border hit-and-run raid. A large Iraqi force had entered al-Khafji and powerful reinforcements, estimated at up to two divisions, were moving up on the Iraqi side of the border. I decided to fly north at once.

I headed for Rish al-Manjur, the JFC-East forward headquarters of Major General Sultan 'Adi al-Mutairi, which consisted of a sand-bagged underground command post and a few tents some 25 miles south of al-Khafji and 15 miles inland from the coastal oil installations of al-Saffaniya. Major General Sultan is a highly capable soldier, but I found his headquarters in a state of some alarm. As the Iraqis advanced into Saudi Arabia, he had repeatedly called on the U.S. Marine Corps for air strikes to stop them. He was in close touch with the Marines because they shared a sector. They had trained together and an American liaison officer was attached to his headquarters. But in spite of his pleas, no air strikes had taken place. Coalition aircraft had not moved. My whole strategy of leaving the immediate border area virtually undefended was being undermined.

Major General Sultan had spent much of the previous night on a long reconnaissance up to al-Khafji and had seen Iraqi deployments for himself. On hearing this news, I realized that the situation was a good deal more threatening than I had at first assumed.

It will be recalled that, following my first trip to the field on August 16 at the start of the Gulf crisis, I had declared al-Khafji a "dead city." An evacuation plan had been prepared for the town's entire population of some 15,000 in the event of an Iraqi move south. But, in order not to create unnecessary panic, we had decided not to implement the plan immediately. There was to be no mass evacuation. No edict was ever issued instructing people to get out. But by December 1990 most of the town's inhabitants had moved to more secure areas inland, some waiting for the school holidays to do so. Some government officials remained behind together with a company of Saudi Marines on guard duty to protect people's property and vital installations, but the town was virtually abandoned. Its heart had gone and, after the start of the air campaign on January 17, the last remaining inhabitants were evacuated.

This proved to be a wise decision because, once the air

campaign started, al-Khafji faced incoming artillery shells, rockets and missiles almost every day. The fear that Saddam might use chemicals was on everyone's mind. Oil storage tanks on the southern outskirts of the town were hit, sending up dense clouds of smoke. The desalination plant, on which the population depended for its drinking water, was situated north of the town, a mere four miles from the Kuwaiti border and well within range of Iraqi artillery. Al-Khafji became a ghost town.

As I explained in an earlier chapter, I had pulled my main force back some 25 miles from the Kuwaiti border to a defense line west of Ras Mish'ab, leaving only a light screening force in the vicinity of al-Khafji some three miles from the frontier. In addition, a company of Saudi Marines was positioned astride the coast road north of the town, while farther north still our coast guard post was just 800 yards from the Iraqi positions. In the long months of stalemate before the start of the air campaign, the coast guards could see the Iraqis swimming in the Gulf.

The mission I had given these forward forces was to observe the movement of Iraqi troops and report the approach of hostile columns. They were not to engage the Iraqis or risk being taken prisoner. I did not want to give Saddam a propaganda victory. If the Iraqis crossed the border, they were to rejoin our main force farther south. My strategy was to defend the border region with firepower not manpower. If the Iraqis ever attacked, we would take them on with air power and with our supporting arms.

The Americans, too, sent small reconnaissance patrols of Marines and Navy Seals to keep an eye on the coastal highway which was the main avenue of approach into the Kingdom, and every so often the U.S. Marine Corps or the U.S. Navy sent up an unmanned aerial vehicle (UAV) to take a look at what was happening on the Kuwaiti side of the frontier.

(I should here digress for a moment to take issue with Schwarzkopf's claim that the strategy to pull back from al-Khafji was his not mine. In his book he writes: ". . . very early in Desert Shield, I'd pointed out to Khalid that al-Khafji was indefensible: 'The enemy can shell you from his side of the border anytime he wants.' Khalid had wrestled with that – his directive from King Fahd was to defend every square inch of the Kingdom

– but finally he agreed and pulled his forces out."* The decision to pull back my forces and leave al-Khafji undefended was taken by me on August 18, eight days before Schwarzkopf even arrived in the Kingdom on August 26, and before I had had any communication with him.)

❧⟨⟩❧

As I studied the situation maps in Major General Sultan's underground bunker on the afternoon of January 30 and scanned the latest intelligence reports, I was naturally very concerned to hear that he had not got the air support he had called for. This was a problem I had to address very soon. But first I wanted to assess the situation as best I could from the information available.

This was the picture that took shape in my mind from the briefings I received. The front had been inactive for months but, since the start of the air campaign 12 days earlier, had sprung to life with numerous small skirmishes and nightly exchanges of missiles and artillery fire between Saudi and Iraqi troops. The U.S. Marines had approached Major General Sultan to ask if their 155mm howitzers could join in. For several days he had sent them forward at midnight to fire at the Iraqis and then withdraw as fast as possible – so-called "shoot-and-scoot" operations. A week earlier an Iraqi deserter had warned that a column of more than 100 vehicles was heading for the border between their minefields. Saudi MLRSs (Multiple Launch Rocket Systems) had opened up, hitting the lead vehicle and bringing the column to a halt. Coalition aircraft had then intervened, destroying most of the vehicles.

On the afternoon of January 29, the day before my arrival, Major General Sultan had received reports of large-scale Iraqi armored movements along the border inside Kuwait. Later that evening, he heard from his American liaison officer that Iraqi forces, supported by tanks and armored vehicles, had made several border incursions at battalion strength farther west, opposite Marine positions at al-Wafra, al-Zubar, and between al-Raghwa and al-Rafi'iya, but were being engaged with artillery

---

* Schwarzkopf, op. cit., p. 424.

fire, antitank missiles, and air strikes. Several Iraqi vehicles had already been destroyed, but fierce engagements were still raging. Later I was to learn that in one of these firefights, seven Marines were killed when one U.S. light armored vehicle shot another in the heat of battle. In the confusion of battle, it is a very easy thing to do.

Then, shortly before midnight on the 29th, Major General Sultan heard from his forward post up on the border that Iraqi mechanized forces were heading down the road towards al-Khafji. He immediately called for an air strike to stop them, and was assured by the U.S. Marines that Cobra helicopter gunships were on their way. Fifteen minutes later, he learned that there had been no air attack but that some 17 Iraqi armored vehicles had crossed the border. Again he called for air strikes, but again nothing happened. Soon he received another report that some 57 Iraqi armored vehicles, including T-55 tanks, were heading towards the desalination plant within the northern perimeter of the town.

Again he called for air strikes to prevent the Iraqis reinforcing their positions, but this time the U.S. Marines replied that they could not comply until the light Saudi screening force west of al-Khafji was pulled back at least one and a half miles. As the right flank of this force was close to the Iraqis and was attempting to engage them, it risked coming under American fire from the air. Wondering why the Marines had not raised this matter earlier, Major General Sultan promptly pulled the force back, and repeated his call for air strikes.

Meanwhile, the company of Saudi Marines was still at al-Khafji, but their short-range antitank weapons were no match for the longer-range Iraqi tanks. Major General Sultan was in touch with these men by radio and also by line telephone: when they came under pressure after midnight, he ordered them out too. But once they had withdrawn, information from the front dried up.

Major General Sultan was understandably bitter that two Iraqi battalions (from the 15th Brigade of the 5th Mechanized Infantry Division, as we subsequently learned) had been allowed to move across the frontier in attack formation and advance over seven miles on al-Khafji without being spotted and intercepted from the air. When I heard about it from him on my arrival at his headquarters, I too was surprised and incensed at the American failure to give our troops air support – a failure which was to extend from midnight on January 29 until well into the afternoon of the next day. As I shall recount in a moment, I immediately contacted the air operations center in Riyadh to demand action, which was then taken.

The U.S. Marines were to advance several reasons why their air wing had not responded faster to Major General Sultan. They said the fear of hitting our troops had been inhibiting: before dropping bombs, the Marines needed to know who was where and who was doing what. They suggested that, once the Iraqi vehicles were among the buildings inside al-Khafji, they were not easy to spot. They explained that the U.S. Marines are organized to fight as an air-ground team and are, as a result, reluctant to use their air force separately from their ground troops. Indeed, even before this episode, I had got the feeling that they only grudgingly committed their air assets to Lieutenant General Horner's central control.

I did not find these reasons wholly convincing. I would have liked to have heard about them at the very start when I could have organized air support from elsewhere. The Marines' air wing had been tasked to provide Close Air Support to the Joint Forces when needed. But when the crunch came, the Marines found it difficult to deliver. As for our own Royal Saudi Air Force, it was already committed to other planned Coalition missions and was therefore not available at the time.

I believe the main reason for the delay in providing us with air support was that the Marines were fighting their own battles farther west – battles which in their eyes at the time were of greater significance than the crisis we faced. At al-Khafji, we were contending with the 15th Mechanized Brigade of Iraq's 5th Infantry Division, but farther west the Marines were struggling to turn back elements of the 20th Mechanized Brigade and the 26th Armored Brigade which were also trying to fight their way across the frontier.

The U.S. Marines had set up a major logistics base at al-Kibrit, about 70 miles west of Ras Mish'ab, where they had stockpiled all the supplies they needed for the coming attack into Kuwait.

The prime concern of Lieutenant General Walter Boomer, the Marine commander who had established his own headquarters out west in the desert, was the security of this logistics base. His fear was that, if the Iraqis in his sector were not thrown back across the frontier at once, they might manage a deep penetration and cut the Marines off from their base. This is where his efforts were directed that night and the following day. No doubt Lieutenant General Boomer thought that if his air wing focused too much on our problem at al-Khafji, the Iraqis might turn their flank and come in from the west, where they felt vulnerable. This, at least, is my reading of the situation. But, by committing their air force to the battles in their sector, the Marines starved us of the air support we needed and had expected to get.

My judgment of these events did not affect my personal admiration for Lieutenant General Boomer. Self-effacing, even a touch austere, he was an aggressive and highly competent battlefield commander who yet showed a deep concern for the welfare of his troops. He was one of the most impressive American generals I met.

Starved of information as well as of air support, Major General Sultan decided to go to al-Khafji himself that night to see what was going on. At 3 a.m. on January 30, he set out from his forward headquarters, making first for the coast guard post at al-Zarqani, just south of al-Khafji. The moon was full, the storm clouds had lifted and visibility in the desert at night was good over long distances.

But before describing Major General Sultan's reconnaissance, I shall for greater clarity say a word about the troops we had available for the defense of our Eastern Area, of which the core consisted of three Saudi brigades reinforced by contingents from our GCC allies.

I had organized these forces in four task forces, named Abu Bakr, Othman, Omar and Tariq. (For Western readers I should explain that the first three were named after the three Caliphs who immediately succeeded the Prophet Muhammad, while

Tariq bin Ziyad was the Muslim conqueror of Spain, after whom Gibraltar – Jabal Tariq – was named.)

- Abu Bakr task force consisted of the 2nd Saudi National Guard (SANG) Mechanized Brigade, plus one Qatari mechanized infantry battalion.
- Othman task force consisted of the 8th Royal Saudi Land Forces (RSLF) Mechanized Brigade, plus one Bahraini infantry company and one Kuwaiti infantry company.
- Omar task force consisted of the 10th RSLF Mechanized Brigade, plus one Omani infantry battalion.
- Tariq task force consisted of two Saudi Marine battalions, plus one Moroccan infantry regiment and one Senegalese infantry battalion (less a company).
- In reserve, a Qatari mechanized infantry battalion and an Emirates infantry battalion.

Before the battle at al-Khafji, the two Saudi Marine battalions of Tariq task force had been given the mission to defend the Gulf coast from Ras al-Safaniya up to Ras Mish'ab, with a company up at al-Khafji itself, while the Senegalese and Moroccans held adjacent strongpoints securing the al-Safaniya area, site of oil installations belonging to the Arabian Oil Company, an important Saudi–Japanese concern. (Some Japanese oil workers stayed in place until January 16, the very eve of the air campaign, when they were persuaded to move to safety farther south.)

As I have said, our main forces – the Abu Bakr, Othman and Omar task forces – were positioned from right to left in defense some 25 miles south of the Kuwaiti frontier, each group sending forward a battalion and a reconnaissance squadron as a screen three miles from the frontier.

Before setting out on his reconnaissance early on January 30, Major General Sultan arranged for two tank companies – one from the 8th RSLF Brigade and another from the Qatari battalion, each company supported by a platoon of antitank missiles – to rendezvous with him at a point four miles west of al-Khafji.

At about 5 a.m., Major General Sultan and his party moved

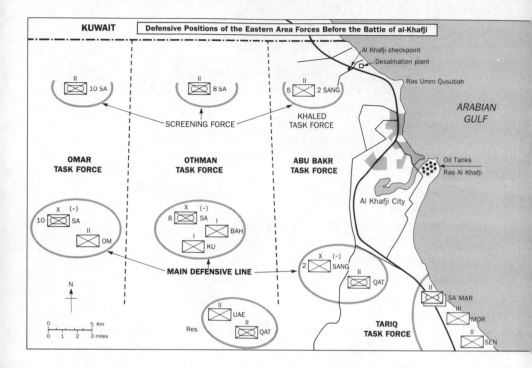

Defensive Positions of the Eastern Area Forces Before the Battle of al-Khafji

KUWAIT

Al Khafji checkpoint
Desalination plant
Ras Umm Qusubah

ARABIAN GULF

10 SA

8 SA

5 ⊠ 2 SANG

SCREENING FORCE

KHALED TASK FORCE

OMAR TASK FORCE

OTHMAN TASK FORCE

ABU BAKR TASK FORCE

Oil Tanks
Ras Al Khafji

Al Khafji City

10 SA

OM

8 SA

BAH

KU

MAIN DEFENSIVE LINE

2 SANG

QAT

SA MAR

MOR

N

0   5 Km
0   1   2   3 miles

Res

UAE

QAT

TARIQ TASK FORCE

SEN

KEY TO MAP SYMBOLS

Abbreviations:

BAH	Bahrain
EG	Egypt
FR	France
GCC	Gulf Cooperation Council
JFC	Joint Force Command
KU	Kuwait
MEF	Marine Expeditionary Force
MOR	Morocco
OM	Oman
QAT	Qatar
Res	Reserve
RG	Republican Guard
SA	Saudi Arabia
SA MAR	Saudi Arabian Marines
SANG	Saudi Arabian National Guard
SEN	Senegal
SY	Syria
UAE	United Arab Emirates
UK	United Kingdom

Size of unit:

XXX	Corps
XX	Division
X	Brigade
III	Regiment
II	Battalion
I	Company

Infantry

Mechanized Infantry

Marines

Special Forces

Armored

RGR

Ranger

Airborne

Air assault

Armored cavalry

Iraqi Forces

Number to left of box is unit identifier

Number to right of box denotes a higher command level

Example:

5 ⊠ 2 SANG

Saudi Arabian National Guard 5th Battalion 2nd Brigade

towards al-Khafji from the west. Leaving their vehicles, they advanced on foot for about 500 yards until they could see the forward Iraqi positions through their binoculars – some 12 tanks and personnel carriers on the western edge of the town. The main Iraqi force was by then inside the town.

As he had received several confused and contradictory reports, Major General Sultan was glad to have firsthand confirmation that the Iraqis were in fact there. Even as he observed the Iraqis he received a radio report from his command that U.S. aircraft were bombing al-Khafji. He was able to reply, "I am at al-Khafji and there is no sign whatsoever of any air activity." He then withdrew and met up with the two tank companies at the rendezvous. Joining the nearby Qatari tank company and its HOT antitank missile platoon, he ordered them to advance and engage the column of Iraqi tanks then moving along a road. The odds seemed reasonable. After exchanging fire for about six minutes, the Qataris scored some direct hits. An Iraqi lieutenant and 20 men then jumped from their vehicles – five tanks and six APCs – and, raising their hands above their heads, ran forward to surrender.

Major General Sultan had planned to advance and engage the Iraqis in the town itself, but when he learned from the prisoners that the Iraqis had entered al-Khafji with two battalions, or about 1,500 men, he had second thoughts. The odds were no longer reasonable. He left the Saudi tank company of the 8th Brigade to control the road going north, and moved the Qatari company to its initial position at the al-Zarqani post south of al-Khafji.

As he was speeding back through the outskirts of al-Khafji he came on a small group of Iraqi soldiers who, he thought, wanted to surrender. But as they approached, the Iraqis fell to the ground and opened fire. His vehicle managed to swing round at speed and escape unharmed, returning to the command post by another route.

Major General Sultan later learned that the group of Iraqis included a number of Saudi prisoners. A Saudi civil defense officer, who had been stationed in al-Khafji before being posted to Dammam, had returned to collect some equipment he had left behind. Thinking al-Khafji was deserted, he and his companions had speeded in a closed car through our roadblock, ignoring attempts to stop them, and had landed in the arms of the Iraqis. After the war, the civil defense officer told Major General Sultan that, seeing his vehicle approach, he had wanted to cry out to warn him, but had not dared do so as the Iraqis threatened to kill him.

❖

Major General Sultan returned to his headquarters at Rish al-Manjur at 1 p.m. on January 30, and it was there that I found him on my arrival two hours later. We were soon joined by Major General Salih al-Muhaya, the Eastern Area Commander who had flown up from his headquarters at Dhahran.

After hearing Major General Sultan's account, my first task was to resolve the vexed question of air support. I rang the Saudi Air Force Commander, Lieutenant General Ahmad al-Buhairi, at the air operations center in Riyadh. I told him I wanted action *now*. He passed the phone to Lieutenant General Horner who was sitting beside him. I told him I wanted air support as well as strikes by B-52s to break up Iraqi concentrations and prevent reinforcements reaching al-Khafji, even if it meant diverting air assets from the air campaign against strategic targets inside Iraq. Minimize raids on strategic targets and maximize them at al-Khafji, I urged him.

To this day I do not know what happened between Lieutenant General Horner and the Marine Corps, because from the way he responded I sensed that he was not in full command of the Marine air wing.

When there was no action within the hour, I phoned Brigadier General Ahmad al-Sudairy, the Saudi Director of Air Operations. By this time my blood was up. An Iraqi armored column heading our way was reported to be stretched out over 12 miles.

"Forget about the Joint Forces," I cried. "If the U.S. Air Force or the Marines don't come at once, I want you to take our air assets out of the Coalition and send them all to me! I need the Tornados, the F-5s, everything you've got!"

I had delivered something of an ultimatum – and it worked. Within minutes, Horner had diverted to the approaches to al-Khafji much of the air power that was going elsewhere. A steady stream of Coalition aircraft struck at the advancing Iraqis, delivering precision weapons and cluster bombs. A single strike by three B-52s decimated more than 80 Iraqi vehicles, lighting up the sky for miles around. Throughout the night of January 30–31, Coalition planes, taking full advantage of their night-fighting ability, also hammered two divisions of Iraq's IIIrd Corps which were detected assembling inside Kuwait for a follow-on attack into al-Khafji. Naval guns out in the Gulf also joined in.

Particularly effective against such targets were the U.S. Air Force's AC-130 Specter gunships which fire 105mm howitzers out of the side. But these planes are vulnerable to optically aimed ground weapons and can only operate at night. Just before dawn on January 31, the pilot of one AC-130 on station was warned by his AWACS controller that he should return at once to base as it would soon be light. "I can't," he replied. "There are too many targets." Minutes later he was shot down by a Stinger-type, infrared missile, with the loss of 14 men on board. Their bodies were recovered only after the war.

Some Iraqi tanks and APCs got through the barrage, but there is little doubt that had the two divisions crossed the border in good order, they would have greatly outnumbered us. They could have inflicted significant casualties on our forces in that sector and perhaps even precipitated the large-scale ground combat which Saddam seemed to want.

But, useful as they were, such air attacks on Iraq's second echelon and reserve units were not going to dislodge the Iraqis already in al-Khafji. That was up to us. Ably assisted by Major General Sultan 'Adi al-Mutairi, I was faced at Rish al-Manjur with the urgent task of analyzing the fast-moving situation, drawing up a plan of counterattack, and allocating troops to a task force to retake al-Khafji. It was a challenging moment.

Recollecting these events in tranquillity long afterwards makes no allowance for the stress, confusion and anxiety of war. As any commander will verify, one is never quite sure what one's own troops are doing, much less the enemy's. However effective one's command, control and communications, there are always gaps in one's information. It is easy to give an order, more difficult to be certain it is obeyed. This was the first time that I had tested my Saudi troops in battle.

I must also admit that I, too, had no previous experience of war. I was a commander who had never been in a real battle and I did not know how I would behave under stress. I discovered that there are two types of men in war: some panic, become overexcited and seem incapable of self-control. It is best to remove them at once from any position of authority because they infect those around them. Others experience extreme fear in the first few minutes – that is quite usual for most people – but then manage to calm down and behave normally. There seems to be no middle ground between the two.

The Coalition could boast of some highly experienced officers – Schwarzkopf himself, de la Billière, Roquejeoffre, the Egyptian and Syrian commanders battle-hardened by their wars with Israel, the Moroccan commander who had won his spurs in the Western Sahara fighting the Polisario. I was very conscious that all of them would be closely observing my performance.

But perhaps my greatest worry was how to reassure my own side that I had everything in hand. King Fahd wanted quick results, and rightly so. He wanted the enemy force expelled at once. He wished to deny Saddam the chance of showing the world that he could invade Saudi Arabia and get away with it. He telephoned me a number of times, calling for action. I also received calls from Prince Sultan. It was my first command in war, this was a highly important crisis, and they were probably not sure how well I could manage. I was relieved when I heard that Prince Sultan had said: "The matter is now in Khaled's hands. We must let the man do the job without interference."

The King's instructions were etched on my mind. He wanted me to recover al-Khafji with all possible speed. He wanted me to be decisive at any cost. To me at that moment, my own life became of no importance. Whether I survived the battle was no longer a consideration. The King was not trying to force my hand, but I could tell he was extremely perturbed.

I begged him not to worry. I knew there was no doubt about the outcome of the coming battle, but I also wanted to save lives. I tried to explain that I wanted to do the job with the minimum of casualties. I knew that hand-to-hand fighting in the city at night could be lethal to my troops who were not trained for combat in urban areas. I wanted to wait for first light before launching the attack. But as I could not show the King immediate results, I am lucky he did not strip me of my command that night!

Meanwhile, the radio stations of Baghdad, Amman and Sanaa were describing the Iraqi incursion in triumphalist terms. Saddam visited his front-line troops in Kuwait and was himself reported to be directing the battle. A few weeks earlier, in the run-up to the air campaign, I had declared that if he did not withdraw from Kuwait, we would teach him "a lesson he will never forget." I now had to prove this was no empty threat.

⤐⤏

While we were putting the finishing touches to our battle plan to liberate al-Khafji, an American liaison officer brought me a piece of news which forced me to think again. He told me that two U.S. Marine fire support teams – six men in one team and five in another – were trapped on the rooftop of a building on the southern perimeter of al-Khafji. It was at once clear to me that we had to rescue them before we did anything else.

Known as ANGLICOs (air naval gunfire liaison companies), the mission of such Marine Corps teams is to identify enemy targets, and then direct fire against them from aircraft, naval guns or ground artillery. In the weeks before the Iraqi incursion, when there was still some traffic in and out of al-Khafji, I knew that the Marines had been sending such reconnaissance teams into the town and up to the border to monitor Iraqi movements. They would drive around the town to see what was going on, and then find a suitable vantage point from which to observe enemy movements. They had the capability to call for fire. Equipped with binoculars, night vision devices and secure radio links to their headquarters, they would normally stay for a couple of days at a time. But once in place, their vehicle would be taken out, so they would have no way to come back until they were fetched. Clearly, no one had anticipated that the Iraqis would move in to al-Khafji. When all other Special Forces had withdrawn, including the company of Saudi Marines, the ANGLICO teams had been cut off by the swift Iraqi advance, or had chosen to stay put. I was told they had laid mines around their hiding place, and were prepared to fight it out if discovered.

As soon as I heard the news, I told Major General Sultan, "Our first priority is not to free al-Khafji. It is to get the Marines out." The nature of the problem had changed.

I determined to rescue the Marines for two main reasons. First, the main priority of any commander is to accomplish his mission, while minimizing his casualties. We had the means to drive the Iraqis out of al-Khafji without sacrificing the lives of our own troops or those of our allies, and I intended to do just that. For me, it was not a matter of Saudi or American. We were fighting the same battle and, while they were in my sector, I was responsible for their safety. Secondly – and I must admit this reason weighed more heavily still – I was extremely worried that Schwarzkopf might use American troops, either U.S. Marines in an amphibious attack or a heliborne U.S. Army unit, to free *my* town in *my* sector. The shame would have been difficult to bear. Worried that Schwarzkopf or Boomer might feel compelled to act to free the trapped Marines, I called my deputy, Major General Abd al-Aziz al-Shaikh, and told him, "Stick with Schwarzkopf. Make sure no one acts. This is my battle!" I also made sure the U.S. Marine Corps got the message that freeing their comrades was now my top priority, before anything else.

In view of the new situation, I asked Major General Sultan to draw up plans for two separate operations: the first was to be a raid that very evening on the southern fringes of al-Khafji. The objective was to isolate the building where the trapped Marines were hiding and push back or destroy the Iraqi troops in the immediate vicinity, so as to free the Marines and then withdraw. The second operation was to be a full-scale attack in the morning on the Iraqi force in al-Khafji.

In forming the task forces for these operations, we decided to give the prime role in both cases to troops drawn from the 2nd Mechanized Brigade of the Saudi National Guard, a highly effective unit equipped with 500 American-built Cadillac Gage light armored vehicles and TOW antitank missiles. After Saddam's invasion of Kuwait, this National Guard brigade had raced to the front from its peacetime locations near Dammam in the Eastern Province. Most of its soldiers were seasoned

Bedouin tribesmen who knew how to live and fight in a desert environment and had already spent several months training in my sector.

Crown Prince Abdallah bin Abd al-Aziz had been given command of the National Guard by King Faisal in the early 1960s when the Guard was little more than a levy of tribal irregulars with poor weapons, no uniforms and little discipline. From this material he had built a well-trained modern fighting force of two mechanized and four infantry brigades. The mechanized brigades had a mobile strategic role able to respond rapidly to any emergency within the Kingdom, while the infantry brigades provided in-place security at key installations across the country, such as the Kingdom's oil infrastructure, desalination plants and electricity generating stations. When the Gulf crisis erupted, Crown Prince Abdallah transferred the operational control of his National Guard units in the theater of operations to the Saudi land forces. I therefore had the honor to command them.

The task of freeing the U.S. Marines was assigned to a company from the 2nd Saudi National Guard Brigade, supported in reserve by a company from the 8th Royal Saudi Land Forces Brigade. Unfortunately, their first assault at dusk on January 30 on the southern perimeter of al-Khafji did not go well. The wide boulevards of al-Khafji provided little cover. Iraqi troops occupied buildings surrounding the one where the U.S. Marines were hiding and Iraqi headquarters were located in a hotel a mere couple of blocks away. When light armored vehicles of the National Guard pushed into the area, Iraqi snipers shot at their tires and managed to immobilize about ten of them. We then decided to bring forward the armor of the RSLF reserve company, and this second attempt was successful. After a fierce firefight, the Iraqis were pushed back and the American Marines were freed. One of them suffered a minor shrapnel wound. We lost no men, although we had to abandon some wheeled vehicles. It had been a mistake to send them in the first place.

Yet, back at the command post, I was jubilant. My fears of an American intervention had been put to rest. Major General Sultan then regrouped his forces south of al-Khafji and spent the night exchanging artillery fire with the Iraqis.

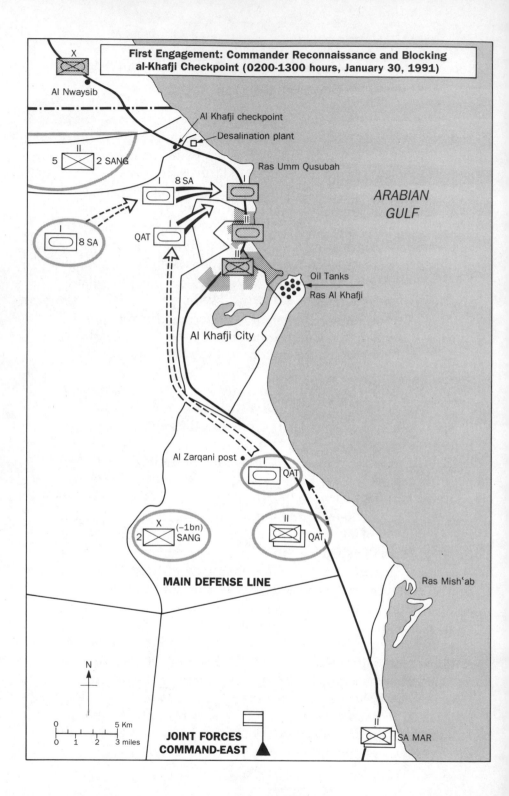

First Engagement: Commander Reconnaissance and Blocking al-Khafji Checkpoint (0200-1300 hours, January 30, 1991)

Al Nwaysib

Al Khafji checkpoint

Desalination plant

5 | 2 SANG

Ras Umm Qusubah

8 SA

ARABIAN GULF

8 SA

QAT

Oil Tanks
Ras Al Khafji

Al Khafji City

Al Zarqani post

QAT

2 X (−1bn) SANG

QAT

MAIN DEFENSE LINE

Ras Mish'ab

N

0   5 Km
0   1   2   3 miles

JOINT FORCES COMMAND-EAST

SA MAR

By this time, our preparations for the main attack were complete. Our task force was in position in the assembly area south of al-Khafji. It consisted of:

- two battalions, the 7th and 8th, from the 2nd Saudi National Guard Mechanized Brigade (drawn from the Abu Bakr task force);
- a Qatari force composed of a company of AMX tanks, a mechanized infantry company and a HOT antitank missile platoon (also drawn from the Abu Bakr task force);
- one battalion from the 8th RSLF Mechanized Brigade to act as a reserve (drawn from the Othman task force).

To tighten the noose around the Iraqis inside the town, we decided:

- to reinforce to battalion strength the Saudi tank company already in place astride the road north, adding a double TOW antitank missile platoon from the 8th RLSF mechanized brigade. The mission of this force was to move around al-Khafji from the northwest and cut the main road north from Saudi Arabia to Kuwait; and
- to send a battalion of Saudi Marines up the coast towards al-Khafji to hold a strategic bridge and prevent any southward movement by the Iraqis.

I had first planned to attack at sunrise on January 31. But, hearing from Major General Sultan that Iraqi troops usually rose early and went about their duties for an hour or so before taking a break at about 8 a.m., I decided that 8 a.m. was the best time to attack.

I was confident that victory would be ours. Everything had been attended to: the plans, the task forces, the briefing of the commanders. Our troops were in position and their morale was high.

To Major General Sultan I said, "It's all yours now. I will not interfere. But if you need anything, I am here." I must pay tribute to his excellent execution of the plans over the subsequent 24 hours.

With Coalition aircraft pounding Iraqi reinforcements throughout the night and Close Air Support promised for the next day, I decided to go to bed. Back in Riyadh I rarely slept more than three hours at a stretch. As my bedroom in the Ministry of Defense basement was next to my office, I would get up in the middle of the night to take calls and scan the maps. But at Rish al-Manjur that night I slept without interruption for a full six hours. On the eve of my first battle, I enjoyed my best night's sleep of the war.

⋙⋘

Battles bear little resemblance to the neat, well-orchestrated affairs taught on sand tables at staff college. Invariably, there are moments of confusion, of fear, of dangerous error. The struggle to recapture al-Khafji was no exception. Air and artillery support from friendly forces was vital and welcome, but to the men on the ground it often seemed to come too late or too close. For example, after destroying an Iraqi tank that morning, a U.S. helicopter gunship fired by mistake at a Saudi National Guard armored car, killing the driver and badly wounding some of the crew. Although U.S. forward air controllers assigned to Saudi units generally did a good job, not all air crews were familiar with National Guard vehicles and there was evidently some confusion over identification.

Our own troops were not blameless. Even before the battle, as units moved that night to their assembly areas, Qatari tanks opened fire on National Guard armored cars which they mistook for the enemy. Fortunately there were no casualties, but some last-minute reorganization was required. Also that night, in the confusion of battle a U.S. supply truck missed its rendezvous with a small reconnaissance detachment of U.S. Marines moving south of al-Khafji. Driving into the town, the supply truck was immediately stopped by Iraqi gunfire. The two American drivers, one male and one female, were captured, giving Baghdad Radio something to crow about. I cite these examples at random to demonstrate that, while a commander can seek to shape the general outline of a battle, he cannot hope to control the hundreds of individual decisions – some heroic, others cowardly, some prudent, others foolhardy – which in the end determine the outcome.

The battle for al-Khafji was brief but very fiercely contested. It was fought more or less simultaneously in different locations and in different modes. We opened the action shortly after 8 a.m. on January 31 with a two-pronged attack: a right axis by the 8th Mechanized Infantry Battalion of the National Guard, reinforced by a Qatari tank company and a HOT antitank platoon, also from Qatar; and a left axis by the 7th Saudi National Guard Battalion. The objective was to reach deep into al-Khafji and destroy the main Iraqi concentrations there. Meanwhile, moving up the coast road, Saudi Marines were to block any southward movement by the Iraqis.

Probing forward towards the entrance of the town, National Guard armored cars soon made contact, drawing heavy Iraqi tank and rocket fire. Hidden alongside buildings or well dug in, Iraqi armor and infantry had built strong defensive positions. Snipers commanded all the approaches. In that first violent clash, National Guard units were fortunate to take only light casualties – one killed and four wounded. About 10 a.m., they regrouped and dug in on the southern edge of al-Khafji.

The crucial question facing our forces as they prepared to renew the attack was whether the besieged Iraqis would be able to bring up reinforcements. To my alarm, I then received a report that an Iraqi armored brigade with about 100 tanks and APCs was racing down the road from Kuwait towards the frontier and al-Khafji. The Iraqis had spread out over two miles in an attack mode. There was no indication of any serious attempt to stop them from the air. This was a most critical moment for us. We knew that if the Iraqi armored column were able to reach the town, our attacking force would be in grave danger. The balance of forces would have been in Iraq's favor.

The Iraqis had to be stopped. The tank battalion and the reinforced TOW platoon of the 8th RSLF Brigade which had been sent to cut the road into al-Khafji were ordered to engage the enemy, and did so with great spirit. After a 30-minute battle, the commander reported that he had destroyed 12 Iraqi vehicles,

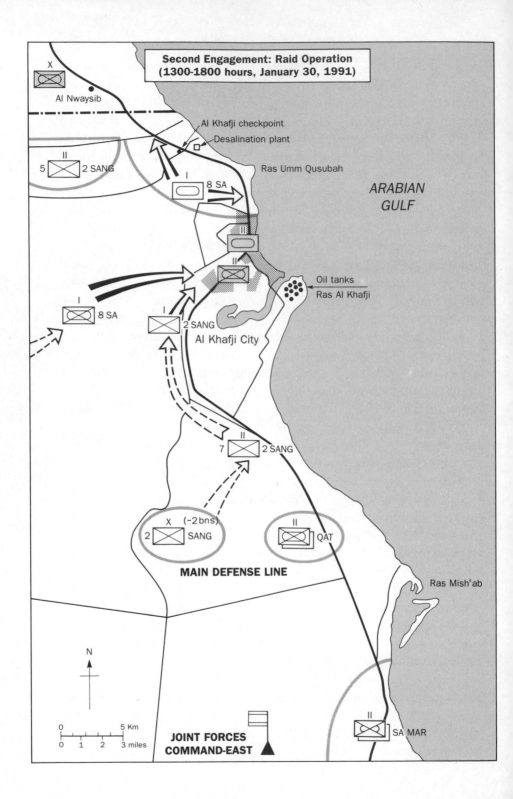

Second Engagement: Raid Operation
(1300-1800 hours, January 30, 1991)

and that the Iraqis were pulling back to regroup beyond the frontier berms. This time Coalition aircraft were ready for them, and inflicted heavy damage, forcing the rest of the column to beat a hasty retreat. When one of our officers, a rash young lieutenant, saw them in flight, he chased after them with two or three vehicles. Unfortunately, he entered a free fire zone which was then being strafed. He escaped but two of his men were killed by friendly fire from the air. He should not have gone forward – but he did. Such are the unpredictable hazards of war.

Freed from the threat of massive Iraqi reinforcements, the 7th and 8th National Guard mechanized infantry battalions supported by two Qatari companies, one a tank company, the other a mechanized company, then broke into the sprawling town where they were harried by Iraqi snipers and faced tank and heavy machine gun fire. Their advance was also hampered by Iraqi artillery fire from north of the town. But for the rest of the morning, they fought numerous skirmishes, advancing street by street, often house by house, taking prisoners and inflicting casualties on the Iraqi defenders.

At one point around midday, when the forward National Guard forces called for ambulances to evacuate their own dead and wounded, Iraqi tanks mounted a sharp counterattack, destroying two ambulances and scattering the relief convoy with machine gun fire. It was at this point, as already related, that a U.S. helicopter gunship hit a National Guard armored car by mistake after destroying an Iraqi T-55 tank.

At about 1330, I learned to my great joy that our forward troops had fought their way through to the far side of al-Khafji and that Iraqi resistance had more or less collapsed. However, fighting in a city is always dangerous and difficult. Pockets of the enemy remained holed up here and there, some not daring to surrender, others determined to go on fighting. Bursts of gunfire continued to be heard. The retreating Iraqis were still directing artillery and MLRS fire at the town. Knowing that all was lost, some Iraqis tried to flee north along a rough coastal road, but they were attacked from the air and lost another dozen tanks. Some vehicles were simply abandoned. With no air support of their own, the Iraqis were highly vulnerable to air attack

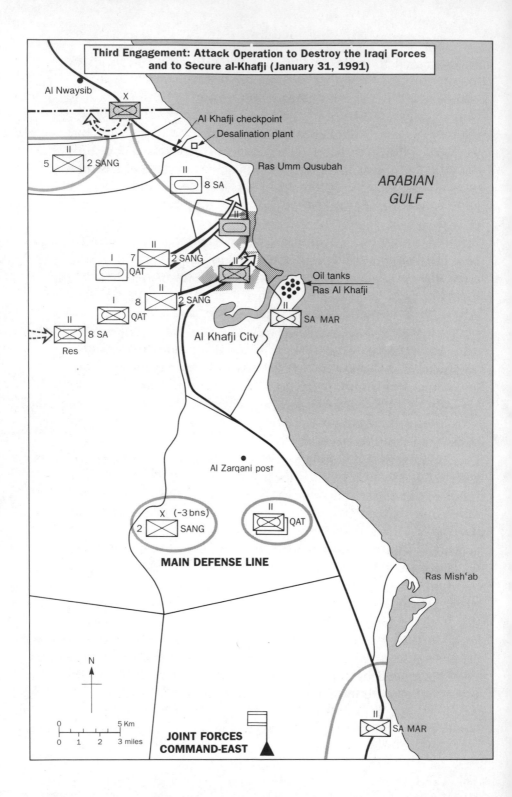

Third Engagement: Attack Operation to Destroy the Iraqi Forces and to Secure al-Khafji (January 31, 1991)

Al Nwaysib

Al Khafji checkpoint

Desalination plant

Ras Umm Qusubah

ARABIAN GULF

5 | 2 SANG

8 SA

7 | 2 SANG

I QAT

8 | 2 SANG

I QAT

8 SA

Res

Oil tanks
Ras Al Khafji

SA MAR

Al Khafji City

Al Zarqani post

X (−3 bns)
2 | SANG

II QAT

MAIN DEFENSE LINE

Ras Mish'ab

N

0   5 Km
0   1   2   3 miles

JOINT FORCES COMMAND-EAST

SA MAR

and appeared to make little use of their Russian 57mm anti-aircraft guns.

But on the whole, the battle had been fierce: the Iraqis had fought bravely and put up stiff resistance until their morale cracked. General Sultan reported to me that 32 Iraqi troops had been killed, 35 had been wounded, and 463 taken prisoner. Eleven T-55 tanks and 51 APCs had been destroyed and another 19 APCs captured. Saudi losses at the end of that day were 18 dead, 32 wounded and 11 missing – who fortunately eventually turned up unharmed. There were no Qatari casualties. We also lost three tanks, one missile launcher and two ambulances. The battle was over and we had won.

With great pride, I was able to telephone the King with the news.

"Sir," I said, "al-Khafji has been freed. It is yours. The casualties are so-and-so . . . The prisoners are such-and-such a number . . ."

He was very happy. He knew I had been in the thick of it. He laughed and said, "I may have been tough with you in the last day or two, but I know you can take it." I was deeply moved.

"What are you going to do now?" he asked.

I told him we were going to interrogate the prisoners. I liked to hear their accounts at firsthand. We were getting ready for the ground campaign to liberate Kuwait and we needed to learn as much as possible about the state of the Iraqi forces.

The King's instructions were very specific. "Don't forget," he said, "that these men fought us against their will. Before you interrogate them, make sure they take a shower and are given clean clothes and a meal. Don't question them before that." I did exactly as he directed.

I went to see a first batch of prisoners. One of them threw himself at my feet and, attempting to kiss my boot, pleaded for mercy. He had five children, he wailed. He was their only means of support. He had not wanted to fight. I ordered him to get up at once and assured him that no harm would come to him. But I was so moved by the scene that I decided to have no more direct contact with Iraqi prisoners in case my heart was softened.

❧✂❧

Within hours of the battle, the King ordered me to meet the press at al-Khafji to show the world that the town was back in Saudi hands. In euphoric mood, I traveled up with my staff from the forward command post. Our sidelights were dimmed so as not to attract attention. Iraqi flares lit up the night sky, no doubt to observe the movement of our troops and direct fire at them. The thump of exploding artillery shells could be heard in the distance as the remnants of the Iraqi invading force struggled back across the frontier.

At the entrance to al-Khafji, I was stopped at a Saudi Marine checkpoint. The officer in charge, Colonel Ammar al-Qahtani, pleaded with me not to go farther. It was dangerous, he said. I had known him since childhood: he was an exceptionally brave man. He explained that the mopping up of Iraqi troops in the town had not been completed. Snipers were still hiding in buildings and the dead had not yet been collected for burial. At that very moment, incoming Iraqi shells exploded not far from us, while just beyond the town B-52s were pounding the retreating Iraqis, lighting up the sky. The Colonel became almost hysterical. "Court-martial me if you like," he said, "but I will not let you through!" With arms outstretched, he stood in front of my vehicle, trying to block the way. Then, when he saw that I was determined to go on, he suddenly reached into the jeep and, to my surprise, kissed the top of my head, almost like a blessing.

We arrived in the main street of the town ahead of the press party. An Iraqi tank was still smoldering. Farther up the road, I counted five bodies. Spreading out my maps on the hood of a disabled Iraqi APC, I waited for the press.

Suddenly, on the edge of our group, a captain inadvertently set off a small explosion with his boot. I have never seen a man jump like that. Some sixth sense must have alerted him because he was up in the air when the explosion occurred, and he was mercifully unhurt. It must have been a booby trap, but it sounded more like a firecracker. Five of my overzealous guards then pounced on me and carried me bodily in the other direction, an experience a good deal more alarming than the explosion itself. I tried in vain to get them to put me down, but they insisted on running about 50 yards.

Some 40 press and television reporters had that afternoon

flown up to Ras Mish'ab from Riyadh and from the media information center at Dhahran. They were then put on board a bus
for al-Khafji. But they made slow progress and night fell, as it
does very suddenly in the desert, while they were still on the
way. Not daring to switch on his headlights for fear of attracting
Iraqi fire, the driver crawled along, afraid of straying off the
road. Torrential rains had made the desert floor as treacherous
as an ice rink.

But when the journalists arrived I was able to give them a
first account of a battle which made history. This was the largest
land battle fought on Saudi soil in modern times, the first battle
fought in an urban area, the first test of the combat efficiency
of Saudi and Qatari troops. It was also the first battle of the war
commanded by a Saudi prince. It meant a lot to me personally.

Although I enjoyed meeting foreign correspondents, these
press conferences in the field were not always wholly satisfactory
occasions. In a sometimes rough scrimmage, reporters and TV
cameramen tended to fight for position as they thrust their
microphones into my face. The bright TV lights picked me out
as a target for miles around. The next day I learned that some
20 armed Iraqis with a clear view of the main street had been
hiding in a building about 300 yards away from where I was
speaking, and had me in their gun sights. When they gave themselves up they asked to be treated as military refugees not
prisoners of war – a reward for not shooting me!

After the press conference I spent a second night at General
Sultan's forward headquarters and, on Friday morning, flew off
to Dhahran to decorate Captain Shamrani for his exploit, as I
had planned to do before the Iraqi incursion at al-Khafji claimed
my attention.

❧❧

In my view, al-Khafji was a pivotal battle of the war. It was
a turning point as significant as the Coalition's battle for air
supremacy in the first few minutes of the air campaign. Before
al-Khafji, the Coalition's mood was somber. In numbers and
firepower, the Iraqi army still commanded considerable respect.
Saudi troops had never experienced battle. Qatari forces had

never deployed outside their country for training purposes, let alone in war. Had the battle gone badly, the blow to our morale would have been severe. But victory changed the mood of our soldiers to an amazing degree: they had been given a chance to prove themselves and had done so splendidly. They had successfully mounted a major counterattack against a tough invading force. V-signs sprouted everywhere. The Arab troops who had fought and won the battle became instant heroes.

Conversely, the battle robbed the Iraqis of the will to fight. They knew that Saddam Hussein was leading them to destruction. All the captured Iraqis — and we took 463 in less than six hours — told the same story. To quote Tolstoy again: "The strength of an army depends on its spirit."

There were also some important intelligence lessons. The three or four Iraqi incursions across our frontier in the last days of January 1991 taught us that, although the Iraqis could move, they were not skillful at coordinating their attacks. Without motivation or air cover, their troops had no desire to stand toe to toe and slug it out with us. That is why they gave themselves up in large numbers. It followed that collecting prisoners was going to be an important aspect of the coming ground campaign. If our advance were not to be slowed down, we needed to make large-scale preparations for processing POWs and moving them back to camps in the rear of the theater.

The battle had been a triumphant test for Saudi and Qatari units and for Coalition air power. The cohesion and effectiveness of the Coalition were clear for all to see. Our forces were now equal partners with our allies, ready to play a full role in any future battle — and in particular the battle to liberate Kuwait.

CHAPTER XXI

The War to Free Kuwait

THROUGHOUT THE WAR, my public relations director Colonel Shakir Idris produced a four-page daily newspaper called *The Voice of Battle* (*sawt al-m'arakah*). It was distributed free of charge all over the Kingdom.

"When does your paper go to bed?" I asked Colonel Shakir.

"At one a.m.," he replied.

"Hold the press tonight," I said. "Come and see me at five minutes past four. I may have some news for you."

At exactly 0405 on February 24, 1991, Colonel Shakir appeared at the door of the War Room. I was able to tell him that the ground campaign had started five minutes earlier.

He splashed the news across the front page and doubled the print run. He asked me if he could change the name of the newspaper to *Victory* (*Al-Nasr*). I signed the order on the spot.

The choice of February 24 for the launch of the land war was determined by many factors – by weather reports; by the need to bring reinforcements in from Europe (some American units only arrived in mid-February); and by our keen wish to get the fighting over before the month of Ramadan, due to begin that year on March 17. The obligation to fast throughout Ramadan profoundly affects the life of every Muslim, and nowhere more so than in Saudi Arabia, the birthplace of Islam. But to have delayed the war until after Ramadan would have meant fighting in the fierce summer heat which comes early in Saudi Arabia.

391

So a date in the latter part of February seemed the most suitable.

Also important in determining the timing was the judgment we made of the impact of the air campaign on Iraq's ability to fight. Few people had expected the air war to continue for more than a week or two. As it turned out it lasted for nearly six weeks. This was because we did not want to launch the ground war until we were sure that Iraq's combat effectiveness had been reduced by at least 50 percent. It was a point I raised repeatedly with Schwarzkopf. As I have already mentioned, I felt the air planners were giving too much attention to hitting targets inside Iraq and not enough to degrading Iraq's front-line forces. My units in JFC-East and JFC-North were preparing for the difficult task of breaching Iraqi defenses around Kuwait: I made clear we would not move until the desired attrition rate had been achieved.

Soldiers have a neutral-sounding phrase to describe the measures they take to soften up the enemy before engaging him in combat: we call it "preparing the battlefield." In the Gulf War, these preparations were particularly thorough. They included the following main items: the 38-day air campaign to degrade the Iraqis' physical capability to wage war; psychological operations to demoralize them and destroy their will to fight; deception operations to conceal from them preparations for the Coalition's left hook and persuade them that the main attack would be up the coast directly into Kuwait, supported by an amphibious attack from the Gulf by U.S. Marines; finally, an extensive repositioning of the Coalition's major strike forces ahead of the deep flanking action from the west which was the heart of Coalition strategy.

I have given some account of the air campaign in an earlier chapter, but it may be worth recalling its extraordinary dimensions: over 100,000 combat and support missions were flown and 288 Tomahawk Cruise missiles launched against key targets in Iraq and Kuwait.

We had to assume that this unparalleled bombardment had gravely weakened Iraq and profoundly shaken its troops. We had evidence that Iraqi commanders at all levels – and even Saddam himself – had difficulty communicating with forward units. Allied bombing had devastated Iraq's C3 networks. Iraqi troops in the field were isolated, frightened, shell-shocked and hungry, with little knowledge of where their own forces were, let alone the Coalition's. Vast quantities of Iraqi equipment and supplies had been destroyed. Damage to bridges, roads and railways had virtually severed Baghdad's links with the front, so that the flow of supplies had dwindled to a trickle.

It required no great effort of the imagination to guess what life was like for the troops on the Iraqi side of the front. A few deserters had already reported that morale was crumbling and that it was only the fear of execution squads roaming around between the lines which prevented large numbers of men from crossing over to us. In addressing the press, I called these squads "execution battalions." Some American reporters did not believe me, and even General Neal, the American spokesman, would not confirm their existence when he was questioned. But the existence of these squads was established after the war.

The Coalition knew Iraq was losing the will to fight, and yet there were still considerable areas of uncertainty. Our intelligence agencies made elaborate computations of the numbers of Iraqi tanks, APCs and artillery pieces destroyed, but there was wide disagreement over the accuracy of these tables. In spite of our victory at al-Khafji, and the evidence that battle provided of Iraqi demoralization, we still felt we were facing the unknown.

As the ground war approached, a question which had worried us from the beginning was now posed more insistently than ever: would Saddam use chemical weapons? I myself believed he would not dare. He must have known that if he did so an enraged United States would go all out to destroy him, as Secretary of State James Baker made clear to Tariq Aziz, the Iraqi Foreign Minister, at their abortive meeting in Geneva on January 9. As Saddam's own personal survival was paramount in his mind, I reckoned that the chance of his using such weapons was remote.

Nevertheless, here again we could not be certain. We knew that by 1990 Iraq had acquired the capability to produce thousands of tons a year of chemical agents, and that it had the means to deliver them in aerial bombs and artillery shells. It had, after all, used nerve and blister agents in its final offensives against Iran in 1988. Would Saddam, in suicidal mood, spring one last surprise on us, one last act of supreme defiance? We had to take the threat of chemical weapons very seriously, and we went to great lengths to issue protective clothing and anti-dotes to our forces.

So far as I know, no stocks of chemical weapons were issued to Iraqi forces in the field. The Czechoslovak decontamination unit under my command detected no trace of either nerve gas or mustard gas. However, months after the end of the Gulf War, many U.S. veterans claimed to have suffered from headaches, skin rashes, coughing, diarrhea and other mysterious illnesses allegedly connected with the war – and sometimes referred to collectively as the "Gulf War syndrome."

In June 1994, although proof of the existence of the syndrome was still lacking, the Clinton Administration announced its support for legislation to compensate all U.S. servicemen suffering from the "syndrome." In Britain, however, Sir Peter Beale, Surgeon General of the Ministry of Defense in London, dismissed the existence of such an illness. In a letter to the *British Medical Journal* he wrote that "We have no evidence to support the claim that a medical condition exists that is peculiar to those who served in the Gulf conflict." However, it was reported in November 1994 that over 400 British servicemen were planning to take the Ministry of Defense to court to prove that their health had been damaged.

It would seem that the ailments may have been caused by the tablets and injections the American and British troops were forced to take as precautions against biological and chemical attack, rather than by any Iraqi action. Troops under my command took no pills and suffered none of the symptoms of the so-called syndrome, although they went into Kuwait and would have been exposed to Iraqi chemical and biological agents had there been any. I had asked our American allies if they could provide antidotes for our troops but – perhaps providentially – there were not enough to go round.

Faced with the possibility that Saddam might use such weapons, the Coalition could take no chances. In the last week before the land war, our attention focused on Saddam's artillery which, following the grounding of his air force, was considered the most likely delivery system for chemical weapons. Eleven thousand artillery rounds and heavy fire from other sources were directed against the breaching area around Kuwait, and especially against Iraqi artillery positions. Hundreds of Iraqi guns were destroyed.

Although we did not have to face chemical weapons, the special suits issued to the troops were to prove useful in ways we had not foreseen, not only against the cold – and it was unusually cold and very wet that winter of 1991 – but against smoke and pollution from the burning oil wells in Kuwait. The suits included shoes, gloves and a headpiece that could be tied in place, so they were totally protective against the elements. To be muffled up in them in August would have been intolerable but, as it turned out, in January and February they provided welcome warmth.

In the early weeks of the crisis, my view had been that we should do nothing to taunt or provoke Saddam. I recommended that, while we built up our strength, we should be civil in our references to him, stressing that we were merely defending our country and that, if he did not threaten us, we would not attack him. But by October, our defenses looked impregnable and, by November, I had almost come to wish that he would attack because it would have cost him dear. My tone changed at that time, and my public references to him became more aggressive.

I began to pay particular attention to psychological operations (or "psyops," for short) to demoralize Iraqi commanders and troops and encourage them to surrender. Psyops served two purposes: an obvious military one, but also a bid to save Iraqi lives. We had no interest in the wholesale slaughter of our brothers in Iraq. Such psychological operations had never been attempted in the Kingdom before. A joint team of Saudi, American and Egyptian experts was set up, led by Major General Muhammad 'Id al-Otaibi. I held several meetings with them and was impressed by their ingenuity. However, in the event, the ground war was over so quickly that there was little time to see the full fruit of their efforts. For instance, we decided that every front-line unit under my command should be issued with loudspeakers and amplifiers, so that the Iraqis could be called upon

to surrender before being attacked. It was an attempt to minimize Iraqi losses. We bought a great deal of equipment and
issued it to the troops but, as the campaign moved fast, it was
not put to much use.

In a more ambitious effort, we set up a number of radio
stations run by Iraqi opposition groups, with help from our own
intelligence behind the scenes. One station broadcasting from
Riyadh proved very popular. We secured Syrian permission to
establish a relay station on their territory. Other relay stations
were positioned around Iraq – on Bahrain, in Turkey, on our
own coast north of Jubail. Our intelligence did a great job beam-
ing these broadcasts to Iraq, but I suspected that few Iraqi troops
had radio sets to listen to. At one point the thought crossed my
mind that we should drop transistor radios over their lines, but
there was no time to put the idea into effect.

Undoubtedly the best psyops weapons we produced were the
leaflets dropped by the million over Iraq and Kuwait. Some told
Iraqi soldiers exactly where the allies intended to bomb and
urged them to flee. Others warned them to stay away from their
equipment. All called on them to surrender. Working on their
own and without my knowledge, the Americans produced some
early leaflets, but the Arab members of the team considered the
wording too threatening and not in tune with Arab sentiment.
The leaflets had a negative effect. I then insisted that the messages should stress the warm welcome our Arab brothers could
expect in the Kingdom if they gave themselves up. Considering
the hell Iraqi troops were enduring, it was not surprising that
huge numbers responded positively to our promise of food,
water, and medical treatment. A gifted Saudi cartoonist, al-
Wuhaibi, drew the sketches on the leaflets to illustrate our message. The most effective and by far the most popular of the
leaflets was designed like a safe conduct pass signed by me:
thousands of Iraqis, clutching the pass and holding it high,
surrendered to the Coalition as soon as the ground war was
launched.

The deception operations to get the Iraqis to focus on the
southern and eastern approaches to Kuwait, rather than on the
undefended open desert to the west, were largely the work of
the Americans and proved extremely effective. There were feints

by Special Forces up the Wadi al-Batin – the wide valley running along Kuwait's western border with Iraq; noisy tank movements broadcast from the vicinity of the coast road to suggest the Marine divisions were still there; naval bombardments of the Kuwaiti coast and other supporting activities to threaten Basrah; above all, aggressive demonstrations by boatloads of U.S. Marines offshore, suggesting that amphibious landings were imminent.

Iraqi defenses were overwhelmingly static and heavily weighted towards the south and east. It was clear that the Iraqis were convinced the Coalition would attack up the coast road, up the Wadi al-Batin and from the sea. That was where we wished to pin down their forces. Of the 43 Iraqi divisions committed to the Kuwaiti theater, six guarded the northern exit of the Wadi, an equal number the approaches to the coast road, and a dozen took up heavily fortified defensive positions facing the sea. Armored reserve divisions arrayed in depth behind dug-in infantry were poised to counterattack in these directions.

I contributed to the deception plan by declaring quite early on that the main battle would be decided on Kuwaiti, and not on Iraqi, territory. In making such statements, my aim was not only to fox the Iraqis but to reassure the Arab forces under my command that they would not find themselves in the role of an occupying army on Iraqi soil. The Syrians had told me very clearly, and the Egyptians somewhat more tactfully, that they could not consider entering Iraq, nor indeed could any Arab troops including our own.

The final phase in the preparation of the battlefield was the vast repositioning of Coalition armies which took place, as I have mentioned, under cover of the air campaign. More than 250,000 American, British, and French troops, with some 60,000 wheeled and tracked vehicles and supplies to match, moved to their attack positions in the west far beyond Iraq's defense lines on the Kuwaiti–Saudi border.

From left to right, the Coalition front was nearly 350 miles wide.

On the far left flank was the French light division, the speed and flexibility of which I had come to appreciate when it was

under my command during Desert Shield. It had now transferred to the operational control of the American XVIIIth Airborne Corps, of which the principal strike forces were the highly
mobile 82nd Airborne and 101 Air Assault Divisions, as well as
the redoubtable 24th Infantry Division which was attached to
the Corps. The mission of this Corps was to drive deep and fast
into western Iraq, so as to control Iraq's lines of communication
along the Euphrates River, notably Highway 8, and bottle up its
forces in the Kuwait Theater of Operations. Able neither to
retreat nor to be resupplied, they would then be at the mercy
of the Coalition. That, at least, was the plan. As will be seen,
however, things did not work out quite so neatly.

In the center of the front were the armored and infantry divisions of the U.S. VIIth Corps, reinforced by Britain's First Armored Division – in all some 1,300 tanks, the most powerful
armored concentration in the history of warfare. This steel fist
was to punch north into Iraq and then, wheeling sharply east
in a left hook, was to destroy Iraq's elite Republican Guard
forces. In navigating at speed through the open, nearly featureless desert, XVIIIth and VIIth Corps had the inestimable benefit
of the Global Positioning System, a small device which, with
help from satellites, allowed units to determine their position to
within a few feet.

On the right of the front, immediately south and west of
Kuwait, were my own forces of JFC-North and JFC-East, positioned on either side of two U.S. Marine Corps divisions
reinforced by an armored brigade. JFC-North comprised one
Egyptian Corps and one Syrian division, together with their
rangers and Special Forces, and two Royal Saudi Land Forces
brigades, reinforced by a Kuwaiti brigade. JFC-East comprised
the 2nd Saudi National Guard Brigade, the 8th and 10th RSLF
Brigades, and smaller units from Qatar, Oman, Bahrain, the
Emirates and Kuwait.

Together with the U.S. Marines, our joint role was to breach
Iraqi defense lines around Kuwait, encircle and destroy Iraqi
forces and liberate Kuwait City. Although ours was described as
a supporting role, intended to fix Iraqi operational forces in place
and distract attention from the main attack by VIIth Corps, we
in fact assumed responsibility for attacking just where Iraq

expected us to attack and where we faced the most formidable of its fortifications.

These fortifications were modeled on those that had served Iraq well in its war against Iran. Facing us along the border were two defensive belts, one three to seven miles inside Kuwait, the other some 15 miles farther in. Each of these belts was composed of dug-in infantry strongpoints behind elaborate obstacles of barbed wire, antitank ditches, trenches filled with oil and mine-fields 100 to 200 yards deep. The Iraqi strategy, as it had been in the Iraq–Iran war, was to trap any attacking force in kill zones between the two belts. Armored reserves stood ready to counterattack any force that managed to breach the second defensive belt.

Evidently, the Iraqis had little or no knowledge of Coalition deployments. Without an air force, they were "blind." They appear not even to have detected the enormous volume of traffic heading west along the Tapline road only a few miles from their frontier. At the start of the crisis, they had attempted to infiltrate agents into the Kingdom among the flood of Kuwaiti refugees, but most if not all of these had been picked up by our security. The Iraqi military attaché in Riyadh, Brigadier General Muhammad Jasem al-Habash, had remained at his post until late August 1990, as had the Jordanian and Yemeni military attachés. The Iraqi was a very shrewd man. I received an intelligence report (derived no doubt from reading his communications) that he had advised Baghdad not to release the Western hostages – that is to say, the large numbers of foreigners whom Saddam was holding against their will in Iraq – but to disperse them to strategic sites around the country. Had Saddam taken this advice, the war might have taken a different turn. Certainly, it might have been politically difficult to launch the strategic air campaign, the Coalition's war-winning ace. I wondered why Saddam had chosen a top man as his attaché in the Kingdom. Was it a clue that he had been planning an offensive long before his invasion of Kuwait?

Because he was being closely watched, the Iraqi could not

move about very much. But I then received a report that his
Jordanian colleague was being particularly active. He was dash-
ing about asking questions and collecting information about the
location of Coalition forces and command posts. We suspected
that Jordan was passing this information on to Iraq. I recommended to Prince Sultan that these two defense attachés be
expelled. Wise as ever, Prince Sultan's first concern was to bring
home from Baghdad our military attaché and his family. The
Saudi government then decided to expel the Iraqi attaché in the
belief that this would give the Jordanian a warning, because at
this juncture we did not want an open quarrel with Amman. But
when further evidence was received of the Jordanian's spying,
I repeated my recommendation. Prince Sultan discussed the
matter with King Fahd and, within 24 hours, the Jordanian
was out.

On another occasion, shortly before the air war, we captured
an Iraqi Special Forces agent at Hafr al-Batin who pretended to
be a refugee from Kuwait. He was equipped with a radio transmitter with which he was sending messages to Baghdad.
Attempting to play him back against the Iraqis, we instructed
him to continue his transmissions under our direction. We
moved him around the country, feeding him tidbits of misinfor-
mation to relay back. But he was tough and well-trained. Not
long after his capture, he broke away from his guards and,
throwing himself into the sea, tried to make his escape. A guard
spotted him swimming away into the Gulf, opened fire and killed
him.

Clearly, we knew a great deal more about Iraq's forces than
Saddam knew about ours. Nevertheless, we too had our blind
spots. There was, for example, little agreement inside the
Coalition about how many Iraqi troops were deployed in the
Kuwait Theater of Operations. This was to be the subject of
much debate and controversy after the war. Intelligence analysts
had come up with a figure of 547,000. As I understand it, this
estimate of Iraqi troop strength was arrived at by multiplying
the number of Iraqi divisions known to be in the theater by the
number of troops an Iraqi division was supposed to have – or
had had in the Iraq–Iran war. However, postwar research has
suggested that these intelligence estimates were hugely inflated,

and that Iraqi forces at the start of the ground war may have
numbered no more than 183,000.*

Not knowing how many Iraqis were there, we still expected
a stiff fight. The prospect of breaching Iraq's elaborate defense
lines and then perhaps of having to recapture Kuwait City in
house-to-house fighting was a daunting one.

My forward commander, Major General Sultan 'Adi al-
Mutairi (who had distinguished himself in the battle for al-
Khafji) was understandably concerned when he studied the
minefields, trenches and tank traps facing our forces. We were
desperately short of mine-clearing, breaching and other equipment. The U.S. Marines on our left flank were stronger and
better equipped. At one of his meetings with Lieutenant General
Walter Boomer, the U.S. Marine Corps Commander, Major General Sultan had asked what level of casualties he might expect
from a breaching operation against Iraq's lines. To his horror,
Boomer had replied that, judging from his engineers' reports,
casualties could be high. Major General Sultan was equally perturbed to learn that the Marines could not spare any of their
specialized mine plows and mine rollers.

Earlier, Schwarzkopf had conveyed to me offers of help from
Marine field commanders. He suggested that, because of our
shortage of breaching equipment and to minimize casualties, the
Marines could go in first and cut a path through Iraqi defenses,
and my Joint Forces could then follow along behind. I told him
there was no way I could accept that. Our Saudi forces would
have to go in first. Breaching was a job we had to do for ourselves. If, however, the U.S. Marines wished to follow in our
tracks, we would have no objection!

To prepare for the task ahead, we immediately put together
two Saudi engineering battalions. For weeks in the desert, these

* See Les Aspin and William Dickenson of the U.S. House of Representatives
Committee on Armed Services, *Defense for a New Era: Lessons of the Gulf War*, U.S.
Government Printing Office, Washington DC, 1992, p. 33. Les Aspin, who was
later to serve briefly as Bill Clinton's Secretary of Defense, and William Dickenson
arrived at their figure of 183,000 by subtracting from 547,000 the following:
185,000 (number by which Iraqi units were understrength), 153,000 (desertions),
17,000 (injured in the air war), and 9,000 (killed in the air war). As these figures
were themselves "guesstimates," Iraqi troops in the KTO may have been even
fewer than 183,000.

units trained under the most realistic conditions, including live mines and booby traps. Barriers were erected similar to the ones built by the Iraqis, and my troops made two practice daytime crossings and one at night. To strengthen the breaching team, I attached a Syrian engineering battalion to my Saudi forces, and scoured the world for breaching equipment. We bought some useful machines from Egypt and Turkey.

Just days before the ground war, the U.S. Marines on our left flank moved a little farther west to positions closer to the Al-Jaber airfield in Kuwait which was the first objective assigned to them. But this move opened up a 30-mile gap between their right flank and the left flank of JFC-East. Major General Sultan feared that, if the Iraqis still had any will to fight, they might seize the chance to attack through the gap and turn our flank. However, when he raised the matter with Lieutenant General Boomer, he learned that the Marines had no men or air assets to spare to defend this area, nor could they provide close air support for our units on their move up the coast towards Kuwait. It seemed a replay of the problems we had faced at the start of the battle for al-Khafji. I had to intervene with Schwarzkopf and Horner to make sure air support was made available.

I mention these details to illustrate the point that, whatever intelligence the Americans may have obtained about Iraqi combat effectiveness before the start of the ground campaign, this intelligence was not passed down fast enough to the people who needed it most. Front-line commanders had little hard information about the effects of the air campaign on the Iraqi troops facing them, and feared the worst. Both Major General Sultan and I were deeply worried at the thought of sending men to die in the minefields. I reckoned we might lose more than 200 men. As I have said, the mission assigned to us seemed far more dangerous than that, say, of XVIIIth or VIIth Corps which, with helicopters and tanks, were going to leapfrog and storm into relatively undefended open desert.

Four days before the attack, because we were receiving confusing reports of the state of Iraqi defenses, we decided to send forward into Iraqi positions a strong patrol of tanks, artillery, Special Forces and engineers. About eight miles inside Kuwait, our patrol encountered minefields and tank traps. Although they came under artillery fire, one of our engineer officers with a single platoon of 30 men started lifting mines by hand and managed to open a 30-yard gap to the end of the minefield – a distance of about 150 yards. They recorded the position on video tape and returned to their own lines with 70 mines, to the amazement of the American liaison officers with our forces. The next day another reconnaissance patrol managed to open up three gaps and brought back 600 mines! Working by hand proved more effective than, say, sending in B-52s to bomb the minefields which, we discovered, often disturbed, buried or uncovered the mines, but did not always explode them.

These courageous mine-clearing operations on the eve of G-day were immensely reassuring and a great boost to morale.

At about the same time, one of our units, conducting a reconnaissance-in-strength operation, captured al-Nwaysib, a Kuwaiti border post opposite al-Khafji. It was the first piece of Kuwaiti territory liberated from Iraq. The Kuwaiti commander, General Jaber, asked if he could raise both the Kuwaiti and the Saudi flags there, but I insisted it should be the Kuwaiti flag alone. I sent up a Saudi army band for a celebratory parade and, once again, I insisted that it should play only the Kuwaiti national anthem and not ours as well, as General Jaber had politely proposed.

＊＞＜＊

Coalition forces did not cross the line into Iraqi-held territory at the same moment: the launch of the land war was phased or sequenced. At 4 a.m. on G-day, February 24, the U.S. Marines immediately to our west started breaching Iraqi lines. At the same time, my own forces in JFC-East cut six lanes through Iraqi defenses in their sector south of Kuwait, while the 2nd Saudi National Guard Brigade advanced up the coastal highway to al-Khafji with the mission of defending the city. Our right flank facing the sea was protected by a battalion of Saudi Marines, commanded by Colonel Ammar al-Qahtani. Nearly 300 miles away on the western flank of the front, the French light division, together with the U.S. 82nd Airborne and 101st Air Assault divisions, surged forward on their wide flanking movement to cut the Euphrates lines of communication and close Iraq's escape route.

The main attack in the center by the U.S. VIIth Corps and the British armored division was not due to begin until 24 hours later, at G+1, at the same time as the attack by my Egyptian, Saudi, Kuwaiti and Syrian forces in JFC-North.

My JFC-East troops and the U.S. Marines to their left penetrated the first Iraqi defense line fairly rapidly without encountering significant opposition. But, by mid-morning on February 24, finding themselves temporarily trapped between the two barriers, they were understandably concerned that the Iraqis would target them with artillery, or that they might be caught by an Iraqi armored attack, either from the east or the west. Should they go ahead and attack the second barrier? A critical element in that decision was aviation support. They had to know whether the Iraqis were concentrating for a counterattack.

At that time of the year, the wind normally blows from the northwest to the southeast, and the sky is usually clear. But on the day of the attack, it rained heavily. The sky was overcast. In addition, dark clouds of smoke from the burning oil wells in Kuwait reduced visibility to 100 yards. My forces and the U.S. Marines contemplated the prospect of having to make a blind attack against a numerically superior enemy. American intelligence was reporting that we faced anything from nine to eleven Iraqi divisions. These were the circumstances in which we had to make a quick decision that morning whether or not to move against the second barrier.

Suddenly the wind shifted direction and started to blow from southeast to northwest. Within an hour, visibility improved dramatically. Coalition aircraft, waiting above the battlefield, suddenly had a clear field of vision and attacked Iraqi positions with great ferocity. Acrid smoke, poisonous fumes from burning oil, all the noxious vapors of the battlefield were blown away from our lines. I knew that even if Saddam were now to use chemical weapons, the change in the wind direction would protect my forces and expose his. I felt at that moment that God was on our side, and I was overwhelmed by an immense feeling of relief. But, if it had not been for that change in the wind that morning, both the U.S. Marines and my own forces could have been in serious trouble.

Both psychologically and physically, it must have been terrible to be on the receiving end of Coalition air power. From the start of the war the dilemma facing Iraqi troops was acute: they got hit if they stayed in their fortifications, they got hit if they fired their heavy guns, they got hit if they moved, and they got hit by Iraqi execution squads if they tried to cross over to us.

Our troops pressed forward and were through the second barrier before nightfall on the 24th. They faced Iraqi artillery fire, but, with only a few exceptions, Iraqi infantry surrendered as our forces approached their positions. This pattern was repeated the next day. Although some small engagements were fought, fears of a major Iraqi counterattack evaporated. Instead, handling the large number of prisoners and escorting them to the rear became a major problem, slowing our advance. It was clear that the 38-day air campaign had done far more damage than we had imagined. There was very little fight left in the Iraqi divisions facing our troops. Indeed, they must have realized that the war was over.

Around midnight on February 25 — in possibly his only sensible decision of the crisis — Saddam ordered his troops to withdraw from Kuwait. But by this time they were already in full flight.

It has often been said that no one hates war more than the soldiers who have to wage it. One has to experience it at first-hand to appreciate its full obscenity. For me, visiting badly burned troops in the hospital some weeks later — such as Sergeant Yahya Ahmad Muhammad al-Bariqi of the Engineer Corps who lost his eyes and his hands — brought home the horror of it, and the supreme courage of those who endured it.

❖➤✕❖

The unexpectedly rapid advance into Kuwait by my forces and the U.S. Marines disrupted the timetable for the ground campaign. The main attack by VIIth corps had been due to begin at G+1, at the same time as that of the Egyptians, Saudis and Kuwaitis of JFC-North. But the speed of our attack made clear

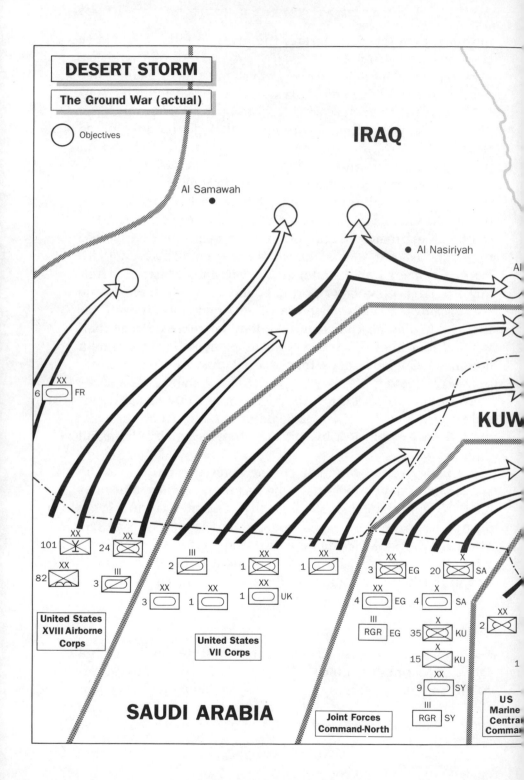

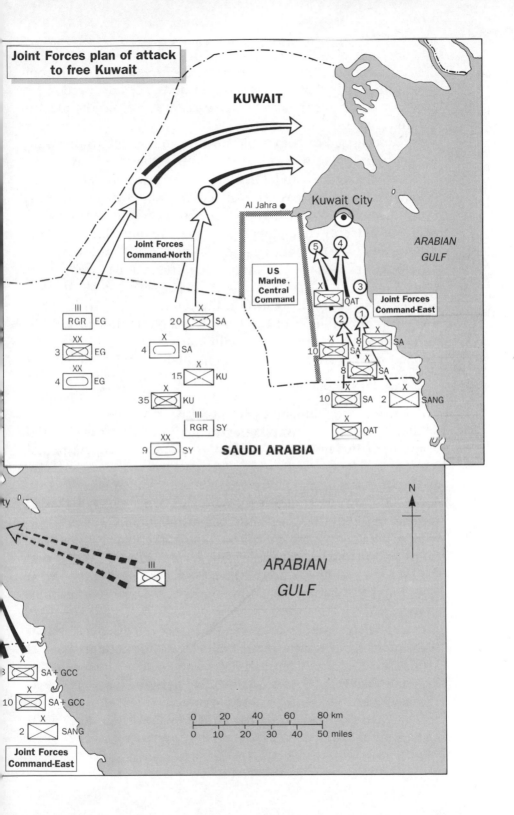

Joint Forces plan of attack to free Kuwait

KUWAIT

Al Jahra •

Kuwait City

ARABIAN GULF

Joint Forces Command-North

US Marine Central Command

Joint Forces Command-East

III RGR EG

X 20 SA

X 4 SA

X QAT

XX 3 EG

XX 4 EG

X 15 KU

X 35 KU

X 8 SA

X 8 SA

X 10 SA

X SA

III RGR SY

X 10 SA

X 2 SANG

XX 9 SY

X QAT

SAUDI ARABIA

N

ARABIAN

GULF

III

X SA + GCC

X 10 SA + GCC

X 2 SANG

Joint Forces Command-East

| 0 | 20 | 40 | 60 | 80 km |
| 0 | 10 | 20 | 30 | 40 | 50 miles |

that our original timetable had to be compressed. Schwarzkopf saw immediately that the main attack had to be advanced if the Coalition were to exploit its early successes. He put the idea to me and I agreed.

So we changed the timetable for the main attack from 4 a.m. on February 25 to 4 p.m. on the 24th – that is to say by 12 hours. Schwarzkopf and I issued the relevant orders to our respective forces – and waited for action. But nothing happened. Nothing moved. We had come face to face with the practical reality of suddenly changing the schedule of a huge fighting force.

For a main force to move at a planned time – referred to as "H-Hour" in military parlance – requires a long checklist of steps, ranging from sending out reconnaissance patrols, to confirming the supply of food, fuel and ammunition, to insuring the physical condition of the troops. It is very difficult for any army to compress this list of preliminary steps.

I had to deal with Major General Salah Halabi, Commander of the Egyptian Corps, and Schwarzkopf had to contend with Major General Fred Franks, Commander of VIIth Corps. In a peculiar way, the difficulties we faced were similar.

I had heard that Schwarzkopf was not on easy terms with Fred Franks. The two men were very different, in fact temperamental opposites: Schwarzkopf was big, extroverted and given to noisy explosions of temper; Franks was quiet and academic, a thinking general. He was from America's European army which had been trained to fight the giant Russian army. Before moving, he wanted to be sure that all his supplies were in place and that there was no possibility of an enemy counterattack. But fighting the Iraqis, then more concerned with saving their skin than with stopping the Coalition, called for speed and daring, rather than caution.

Once Desert Shield was in place, Major General Salah Halabi had replaced the more politically astute Major General Muhammad Bilal as Commander of the Egyptian forces. Major General Halabi was a well-qualified soldier who, back in Egypt, had commanded the 2nd Field Army, a force of some four or five divisions. He understood his mission in Saudi Arabia, had carefully trained his troops and appeared anxious to perform well.

Halabi was worried about the obstacles facing his front, in particular the oil-filled trenches which the Iraqis had set alight. He wanted to minimize casualties and he was concerned about the possibility of an Iraqi counterattack. So he moved slowly.

In those tense hours in the afternoon of February 24, Schwarzkopf hinted to me that he might, to protect his Marine flank, send some forces from VIIth Corps into my sector. I thought at the time that he was bluffing and that he must have known we would take whatever steps were necessary to correct the problem ourselves. I knew the change in timetable had disrupted Halabi's plans, but I demanded immediate action. I did not want history to record that our professional Egyptian forces had not breached Iraq's defenses on time.

Meanwhile, the remnants of Iraq's IIIrd Corps had fallen back in disorder on Kuwait City where, together with the local occupation forces, they grabbed whatever loot they could lay their hands on and whatever civilian or military vehicles they could find, and scrambled to get out along the northern highway. When this huge, panic-stricken traffic flow was immobilized by air strikes on the afternoon of the 26th, and then devastated from the air on the morning of the 27th, it was to become known as "the highway of death," a tragic end to Saddam's Kuwaiti adventure.

After a stiff fight – one of the few serious clashes in the sector – the 1st U.S. Marine Division took Kuwait International Airport before dawn on February 27 and then moved to secure the Al-Mutla' ridge which dominates the roads leading out of Kuwait. Later that morning, with the city thus virtually isolated from the retreating Iraqis, forces of JFC-North entered Kuwait unopposed from the west and linked up with forces of JFC-East which had secured their objectives south of the city. Iraqi opposition was negligible. Iraqi forces had either fled, been killed or gone south in one of the long convoys of prisoners of war. My troops alone took some 25,000 prisoners, and the Coalition as a whole nearly 90,000.

On the left flank of the front, the French, the Americans and the British conducted what were, in effect, large-scale exercises against a routed Iraqi army which had lost much, if not all, of its combat effectiveness. For instance, as they stormed towards the Euphrates, the 101st Airborne Division, the "Screaming Eagles," carried out the biggest helicopter operation in history – but against an enemy that had already given up the fight. On the few occasions when the Iraqis tried to make a stand, they were destroyed by the Coalition's longer-range and more sophisticated weapons, often without seeing their enemy. The French Commander, Lieutenant General Roquejeoffre, was I believe the only commanding general in modern times actually to take prisoners himself. Returning from a recce by helicopter he spied a group of Iraqi soldiers on the ground. He landed and accepted their surrender.

Schwarzkopf and I had hesitated to launch the ground campaign before we were sure that Iraqi troops had been sufficiently degraded by the air campaign. Then came a sudden change of mood. When it was obvious to us that the Iraqis were collapsing, there was something of a scramble to send in ground troops. A cry went up at headquarters: "Follow them! Chase them! Exploit the success!" Taking prisoners and burying the dead turned out to be the main tasks of the ground campaign. I had attached a 12-man Saudi section to each American, British or French brigade or battalion with the express duty of giving the Iraqi dead a Muslim burial.

When my forces reached the outskirts of Kuwait, I issued orders to both my forward commanders – Major General Sultan 'Adi al-Mutairi of JFC-East and Major General Sulaiman al-Wuhayyib of JFC-North – on three military matters which had political implications. The first was the most important. I ordered the JFC-East commander to form a task force made up of contingents from all six GCC countries; and the JFC-North commander to form a task force made up of contingents from Egypt, Syria, Kuwait and Saudi Arabia. These two task forces were to march on Kuwait City from the west and the south and rendezvous at a predetermined place near the center. My directive was intended to ensure that contingents from all the Arab forces were present. I wanted everyone to participate in the parade, so that all could share equally in the honor of having liberated Kuwait and that no one country could later claim to have done the job alone.

My second order was that I barred Saudi troops from entering al-Jahra, a region west of Kuwait City, because this had been the site of a clash in 1920 between the Kuwaitis and the *Ikhwan* of King Abd al-Aziz. Not wishing to revive old memories, I assigned Egyptian forces to this sector.

Thirdly, I prevented Saudi naval vessels from approaching some small offshore islands, the ownership of which has still not been agreed upon between Saudi Arabia and Kuwait. I did not want anyone to think that we might take advantage of the situation.

Escorted by the Kuwaiti armed resistance, which had emerged from underground as the Iraqis departed, our troops entered the city to rapturous applause from its sorely tried inhabitants.

As early as the morning of February 25, Schwarzkopf had informed me, to my great surprise, that he might soon receive an order from President Bush to stop the war. By this time Iraqi troops were fleeing from Kuwait, but farther west the Coalition's battles with Saddam's Republican Guard divisions were far from over and a sizeable part of Saddam's war machine still remained intact. It was then, however, that Iraq's lethal Scud attack on the U.S. barracks at Dhahran had the indirect effect of postponing the cease-fire by a few days. It was not until 8 a.m. on February 28 that President Bush's order suspending military operations brought hostilities to a close – and even then there were some who thought that an extra 24 hours of fighting would have completed and consolidated the Coalition's victory.

The ground war proved easier than we had imagined. There was no comparison between the forces deployed on either side. On the Iraqi side, poorly trained conscripts no better than cannon fodder were pinned down without air cover in static defenses. Before the ground war even started, they were cut off and devastated by one of the most ferocious air bombardments in the history of warfare. On our side was an American army – to mention no other national contingents – which had been built to fight and beat the Russians and which, in the years since Vietnam, had been reformed, even revolutionized, by new battle doctrines and the introduction of an array of advanced weapons systems – AWACS, the Stealth bomber, Wild Weasels, Tomahawk missiles, the Bradley fighting vehicle, the M1A1 tank, the Global Positioning System, and many many others.

On the Iraqi side, supply lines were severed and the whole infrastructure of the Iraqi economy was shattered. On the allied side, the deployment of men and supplies was unhindered by any threat of enemy activity. At the ports, unloading went smoothly with the help of modern equipment. Even forward supply dumps did not need protection.

But perhaps the main difference between the two sides lay in the leadership. Iraq had a leader whose whole perception of the conflict from the beginning was hopelessly wrong. I suspect Saddam believed that we were bluffing, that the Coalition would never attack him, that he could sit out the crisis and emerge with some political dividend. How else can one explain his total inactivity after the invasion of Kuwait? Almost immediately he started digging in! He failed to exploit the Coalition's moments of vulnerability, either at the start before the heavy ground and air deployments, or later in January when Coalition forces were moving into position for the ground campaign. On the allied side, political leaders such as King Fahd and President Bush were totally committed to restoring the status quo in the vital Gulf region, and removing the threat posed by Saddam's Iraq. They were prepared to take the necessary risks and devote the necessary resources to the task.

However, when the fighting ended our victory celebrations were not unreserved. Although XVIIIth Corps had moved fast, it had not moved fast enough. Nor had VIIth Corps completed its destruction of the Republican Guard. The noose had not been pulled tight around the Iraqis. Up to 100,000 Iraqi troops, including complete Guard units, managed to escape to Basrah, and then flee along the Shatt al-Arab to al-Qurna. Others escaped on the causeway across the Hawr al-Hammar. Whole Iraqi divisions simply disappeared in the northeast corner of the theater. On these matters we were largely reliant on what the Americans told us. But as no authoritative statement on battle-damage assessment was ever issued, we were left in the dark. The truth was that we had little precise information about what happened on the left flank of the ground campaign. There was a strong feeling at the end of the conflict that the United States had not been entirely candid with its allies and had kept a good deal of information to itself. But perhaps that was only to be expected in dealings with a superpower.

❖

As soon as I learned that the Iraqis had fled I was anxious to put into effect a security plan I had devised for Kuwait. It was an ambitious plan which involved surrounding and sealing off the city; dividing it into four sectors; emptying each sector in turn of its inhabitants; sending in troops to collect weapons, and remove mines, booby traps and other obstacles which the Iraqis might have left behind; and cleaning up the debris of war. While this was being done, we planned to assist the Kuwaiti authorities to restore essential services – water, electricity, sewerage, food supplies. I reckoned the whole operation could be completed within three months. To provide temporary housing for the displaced inhabitants of each sector, I had had built a vast tented city at al-Wafra, northwest of al-Khafji, large enough to house 50,000 to 100,000 people, making use of tents which we had in store for the annual pilgrimage. We had heard terrible tales of torture and vandalism by the Iraqis and I felt our help would probably be needed. After months of a brutal occupation, the situation was likely to be anarchic. I suspected that vast quantities of weapons had been hidden in Kuwait which could later pose a problem to the legitimate government. But before implementing the plan, I wanted to get a firsthand account of the situation in Kuwait from my forward commanders.

So, overruling various members of my staff who thought I should defer my visit for a few days as the situation in Kuwait, so soon after its liberation, was still dangerously uncertain, I determined to fly up on February 28. However, just before leaving Riyadh for Ras Mish'ab, where I was due to meet a press party and proceed north by helicopter, I heard from Prince Sultan that the Kuwaiti government had declared a state of emergency and that Shaikh Saad, the Crown Prince, had been appointed military governor. It was at once clear to me that my plan would have to be shelved, and that I had better hand over to the Kuwaitis and get my troops out of the city as soon as possible.

My own entry into Kuwait was hardly glorious. In the run-up to the war, I had been in the habit of taking groups of journalists on tours of the theater, usually traveling with a fleet of four or even five helicopters: one for me and my subordinate commanders; another for my staff; a third for my security team; and a fourth or even a fifth for the press, depending on their numbers. To boost morale and also to vary my travel routine for security reasons, I might suddenly decide to change helicopters. If I saw a keen young pilot at the controls of one of the machines, I would say, "I'm coming with you!" And that is what I did that day. Three Super Puma helicopters of the Saudi Navy were waiting for us at Ras Mish'ab. My security and headquarters staff had gone ahead by road. They were to set up my communications in Kuwait and make other arrangements. I followed by plane with Major General Salih al-Muhaya, the Eastern Area commander, and the rest of my staff.

We had only been flying for 10 or 15 minutes when the pilot in the plane ahead reported that he had entered a thick pall of smoke from burning oil wells. The Iraqis had blown up all the wellheads in the Burgan and Kuwait West oil fields and the dreadful result of their work engulfed us, as we too flew into dense smoke. It was black as night. I heard on my headset that the pilot of the first plane was proceeding with difficulty. With no visibility, he was flying on instruments and had decided to return to Ras Mish'ab.

I could see that our own young pilot was beginning to panic.

"Is everything OK?" I asked him over the intercom.

"I haven't done any night flying," he answered with a catch in his voice. "I've never been in anything like this before." Trying to see his way through the oily smog, he made some nervous maneuvers and we were tossed about a bit. I thought it would probably be wise if we, too, landed as soon as possible. The thought crossed my mind that having survived the war I might now die in a banal flying accident.

"Look," I said, "why don't you head east for the coast and land by the road."

But where to land? I knew there were uncharted minefields below. A few moments later, we saw the Kuwait—al Khafji highway beneath us. Tanks and trucks of all sorts were roaring up and down. We clearly could not land on the road itself.

I asked the pilot to circle around while I looked for a suitable landing site, which we soon found some 50 yards from the road. We came down. I was about to step out of the plane when the commander of my military police battalion, Colonel (Prince) Turki bin Abdallah, jumped out ahead of me and utterly refused to let me put a foot on the ground. He insisted on tramping round to check for mines, a display of selflessness which I found very moving. As we had landed at about 12:30 p.m., I decided that the most useful thing we could do was to perform the noon prayers together.

We were then reduced to hitchhiking! Colonel Ahmad Lafi, my ADC, and Colonel Abdallah Suwaylim, my office director, went to the main road to try to stop a vehicle. They were wearing dark green fatigues of the air defense forces, the same color as Iraqi uniforms. Seeing them gesturing from the roadside, and no doubt taking them for Iraqi deserters, drivers would not stop. Passing vehicles accelerated past them. There was nothing for me and Major General Salih al-Muhaya to do except wait. I had no means of communicating with my headquarters or with my forward commanders. For all effective purposes, I had lost my command.

An hour passed. At last a jeep stopped. In it were a lieutenant colonel in the Saudi Marines from the naval base at Ras Mish'ab and an American lieutenant colonel, an adviser to the Saudi Marines.

"Oh my God," the American exclaimed when he saw me. "Is that General Khaled?" For several minutes he was unstoppable. "This is the greatest thing that ever happened to me. I must tell my family . . ." He was so taken by the occasion that I promised to send him a memento of our meeting. Unfortunately I mislaid his name and address, but I hope this book will encourage him to make contact.

More vehicles were then summoned. Climbing aboard them, we headed north, following the signs pointing to Kuwait. It was dark, windy and wet, the air heavy with the acrid stench of burning oil. Eventually, we stopped at a checkpoint manned by armed members of the Kuwait resistance, ragged and filthy from their long game of cat-and-mouse with the Iraqis. I was hoping they would be able to direct me to where my commanders were waiting. Instead, they led us to the international airport where, picking our way through the rubble, we found no one but tired American Marines sheltering from the rain in the main terminal.

Turning back towards Kuwait City, we came at last upon a contingent of Qatari troops near a bridge. When the Qatari contingent first came to Saudi Arabia, my friend Shaikh Hamad, the Crown Prince, sent his eldest son along as the youngest officer in their force. I had thought of inviting him to a meal in Riyadh, but Shaikh Hamad had said, "I want him to learn to be a professional soldier. You must give me your word, as a friend, that you will treat my son like any other junior officer. I don't even want you to speak to him."

To my astonishment, the man who came to greet me when I stopped at the Qatari unit was Shaikh Hamad's son. I was delighted to see him but, remembering my promise to his father, I was careful not to pay him undue attention.

After I had spent a couple of happy hours talking to the Qatari troops, Major General Sultan 'Adi al-Mutairi, my forward commander, came to escort me to his headquarters, and some order was restored to my life after the fog and confusion of war. But on my way there, a worrying thought struck me. I had arranged to meet the international press at 1 p.m. It was now 5 p.m. What sort of stories would they be filing? Would they report that the Joint Forces Commander had gone missing? I started to sweat. But my fears proved groundless. I discovered to my relief that the journalists had been taken to the wrong place and knew nothing of my adventures. For once I was glad that my public relations office had goofed.

Major General Sultan had established his headquarters in a school building in a quarter of Kuwait called Umm al-Hayman, near al-Shu'ayba port. It was there, at a meeting with all the commanders – the Egyptian, the Syrian, the commanders of the GCC contingents, and of course my two forward commanders – that I was given a detailed briefing of the military operations in the previous four days. And it was there, after long discussions, that we spent a cold night. I never knew that Saudi rations – dates, tinned cheese and biscuits – could taste so good. Unfortunately, the Iraqis had been there before us, and had stripped the school of electrical plugs and switches, pulled wires out of the walls, broken windows and furniture and defecated carelessly. Major General Sultan kindly gave me the best room in the building – the headmaster's study – but it had been vandalized too. I learned the next morning that one enterprising Saudi journalist, Abdallah al-Shahri, had crept into a helicopter parked close by and had spent a snug night under seven blankets!

I realized soon enough that, if I kept my forces in Kuwait for very much longer, I would face some awkward political problems. Armed Kuwaitis were everywhere, clearly anxious to regain full control of their state. They were driving round and round the city in noisy convoys firing off guns in celebration. Several people had already been wounded by stray bullets and I myself had very nearly been hit in one such joyful fusillade. It was a dangerously undisciplined situation. I worried that my men might be accused of some misdemeanor. The Syrians were in an area surrounded by Palestinians, and I was concerned that clashes might occur between them. I feared that there might be trouble between my regular troops and the local irregulars.

The Amir of Kuwait had declared a state of emergency, but what force was to implement the emergency decree? For the moment all the regular forces in the city were under my command. In the circumstances, I felt it better to give the Kuwaitis their own separate command before my hand was forced by events.

That night I issued a verbal order – which I confirmed in an official statement the next day – transferring all Kuwaiti units in the Joint Forces Command to a separate independent Kuwaiti command. My units spent the next three days clearing up their respective sectors before handing over their positions to the Kuwaitis. I ordered them not to interfere in any way in Kuwaiti affairs. However, the Crown Prince of Kuwait, Shaikh Saad, requested me to deploy some Saudi troops to defend Kuwait's western border. They were to remain there for seven months. He also asked me to protect some vital Kuwaiti installations during the month of Ramadan (which occurred that year just after the end of the war), such as al-Shu'ayba port, the main desalination plant and the main power station. I also offered the

Kuwaitis the support of an engineering battalion to help them
clear mines and unexploded ordinance, and petrol was brought
in to supply the long lines of cars waiting to fill up at local gas
stations. There was as yet no electricity in the city, no shops
open, no markets. The Iraqis had even damaged the water supply before withdrawing. More than 300 trucks carrying meat,
vegetables, rice, cooking oil and other staples were sent up as a
gift from the Kingdom to keep the city going.

It was perhaps just as well that my security plan for Kuwait
was never adopted. It would have required strict overall control
by a single military commander. Militarily, it made sense at the
time, but politically it would have been a minefield. The
Kuwaitis had no wish to exchange one occupation for another,
however brief and benign it might be. And they were right.

❖⟫⟪❖

The ground campaign brought the Gulf War to a close in a
spectacular 100-hour demonstration of allied military power.
With this action, the members of the Coalition reversed Iraq's
invasion of Kuwait and reaffirmed their commitment to the
existing order in the Gulf. Some critics were to complain that
we left the field before finishing the job but, in any event, the
consequences were profound. Politically, the campaign over-
turned Saddam Hussein's bid for regional hegemony: his preten-
sions to dominate the region were decisively punctured.
Militarily, it robbed him, for the foreseeable future, of the means
to project force against his neighbors. A major attempt to subvert
the Gulf and change its nature thus ended in destruction and
humiliation for its perpetrator. Our war aims were achieved:
Kuwait's legitimate government was restored, while Saudi
Arabia and its Gulf allies recovered that freedom from external
pressure which is a necessary condition for true national independence.

There were limits, however, to our agenda. As King Fahd
made clear, we, the Arab hosts of the Coalition, had no wish to
destroy Iraq's domestic economy or inflict unnecessary suffering
on its population, still less to invade or conquer its territory.
Troops under my command had strict orders not to set one foot

inside Iraq. We fought Iraq only in so far as it was necessary to free Kuwait and protect our own independence. Permanent enmity between Saudi Arabia and Iraq was neither our desire nor our interest. Iraq is, after all, our neighbor and a brotherly Arab country whose important role in our regional Middle East system cannot be denied, whatever the folly of its leader.

It was Saddam Hussein who forced war upon us. We had no alternative but to fight. And so long as he remains in power it is hard to imagine a durable peace between us. He has made too many blunders, told too many falsehoods, infected our relationship with too much hate and stained it with too much violence. Yet my hope is that we can eventually justify to the Iraqi people what we fought for. I trust that, once Saddam has passed from the scene, they will come to understand that we only did what we had to do, and that we bear them no permanent ill will.

Countries participating in Desert Shield/Desert Storm by country, command and casualties (March 6, 1991)

Country	Air	Ground	Naval	Joint Forces Command	U.S. Command	Killed in action	Wounded in action
Afghanistan		*		308			
Argentina			*		450		
Australia			*		1,622		
Bahrain	*	*		223			2
Bangladesh		*		2,231			
Belgium			*		600		
Canada	*		*		2,275		
Czechoslovakia		*		198			
Denmark			*		100		
Egypt		*		33,677		11	84
France	*	*	*	14,600		2	34
Greece			*		200		
Hungary (M)		*		38			
Italy	*		*		1,950		
Kuwait	*	*		9,643		1	7
Morocco		*		1,327			
Netherlands			*		132		
New Zealand	*				106		
Niger		*		481			1
Norway			*		227		
Oman	*	*		957			1
Pakistan		*		6,406			
Philippines (M)		*		156			
Poland (M)		*	*	488			
Qatar	*	*		1,581			2
Romania (M)		*		384			
Saudi Arabia	*	*	*	95,400		38	175
Senegal		*		496			8
Sierra Leone		*		24			
Singapore (M)		*		30			
South Korea (M)		*		154			
Spain			*		1,956		
Sweden (M)		*		525			
Syria		*		14,300		3	
UAE	*	*		1,497		5	
UK	*	*	*		45,300	17	45
U.S.A.	*	*	*		540,331	146	338
TOTAL	12	26	15	185,351	595,022	223	697

M = Medical unit / personnel (military and/or civilian)

CHAPTER XXII

❧✢❧

Failure at Safwan

I N MY PERSONAL VIEW, the manner in which the Gulf War
was concluded did not match up to the way it was waged.
Whereas the military operations were, on the whole, mas-
terly and decisive, the arrangements for the peace that followed
were uncertain and equivocal. They must be held in part responsible for allowing Saddam Hussein to survive the conflict. At the
time of writing, four years after the invasion of Kuwait, the Iraqi
leader continues to oppress his own people and, by his very
presence in power in Baghdad, prevents the emergence of a
coherent security structure in the Gulf, and even the restoration
of normal interstate relations.

The Gulf War was brought to an unsatisfactory conclusion
because there was no agreement, nor even real discussion,
among Coalition members about how to end it. Part of the problem can, in my judgment, be traced back to the Safwan talks;
that is to say, to the hurriedly convened and curiously inconclus-
ive meeting on March 3, 1991, which Schwarzkopf and I
attended with two Iraqi generals at an Iraqi air strip some three
miles north of the Kuwaiti border. I believe the occasion to be
of sufficient importance to merit a somewhat fuller treatment
than it has so far been given.

❧✢❧

Three days before the Safwan meeting, on the night of February
28, 1991, I was in the vandalized headmaster's study of the
schoolhouse in Kuwait which had become my forward headquarters when Schwarzkopf called me from Riyadh on my

secure satellite telephone. Outside my window, the rat-a-tat of gunfire mingled with the raucous blare of car horns as jubilant Kuwaitis celebrated their newfound freedom. I had arrived in Kuwait that morning and my mind was full of local problems. The Iraqis had fled but, as I have mentioned, I was worried about the possibility of incidents between troops under my command and members of the gun-toting Kuwaiti resistance who now controlled the streets, or with the large and nervous Palestinian community which was suspected, sometimes unfairly, of having sided with the Iraqi invaders, and whose relations with the Kuwaitis were necessarily strained. In the prevailing anarchy, I had instructed my commanders to be exceptionally vigilant. I was due to tour the city the next day and I was still half hoping that my plan for making Kuwait safe would be adopted.

"I've just received an important message from the President," Schwarzkopf said. "He wants us to hold a meeting with the Iraqis as soon as possible. You and I should sit down together and plan it."

President Bush had ordered a cessation of hostilities to come into effect that very morning – 8 a.m. Riyadh time on February 28 (or midnight on February 27, U.S. Eastern Standard Time) – bringing military operations in the Gulf War to an official close. I assumed that the President now wished to arrange a meeting at which the Iraqis would formally surrender to the Coalition. I had a vision of a solemn scene like the one in Tokyo Bay in September 1945 when General Douglas MacArthur accepted the Japanese surrender.

But I had, as yet, received no instructions from my government on this matter.

"Has your President talked to my government about it?" I inquired. "I can't discuss or plan anything with you, until I'm told to do so."

"I don't know."

"Unless I receive orders from the King or Prince Sultan to return immediately to Riyadh, I intend to spend the day in Kuwait tomorrow, and proceed with my program as planned."

And this is what I did, returning to Riyadh in the early evening of March 1. It was there, shortly after my arrival, that I learned that the proposed meeting with the Iraqis was due to take place the following day, March 2, and that I was to work with Schwarzkopf to make the occasion a success.

We got together that night about 11 p.m. in the big operations room.

"I'm now ready to talk in detail," I told him. "But I have two preliminary questions: whom are we going to meet? And where will our meeting take place?"

"Let's discuss the location first," Schwarzkopf said. "How about a U.S. carrier? Would that be acceptable to you?"

"No," I said very firmly. "That would be out of the question." To my mind, holding a meeting with the Iraqis on board an American warship would have made it seem like an all-American show.

"If that's the case," Schwarzkopf said, "we could meet in Riyadh if you like, or indeed anywhere else."

"Riyadh or Geneva, for example, would be perfectly acceptable."

"How about a place in Kuwait or inside Iraq itself?"

"We wouldn't mind that either."

It was then that he put to me the idea of holding the talks at Safwan, pointing out that the place had many advantages. It was close to Kuwait, in fact just north of it. It had its own airstrip. Allied commanders could travel there easily and securely. And yet, being on Iraqi soil, it would highlight to the world, and to the Iraqi people, Saddam's defeat and the Coalition's victory.

When we came to discuss the identity of the Iraqi delegation, Schwarzkopf told me that he still did not have any names.

"But how can we consider holding a meeting without knowing whom we are to meet?" I protested.

"Even my government doesn't seem to know whom Saddam will be sending," Schwarzkopf replied.

I found this very unsatisfactory. I told Schwarzkopf we should insist that the Iraqis send to the talks a member of the RCC – the ruling Revolutionary Command Council – so as to project the right political symbolism and underline the reality of Saddam's defeat. We had won the war, so it seemed right to me that we should meet Iraqis of a higher, rather than a lower, rank than ourselves, if for no other reason than to deflate Saddam's ego and help bring him down.

"That's a good idea," he said.

There and then, as I sat beside him, Schwarzkopf telephoned General Colin Powell at the Pentagon to explain my views.

When he put down the phone, he said to me, "All of us agree with you."

"When you say 'All of us agree,' whom do you mean?" I asked.

"Powell, Cheney and myself," he answered.

I was reassured. I thought my point of view had been taken on board, and that I had at least secured a delay in the convening of the talks to give more time for suitable arrangements to be made. In accordance with what I assumed to be my government's position, I had ruled out a meeting on a U.S. carrier, I had insisted on knowing the names of the Iraqi delegation before we went to the talks, and I had strongly suggested that they be of high rank.

On the afternoon of March 2, there were further exchanges between Riyadh and Washington about the proposed meeting – following which Schwarzkopf and I were formally instructed to attend on March 3. We held another meeting in the operations room to tie up the details.

Although the talks were due to take place the very next morning, Schwarzkopf still did not know the names of the Iraqi delegation. Under the circumstances, I did not see how we could possibly go. I suggested that it would be wiser to send our deputies, especially if the Iraqis turned out to be of lower rank than ourselves.

It was at this point that Schwarzkopf's chief intelligence officer came running in with the names of two Iraqi generals. We examined them with some puzzlement. One was Lieutenant General Sultan Hashim Ahmad, the other Lieutenant General Salah Abbud Mahmud. The names meant nothing to us. We did not know who they were or what position they held in the Iraqi armed forces. Schwarzkopf put the question to his intelligence officer but he did not seem to know either. I still find it hard to believe that the United States did not know the identity of the two Iraqi three-star generals.

It was only after I instructed the head of our Military Intelligence, Major General Nasser al-'Arfaj, to provide background information on the two men that we learned that Lieutenant General Ahmad was a deputy chief of staff, while Lieutenant General Mahmud was the Commander of the 3rd Corps – or rather of what remained of it after the devastation of the Coalition's air and ground campaigns.

My own view was that I did not think we should do business with two unknown Iraqi generals. But, not wishing to risk a breach in the Coalition at this eleventh hour, I felt I could not put up further resistance.

"I don't like it," I told Schwarzkopf. "I think it's a mistake. But I have no option but to attend."

With hindsight, however, I still think that had the allies insisted on the presence at Safwan of an RCC member as I had recommended, and had the pressure on Saddam been kept up for a little longer, he would have had to comply – and the face of Iraq and the Gulf might well have been changed for the better.

But the U.S. was evidently not prepared to press the point. By this time, I had the strong feeling that, just as the President's cease-fire had been timed to provide the catchphrase of a "one hundred hours war," so the meeting at Safwan was planned as an exercise in propaganda, a media event of little political, or even military, substance. Rather than a formal surrender, or any sort of public recognition that Saddam had lost the war, it was proposed that we "discuss" with the Iraqis a number of technical problems, such as the release of prisoners of war, the collection of dead bodies, the location of minefields, the separation of forces, all of which could, in my opinion, have been handled more effectively by our staff.

I was left with the feeling that the U.S. was not seeking a formal Iraqi surrender, or did not think one appropriate. I could only speculate about the reasons. Perhaps believing that Saddam could not long survive the punishment he had received and would shortly be brought down by his own people, President Bush and his advisers may have wanted to heal the wounds of war in a way consistent with the "new world order" Washington was hoping would emerge from the conflict. They may have judged that Iraq should be allowed to remain strong enough to defend itself and serve as a regional counterweight to Iran.

Alternatively, the explanation could have been a good deal simpler: the war was over. There was little enthusiasm for more fighting. With the Iraqis in headlong flight, world opinion was beginning to rebel against further killing in what was now seen as an unequal battle. Moreover, the Coalition had taken very few casualties, and the view of our American and British allies was: "Let's not take any more. Let's wrap up the loose ends and get out fast."

These may have been some of the reasons why the arrangements for the Safwan meeting were made in a hurry with apparently little regard for the longer-term consequences.

I should add, in all fairness, that our own input to these arrangements was limited. Once Kuwait was liberated we, and our Arab partners in the Coalition, virtually withdrew from the conflict. When the action moved into Iraq, I personally had nothing further to do with it. My troops were not engaged there. My sector was restricted to Kuwait. In the last few days of the conflict, I had tried to follow the ongoing battles in southern Iraq but I had little intelligence from there and, as I have already mentioned, the United States was not very forthcoming about the detailed results of the "left hook."

There was never any suggestion of marching on Baghdad nor, so far as I know, was the subject ever discussed. Needless to say, any such move was out of the question for the Arab members of the Coalition, and indeed would have been vigorously opposed by Saudi Arabia.

We were anxious to set the stage for the Iraqi people to rid themselves of Saddam, but without our direct intervention. Iraq was, after all, an Arab neighbor whom we had fought with the greatest regret and with whom we would now have to live. At that stage, few could foresee the uprisings against Saddam in the south and the north of the country, and the savagery with which they would be suppressed.

These considerations shaped my approach to Safwan. As I have said, I was disappointed that there was to be no formal document of surrender which, I believed, might have helped remove Saddam. Late on March 2, as Schwarzkopf and I reviewed the limited agenda for the talks the next morning, I tried to draw a line between us. I said that I would raise items within my area of authority, such as the repatriation of Kuwaiti civilians taken to Iraq against their will, leaving to him matters which were within his sphere of responsibility, including the return of POWs and the separation of forces. The latter, in particular, was an issue with which I did not wish to get involved. American troops, not mine, were then occupying a substantial slice of Iraq and continued to confront, and even to fight, the Iraqis. We ourselves had no direct contact with Iraqi troops, seeing that U.S. forces were positioned between us and them.

The cessation of hostilities announced by Bush for February 28 had not prevented a number of clashes, of which the most serious had taken place that very morning, March 2, when units of the U.S. 24th Mechanized Infantry Division devastated an Iraqi column near the Rumaila oil fields, destroying scores of armored vehicles and artillery pieces. Another clash nearly occurred at Safwan itself. When it was chosen as the location for the talks, Schwarzkopf thought the area was controlled by VIIth Corps' 1st Infantry Division – known as "the Big Red One." But, when the Americans came to make the arrangements, they found the Safwan airstrip still occupied by an Iraqi unit, apparently ready to fight! After some angry exchanges with the commander of VIIth Corps who, he felt, had misled him about the situation on the ground, Schwarzkopf called me to say, "We have a problem." The cease-fire ruled out any offensive action to expel the Iraqis, but the press had already been told the meeting would take place at Safwan. What was to be done? To resolve the dilemma, Schwarzkopf ordered a strong American force to surround the area and issue an ultimatum to the Iraqis: "Get out or we'll shoot!" The Iraqis thought better of it and withdrew in good order, taking their tanks with them.

This last development took me by surprise, as it seemed to contradict an understanding I had earlier reached with Schwarzkopf: seeing that the Coalition had already taken tens of thousands of prisoners and could not easily accommodate many more, we had agreed that Iraqi units we encountered would be disarmed and sent home by truck or on foot – leaving their heavy equipment behind. However, the Iraqi unit at Safwan was allowed to withdraw with its equipment, joining the many well-armed Republican Guard units that had somehow managed to escape the American net.

I was due to leave for Safwan by helicopter on the morning of March 3. But, realizing that it was going to be something of a media event, I told my director of planning, Major General Yusuf Madani, and his team to go on well ahead at 4 a.m. to check the arrangements. I wanted him to make sure that Schwarzkopf and I were given equal billing at the talks, that neither of us would be placed "at the head" of the negotiating table. Funnily enough, on arrival Madani found Schwarzkopf's people already there, with the same mission!

Another small clash of egos occurred when I landed at Safwan shortly before 11 a.m., in time for the talks which were due to begin at 11:30. As we came in, I could see that the dun-colored desert was beginning to turn into sparse grassland. On the southern horizon, a pall of smoke rose from the burning Kuwaiti oil wells. When the doors of the white royal helicopter opened, my air force representative, Lieutenant Colonel Ayedh al-Ja'id, told me that the cluster of military tents where we were to meet was situated a long way away, at the end of the concrete airstrip, and that an American lieutenant colonel was waiting in a jeep to accompany me there.

"Where has Schwarzkopf's helicopter landed?" I asked.

Lieutenant Colonel Ayedh told me that his machine was parked well forward, close to the tents.

"My helicopter must taxi up there too," I said, "or I will return to Riyadh." I knew that representatives of the media were there and would witness my arrival, so I decided to sit tight.

After a brief pause, my helicopter was allowed to move right up to the tents where, on arrival, I was met and escorted by Lieutenant General Gus Pagonis. It was one of my last attempts to give public expression to the notion of a "parallel command!"

The Iraqi delegation had been met some two miles outside Safwan and was brought to the meeting in humvees, flying the

After the cease-fire, General Schwarzkopf and I faced two Iraqi generals in a tent at Safwan but, regrettably, this was not a ceremony of surrender. It was a media event rather than a meeting of real political or military substance. Colonel Ahmad Lafi, my ADC, is on the far right of the picture taking notes. My two security officers, Captain Zaki and Lieutenant Sultan, are standing behind me.

Addressing the press after the Safwan meeting, I was interrupted by whispered promptings from Schwarzkopf that I ignored but which caused me some public embarrassment. On the extreme right of the picture with his arms folded is Major General Jaber al-Sabah, commander of Kuwaiti forces.

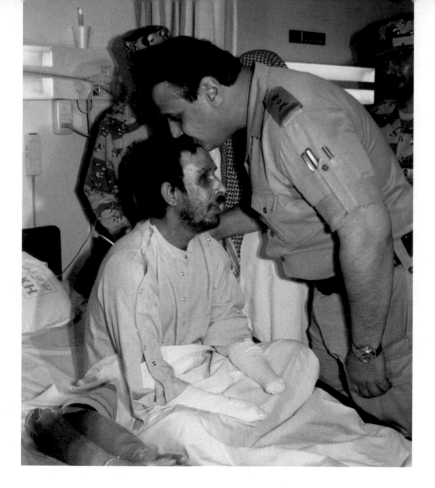

ABOVE: The ugly and tragic face of any war. Sergeant Yahya Ahmad Muhammad al-Bariqi of the Royal Saudi Corps of Engineers lost eyes and hands on the battlefield.

RIGHT: Welcoming home Coalition POWs after their release by Iraq.

LEFT: At Rafha, a model camp we created in northern Arabia for some 25,000 Iraqi civilian refugees, I conferred with Shaikh Shaalan, one of the camp's leaders.

At a simple, but emotional, ceremony, General Schwarzkopf presented me with the American Legion of Merit, together with a personal letter from President Bush, while I presented him with the King Abd al-Aziz Order of Merit (First Degree), the first time this high decoration has been awarded to a non-Saudi officer.

A last bearhug for Norman Schwarzkopf, my companion in arms, on his departure from the Kingdom in April 1991.

With Shaikh Jaber, of Kuwait.

With Shaikh Khalifa, of Qatar.

With Shaikh Isa
of Bahrain.

After the liberation of Kuwait, I toured member states of the Gulf Cooperation Council to celebrate our victory and thank the rulers for their contribution.

With Sultan Qabus of Oman.

LEFT: With Shaikh Zayid of the United Arab Emirates.

Conferring with Shaikh Hamad, Crown Prince of Bahrain (*below right*) and Shaikh Khalifa, Crown Prince of Qatar (*below left*), both childhood friends.

ABOVE LEFT: I traveled to Cairo to thank President Husni Mubarak for the Egyptian corps he sent to our aid. ABOVE RIGHT: In Damascus, I thanked President Hafiz al-Asad of Syria for the division he sent us. *(This picture is taken from a videotape of the meeting.)* Egypt and Syria reinforced the coalition's legitimacy by joining it from the very beginning.

ABOVE: Niger's President Colonel Ali Saïbou presented me with a medal and a warrior's spear when I thanked him for his help. Our interpreter was a French-speaking Saudi graduate of Saint Cyr, First Lieutenant Ahmad Hassan Asiri.

LEFT: King Hassan of Morocco, one of the Arab leaders I most admire, in his Palace in Rabat with his two sons, Crown Prince Sidi Muhammad and Prince Moulay Rachid. Battle-hardened Moroccan rangers were among the very first forces to rush to our defense.

BELOW: At the Elysée Palace in Paris, I had the honor of being received by President François Mitterrand who conferred on me the insignia of a Grand Chevalier de la Legion d'Honneur.

LEFT: General Sir Peter de la Billière accompanied me to Buckingham Palace where the Queen graciously conferred on me the honor of Knight Commander of the Most Honourable Order of the Bath.

BELOW: At Joint Forces Command headquarters on June 3, 1991, half an hour before leaving the command for the last time. With me *(from left to right)* are my deputy, Major General Abd al-Aziz al-Shaikh, and the Director of Planning, Major General Yusuf Madani.

My brother Fahd and myself in 1979. Between us are my two older children, Faisal and Sara.

ABOVE: My five younger children. *From left to right:* Hala, Fahd, Salman, Mishael and Abdallah.

RIGHT: As a proud father with Salman, my youngest child.

flag of the Red Crescent Society, under strong American escort. Roaring alongside their trucks were two Bradley fighting vehicles and two M1A1 tanks, while two Apache attack helicopters hovered overhead.

Schwarzkopf and I had worried about the weapons the Iraqi officers might bring with them: for all we knew, they might have been killers on a suicide mission. So, in order to search them without causing them undue humiliation, we had agreed that we would all submit to being searched – by our own guards, of course. Schwarzkopf was searched first. I then handed over my pistol to my security commander, Captain Zaki, and was searched in front of the Iraqis. Then, with some evident reluctance, the Iraqi party agreed to be searched in turn. They had to walk between a row of sniffer dogs trained to detect explosives. We filed into the canvas meeting tent, ringed by U.S. tanks, armored fighting vehicles and rows of U.S. troops in full combat gear, and took our places at a plain redwood table. Only Captain Zaki and his assistant, 1st Lieutenant Sultan, and two of Schwarzkopf's guards were allowed to keep their weapons inside the tent.

Schwarzkopf and I sat side by side, flanked by his interpreter, opposite the two Iraqi generals and their interpreter, in their dark green winter uniforms. Behind the Iraqis was a row of metal folding chairs intended for the rest of their party. However, as Lieutenant General Ahmad explained, bomb damage to Iraqi roads and bridges had prevented other members of the Iraqi delegation from attending. Behind Schwarzkopf and me sat all the allied commanders – senior U.S. generals, Britain's Sir Peter de la Billière, France's Michel Roquejeoffre, Italian and Canadian generals, the Egyptian Salah Halabi, the Syrian Ali Habib, Major General Jaber al-Sabah, the commander of Kuwaiti forces and many others from the GCC and elsewhere. It was hot in the small and overcrowded tent.

Pagonis had worked all night with a squad of U.S. sergeants to prepare the site and pitch the tents. He was evidently very tired. As our discussions with the Iraqis rambled on, he was overcome by tiredness and the heat – and whoom! He dozed off, fell out of his chair in a row behind us and was on the floor. Fortunately the TV cameras which had filmed the opening minutes of the meeting were no longer there, and his little upset was not recorded.

❖❖❖

From the very first exchanges in the tent, it became apparent that the Iraqis had instructions to be conciliatory: Saddam was obviously anxious to relieve himself of military pressure from the Coalition as soon as possible. Replying to Schwarzkopf's opening remarks, Lieutenant General Sultan Hashim Ahmad – who emerged at once as the main, indeed the only, spokesman for the Iraqis – declared that he had the authority to make the meeting "a very successful one in an atmosphere of cooperation."

Two documents shaped our discussions. The first were Terms of Reference for the meeting which had been communicated by the Americans to the Iraq government on March 1. The second was Resolution 686, adopted by the UN Security Council on the night of March 2, a few hours before our meeting, by 11 votes to one (Cuba), with three abstentions (China, India and Yemen). Among other provisions, it demanded that Iraq:

- Cease hostile or provocative actions by its forces . . . including missile attacks and flights of combat aircraft;
- Designate military commanders to meet with (Coalition) counterparts . . . to arrange for the military aspects of a cessation of hostilities . . .;
- Arrange for immediate access to and release of all prisoners of war under the auspices of the International Committee of the Red Cross and return the remains of any deceased personnel . . . .

With these two sets of guidelines, the course of the meeting was largely predictable – although, as I shall recount, there was one unscheduled item of substance which was to have important consequences.

Schwarzkopf chose to start with the POWs.

"The first thing we would like to discuss is prisoners of war," he said. "We would like to ask you the following things. We would like to ask first that the International Committee of the

Red Cross be allowed immediate access to our prisoners of war that are being held by you."

Lieutenant General Ahmad was quick to agree. "This will be accomplished," he said, adding that this had been, and would always be, Iraq's intention. Schwarzkopf then raised the matter of arrangements for the release of all POWs, whereupon Lieutenant General Ahmad said:

"We are fully ready now to release all POWs at once and in any convenient way for the Red Cross."

General Schwarzkopf: "Are you saying that we should put this entire matter in the hands of the Red Cross to decide?"

Lieutenant General Ahmad: "Absolutely and right now." He was ready, he said, to begin the release at once at any place convenient to the Red Cross.

I then raised the question of Kuwaiti civilian hostages detained by Iraq, a subject which concerned me greatly. "How will they leave Iraq when they are not considered enemy prisoners of war?" I asked.

Lieutenant General Ahmad: "Be specific please."

Myself: "I am talking about the 5,000-plus Kuwaitis that were taken from Kuwait. What about them? Are they prisoners or not?"

Lieutenant General Ahmad answered that we would be given the full number of Kuwaiti POWs. But this did not satisfy me. He seemed to be fudging the difference between military POWs and abducted civilians. I said I wanted to know about the Kuwaiti civilians who had been taken to Iraq by force, and whom I considered as important as the POWs.

Lieutenant General Ahmad: "Once the war started, many Kuwaitis of Iraqi origin chose to go to Iraq . . ." What was important, he added – once again fudging the issue – was the exchange of POWs, and the Red Cross would take charge of that.

I retorted that what was important to us was the number and names of Kuwaiti civilians taken to Iraq. These should be added to the exchange of POWs.

Lieutenant General Ahmad: "For us, all POWs will be released. Those Kuwaitis who are residing in Iraq can leave or stay as they wish."

Myself: "We must know of all the Kuwaitis residing in Iraq.

They need to be identified by an international committee to check whether they wish to stay or not."

Lieutenant General Ahmad: "Yes. The International Red Cross will handle this matter and those who wish to leave Iraq can contact the Red Cross."

General Schwarzkopf: "I think the important point is that anyone who is taken against their will, what we agree to, should be treated as a POW and that is in principle what we agree to."

Lieutenant General Ahmad: "We have not taken anybody against his will, but if there is a case like that then he will be treated as a POW. If it is because some of them are of Iraqi origin living there and they have the right to go back or stay as they please."

General Schwarzkopf: "Of course. Certainly, if someone of his own free will chooses to live there, that is not a question."

Lieutenant General Ahmad: "We will give you the list of POWs and this will be very accurate to the man, and we don't have any other numbers other than these people."

A moment later, Schwarzkopf turned to me and said, "I think on both sides, the question is who wants to go back and who wants to stay. And we probably end up having some intermediary to see that the Kuwaitis have access to the Red Cross." Turning to the Iraqis, he continued: "Then we have agreed that we will let the Red Cross determine whether people want to come back or not, and if they tell the Red Cross they want to come back then they come back."

Lieutenant General Ahmad: "The Geneva Treaty is very clear to us and to you ... We are ready from this very moment to exchange through the Red Cross. Any suggestions outside this subject then we'll have to agree upon discussing the questions."

General Schwarzkopf: "Good. Then I have no problem if we are going to immediately exchange prisoners through the Red Cross."

Turning to me a moment later, he asked: "Any more discussions about prisoners?"

Myself: "When we talk about prisoners of war are we talking about the civilians?"

General Schwarzkopf: "Yes. I believe we agreed to that."

Myself: "What about the Kuwaitis that entered Iraq with the Iraqi army?"

Lieutenant General Ahmad: "I have told you. Whoever entered our land on his own will leave it on his free will. As to the POWs, we will provide you with names and numbers."

Myself: "I just want to emphasize the importance of this point at these talks."

Lieutenant General Ahmad: "I repeat that everybody who comes to Iraq has the freedom to go back. Any POWs who were captured then they will be sent back or released and this will be announced and we have no problem."

General Schwarzkopf: "But everyone who has come to Iraq since the beginning of this conflict will at least have access to the Red Cross to determine if they want to return and, if they do, they will be returned."

Lieutenant General Ahmad: "This is very clear that the Red Cross will be able to see whether they want because we said through the Red Cross, and we from our side will announce it and the Red Cross will very well announce it."

I have quoted in full these exchanges about Kuwaiti civilians abducted by the Iraqis to show that, in spite of our repeated efforts, the matter was not resolved wholly satisfactorily. We did not secure a clear Iraqi commitment to give us the names and numbers of Kuwaiti civilians taken to Iraq: in fact Lieutenant General Ahmad said that the Iraqis had no numbers of Kuwaiti civilians other than POWs. Nor did we obtain a firm promise that all the civilians would be returned. It was to be left to the Kuwaitis in Iraq to contact the Red Cross if they wished to return home – which, in a regime like Iraq's, meant in effect that their fate would to some extent depend on the whim of the Iraq government. Ominously, Lieutenant General Ahmad declared that "We have not taken anyone against his will" – which, of course, was a blatant lie in view of the numerous arrests and deportations of Kuwaiti civilians during Iraq's occupation, including a large group seized and deported only days before the end of the conflict.

Immediately after the Safwan meeting, Iraq hurriedly freed over one thousand internees from this latter group – as a so-called "confidence-building measure" – and allowed the International Committee of the Red Cross to visit, register and repatriate many others. Over 6,500 Kuwaitis, both civilians and POWs, were released. And in the weeks that followed other Kuwaiti prisoners managed to escape from Iraqi jails and make their way home, often on foot, in the confusion following the uprising in the south of the country.

But, at the time of writing, some 600 Kuwaitis are still missing and are still thought to be languishing in Iraqi prisons, although some may be in hiding and others dead. The Iraqi government refuses to account accurately for them and continues to deny that it is holding any Kuwaitis in its jails. Yet, on September 8, 1993, Amnesty International reported that "there is strong evidence to suggest that many people arrested by Iraqi forces during the occupation, and who were subsequently transferred to Iraq, are still being held."

With hindsight, it is clear that, by promising to return POWs immediately, Lieutenant General Ahmad managed to avoid giving a clear answer about the fate of Kuwaiti civilians. We should have forced the Iraqis to reveal the number and names of all the Kuwaitis they had taken. I regret that this issue was not addressed still more forcefully. This may have been due to the relatively informal, even friendly, nature of the talks: instead of telling the Iraqis what we expected from them, we chose to engage them in discussion. I felt it my duty to avoid public disagreement between Schwarzkopf and myself. If I had continued to press the issue of the Kuwaiti detainees, I risked a dispute. Schwarzkopf in turn proposed limiting the discussion because he evidently wished to avoid any angry exchanges between Lieutenant General Ahmad and myself.

Yet I was far from satisfied. The United States was in a position to give Saddam an ultimatum: "Release all these people at once or the war will go on!" But it did not do so, and the opportunity was lost.

Other matters were dealt with more successfully. The Iraqis gave us a list of POWs they were holding as well as of dead bodies, some unidentified, some still unburied. They were clearly astounded when we told them we were holding over 60,000 Iraqi POWs. They handed over maps of minefields in

Kuwait and the surrounding waters. They informed us of the locations of their main ammunition dumps. And they undertook to stop all further Scud launches.

There followed a discussion about the need physically to separate front-line forces to prevent further clashes. Referring to the battle on the morning of March 2 in which many Iraqis had been killed, Lieutenant General Ahmad complained that Iraqi troops had been attacked when they were withdrawing. He reminded us that, at Safwan itself, the Iraqi unit occupying the airstrip had also been forced to pull back in spite of the cease-fire. More generally, he said he had not expected Coalition troops to enter Iraqi territory once Iraq had announced its withdrawal from Kuwait. Very sensibly, Schwarzkopf refused to be drawn into a discussion of these complaints.

Lieutenant General Ahmad wanted an assurance that the line Schwarzkopf was proposing to draw between the opposing armies – and from which each side would withdraw 1,000 yards to ensure their physical disengagement – would not be a permanent line and had nothing to do with borders.

"Absolutely!" General Schwarzkopf replied. "I assure you it has nothing to do with borders. It has nothing to do with permanent borders. It is only a safety measure, and I also assure you we have no intention of leaving our forces permanently in Iraqi territory once the cease-fire is signed."

A few minutes later, he returned to the same point: "You have my word, I swear to God, there is no intention of that being a permanent line at all. None!"

In between these interventions, there occurred a brief exchange between Lieutenant General Ahmad and General Schwarzkopf which yielded the one important point of substance of the talks.

Lieutenant General Ahmad asked if we would permit helicopter flights inside Iraq which, he claimed, were "needed to carry some of the officials, government officials, or any members that need to be transported from one place to another, because the roads and bridges are out."

General Schwarzkopf replied, "As long as it is not over the part we are in, that is absolutely no problem. So we will let the helicopters, and that is a very important point, and I want to make sure that's recorded, that military helicopters can fly over Iraq. Not fighters, not bombers."

Lieutenant General Ahmad: "So you mean even the helicopters that are armed in the Iraqi skies can fly, but not the fighters? Because the helicopters are the same, they transfer somebody or . . ."

General Schwarzkopf: "Yeah. I will instruct our Air Force not to shoot at any helicopters that are flying over the territory of Iraq where we are not located. If they must fly over the area where we are located in I prefer that they not be gunships, armed helos and I would prefer that they have an orange tag on the side as an extra safety measure."

Without further prompting from Ahmad, and just as the session was being concluded, Schwarzkopf repeated the undertaking he had given. "From our side," he said, "we will not attack any helicopters inside Iraq."

As is now widely acknowledged, this important concession was to have dire consequences – especially for the people of Basrah and southern Iraq who found themselves facing Saddam's helicopter gunships when they rose in rebellion shortly after the end of the war.

Lieutenant General Ahmad had slipped in his request without fanfare, as if it were a matter of little importance, and equally abruptly Schwarzkopf had agreed to it. He did not discuss it or seek my views either before or during the meeting. No doubt he should have qualified his agreement by saying that the helicopters could fly only on peaceful missions or should not be armed. But he did not. It was, I believe, a lapse he later regretted.

For my part, I was taken aback when I heard him give the Iraqis permission to fly armed helicopters. I felt it was wrong. But I did not express my views on the spot – for much the same reason that I did not press still harder for the return of the Kuwaiti civilians. I did not want to risk a public disagreement with Schwarzkopf, and I did not know what line my government would take on the matter. Nor did I raise the subject after the talks because there seemed no point in doing so. The damage had been done.

As I have said, on the night before the Safwan talks Schwarzkopf and I had agreed on the topics to be discussed and had divided them between us. Helicopters had not come up. The item was not on the agenda. Suspicious minds might believe that Lieutenant General Ahmad's exchange with Schwarzkopf sounded like a preplanned question and answer. On this theory, the Americans may have expected the subject to come up, and had prepared their response. It may be that, in the reasonably civil atmosphere of the talks, Schwarzkopf felt the Iraqis deserved a concession, seeing that they had agreed to cooperate on other matters, such as the exchange of POWs, the return of the remains of men killed in action, the separation of forces, the location of minefields.

According to one somewhat far-fetched hypothesis, advanced in an article in the American press,* Schwarzkopf gave the Iraqis permission to fly armed helicopters in the mistaken belief that the helicopter forces would lead an anti-Saddam coup. The article even suggested that this miscalculation might have been planted in the minds of the U.S. high command by an Iraqi agent in a London-based Iraqi opposition group who was a relative of an officer commanding Iraqi helicopter gunships. So far as I know, this hypothesis remains unconfirmed.

The talks on March 3 lasted two hours, from 11:30 a.m. to 1:30 p.m. When I shook Lieutenant General Ahmad's hand, I told him I hoped that, as Arabs, we could return to the relationship we had before the conflict. But when we filed out of the tent into the sunlight, I had a sense of anticlimax. No document of any sort had been signed by the Iraqis, let alone a document of surrender. Very little of real substance had been achieved – save by the Iraqis in securing the freedom to fly their gunships. It was a strangely fluid and uncertain way to bring to a close a war which on the battlefield had been so decisive. It was as if, watching a great movie in a theater, one gears oneself up expectantly for a grand finale, only to be let down by a feeble, unconvincing ending. Safwan, I felt, was a mistake.

↝↜

* See Laurie Mylroie, "Iraq's Real Coup: Did Saddam Snooker Schwarzkopf?," *Washington Post*, June 28, 1992.

In spite of the congratulations which Schwarzkopf and I then exchanged with the other Coalition commanders, I believe our inner sense of unease was reflected in an incident which occurred when we addressed the press after the talks. I followed Schwarzkopf to the press podium to answer questions from Western and Arab reporters. An Arab journalist asked, "Do you think that peace has been achieved?"

"Yes," I exclaimed spontaneously. "I take off my war helmet and put on my peacetime cap." And, as I spoke, I did just that.

But the incident I am referring to occurred a moment or two earlier when a Western journalist asked me if any POWs had died in captivity. Interrupting me before I could answer, Schwarzkopf growled, "I would not answer that." I pretended not to notice, but then he did it again – and then again. "I would not answer that . . ." he said when the question was repeated, and, "Don't go into any details on this." To most people his graceless interruptions, delivered through clenched teeth, were inaudible. But CNN, using a directional microphone that can pick up a voice at about 20 feet, broadcast them to the world, causing us both some embarrassment.

Why did he do it? I believe that Schwarzkopf acted out of nervousness and friendly concern for me. He knew that Safwan was not what I had wanted, and he may have suspected that I was none too happy with the outcome. He may have worried that, out of anger or disappointment, I might say something to cast doubt on what had been achieved. But, because of our generally cordial relations, I paid no attention to his interruptions.

One view I have heard, however, is that, with the war over, he may have felt he no longer needed my cooperation. I had sensed that his staff were not keen on my addressing the press at all. Very probably, he wanted to be seen as the sole hero of the Gulf War!

CHAPTER XXIII

After the Storm

THE LIBERATION OF KUWAIT and the end of military operations brought about a radical change in my duties and in those of my Joint Forces Command. As Desert Storm gave way to Desert Farewell, I found myself once again principally concerned with logistics, as I had been at the very start of the crisis. But this time it was a case of winding down rather than of cranking up the great Coalition war machine.

President Bush had given King Fahd an undertaking that, once the war was over, American forces and their equipment would at once be withdrawn from the Kingdom. The Americans were anxious to honor this promise. But, just as they had needed our help in building up their forces in the theater, so they now needed our help in building them down. In this, I again worked closely with Lieutenant General John Yeosock, the CENTCOM Army Commander with whom, in the hectic days of August 1990, I had first planned the Kingdom's defenses, and also with Major General Gus Pagonis, the U.S. logistics chief, who had been designated to stay behind to supervise the American departure.

Some 5,000 American troops were moved out each day – over 300,000 in 90 days – which I believe is the fastest the United States has ever deployed out of a conflict. Over 400 huge ships were used, with enough space for vehicles and equipment to maneuver inside, and once again our modern port facilities proved invaluable.

I am told that at the end of World War Two, the departing U.S. armies left much of their combat equipment behind in Germany. They took very little home. At the end of the Korean War, there was very little to take home. In Vietnam, the U.S. left so abruptly that billions of dollars' worth of goods were left behind in ware-houses – tanks, artillery pieces, armored personnel carriers, whole workshops, and much else besides. The Gulf War was the first war in American history in which the United States took their soldiers and the bulk of their equipment home. Surplus stores, of which there were great quantities, were sold at public auctions held near Dhahran airport in the Eastern Province. There was every sort of building material – lumber, roofing, electrical fittings, tools, plumbing – and vehicles and engineering equipment of all types. Spread over a vast area, these stores and vehicle parks were a sight to behold.

At the start of the crisis, when Saudi resources were being mobilized in support of the Coalition, I had had little direct contact with Pagonis, as he had dealt mainly with my staff in negotiating and concluding contracts for the supplies he needed. But during Desert Farewell, we worked more closely together. He used to come to see me once a week, to tell me how many U.S. troops were left in the Kingdom, how many contracts were still unexpired, which contractors' claims remained to be settled, and to seek my help and that of my staff in solving the numerous problems that arose. To cite a single example, many trucks and buses we had leased for our allies were lost or damaged during the conflict. Some of the buses had gone all the way up into Iraq to collect prisoners of war. Some had broken down or been blown up or had been abandoned in the desert. At one point we were missing 1,000 buses out of the 4,000 we had used. Teams had to be sent in to find them, and if possible recover them, before contracts could be closed and claims met. Each contractor's claim had to be examined on its merits and a decision taken about payment.

The Kingdom itself ended the war with huge stocks of tents, blankets, clothing, vehicles of all types, spare parts, generators, and much else besides, which had been purchased in the belief that the war might last longer than it did. As I have mentioned, Prince Sultan suggested that we express our appreciation to the national contingents that had come to our aid, some from far away in Africa, by letting them take a great deal of this equipment home with them. They had done us a tremendous political and military service and deserved our gratitude. We also allowed them to take away some captured Iraqi equipment. Some just took trophies or samples, others more substantial supplies. These were the legitimate spoils of war.

But it was a source of pride to me – and surprise to our allies – that, unlike almost every other war in history, no black market in military supplies emerged in Saudi Arabia. In the confusion and wastefulness of war, one might have expected goods to be stolen or purchased illegally from allied armies, and then to resurface for sale on the black market, as usually occurs in the course of conflicts. But I cannot recall more than two or three cases of such irregularities coming to light in the Kingdom, either during the war or in the months which followed it.

I was also proud to note that, when we came to inspect the desert locations occupied by our troops, we found hardly a single round of live ammunition left behind. Our men may have lacked combat experience but their care for their equipment was beyond reproach. This was not always the case with our more powerful allies. When we inspected some Coalition locations, we found huge mountains of live ammunition, abandoned and unguarded – tank ammunition, field artillery ammunition, MLRS missiles, even personal weapons and ammo just thrown away as garbage. In the heat of battle, the troops had simply taken what they needed and left the rest behind. We took photographs and videotapes of what we had seen, and told our allies about it. Certain areas had been set aside for trash to be burned, but within these huge dumps we also found live ammunition. There were explosions everywhere. I must record that there were a great many violations of basic security rules. After the war, it took more than two years' work and tens of millions of dollars to clear up the debris of war from grazing land in the north of the Kingdom, so as to preserve the future safety of people and livestock in that area.

⟡

One of my greatest preoccupations in the last months of my command was with deserters, POWs and civilian refugees. When the first Iraqi deserters came over to us in September 1990, I asked Prince Sultan whether we could announce their arrival, but he wisely advised me that it was not the right time. First, we should not provoke Saddam until we were ready to confront him; and secondly, as we wanted more deserters to come over, a premature announcement, leading to reprisals against their families, might dry up the flow.

By November, we were holding some 350 deserters from the Iraqi army. They came across in ones and twos – out of fear of the coming war, out of disillusion with Saddam, or for personal reasons. We took an early decision to treat them more like refugees than prisoners of war, giving them good accommodations, a monthly stipend, and other privileges. But fearing that a number of Iraqi spies might be among them, we evacuated them rapidly to the rear for questioning by Saudi military intelligence and kept them confined in a camp. They proved a valuable intelligence asset, and thanks to them we started to build up a more accurate picture of the Iraqi forces facing us. The tentative conclusion we reached, even before the devastation of the air campaign, was that there was not much fight in the Iraqi army. Other intelligence sources confirmed that large numbers of men were waiting to surrender.

These reports led me to believe that we would need a lot of accommodations for POWs and, to the amazement of some members of my staff, I gave instructions to build camps to house 100,000 men. One camp was built at al-Nu'ayriya, another close to Hafr al-Batin; and a third larger camp able to take 45,000 men at al-Artawiya, an isolated location far from any major city. Roads had to be built to these camps, tents erected, rations stored and water trucked in. Each camp was commanded by a Saudi brigadier general, while I put the whole complex under the control of Major General Hatem Okasi who headed a special department of the Joint Forces Command set up for this purpose. By the end of the war we found ourselves holding more than 60,000 Iraqi POWs – of which no fewer than 14,000 indicated that they had no wish to return home! As I told the international press at the time, our policy was to abide strictly by the terms of the Geneva Convention relating to POWs. They would stay where they were until they chose to go home or emigrate to other countries. In the meantime, we had to process them, provide them with food, shelter, medical attention and all their other needs.

When we first started taking prisoners, I learned that a riot had broken out at one of the camps, so I sent a committee to investigate. I soon realized that the camp commandant (who may have watched a movie about a World War Two POW camp) was overzealous. There were a lot of parades, petty disciplinary routines, and a ban on cigarettes which apparently had been the immediate cause of the disturbance. I instantly replaced the commandant and his team. "Don't be too severe," I instructed the new commandant. "Treat the men decently. Think of the camp as a school, even if it has to be a strict school. Give the men cigarettes, if that is what they want. Place guards around the camp, but inside the perimeter wire let the prisoners have a good deal of freedom so long as they don't misbehave." The truth was that this was a wholly new experience for us. We had never before had to cope with the problem of prisoners of war and we had no precedents to go by.

Many of the POWs had reached our camps in a lamentable state, exhausted, dirty and flea-infested. Most were boys in their teens. They told a dismal story. On the Iraqi side, there had been little food or water. Some had not had a proper wash for months. But, after a day or two of eating, washing and sleeping, they showed a remarkable change in appearance.

I visited one of the POW camps and had a long talk with a group of some 40 or 50 Iraqi officers. Telling the guards to leave us, and accompanied only by the camp commandant and Captain Zaki, my chief security officer, I sat alone with them. These one-time allies and brothers-in-arms were now our prisoners. It was an uncomfortable feeling which gave me no cause for celebration.

I began by asking them if they were being well treated and assured them they would be given exactly the same rations as our own troops. I expressed regret for what had happened. I said it was beyond my control and theirs. I told them that, for my part, I preferred to call them military refugees rather than prisoners of war. King Fahd had ordered that they were to be our guests. He had instructed that if we degraded them, we degraded ourselves.

One of them raised his hand. "General," he said, "we appreciate everything the Kingdom is doing for us, but we would prefer you to call us POWs, not refugees."

I was curious to know his reasons.

"If you call us refugees," he answered, "my family will be killed. I'll give you an example. Some soldiers deserted to your side before the air war. I know one of them. The authorities went to his family. They raped the women in front of everyone and then killed the whole family. So we beg you not to call us refugees."

They pleaded with me not to publish their names or have them photographed or filmed. Accordingly, when I visited a hospital ward full of wounded Iraqis, I dismissed the reporters and cameramen following me and gave orders that any video film showing Iraqi troops thanking me or praising Saudi Arabia should be destroyed. I could not bear to think of what might befall their families. In Saddam Hussein, we were not dealing with a normal man.

⊱⊰

Although we were reasonably well prepared to deal with POWs, I must confess that I never envisaged that we would also have to accommodate a flood of civilian refugees from Iraq. I had not anticipated the uprising in southern Iraq of March 1991, nor the thousands who would subsequently need protection from Saddam's repression. The scenario I had envisaged was that, with Kuwait liberated and Western troops occupying a third of Iraq, Saddam would be swept from power by a popular revolution and a new more representative government would then emerge. I was soon to realize that this was an inadequate analysis.

In the weeks following the end of Desert Storm, large numbers of Iraqi men, women and children, mainly Shias from southern Iraq, gathered in makeshift camps just inside Iraq close to the Kuwait border. Fleeing from Saddam's persecution, they sought the protection of American forces. Some of the refugees were deserters from the Iraqi army and, to our surprise, we discovered that a number of them had been in our hands, not once but twice. Having captured them during the ground war, we had returned them to Iraq in the exchange of prisoners after the cease-fire. But the Iraqi authorities had forced them back into uniform and sent them down to Basrah to help quell the uprising there. Those who had refused to go were shot on the spot. From that front some had fled to us as refugees.

I sent my deputy, Major General Abd al-Aziz al-Shaikh – a pillar of a man – to assess the situation of the refugees on the ground, with instructions from me to provide them with tented accommodations and emergency rations for a few weeks. I imagined that Saddam would soon fall and that they could then return home.

There were about 6,500 of them at Safwan and many more at Saddah, a point farther west. Kuwait, having suffered a great deal from the Iraqi occupation, was evidently in no position to take them in. Their plight seemed desperate because, with the cease-fire holding, the Americans were preparing to withdraw from Iraq – which would have left the refugees at Saddam's mercy.

"We've got a problem," Schwarzkopf said to me. "I've got to pull my troops out, but the Kuwaitis refuse to take the refugees. If they stay where they are, they will be dead. What can we do about them?"

I faced a most difficult dilemma. I felt that we, in Saudi Arabia, should take them in, but I realized I might meet considerable opposition. After carefully weighing the pros and cons, I came to the conclusion that we Saudis had to be better protectors of Arabs than the Americans. I wanted the Kingdom to get the credit for a humanitarian gesture. We had fought Iraq, but we would protect Iraqis. It was the least we could do to try to heal the wounds between our two countries. I felt I had to do it.

So I urged Schwarzkopf to keep his troops in place for a few more days while I made the necessary preparations, and then I asked John Yeosock to fly the refugees down to a hurriedly constructed camp near Rafha, some 10 miles inside our borders. Saved from Saddam's bloody revenge, the refugees were overjoyed. Within a very few days, we had some 25,000 Iraqis to feed, clothe, house and generally look after.

After visiting them, I chose as camp commandant Major

General Attiyah al-Touri, Commander of the Saudi Air Defense 5th Group in the Eastern Province, an officer of proven administrative talents. I also knew him to be wise and humane. My choice was fully justified. When he left some months later to resume his air defense duties, he was much missed. He had won the trust and affection of the refugees. His job turned out to be one of the most demanding and politically sensitive of the war.

I was anxious to create a model camp. With instructions from the King and Prince Sultan, and cooperation from several Saudi government agencies and charitable bodies, a massive flow of supplies to the refugees soon got underway – hundreds of sheep a day, truckloads of fruit and vegetables, tens of thousands of bottles of water, cooking utensils, powdered milk for babies, clothes, blankets, bedding and furniture, even underwear and make-up for the women. A great deal of help was received from the Islamic Relief Agency, an international body with headquarters in Riyadh. In planning the camp, we put up separate tented accommodations for single men, for married couples and their families, and for single women. But these were not neat categories. There were many women who, in their flight from Saddam's bombs, had lost contact with their fathers and husbands; men who did not know what had happened to their wives and children; children who had been separated from their families, and were no better than orphans. There were many anguished, tearful people in that camp.

For greater ease of control and to help reunite divided families, we grouped the camp population into separate "quarters," according to their province of origin in Iraq, appointing in each case a local notable or tribal chieftain to act as leader, and to serve as an intermediary with the camp authorities in solving problems as they arose. Each of these camp leaders was given a meeting tent, a generous stipend, and supplies of coffee, sugar, dates, and fresh fruit to enable him to extend hospitality to his visitors. These centers of authority and influence were a great assistance to us in the harmonious management of the camp.

We also rented a hotel in Riyadh for use by the refugees if they needed to consult a medical specialist or if they needed to call at the visa sections of foreign embassies. With help from us and from international aid agencies, several thousand were in due course able to start a new life in no fewer than 31 foreign countries.

I was interested to discover that among the mass of Iraqi refugees were some 250 engineers, over 100 medical doctors, numerous former senior civil servants, diplomats, teachers, factory owners, mayors and other notables. I held several meetings with them, and we did our best to provide gainful employment in the camp to those who were qualified. But the camp also contained its share of escaped convicts, troublemakers, professional saboteurs and agents of Saddam Hussein's secret police. After making a number of arrests, we learned that some of these men planned to start fires in the camp, poison the water supplies, set one tribal group against another, murder officials and steal the ID cards of notables we had appointed, so that the Iraqi authorities could then identity them and hunt down their families.

We were greatly assisted when one of these informers, apparently suffering from a troubled conscience because of the families he had sent to their death, gave himself up to the camp authorities. He helped us identify several Iraqi agents, including a "doctor" at one of the camp clinics – who turned out to have been a mere salesman of spectacles – and who was in the habit of sending information out of the camp by referring his "patients" to the general hospital in the nearby town of Rafha where they were apparently able to make contact with Iraqi couriers. He was assisted by a nurse who claimed to be his wife, but it emerged that she was neither a nurse nor his wife, but an Iraqi agent. We placed the "doctor" and the "nurse" under surveillance and soon put a stop to their activities.

More dangerous, however, was their "minder," an Iraqi army lieutenant, whom our intelligence had been unable to arrest because he moved around the camp a great deal. With considerable ingenuity, the camp commandant, Major General Attiyah al-Touri, recruited two ex-convicts to do the job, one of them a particularly strong man. After briefing them secretly in his office, he gave them a sum of money, and lent them an ambulance. They returned a short while later with the lieutenant trussed up inside. They had lured him out of a tent by telling him that a sick man – whom he took to be one of his informers – wished to speak to him. He was then overpowered and tied up.

There were many such incidents at the camp, some poignant, some bizarre, some potentially dangerous. One night Major General Touri called me to say that an Iraqi woman with three little girls had been picked up by our guards in the desert outside the camp. She claimed that her husband was inside and pleaded to be allowed to join him. The woman and her children were in a desperate state. What was to be done?

I told Major General Touri to let them in and then to check whether the woman's story was true. They were kept under guard that night. In the morning the husband was located and summoned and the family was tearfully but joyfully reunited. A crowd of refugees witnessed the reunion and wept to see the children racing to embrace their father. It was, Major General Touri reported, a most moving scene.

On another occasion a large group of refugees – some 70 men, women and children – cut a hole in the perimeter wire, and escaped. The camp guards gave chase, soon caught up with them and, after much argument, brought them back in two buses. But, once they arrived at the camp gates, they utterly refused to disembark, and seemed to be in a state of collective hysteria.

Major General Touri interviewed the ringleaders to discover what had prompted such a foolhardy, even suicidal, enterprise. Without shelter, food or water, the refugees could not long have survived in the open desert. To his astonishment, he learned that they had held a séance and seen visions. One of the spirits they had summoned up from the dead had told them to expect an attack on the camp by Iraqi Scuds at 5 o'clock the following morning! The spirit had told them they would die and they believed him implicitly. So they had fled to save themselves and their children.

Wailing and weeping, in an evident state of panic, they refused to leave the buses. They pleaded with Major General Touri to let them go. He spoke to them at length, appealing to them as Muslims to set superstition aside, but they would not be swayed. It was as if they were under hypnosis. Wisely, he decided to let them spend the night in their buses outside the perimeter fence. The next morning the sun rose and 5 a.m. passed without incident. No Iraqi missile made its appearance. As the sun climbed in the clear sky, temperatures soared inside the buses. Hungry children screamed, women cried, and arguments among the refugees turned into fights. It was not long before everyone was happy to return to the relative comfort of the camp.

On my visits, I was struck that the requests put to me by the refugees were hardly ever about their living conditions, but almost invariably about politics. Would I ask King Fahd for help against Saddam Hussein? Why had the Coalition not over-thrown him? This was the recurrent theme of the refugees' demands. As the population of the camp was overwhelmingly Shia Muslim, the notables among them clamored for our help to replace Saddam with a leader of their choice.

There were two main political currents inside the camp. One, led by Shaikh Saadi, consisted of followers of Baqer al-Hakim, a prominent Iran-based opponent of the Iraqi regime. Another was made up of followers of Shaikh Shaalan, a tribal dignitary and member of the Iraqi National Council, an opposition move-ment. We soon discovered that Iraqi agents were attempting to stir up trouble between these two currents. We uncovered a plot to kill Saadi and then accuse the Shaalan faction of the murder, so as to trigger an all-out fight between them.

On one occasion, a 14-man delegation from Baqer al-Hakim, including several turbaned clerics, arrived on a visit to the camp. But, on being let in, their bus was surrounded and brought to a halt by a rowdy crowd, over 1,000 strong, beating their breasts and chanting, "No leader but Hakim!" The bus could neither advance nor retreat, nor could the passengers get out. The mob banged on the windows, climbed on the roof, and seemed in danger of overturning the bus altogether. So overexcited were the refugees, that it was not easy to say whether their mood was friendly or hostile to the delegation inside the bus. As a precaution, Major General Touri deployed armed units around the camp. Eventually, with great difficulty, he managed to get a loudspeaker into the hands of the delegation's leader, who was able to calm the crowd and at last disperse it.

It was only later, after further arrests of Iraqi spies, that we learned that the riot had been deliberately instigated by Iraqi *agents provocateurs* who planned to kill the entire delegation, inflame opinion inside the camp, start a mutiny and bring about international condemnation of the Saudi government.

Once the camp had settled down to something like a normal routine, King Fahd ordained that the Kingdom should provide still better conditions for the refugees. Accordingly, Prince Sultan ordered me to start building a new camp to house 35,000 people on an excellent site some three miles from the old one. I called in civilian contractors and, from the start, we planned it as a model city linked by an asphalt road to Rafha, with proper electricity supply and sewerage, several desalination plants, permanent living accommodations for the refugees, elementary and secondary schools for boys and girls, a major hospital and several clinics, libraries, gymnasiums and sports fields and many other facilities for work and play. Each year we arrange for large numbers of refugees to go on the pilgrimage to Makkah. We earned the plaudits of the press and of the International Committee of the Red Cross who told us that the money we spent on our Iraqi refugees amounted to some 30 percent of the sums which the ICRC spent on 18 million refugees worldwide. The Rafha camp is indeed a showpiece, a five-star refugee facility such as exists nowhere else and of which we are justly proud.

✦≫╾╼≪✦

In handling the media, the principle I adopted was to treat correspondents with fairness and respect, recognizing their right to know, so long as the secrecy of military operations was not compromised. If journalism is the first draft of history, by denying access to journalists you cut off that first draft.

Once the crisis was underway, I came under some pressure to agree to be interviewed live by Ted Koppel of *Nightline*. Although it was my first appearance on camera, it went well, encouraging me to make myself more accessible to reporters. I must pay tribute to Ted Koppel for his courteous and skillful handling of the occasion.

During the war, I related well to a number of American television journalists, of whom John Sweeney of CNN, Forrest Sawyer of ABC News, and Ed Bradley of CBS deserve special mention. Although his questions were tough, Sweeney put together a profile of me which I thought very fair. I met Forrest Sawyer at the time of the *Nightline* program. He wrote me a nicely worded letter asking for a meeting. I responded by inviting him to a meal in my private dining room, next to my office in the Ministry of Defense. It was then that he requested to be allowed to fly in an F-15 during a bombing run. I think he was a bit surprised when I picked up the phone and gave my instructions on the spot. His cameraman flew in an accompanying aircraft. No other air force, including the American, ever took a reporter up. When the time came to liberate Kuwait, I attached Sawyer to my forward troops and arranged for him to take a satellite dish into the country which enabled him to broadcast live from there. I believe he was the first American reporter to do so.

Immediately after the battle of al-Khafji, Ed Bradley devoted a whole segment of a *60 Minutes* program to the war. He went right up to the battle zone and met Major General Sultan and then interviewed me in Riyadh – the first interview by a representative of the Western media to be conducted in the war room at the Ministry of Defense. I remember we had to cover up the maps and charts for fear some secret information might leak out.

I was later heartened to learn of an assessment of press coverage during the war by Jonathan Alter, a senior editor at *Newsweek*. "The Saudi military authorities," he said at a National Public Radio forum, "were more accessible, more cooperative and brought American reporters closer to real news than did the American authorities . . . There were plenty of pools in which reporters were taken out for a feeling of life in the field, but there were hundreds of complaints from reporters involved, many of them detailing cases in which they were taken in directly the opposite direction from where the real action was." Alter's remarks confirmed me in my belief that denying access to journalists is not the best way to get results.

Among print journalists, Judith Miller of the *New York Times* impressed me by her knowledge of Arab affairs, as did her colleague Michael Gordon by his knowledge of defense matters, although I must confess that not everything they wrote about me was as flattering as I would have wished. On a more scholarly level, I was stimulated by discussions with the distinguished military analyst Anthony Cordesman (then acting as a consultant for ABC), and by his subsequent writings on the Gulf War.

I have long felt that, with rare exceptions, the Arabic press lagged behind the great newspapers of the Western world, and needed revitalizing – an enterprise in which I hoped to play a role. The opportunity came in 1988 when I learned of a project to relaunch *Al Hayat*, a celebrated Lebanese daily founded in 1946, and which had won an enviable reputation until the assassination in Beirut in 1966 of its founder and editor-in-chief, Kamel Mroué. In the ideological and political battles of the 1960s between Nasser's brand of radical Arab nationalism and more moderate and conservative Arab leaders such as King Faisal, Mroué had bravely supported the latter, a commitment which almost certainly cost him his life. (I myself first appeared in the pages of *Al Hayat* in the late 1960s when the paper published a photograph of me as a Sandhurst officer cadet. I was passing through Beirut on my way home to Riyadh, and proudly kept the cutting for years.)

The prime movers behind the relaunch of the paper in 1988 were Kamel Mroué's son, Jamil, and Jihad al-Khazen, a talented journalist who, in 1978, had successfully launched another Arabic daily, *al-Sharq al-Awsat*. Impressed by this team, I agreed to fund the project, with the ambition from the start of creating an independent pan-Arab daily which, in its wide news coverage and judicious editorial policy, could stand comparison with leading Western counterparts such as the *International Herald Tribune*. I am glad to say that this ambition has been realized, and that *Al Hayat* is today widely read and well respected. In 1992, we expanded the publishing group with the launch of the weekly news magazine, *Al Wasat*. Since my resignation from the armed services after the Gulf War, I have been able to devote more time to the challenging and engrossing task of being a newspaper publisher.

❖❧

Although I think of myself as a professional soldier, a great deal of my time during the Gulf crisis was taken up with what could broadly be called diplomacy – making arrangements to receive the forces of friendly countries, playing host to them, supplying them with everything they needed, thanking them for their presence, making them all feel they were an important part of the Coalition, no matter how small or remote a country they came from. And, once the crisis was over, I resumed a diplomatic role in a series of official visits I made in the spring of 1991 to convey to foreign leaders the thanks of the King and of the Kingdom. Thus I traveled to Egypt, Syria, Bahrain, Qatar – where the ruler did me the honor of asking me to inspect his troops with him – the United Arab Emirates and Oman, and, in a second phase, to Senegal, Niger and Morocco, where I was deeply touched to find that King Hassan had sent his Prime Minister and several members of the cabinet to receive me at the airport.

In April, the time came for me to bid farewell to Schwarzkopf for whom, despite the ups and downs of our relationship, I felt real affection. In a simple, but emotional, ceremony, he described me, to my great satisfaction, as "a true servant of the Kingdom," and presented me with the Legion of Merit, together with a personal letter from President Bush which recognized in the warmest terms my contribution to victory. I, in turn, presented him with the King Abd al-Aziz Order of Merit (First Degree), the first time this high decoration has been awarded to a non-Saudi officer. I also gave him a personal gift of a handsome watch inscribed with the words, "For lasting friendship" – which genuinely expressed my sentiments.

I have often reflected that we were the two luckiest generals ever to fight a war. Few commanders in history can have been as certain of victory as we were. Schwarzkopf performed his mission admirably but, perhaps immodestly, I sometimes feel I had the more difficult and complicated task, and Saudi Arabia had more problems to handle than the United States. At his disposal, Schwarzkopf had a large staff, elaborate plans, a well-structured command, highly trained combat troops, a clear mission. To create the new Joint Forces Command, I had to bring people in, fight for authority, improvise, create the organization we needed to receive, take in hand, deploy and supply forces from two dozen nations. I had to sign treaties and manage a vast budget. Above all, I had to fight for the image of the

Kingdom, which meant standing up to the Americans to save our country from appearing an American dependency.

Some three weeks after the end of the war, the British government informed me that Her Majesty the Queen wished to confer on me the honor of Knight Commander of the Most Honourable Order of the Bath. After seeking King Fahd's permission, I was allowed almost a year later to accept. Accordingly, I traveled to London where General Sir Peter de la Billière and our ambassador in London accompanied me to Buckingham Palace. We waited for a moment in an antechamber, before I was ushered alone into her presence. I had been told that when one is knighted, one has to kneel before the Queen. Although very conscious of the honor done to me, I could not do that, so the ceremony in my case was quite informal. We had a cup of tea together. In due course, a chamberlain brought in the decoration which she presented to me.

I was able to remind her that in 1967, nearly a quarter of a century earlier during a state visit by King Faisal, I had come to Buckingham Palace in the uniform of a Sandhurst cadet.

I was impressed by the Queen's keen and detailed questions about the war. She asked me about the strategy of the campaign, about the losses suffered on both sides, about Kuwait both before and after the crisis. She wanted to hear an account of the war from our standpoint – which is what I have sought to do in this book.

As chance would have it, I went to the Palace some hours before it was publicly announced that the investigators of the Lockerbie disaster – the downing of a Pan Am airliner over Scotland with great loss of life – had identified two Libyans as the men, it seemed, who had planted the bomb in a suitcase which had found its way into the plane's hold. The Queen was the first to break the news to me, speaking animatedly about it at some length and in considerable detail. It was interesting to learn of these allegations from so distinguished a source. I then went to lunch with the Chief of the General Staff and other high-ranking British officers, before crossing the road on foot to the Ministry of Defense where I was received outside the front door by the Minister, Tom King, for whom I had developed a liking during the war.

Some weeks later, I had the honor of being received at the Elysée Palace in Paris by President François Mitterrand who conferred on me the insignia of a Grand Chevalier de la Légion d'Honneur. (I could not suppress a grin when I learned that Schwarzkopf received his French decoration at the hands of the French Chief of Staff, General Maurice Schmitt. However, Schwarzkopf scored a point over me by receiving a medal from the United Arab Emirates!) In all I received decorations from 12 countries – Bahrain, France, Hungary, Kuwait, Morocco, Niger, Oman, Qatar, Saudi Arabia, Senegal, the United Kingdom, and the United States – something of a record I believe for an Arab soldier in war. I would like to thank those who gave me a medal as well as those who, although they did not decorate me, gave me the honor of commanding their troops.

⊰⊱

War experience is vital for a commander. I learned more in nine months of crisis than I could have learned in a quarter of a century of peacetime soldiering. I had a first hand, close-up view of the largest military organizations of the Western world: the U.S. armed services working hand in hand with the British and the French. I saw how a high-tech war is managed, how huge numbers of combat and support troops, and massive quantities of weapons and supplies, are transported and deployed to remote locations. I had a chance to command troops in battle. Above all, I witnessed the speed and lethality of modern war.

This experience sharpened my sense of what needed to be done to improve our defenses and those of our partners in the Gulf Cooperation Council. Ours is a volatile and dangerous region. The Coalition's victory did not banish all regional threats, nor guarantee our long-term security. We have to be ready for whatever the future may bring. We cannot be sure that, next time round, our friends will be able to come so swiftly to our aid. Realism and self-respect demand that the Arab countries of the Gulf look to their own protection by building professional armed forces. This is a subject on which I feel I can speak with a fair degree of authority (and to which I will return briefly in the next chapter) because, although I was born a prince, I have earned being a general.

When the King, the Crown Prince and Prince Sultan entrusted me with the leadership of the Joint Forces Command, I knew that I faced a choice: either to be a mere figurehead, a puppet in the hands of the powerful friendly forces that came to our assistance, or to be a real commander, exercising to the full the powers that had been delegated to me. My duty dictated that I choose the latter course. I was a military commander, not a politician. My task was to build up the morale and combat-readiness of our troops – to be strong and to *sound* strong – so as to protect the honor and independence of the country.

Needing to get things done in a hurry, it was perhaps inevitable that I should step on a few toes and sometimes arouse resentments, even among those quite close to me. Some may have felt that I had been given too much exposure, others may not have realized how important my job would turn out to be. In any event, once the crisis was over and the danger had passed, there was evidently no further need for a task force such as the Joint Forces Command. Moreover, after the great responsibilities I had shouldered, it was hard to go back to my old position in the military establishment, junior to that of men I had commanded. I also had a notion that, in giving up my command once the job was done, I was setting an example all too rare in the Third World, where positions and titles are sometimes thought to be "owned" for decades, if not for life!

As I have said on more than one occasion in this book, I am the King's obedient servant, a member of a Royal Family team ready to serve my country to the best of my ability. Having served in the Gulf War, it was clearly time to make a graceful exit.

On May 27, 1991, I wrote two letters of resignation, one to the King, the other to Prince Sultan. It was the most difficult decision of my life. In my prime – I was still only 42 years old – I was sacrificing everything I stood for, saying farewell to comrades with whom I had shared the best years of my life, putting an end to the military career I loved.

In writing directly to the King, I transgressed against protocol and against the military chain of command. I should, of course, have submitted my resignation to Prince Sultan, Second Deputy Prime Minister and Defense Minister, who would then have put it before the King. But I did not wish to cause my father any embarrassment or burden him with any share of responsibility for my decision. I was also afraid that he might not accept my resignation, leaving me no choice but to obey his wishes.

To the King I wrote that, in requesting to be relieved of my military duties, I was not aspiring to another position. This had not been my ambition in the past and would not be in the future. The honors he had already bestowed on me were deeply appreciated and more than sufficient. "The only aspiration I have in life," I wrote, "is to serve my faith, my King and my country, and to assist in making our armed services a professional military force."

I sent a copy of this letter to Prince Sultan. In a separate letter to him, I apologized for writing direct to the King, explaining that I had not wished to embarrass him or make a claim on his fatherly emotions. I then outlined the military lessons I had learned from the conflict and the recommendations I proposed for our armed services.

On the same day these letters were dispatched, I made a farewell trip to Kuwait to say goodbye to some of the Saudi and other Arab troops I had commanded, stayed overnight at Hafr al-Batin, and then paid a visit to the refugee camp near Rafha, accompanied by about 30 correspondents. Answering questions, I made a slip of the tongue. I said something like, "This is the last time you will see me. This is my last command . . ." An American woman reporter pounced on this remark, "What do you mean by saying this is your last command?" I tried to retrieve my mistake by explaining that this was my last function as Joint Forces Commander, but I sensed she was not convinced.

On June 2, as a grand finale to the Gulf crisis, there took place a three-hour victory parade at the new King Fahd bin Abd al-Aziz airport at Dhahran, in which every Saudi unit and every major weapons system were represented. It was the first parade in the history of the Kingdom in which the armed forces, the National Guard and Ministry of Interior troops were present together. It was a moment of celebration. The country had taken up the challenge and passed the test of war. On that occasion, the King bestowed on me the sash of King Abd al-Aziz (First Class), the Kingdom's highest award.

The next morning, at 10 o'clock on June 3, I went down to the War Room at the Ministry of Defense for a last update of the situation in the theater of operations and issued my last military orders. It was a sad moment as the officers briefing me knew I was not coming back. Cameras came out and they asked if they could take pictures with their commander. I then went upstairs for a final meeting with the Red Cross representative to review the situation of the POWs and the refugees which had absorbed me for several weeks.

Then, in the presence of some 30 generals, I made some farewell remarks and formally dissolved the Joint Forces Command, the headquarters which I had fought to create and which – as I hope I have shown in this book – made a vital contribution to victory. Shortly after 2:30 p.m., I left the command center for the last time, pausing on my way out to pick up from my desk the nameplate with the motto which has inspired my whole career: "He who dares not climb mountains will spend his life in the pits." Only my deputy, Major General Abd al-Aziz al-Shaikh knew of my decision to resign from the armed services. I noticed that his eyes were moist as he escorted me downstairs to the front door and gave me a last hug.

I went first to my father's house to kiss my mother's hand and see my sisters. Then I went home to my wife and children. Glad to have me back after my long spell at the Defense Ministry, the children had draped the house in "Welcome Home" banners. Normally, I throw off my uniform as soon as I get indoors, but that day it took me more than an hour to take it off. I knew it would be for the last time.

Four months elapsed between my submitting my resignation and its acceptance by the King. In those long months, while my resignation was being considered, my position was anomalous and the uncertainty difficult to bear. Was the military career to which I had devoted my life truly over, or would I be reprieved? As I lay awake at night, my years of service flashed before my mind's eye. The challenge of Sandhurst; the exhilaration of my first command at Tabuk; the years of study in the United States; travels to every corner of the Kingdom, inspecting, training, building, sharing every kind of experience with my men; my widening air defense responsibilities; the long, hard-fought battle to have air defense recognized as a separate force; the acquisition of Chinese missiles and the creation of our Strategic Missile Force; my rise from head of the Projects and Planning Office to assistant commander, then to deputy commander, and finally to Commander of Air Defense Forces. Then, in our great national emergency, my appointment as Joint Forces Commander, the highest honor and responsibility to which a soldier could aspire. Service in the military is not a hobby, nor does one embark on it for personal prestige or gain. It had absorbed all my energies for more than two decades. I had wanted to make my country as nearly impregnable to attack as was humanly possible. Others would now have to take up the burden and complete the journey. The King, our supreme decision-maker, supported by Crown Prince Abdallah and Prince Sultan, would decide who they were to be.

As I awaited the King's decision regarding my own future, I decided to leave the country for a few weeks to recover my composure after the stress of the great events in which I had played a part. I needed time to isolate myself from everyone, including my wife and family. I must confess that I often suffered from nightmares about fighting, about death, about the burdens I had assumed. I used to break out into cold sweats. Was I responsible for the death of my men? Had I done a good job? I leave this to the judgment of my contemporaries – and to history.

On September 24, 1991, the King promoted me to four-star general by royal decree and accepted my resignation. There was an official announcement in the media. This was the occasion for a number of farewell parties including a lunch at the Officers' Club in Riyadh, given for me by Shaikh Othman al-Humayd, the assistant Minister of Defense, and attended by the Chief of Staff and leading Saudi commanders from all services, as well as by Lieutenant Generals Horner, de la Billière and Roquejeoffre. I made a speech which the King generously ordered to be broadcast in full on our national TV network. It was a deeply emotional moment. "I want to thank you for the years we spent together," I told my fellow officers. "They were well-spent years devoted to the defense of our nation. The flower of our youth gave itself willingly for King and country. I have come here to hail you, not to bid you farewell."

I cannot end this account of my military career without saying, from the heart, that no commander can achieve anything at all, in peace or in war, without the help of private soldiers and noncommissioned officers, who are the true backbone of any army and whose loyalty and readiness to sacrifice deserve the highest praise – and my deepest gratitude.

My Thoughts on Gulf Security

I N THE YEARS THAT HAVE ELAPSED since the Gulf War of
1991 I have tried to identify, and clarify in my own mind,
the lessons which we in the Gulf region can usefully learn
from that conflict. This has not been an easy exercise because
the Gulf War was unique. It was totally unlike the conflicts
which have raged in and around our region in recent decades.
It bore no resemblance to the Iraq–Iran war, to the wars in the
Horn of Africa, in the southern Sudan, in Yemen, to the bitter
inter-communal conflicts in the former Yugoslavia in which
whole populations were displaced or massacred, to the insur-
gency in Algeria, to the Arab–Israeli wars of 1967, 1973, and
1982, or to the *intifada* in the Occupied Territories. It was neither
an old-fashioned conventional war between states nor a war of
national liberation; neither an ethnic or religious struggle nor a
low-intensity conflict such as has ravaged and bankrupted so
many parts of the Third World.

The Gulf War was something quite different. On the Coalition
side, the principal actor was a superpower, and the advanced
weapons deployed – satellites, Stealth aircraft, submarine-
launched Cruise missiles – were systems only a superpower can
command. On the opposite side was the absolute dictator of a
relatively small Third World power who, because of his earlier
war with Iran, possessed an abnormally large, if not very sophisticated, war machine which he used in a rash act of aggression.
Deaf to advice, apparently indifferent to the sufferings of his
people, ignoring the basic principles of war as well as plain
common sense, Saddam then led his country to destruction in a
grossly unequal contest with a powerful international Coalition.

461

At first glance, there seems little here that is relevant to our future situation. If indeed, as I believe, the Gulf War was unique, perhaps the first and last conflict of its kind, are there any useful lessons to be learned from it? Perhaps we should be careful *not* to draw too many lessons from it, as they might lead us astray, distracting us from the real dangers we face.

The wars we might be called upon to fight, of which the world around us provides so many examples – low-intensity wars, counterinsurgency, wars against terrorism, or relatively low-tech interstate Third World conflicts – require quite different force structures, weapons, and strategies from the ones deployed in the Gulf. It may be that the computerized, push-button, high-tech, high-speed Gulf War is not *primarily* the model of war we should focus on or the type of war we should prepare for. In our weapons procurement, in the organization of our forces, and in our defense arrangements with our GCC partners, we should not *necessarily* seek to copy the armed forces of the most advanced Western nations as we saw them at firsthand in the Gulf conflict. Rather, we need to shape, train and equip our forces on the basis of a clearheaded assessment of the more likely threats we might face, of our own special strategic environment, and of our manpower and other resources.

This prompts the question: could the Gulf crisis happen again? In theory, the answer would have to be yes, if conditions in Iraq or elsewhere were to be the same as they were in 1990–91. But in practice, it would seem highly unlikely that this or any other Iraqi or regional leader would have the same unfettered power as Saddam Hussein had at that time, or would make the same mistake of challenging the entire industrialized world, or that his armed services would agree to fight under such unequal conditions.

As for the superpower response in a future crisis, we cannot speculate as to what that might be. We need to take note, however, that the United States and its principal Western allies are making deep cuts in their defense capabilities, and that the American military infrastructure in Europe, which proved of such vital importance during the Gulf crisis, is being sharply reduced. We should bear in mind that there is nothing automatic or inevitable about Western intervention in regional disputes.

In Somalia, for example, the United States backed off when it encountered resistance and when its vital interests were not obviously threatened, while in Bosnia it has been singularly reluctant to commit troops. I am mindful of a warning given in 1993 by General Colin Powell who, as Chairman of the Joint Chiefs of Staff, was one of the directing minds of the Gulf War. "I think it is essential," he remarked, "that as we bring the force down, we have a clear understanding of what we will *not* be able to do." In other words, America's present world dominance does not mean that it will be prepared on all occasions to be the world's policeman. All we can say – and it is a principle which guided us in the past – is that if vital Western interests in our region are threatened, then we believe we can confidently count on Western help. If such interests are not threatened, then we might have to make do on our own.

So my first conclusion is that we must be wary of seeing the Iraqi invasion as a model of the threat we may face in the future, and the Gulf War as a model of how that crisis was resolved. Both the crisis and the war were very special and probably non-repeatable.

✦≫≪✦

This said, there are nevertheless some broad lessons to be learned from the events of 1990–91, and perhaps none is more important than the close link between war and politics. When, in the early nineteenth century, the Prussian soldier and strategic thinker, Carl von Clausewitz, wrote that war is "the continuation of politics," he meant that states use organized violence in order to achieve their political objectives. While this is undoubtedly true, one might add that success or failure in war depends on getting one's politics right. Saddam got his politics wrong. Although he made several military mistakes, his main blunders were political. He failed to grasp the importance which the international community attached to Kuwait and, beyond Kuwait itself, to the political status quo in the Gulf.

The precedents were there, but he did not heed them. In 1961, for example, when the Iraqi leader, Abd al-Karim Qassem, threatened to take Kuwait, Britain – then the dominant power in the Gulf – rushed in troops to thwart him. The British force was soon replaced by a combined Arab League force under the command of a Saudi officer, Brigadier General Abdallah al-Mutlaq. When the latter was appointed Saudi Chief of Staff, he was replaced in Kuwait by another Saudi officer, Brigadier General Abdallah al-'Isa. The meaning of the British intervention in the Kuwait crisis, followed by that of the Arab League, was that Britain and the principal Arab states were determined to prevent Iraq extending its influence over the entire Gulf region. This was a dress rehearsal for 1991. Had Saddam made a close study of the 1961 crisis he might well have been deterred from his aggression 30 years later.

Another precedent which Saddam overlooked was the U.S. naval deployment in support of reflagged Kuwaiti tankers in the final stages of the Iraq–Iran war. Although the U.S. action was triggered by an earlier Soviet initiative in support of Kuwaiti tankers, it was proof that Washington was prepared to use force to safeguard access to oil, as well as the political order in the Gulf.

Paraphrasing Clausewitz, one can draw the broad conclusion that military operations cannot be separated from politics. If disaster is to be avoided, the military need to be informed about politics, while the political leadership needs to be given truthful and accurate information about the capability of its own armed forces. In 1967, the Egyptian leader, Gamal Abd al-Nasser, was misled by his military chief, Field Marshal Abd al-Hakim Amer, about the combat readiness of the Egyptian army and its ability to withstand an Israeli first strike. Amer evidently had a poor grasp of politics, both regional and international. He failed to realize that Israel would leap at any opportunity to bring down the one Arab power strong enough to challenge it, and that the United States would raise no objection. Thus, on bad advice and inadequate information, Nasser gambled in Sinai and lost.

In 1990, Saddam Hussein, too, appears to have had little insight into the workings of the international system, and a poor understanding of how his armies would fare in a clash with the forces of a superpower. He was politically mistaken when he imagined that war could be avoided, and militarily mistaken when he believed he could escape defeat. A brutal dictator, inspiring fear in those around him, is seldom told the truth.

The old saying that generals do not need to know about politics was, for me at least, proved decisively wrong by my experience in the Gulf War. To identify and assess potential threats and to give sound advice to the political leadership, generals in our region need to have a good understanding of Middle East politics, indeed of world politics. In coalition warfare especially – which may well be the dominant pattern of future conflicts – generals need to be acutely aware of the political concerns of their allies, as I discovered when commanding and managing different national contingents. I believe we need to train a new breed of "multinational" commanders, skilled in politics as well as the art of war. I hasten to add, however, that while I want generals to be informed about international politics, I am not recommending that they become politicized!

Few wars these days, even in remote parts of the world, let alone in a highly sensitive region like the Middle East, can be fought without reference to the views of the international community. Winning or losing may depend on which side of the conflict the international community chooses to support. It follows that, even before contemplating military operations, leaders must seek to win over world public opinion and convince it of the justice of their cause. It is striking that this too was a lesson Saddam failed to heed. He invaded Kuwait at a time when his image and reputation were at a low ebb. Instead of courting opinion before his reckless move, he managed to alienate it.

Part of the training of our commanders should be in how to handle the media, which is itself a political skill. In this television age, military commanders can no longer ignore the media, any more than politicians can. The impact on public opinion is simply too great. However, in Saudi Arabia we were not used to dealing with large numbers of reporters, and it took us some time to learn how to do it. A key turning point, which opened the door to proper coverage, was the commitment made by the Kingdom at the highest political level to let the international media in and to give them full access.

Another major lesson we learned from the crisis is the vital importance of intelligence. If we are not again to be taken by surprise, we need to devote more resources to studying and understanding the capabilities and intention of all our neighbors, Arab and non-Arab alike. A pithy saying of Mao Zedong sums it up: "Know yourself, know your enemy. One hundred battles, one hundred victories."

Clearly, we did not know Saddam's character well enough or properly understand his situation. We did not pay sufficient attention to the brutality of his regime. We did not realize to what lengths his impulsive temperament, bitter sense of grievance and acute shortage of funds might drive him. As a result, we failed to predict, or gain advance knowledge, of his intention to invade Kuwait, although the plan probably took shape in his mind as early as April or May 1990, and must have been discussed at the time with his top military and civilian colleagues.

When Saddam began to move his forces south, we thought he was simply exercising pressure on the Kuwaitis – a political maneuver rather than a military move. Our own intelligence, and the intelligence services of countries better able to monitor events, concluded that Saddam was bluffing. I have since learned that, three or four days before the invasion, American satellites detected bridging equipment with Iraqi forces north of Kuwait, leading some analysts to conclude that Saddam's objective was the Kuwaiti sand flats obstructing the entrance to the Iraqi port of Umm Qasr, and which he had long coveted. Deploying bridging equipment may have been a deliberate deception on Saddam's part, intending to signal that he was going one way rather than another. At any rate, no one in the Western or Arab intelligence communities predicted that he would seize the whole of Kuwait.

The Coalition knew a lot about Iraq, its armed forces and its military industries, and learned a great deal more in the six months between the invasion of Kuwait in August 1990 and the outbreak of war in January 1991. Yet important gaps in our knowledge remained. From intelligence reports our allies shared with us, we concluded that, while the United States had a good understanding of Iraqi formation tactics, it had an imperfect knowledge of Iraqi tactics at unit and subunit level. I believe that ignorance about how such small Iraqi units were deployed on the ground contributed to the gross overestimate of the size and strength of Iraqi forces in Kuwait. There was a failure to realize that most Iraqi divisions were greatly understrength. Had the Coalition known more about the detailed deployments of Iraqi units it would have concluded that there was simply no room in the Kuwait theater of operations for the numerous full-strength divisions which Western intelligence agencies believed were there.

The "Great Scud Hunt" provided other examples of intelligence gaps, ours and Iraq's. Iraq made the mistake of modifying some of its Scuds without full knowledge of how this would affect their performance. In the event, the missiles lost accuracy and often broke up in flight. The lesson we derived was of the danger of modifying the characteristics of a weapons system without thorough study. For its part, the United States knew the general characteristics of the Scud, but had had no direct experience of its use. It did not know, for example, that a missile launcher could evacuate a launch site within seven minutes of a launch – a vital piece of information in seeking to locate and destroy the elusive launchers. I recall that the Americans believed evacuating the launcher would take 30 minutes! Moreover, had the Coalition known more about Scud tactics it would not have assumed that Iraq would move its mobile launchers during daylight hours and risk their being attacked.

I quote these examples not to find fault but to make the point that military plans must rest on a very detailed knowledge of the enemy, his tactics at unit level and his weapons systems.

This book contains enough references to logistics for me not to need to dwell further on that subject. Yet the supreme importance of logistics in modern warfare was, for me, one of the overriding lessons of the crisis. No military operations can be contemplated or conducted without the back-up of an effective supply system before, during and after the battle. Any country in a vulnerable or exposed situation needs to constitute a logistics war reserve. The high military command needs to maintain close relations with the civilian sectors of the economy so as constantly to update its inventory of national resources. In a general sense, the nation as a whole needs to be prepared for war in all its aspects – politically, socially, economically and, of course, militarily. In undertaking public civil engineering and industrial projects, military considerations need to be borne in mind.

Once again, however, the point needs to be made that the Gulf War was one of a kind, and that its logistics cannot be taken as a guide to what might be required in future conflicts. The consumption rates and loss ratios in the Gulf War were wholly untypical. Because there was plenty of everything, consumption rates were enormous in such items as water, ammunition and fuel. The quantities and types of fuel and ammunition used in the 38-day air campaign boggled the imagination. Similarly, the casualty rates of the Coalition – estimated at below 0.04 percent – were miraculously low because the Iraqis were quick to collapse, surrender and flee. No sensible extrapolation can be made from these rates and ratios.

Frequent reference has also been made in this book to the invaluable role during the crisis of the Kingdom's modern infrastructure – its ports, airports, refineries, desalination plants and so forth. It proved to be one of our main contributions to victory. Indeed, to meet the needs of the campaign we had to make still further infrastructural efforts, upgrading airfields, laying fuel pipelines, and building roads. This preparation of the theater of operations in all its engineering, transport, maintenance and other economic aspects is clearly of the first importance and will require still further attention.

Contrary to some criticisms heard at the time, I believe the crisis largely vindicated the defense policy pursued by Saudi Arabia over the past two decades, of which a central feature was the building of an elaborate infrastructure, together with "military cities" at key points around the country able to provide support for reinforcements at moments of crisis. Without these ambitious and costly preparations – and without the Kingdom's strategic depth, a factor of critical importance – our Arab, Islamic and Western friends would have found it difficult, if not impossible, to come to our aid, and the Kingdom and its Gulf neighbors might well have fallen victim to Saddam's aggression.

Among the strictly military lessons of the war I would give pride of place to the role of air power, to the vital contribution of electronic warfare as a "force multiplier," and to the impact of "smart" and precision weapons. Modern war cannot be waged without air cover, and achieving air supremacy in the early stages of a conflict is of paramount importance.

It was one of Saddam's biggest military blunders to continue the war after the loss of his air force. He would have done better to have accepted defeat and announced his withdrawal from Kuwait in the early days of the air campaign. Instead he waited five weeks, during which his air, naval and a large portion of his land forces were destroyed, before committing the remnants of his army to a suicidal land battle. He was unable to conduct a defensive battle because his command, control and communications (C3) centers had been crippled by air and missile attack. The overall result of these errors was the rout of Saddam's army and the destruction of much of his military machine.

Saddam depended largely on fixed defensive positions which he imagined could not be breached. In planning our own defenses we should not imagine that a fortified defensive line can provide adequate security. A lesson of the war is that there is no line which cannot be penetrated or turned.

It is sometimes said that Iraq's defeat was due to its adoption of Soviet military doctrine. This is to do the Russians an injustice. Much like Western doctrine, Soviet doctrine stresses the need for speed, shock and surprise; the concentration of maximum strength at the enemy's weakest point: Sun Tzu's dictum of smashing rocks against eggs; the coordination of forces; and a high, sustained rate of combat operations – none of which characterized Iraq's military effort. If Iraq had digested and implemented Soviet strategies, the Coalition would have had a harder task.

Another lesson learned from the war was the importance of deception. Successful deception depends on an overall integrated strategy applied harmoniously at all levels – whether strategic, operational or tactical. However, at the sharp end, at the point where our forces make contact with the enemy, it is best if our own unit commanders at tactical level are not aware of the deception plan but fight for real. Only this will convince the enemy that he is facing a genuine threat on this front.

Iraq scored some notable success in deception, suggesting that it had been influenced by Soviet "*maskarovka*" military tactics. Iraqi troops showed considerable skill in building decoy targets and dummies, which in some cases fooled allied bombers and led to wasteful bombing by Coalition aircraft. Plywood and cardboard decoys helped protect Saddam's precious mobile Scud launchers, while dummy aircraft and tanks were also detected. The lesson I drew from these Iraqi efforts was that we need to improve our technical capability to differentiate decoys and dummies from the real thing. To combat enemy deception strategies, we need to know the tactics of his small units, upgrade our detection capability, and develop our information processing and analysis.

In terms of strategic deception, Saddam caught the world off balance by seizing the whole of Kuwait rather than, as some expected, one or two of the low-lying islands opposite Umm Qasr. For its part, the Coalition more than matched this record by deceiving Saddam into believing that its main attack would come in the east rather than the west.

Other lessons of the war include the great role which psychological warfare can play, if in skillful hands, and the vital importance of bolstering the morale of one's own troops. This is a factor which can determine the outcome of a battle even before it is waged.

The Gulf War brought further confirmation of the old lesson that the art of modern warfare demands the combined operations of land, air, naval and air defense forces, carefully coordinated at all levels by effective C3 systems. Air power alone cannot win wars: land forces are needed to occupy the ground and clinch the victory. Critical to modern warfare is the ability to fight faster than the enemy, to move greater distances, to close at greater ranges, to engage with lethal fire while the enemy cannot even acquire you or even know where you are, the ability to fight 24 hours a day, and principally at night. What we observed of Western units during the crisis taught us that we had a good deal to learn.

The Coalition fought an AirLand battle in accordance with the latest U.S. military doctrine. It must be said, however, that the effectiveness of this doctrine could not be truly tested in view of the absence of any real opposition.

In a general sense, the conflict brought home to me that the "principles of war," as elaborated by strategic thinkers down the ages, remain valid, whether the combatants are a superpower or a modest Third World state. Combat operations must always be planned in accordance with the art and principles of war.

❧

In the Kingdom, we have over the past two decades laid the foundations for strong armed forces, paying particular attention to the air force and air defense forces, where impressive standards have been attained. The Royal Saudi Air Force acquitted itself well during the war and was accepted by its peers as a professional force. It was recognized, however, that improvements were necessary in the combat readiness and coordination of our forces – in the ability of our air force to provide close air support to our land forces; in the integration of air force air defense assets and ground air defense forces; in the ability of our land forces to wage mobile warfare; in the more exact definition of the missions of the armed forces, National Guard and Coast Guard.

The Gulf War demonstrated the potency of what I like to call the "triangle of victory," that is to say leadership, discipline and training. All three deserve equal prominence, although leadership could be said to be "more equal" than the other two since they derive from it. My observation of friendly forces led me to conclude that, for our part, training was the side of the triangle to which we should give great attention – continual training, at a demanding, operational tempo to the highest professional standards. Nothing less will do in the dangerous environment in which we find ourselves.

More than half a century ago, in the 1920s and 1930s, the British military thinker Liddell Hart mounted a critique of Clausewitz, his Prussian predecessor. He blamed Clausewitz for the doctrine that one state can break another's will by smashing its army – a view he held responsible for the sterile strategies of World War One in which generals sent massed armies in repeated frontal assaults against each other, leading to senseless slaughter on a vast scale.

Had he lived, Liddell Hart would have been equally critical of the eight-year-long Iraq–Iran war, waged close to our borders, which was itself not unlike the slow-moving European battles of World War One. We observed huge armies facing each other across heavily fortified, largely static defense lines. Now and then, one side would surge forward to grapple with the other in hand-to-hand combat. The Iranians, in particular, seemed to put their faith in "human wave" tactics, sending tens of thousands of poorly armed and poorly trained youths to their deaths in an attempt to storm Iraq's defenses.

In a bid to shake the strategic thinking of British army chiefs after World War One, Liddell Hart preached the merits of flexibility and surprise by relatively small, specialized units rather than of wasteful frontal assaults by large bodies of men. He advocated mobile mechanized warfare, that is to say deep strategic penetration of enemy positions by fast-moving armored forces. He developed his celebrated theory of the "indirect approach," the idea of striking at the enemy where he least expects it, at his most vulnerable rather than at his strongest point. The objective of war he wrote was "to subdue the enemy's will with the least possible human and economic cost" to oneself. As is well known, Liddell Hart's ideas were to influence German commanders of Panzer divisions in World War Two such as Guderian and Rundstedt.

Several of his ideas could still be useful for us today, notably his advocacy of a highly trained and mechanized professional army, as was fully confirmed by the Gulf War. The challenge for the Third World is to build a truly professional army, in which appointments, postings and promotions are based on merit alone, and in which skills and education are fostered, as well as the traditional military virtues of discipline, obedience and loyalty.

Ours is a thinly populated, continent-sized country with long coastlines on the Red Sea and the Gulf, and a number of potentially hostile powers all around us. Today's friends could be tomorrow's enemies, and vice versa. The sheer size of the country and the relative shortage of manpower make it impractical to base large land forces in all parts of the Kingdom. We cannot maintain a presence everywhere. (During the crisis, I and my officers used to fly over the areas where the Coalition was deployed, but had I not known that 750,000 men were down there, I would not have believed it. They were lost in the immensity of the desert.) The danger for us is that, in response to the Gulf crisis, we may attempt to create too large a force, beyond what our demography will support. Large standing armies are not a guarantee of security or a demonstration of power. They are largely irrelevant, even a burden. Far better, as Liddell Hart advised long ago, is to have a relatively small number of highly mobile, well-equipped and highly trained units able to move fast and hit hard, and to serve as the nucleus of any force that we may need in an emergency. In the same spirit, I am also greatly in favor of creating elite Special Forces, a capability which we did not have enough of during the Gulf War, when we were forced to depend on the Special Forces of our allies for intelligence-gathering, Scud-hunting and other operations behind Iraqi lines. In sum, building too large a force is as bad a mistake as building too small a one. Force structures must be based on a detailed analysis of the threats we may be called upon to face.

I like to think of the defense of Saudi Arabia and the Gulf in terms of a series of concentric circles, interacting with and reinforcing each other. At the center is the Kingdom itself, and its national armed forces: this is our "first circle," as it would be for any country. The "second circle" is made up of the six partners in the Gulf Cooperation Council, that is to say Saudi Arabia, Kuwait, Qatar, Bahrain, the United Arab Emirates and Oman. The GCC is the prime source of solidarity for its members. In other words, the first and second circles constitute the main defenses of ourselves and our partners in the Arabian Peninsula. (Outlined below are some proposals for the improvement of GCC defenses.)

The "third circle" is, to my mind, composed of friendly states within the wider boundaries of the Middle East and South Asia. I am thinking, for example, of Egypt and Syria, Arab states who came to our aid during the Gulf crisis, as well as Turkey and

Pakistan, friendly Muslim powers on the immediate frontiers of our region. I believe that if these four countries and the GCC planned their defenses together, and carried out joint training, they could make a very considerable contribution to the security of the area. As a member of the NATO Alliance, and as a considerable military power in its own right, Turkey could serve as a bridge between our regional allies and our Western friends. Conducting training exercises with Turkey would give us exposure to Western standards.

I am not suggesting that we, in the Gulf, should buy military services from others. On the contrary, it is a case of recognizing and building on interests which we have in common: just as these countries can be our shield, so we in the Arabian Peninsula can constitute their strategic depth. We are as important to them as they are to us.

We need to bear in mind that the gravest threats we are likely to face will come from within our Middle East region, so we need friends within this "third circle" to hold in check potential adversaries. A balance of power between the main states of the region remains very probably the best guarantee of long-term stability.

If, however, a crisis erupts which is beyond the capability of ourselves and of our regional friends to handle – as occurred in 1990 – then we would need to turn for help to the "fourth circle" of our defenses, that is to say to the United States, Britain and France, to which Russia and China might also be added, now that the Cold War is no more and that the threat of Communist aggression or subversion has disappeared. China's rapid economic growth must soon make it a formidable military power which we, in the Middle East, must take into account. Some estimates suggest that China will in the coming years become a large customer for Middle East oil, perhaps laying the basis for a future security partnership between us.

Let me now return in my final comments to the "second circle," that is to say to our immediate Gulf neighbors and partners in the GCC. One of the main conclusions I drew from the war was the urgent need for strong collective defenses in the Arab Gulf region. No single GCC member, with the exception of Saudi Arabia, has the potential to build on its own a force strong enough to defend itself and its neighbors against aggression from one or other of the potentially hostile powers close to our borders. In security terms, Saudi Arabia and its Gulf neighbors are truly interdependent. We should remember that the moment Kuwait was attacked, each one of us was at risk. We cannot again allow a GCC member to become a springboard for a potentially hostile assault on us. The number one lesson of the crisis was that had the Gulf states been truly united they would have been able to put up more of a fight on their own.

If Saudi Arabia and the Gulf states were militarily integrated and collectively strong, we would be better able to defend ourselves and we could speak, politically, with greater confidence to the region and to the whole world. Collective security in the Gulf is, I believe, an imperative, with the Kingdom necessarily playing a leading role because of its greater resources and larger armed forces.

However, such collective security cannot take place in a political vacuum. Its necessary political underpinning must be a respect for one another's sovereignty and borders, an end to conflicts between member states and the maintenance of the political status quo.

The crisis taught us that Gulf defenses, as they existed in 1990, were wholly inadequate to deal with Saddam's aggression. Peninsula Shield, the defense wing of the Gulf Cooperation Council, was not strong enough to deter Iraq or to respond on its own once the invasion had taken place. Hence the urgent need to rethink our collective defense arrangements.

In my personal view, the answer cannot lie in a force like Peninsula Shield, shaped as much by political as by military considerations. Nor does the answer lie in a large GCC standing army, such as the suggestion for a 100,000-man force. It would be unrealistic to expect member states to agree to allocate their best units to such a regional defense force on a permanent basis. Where would such an army be based? Who would finance it and who would supply it? How could one resolve the social problems caused by posting officers and men from different GCC countries far away from home?

Inevitably, my thinking on Gulf security has been influenced by my experience during the Gulf War. The Joint Forces Command we then created to mobilize, train and commit to battle our own Gulf troops and the friendly forces that came to our aid could serve as the model for a new GCC military headquarters.

My proposal would be to set up a joint military command, based in Riyadh and staffed by professional officers of the highest caliber. No troops would be permanently allocated to the proposed headquarters. Instead, the various national contingents would stay at home until required for joint exercises or to meet an emergency.

The authority and responsibilities of the command would be determined by directives from the GCC heads of state and their ministers of defense. Such a command would need to be given real authority to speak, plan and act on all military matters in peace as in war. However, as with NATO, the country making the biggest contribution to the joint defense effort would provide the commander.

In war, the mission of the permanent headquarters would be to take operational command of all GCC forces allocated to the command so as to deter a potential aggressor or defeat an act of aggression.

In peacetime, its mission would include the following:

- to assess all possible external and internal threats and prepare contingency plans and scenarios to confront them;
- to ensure coordination between GCC armed forces by close cooperation with the chiefs of staff of member states;
- to advise member states on military doctrine and weapons procurement so as to enhance interoperability between various national forces. (At present GCC states field no fewer than 20 different models of armored personnel carrier and eight different models of main battle tank – a logistician's nightmare.) Standardization would greatly enhance GCC military capability;
- to establish a joint center for military communications, intelligence and operations;
- to conduct regular joint field exercises, to train, inspect and evaluate units allocated from national armies, and to submit reports to each national authority, so as to ensure high combat readiness of these forces;

- to advise on the infrastructural preparation of the theater of operations.

An early task of such a command would be to make a detailed assessment of the military contribution which each member state can make, and then to divide the armed forces of each state into: a) first priority forces, which would be immediately available in the event of a threat; b) reinforcement troops, which would be ready to move once priority forces were assigned; c) remaining forces, which would stay in their home countries to meet internal security requirements.

Clearly, these are only tentative proposals which would need to be refined and modified in the light of past and future experience and to accommodate the views and interests of each Gulf country.

To sum up, Gulf security depends first of all on a strong Saudi Arabia; then on a militarily integrated GCC; thirdly, on relations of mutual support with a number of friendly Arab and Muslim states in our region so as to defuse or eliminate potential threats from within the region. Fourthly, in very grave emergencies, we might need help from our Western friends, as occurred during the Gulf crisis. However, although we relied on them in the recent past, we need to be aware that they may not be available next time, unless it is clearly in their best interests. We should always bear in mind that God helps those who help themselves.

Saddam Hussein's invasion of Kuwait came as a severe shock to us and to our neighbors in the Gulf. The war that followed was a learning experience such as no other Arab countries have had, and from which we must seek to profit if we are to be ready next time. It woke us up to the need to be ready to face aggression from any quarter. It taught us that we have to devise all-round, 360-degree defenses, that we have to plan for the long term and not just for the next year or two, and that, as I have mentioned, the size and nature of our armed forces must be determined by careful, scientific threat analysis.

Today, my concern is that the sense of shock we felt in 1990 may have been dissipated too soon for these lessons of the crisis to sink in. For many people, Desert Storm – one of the greatest military ventures of our time – passed like a film on a theater screen. It was over so quickly, and the great Coalition war machine was withdrawn from the region so smoothly, that for some the temptation has been to behave as if the threat to our independence never occurred. I feel the need to warn against this sort of collective amnesia. My hope is that this record of events as I saw them will serve as a reminder of the need for the utmost vigilance. In our troubled world, national security lies in preparing for the worst.

INDEX

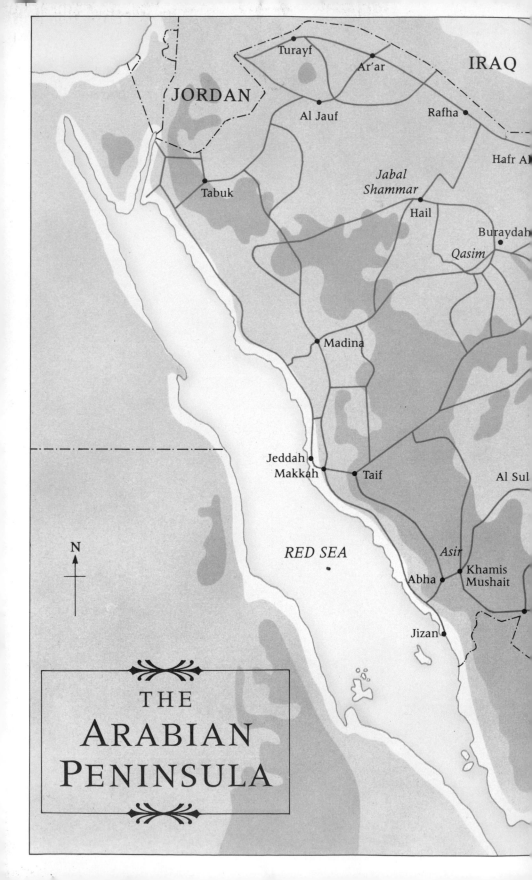

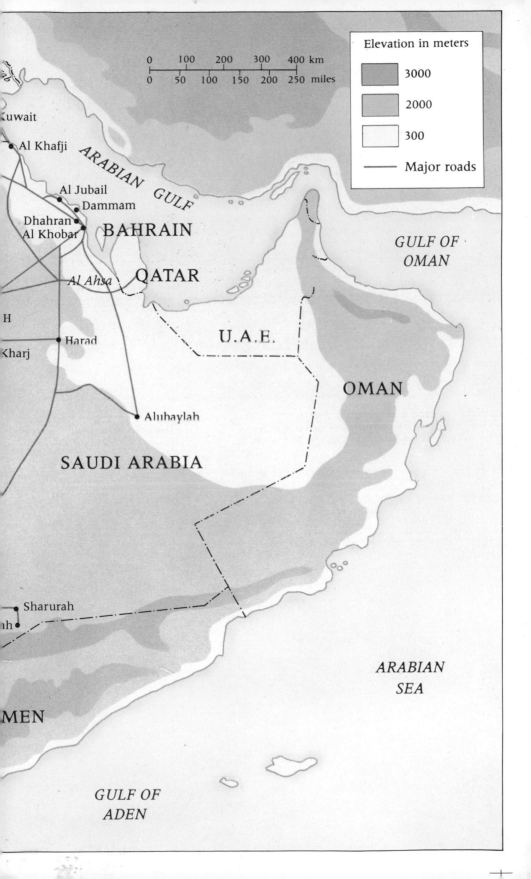

Elevation in meters

- 3000
- 2000
- 300
- —— Major roads

Kuwait

Al Khafji

ARABIAN GULF

Al Jubail
Dammam

Dhahran
Al Khobar

BAHRAIN

Al Ahsa

QATAR

GULF OF OMAN

H

Harad

U.A.E.

Kharj

OMAN

Aluhaylah

SAUDI ARABIA

Sharurah

ah

MEN

ARABIAN SEA

GULF OF ADEN